# THROUGH THE DRAGON'S MOUTH

Journeys Into the Yangzi's Three Gorges

千古奔龍

長江三峽

Ben Thomson Cowles, Ph.D

Fithian Press   Santa Barbara, California  1999

**Copyright © 1999 by Ben Thomson Cowles**

First Edition

Book Editor: Heidi Nye

Manuscript Editor: Douglas Cowles

Cover Design: Ronald Geisman

Lay-out, scanning, typeset by Lynn Wu

Pen and Ink Drawings by Helen Houser

Landscapes by HsiaoPi-yu and Kayo Nakamura

Printed by Pacific Rim International Printing

Printed In Hong Kong

Published by Fithian Press
a division of Daniel & Daniel, Publishers, Inc.
Post Office Box 1525
Santa Barbara, California 93102

**Library of Congress Cataloging-in-Publication Data**

Cowles, Ben Thomson, 1915-
    Through the dragon's mouth : journeys into the Yangtze's three
gorges / by Ben Thomson Cowles.
        p.    cm.
    Includes bibliographical references.
    ISBN 1-56474-294-6 (alk. paper)
    1 . Author--Journeys--China--Yangtze River Gorges. 2. Yangtze
River Gorges (China)--Description and travel.    I. Title.
II. Title:   1946 exprience in China's Yangtze River gorges.
DS793.Y3C69  1999
915.1'20442--DC21                          98-33984
                                           CIP

# DEDICATION

# Wang Shi

### Eager Instructor and Patriot

### Lived and Died for what he believed

# Judith Cowles Owens

### Loving Daughter

### Exhuberant in Life, Courageous in Death

# TABLE OF CONTENTS

Preface WORLD'S THIRD LONGEST RIVER; ACKNOWLEDGEMENTS & ROMANIZATION .I

Introduction THE LURE OF JOURNEYING THE YANGZI GORGES . . . . . . . . . . . . . .1

Chapter 1 YICHANG MISSION HOSTEL'S CAVEATS AND COUNSEL . . . . . . . . . . .12

Chapter 2 RENEWING OLD CITY SERVED BY VIBRANT MISSION . . . . . . . . . . .26

Chapter 3 FIRST NIGHT ABOARD THE JUNK AND YET ANOTHER DELAY . . . . . . .38

Chapter 4 THE YICHANG GORGE BECKONS . . . . . . . . . . . . . . . . . . . . .51

Chapter 5 THROUGH THE XILING'S GATES OF HELL . . . . . . . . . . . . . . . .66

Chapter 6 QINGFAN'S RESTAURATEUR, PHILOSOPHERS AND MONKS . . . . . . . . .80

Chapter 7 MI DAN CHASM AND TEA WITH BANDITS . . . . . . . . . . . . . . . .88

Chapter 8 UNSUNG COMMONER HEROES AND LESSONS OFFERED . . . . . . . . . .101

Chapter 9 NEW LIFE IN THE WITCHES GORGE . . . . . . . . . . . . . . . . . .115

Chapter 10 WUSHAN CITY AND OUR SEARCH FOR ZHOU ANCESTRAL HALL . . . . .127

Chapter 11 AWE AND TERROR, BEAUTY AND DEATH IN THE EMBANKMENT CHASM .137

Chapter 12 FENGJIE, CITY OF BRINE, COAL AND GHOSTS . . . . . . . . . . . . .146

Chapter 13 CLOUD CITY'S TEMPLE, MISSION AND INQUIRERS . . . . . . . . . . .153

Chapter 14 TALKING ABOUT TRUTH WE NEARLY MISSED BEAUTY . . . . . . . . . .166

Chapter 15 UNIQUE SCENES AND SHARNG CROWD LAST DAY WEST . . . . . . . . .174

Color Plates . . . . . . . . . . . . . . . . . . . . . . . . . . . . . . . .176

Chapter 16 A PROMISING WELCOME . . . . . . . . . . . . . . . . . . . . . . .202

Chapter 17 WANXIAN, THE MYRIAD CITY . . . . . . . . . . . . . . . . . . . . .208

Chapter 18 FEMALE ENTHUSIASM AND POWER . . . . . . . . . . . . . . . . . . .218

Chapter 19 A NEW MANDARIN AND WANXIAN MISSION'S "HOLY TRINITY" . . . . .223

Chapter 20 TEACHER'S VISIONS OF A NEW CHINA . . . . . . . . . . . . . . . .234

Chapter 21 DOWNRIVER THROUGH THE QUTANG GORGE . . . . . . . . . . . . . .250

Chapter 22 WUXIA AND XILING GORGE'S RAPIDS AND LEGENDS . . . . . . . . . .269

Chapter 23 TREASURED RECOLLECTIONS MEET TRAGEDY . . . . . . . . . . . . . .283

Chapter 24 DECADES OF RADICAL CHANGES . . . . . . . . . . . . . . . . . . .292

Epilogue THE THREE GORGES IN THE NEW CENTURY . . . . . . . . . . . . . .304

Bibliography . . . . . . . . . . . . . . . . . . . . . . . . . . . . . . . .318

# Preface

*Traditional blend of painting, poetry and calligraphy.*

The focus on China's famed Three Gorges of the Yangzi River is particularly timely at the end of the twentieth century when construction of the long-planned and much-debated mega-dam has already begun. The flooding of large portions of the region and the dislocation of 1,500,000 residents will mean that much of the ethnic, scenic and archeological uniqueness of this magnificent area soon will be lost forever.

The engineering project, as enormous as it is, will not by any manner mean the end of the Long River. Nevertheless, the temptation to call forth Chinese lore about the last days is strong. Chinese apocalyptic literature, drama and painting give rich imaginative description of the last of all days, including graphic depictions of the ultimate judgment of heaven and hell. Any end of human history, however, is not even a moment within the larger development of the universe. The Long River's Three Gorges, according to geologists, have existed for millions of years, and their geological permanence is hardly in question. They transcend all moments of the temporal process and are the beginning and end of time itself–*eternity.* Chinese, for millennia, have associated elements of eternity with the Long River's Three Gorges.

The account of my ephemeral one-of-a-kind 1946 three-week adventure into the Three Gorges offers a glimpse into this Chinese assumption. Although hope for possible intimations of things eternal were not absent, attention was on the present. This approach gives reason for the story to transcend an ordinary travelogue.

In the spring of 1946 no plans for man-made changes in the gorges had been made public, so the journey focused on the immediate now and not on engineers' plans for the gorges' future. The immediacies of the riverscapes and the river people, together with the geographical and sociological contrasts, engrossed us and made deep and lasting impressions. When three Americans, a Chinese professor and a crew of 65 Chinese crowd into a 95-foot-long upper Yangzi junk, all sorts of unpredictable happenings occur. Included were struggles through life-threatening rapids, living with and depending on indentured boatmen and trackers, meeting with innovative workers in frontier missions, being held captive by bandits and dialoguing with pressured and nationalistic middle-school teachers. Set against natural grandeur, the journey provoked reflection on significant aspects of China's long and rich yin-and-yang history and shed light on contemporary events and conditions.

Memories of spectacular panoramas and the striking events encountered have continued flowing like the Long River's current and keep emotions swirling like its whirlpools. The memories of the 1946 odyssey were reinforced and detailed with three subsequent Three Gorges journeys in 1982, '84 and '91. The accumulated saga surges with the immediacy and power of the mighty river sweeping toward the sea.

Each of these adventurous journeys offered a gamut of unique encounters. Much more than routine sight-seeing, strong feelings about places and people were aroused. Ever present were the challenges and responsibilities of "journeying"–disciplined inner and outer exploring.

In these experiences–aesthetically seeking union of self and world–awareness and powers of expression were challenged. Powerful images and their meanings continually impinged upon us. Often one of us would exclaim to a companion, "So this is one of China's famed gorges!" As we faced the gorges' signatures–a chasm, a cove, a pagoda, a temple or a river town–the scene before us seemed to take on not only physical variations but life itself. If we were especially struck with the light–shades, beams or dancing rays reflected off the river's turbulence–we would see more: Shafts of light invaded dark corners; and accented colors, some bold and bright, others soft and pastels. There were shadows, dark like Rembrandt's "Annunciation to the Shepherds." The light and dark we experienced came down to facing the *idea* about light and darkness–in nature's chasms and in human relations.

Our impressions were pressed toward an image that embraced all images. These images, however, didn't stand alone. When intimations of the universal broke through the gorges' environment, they only shined through particular images. The individual gorge we were passing through was a fragment of the universe of meaning. We treasured the paintings seen of the gorges done by Chinese artists in which they depicted his/her dynamic image of the world. We thought of Ralph Waldo Emerson's luminous belief in an imminent higher force embodied in the wonders of nature. In this union there were degrees of depth and authenticity. These were aesthetic encounters in which substantive union of self and world were achieved.

The saga's title, *Through The Dragon's Mouth*, comes from an ancient Chinese poet's verse in which he was creating an image both of gorgeshood and of the universe as reflected in the mirror of one portion of the Xiling Gorge. For us journeyers, the title derives from our successfully navigating the particular Dragon's Cave section of the gorge. The journey brought a number of other hazards so that "going through the dragon's mouth" was a metaphor for meeting and overcoming the river's many other threats.

Represented as a huge, winged, fire-breathing amphibian, the dragon conveys for Chinese both negative and positive meanings. Negatively, the dragon is associated with evil because of its ability to wreak havoc upon a land and is especially manifest in the destructive aspects of water and of nature generally. The dragon embodies powers at work that humans have not figured out how to understand and handle. This aspect of the dragon symbolizes humans' vulnerability to ominous possibilities. Because of this evil side the dragon had to be propitiated to, placated or killed. Positively, Chinese also associated the dragon with the continuity of historical flow and creative forces. The dragon was thought to typify life-giving powers and also to represent fertility and prosperity. Having many human characteristics, the rambunctious dragon was considered to be mercurial and whimsical, capricious and unpredictable, adventuresome and innovative, yet willful and purposive. It is little wonder that for millennia the dragon was a national symbol for Chinese.

During the years since 1946, China has come a long way in understanding and handling the Yangzi's Three Gorges' dragon. The river dragon's mortal dangers and navigational obstacles have been greatly reduced. Relation with the river dragon, as with friendship, requires attention, care and love. For hundreds of millions of Chinese much depends on tending their friendship with the Yangzi's river dragon. Serious and disturbing questions, however, now deepen: Will the construction of the mega-dam really harness the river dragon's power and excesses? Have humans gone too far, causing irreparable ecological damage and irretrievable archaeological loss? Answers will come in the twenty-first century.

In remembering the mid-century journey, I found significant parallels between it and my work as a psychotherapist. The journey into China's Three Gorges and the journey into the psyche provide two modes of understanding and surviving in one's world. In therapeutic exploration some dynamics are clearly understood, but what appears to be reality is often puzzling and threatening. Frequently the therapist is unaware of how the client is growing until the long and painful story unfolds. In psychotherapeutic encounters, as on a river, therapists travel the client's real life events, problems, motives and intentions. Always more than verbal exchanges take place. Metaphors are used to understand and to respond to the nonverbal messages revealed in body movements and eyes meeting on a different plane.

Psychotherapy uses the fantasies (symbols) of what our real-life experiences might become to develop the capacity to make competent decisions and gain the security needed to listen to the odd wisdom of the unconscious. The metaphors of the Chinese *laobaixing* (commoners) opened new vistas of understanding as we traveled through the terrain of real places and events. Their references to the imagined river dragon's activities and intentions shed light on how they viewed their world. The dragon metaphor offered a way, not to escape or evade issues, but to cast new and different light upon issues that were not being resolved by reason or logic.

The journeying of therapeutic work often is identified as dealing with reality. Hopefully, it is that. It is, however, more akin to a metareality because it is always dealing with more than what appears on the surface. In theological language, the process of interaction between therapist and client-journeyer reflects not so much the results of the development of a scientific law as it is an expression of grace unfolding.

The suggestion about "grace unfolding" calls for some indication about my convictions. I expected that the experiences in journeying the Three Gorges would give manifestations to the Creator God.Conceivably, the river's whirlpools, like China's revolutionary caldron, would give intimations of the unfathomable deeds of God in the perplexing world of China for whom God's son also died. There would be intimations of a God whose Kingdom not only mirrors eternity, but contributes to Eternal Life in each of its moments. Journeying in the gorges, as a person of faith, I would be reminded that in the Bible we do not begin with nature. The psalmist does not consider the heavens; he considers "thy heavens"; he has already been somewhere before he starts (Ps. 89:3). Neither do the Biblical writers take off from history. The Bible begins, continues and ends with the God of history, as he ceaselessly works out his gracious plan of salvation. For those of faith, who listen and watch, the Almighty's inner historical influences and transcendence were apparent.

The *eternal* is suggested in memory. Memory is living retention of the remembered person or event. It is holding in transcendent unity the three modes of time–past, present and future. Participation in eternity is not "life-here-after." Neither is it a natural quality of the human soul. It is rather the creative act of God, who lets the temporal separate itself from and return to the eternal. Eternal life, then, includes the positive content of history, liberated from its negative distortions and the fulfillment of its potentials. This view avoids getting bogged down in controversy over whether there is an eternal death and damnation for here-after. Instead of superficial indifference it sees profound seriousness: instead of ultimate despair it sees ultimate hope. This "eternal" life is life in God.

This view sees the world process as meaning something for God. God is "in the fray"–in the texture of human life; in the struggles of life's journeys. He is not a separated self-sufficient entity who, driven by whim, creates what he wants and saves whom he wants. Rather, the eternal act of creation is driven by a love which finds fulfillment only through the other one who has freedom to reject and to accept love. God, so to speak, drives toward the actualization and essentialization of everything that has being. For the eternal dimension of what happens in the universe is the Divine Life itself. It is the content of the divine struggle and blessedness seen in the *qian gu*, the "forever" aspect of China's Three Gorges.

And, being a Presbyterian, I support Max Weber's thesis of the connections between the Protestant ethic and the rise of capitalism–and by inference, this influence on the human changes now being wrought in China's Three Gorges. I would agree that Calvinistic Protestantism legitimized and encouraged behavior consistent with business success. It gave sanction to rationality and encouraged the belief that man could master his environment. Its emphasis on instruction and literacy facilitated the acquisition and spread of knowledge. The result was not just the rise of experimental science, but its coupling with a self-sustaining dynamic of practical, profit-oriented industrial innovation.

Psychotherapeutic or theological approaches meant little, if anything, to the Three Gorges' boatmen confronting the river's dangers. Having a metaphorical view, however, it made sense to ascribe the perils to machinations of the mythical river dragon. Encountering the river dragon's hazards these *laobaixing* (commoners) were sustained by bits and pieces of traditional outlook and approaches filtered down through the millennia. Relying on this conventional and metaphorical outlook they frequently thought, for example, that each day man is born and dies anew, like the sunrise and sunset each day has its manrise and manset. Humans are surrounded with duration-and-cessation, receptivity-and-rejection, the arousing-and-the gentle, the creative-and-the abysmal. They hoped to draw favorable predictions offered through the *I Ching* (Book of Changes). Entrance into the system, at any given moment or any particular circumstance, begins by casting three coin or drawing three yarrow sticks and getting an *I Ching* number.

This expression of the Chinese commoners' outlook and approach to life is watered down from a complex cosmology and divinatory or conjectural texts. The assumptions are that human beings are at the meeting ground and instru ment of active and passive energies. The triad symbol of Heaven-Man-Earth is at the heart of the *I Ching's* system. The *ba gua* (so called "trigrams") are con structed of three lines, one above the other. Each line symbolizes one of the three basic forces: the top line, heaven, and its alternations of light and dark; the bottom line, earth, in its aspects of yielding and firmness; and the middle line, man, in his qualities of love and rectitude. These three lines are either solid or broken, representing respectively the yang–the heavenly, positive, male forces, and the yin–the earthy, negative, female forces. The two qualities may be seen as the light (yang) and dark (yin) forces of the universe. Everything in nature is a blend of these two forces.

Such an all-embracing system includes many processes. The eight basic sym bols of change–the *ba gua*–are doubled and placed on top of the other to form a six line structure–the *gua* ("hexagram"). These combinations yield sixty-four *gua* which symbolize the various stages of change common to all phenomena. Knowledge of the *ba gua* (eight system of changes), starting from the *wu j* (the primordial void), consists of following their growth in individual com plexity and in their developing relationships.

From ancient times to the present, two arrangements of the *ba gua* form have been transmitted: the earlier Heaven or Primordial Arrangement; and the later Heaven, or Inner World Arrangement. In this Primal Arrangement the eight fundamental force symbols of the universe are grouped as four sets o polarities reflecting and complementing each other. The forces complement each other, and are held together by the eternal center, the sum total compris es the archetypal atom of an ordered universe. A verse from the *Xuo Gua* sec tion of the *I Ching* explains how these cosmic forces are harmonized:

> *Heaven and earth determine the direction*
> *The forces of Mountain and Lake are united.*
> *Thunder and Wind arouse each other.*
> *Water and Fire do not combat each other.*
> *Thus are the eight ba gua intermingled.*

Events and experiences occur in cycles, are interlinked and are the expres sion of one immutable law. As basic forces, they create and sustain each other through the mysterious power emanating from the center. All phenomena in a symmetrical manner radiate from this center. When the *ba gua* intermingle that is, when they are in motion, a double movement is observable: first, is a usual clockwise movement, cumulative and expanding as time goes on. Second, is an opposite, backward movement, folding up and contracting as time goes on. To know this movement is to know the future. In figurative terms, if we understand how a tree is contracted into a seed, we understand the future unfolding of the seed into a tree.

Every consideration of the Three Gorges now is dominated by questions about the drastic changes being effected by the mega-dam project. The consequences of the mega-dam, bounteous or catastrophic, in radically modifying the Long River from what it has been for countless millennia are not just an imaginative matter. Whether a boon or cataclysm, radical changes in time and space are occurring.

Stanford University professor Lyman P. Van Slyke, in his book *Yangtze* (1988), uses three kinds of time, three lenses, to view the Yangtzean world: natural time, social time, remembered time. These, he suggests, are only a method, an avenue of entry, not an end. The river dragon metaphor suggests a fourth kind of time: that of *qian gu* (thousand ancients = forever). It becomes an expression of peoples' standing every moment in the face of the eternal. If the mode of past is used for the relation of the temporal to the eternal, the dependence of creaturely existence is indicated; if the mode of future is used, the fulfillment of creaturely existence in the eternal is indicated. Past and future meet in the present, and both are included in the eternal "now."

How radically the massive mega-dam project in this crucial section will alter the Changjiang's (Long River's) full 4,000 mile-length is difficult to estimate. The project's enormous human efforts will improve communications between the Yangzi Valley's eastern and western regions and provide a significant volume of additional kilowatts. Like all man-made geographical alterations, they challenge memories, attitudes, emotions, symbols. In China, where memories go back four thousand years or more, layers of time and memory lie like geological strata deep upon the land. With many being violated, serious questions about the mega dam continue to be raised.

Whatever lens is chosen to estimate the mega dam's consequences, some will see it bringing benefits and blessedness and others will see it as bringing devastation and damnation. Regardless of what view is taken, its massive human effort is but a small event within the temporal process. The fragmentariness of the kingdoms that have come and gone on the Long River's banks are but one testimony. This colossal project to improve navigation and increase hydroelectric production must be viewed also in light of the river's analogous inner-historical (personal and ethical) and transcendent significances.

As to the lens through which the journey into the Three Gorges were filtered another acknowledgement needs to be made: The author is a white, Anglo, Westerner, with Southern parentage, Ivy League College education and Union Theological Seminary (N.Y.) indoctrination. Thus, he sees and hears through eyes and ears conditioned through these experiences. I am aware of the vaunted individualism, sense of self-importance and even arrogance that may come from such a background. Therefore I tried conscientiously to be open and receptive to all lessons and innuendos about Chinese and their remarkable culture. Instead of going to teach, I was journeying to learn. The major, my traveling colleague, and I learned that we did not have to change people. We simply had to be present to others as the people they are. And, as to our need for others, we simply needed those who would be present to us as the people we are. This was how gifts of journeying were called forth.

Several disclaimers are in order: First, names of persons in the narative have been altered to preserve their anonymity. Second, 100% accuracy of names of villages, coves, mountains and rapids is questionable. Many locations could not be confirmed or have been changed since 1946. Third, not being native Chinese, there were many unidentified and/or unspoken messages about China and Chinese that we Westerners did not hear or intuit. And, fourth, the 1946 journey came before the era of tape recorders, so the account was elaborated from sketchy log-notes made forty years before. Thus, like the poet Willam Wordsworth, much of the writings are "emotions recollected in tranquility."

The recovery of memories of the 1946 journey into China's renowned Three Gorges and the present reexploration fifty years later was not begun with the choice of yarrow sticks and consultation with the *I Ching*. Rather, it was undertaken first to renew friendship with China's Long River now undergoing radical surgery of its gorges' heartland. Dr. Samuel Johnson advises us to always keep in repair our friendships, since only in the heart of a friend can we really recognize ourselves and the world. Second, the project was started by proddings of insistent and suppportive friends.

As to these supportive friends I am eager to acknowledge a few among those to whom I am especially indebted. There those who have encouraged me to start and have kept after me to press toward completion of the project. In the beginning there were David Buttrick, John Espey, Grace Fulkerson, Harry and Loma Haines and members of three subsequent study tour groups which I led There were those who graciously and hopefully read preliminary drafts, including Oscar Armstrong, Janet Baker, Mary Nier Butier, Paul Chou, Wayne Ewing, Richard Hayman, Kay Halsey, Mary Clark Howland, Charles Riddle, John Service, David Spilver, Audrey Topping and James Weeks. Production of the work would have beem impossible without the editorial labors of Heidi Ney and Douglas Cowles, the correction of technical rendering of Chinese by Prof. Li San-pao and Cheng Pei Hsin, the art work of Lita Singer, Janet Baker, Helen Houser, Pearl Hsiao Pi-yu and Lynn Wu and the publishing assistance of Ty C. Colbert, Lori Davis and staff of Pacific Rim Company and John Daniels of Fithian Press.

For permission to reproduce and use monochrome pictures and sketches particular thanks are extended to Lyman VanSlyke for selections from his book *Yantze* (1988) and Caroline Walker for selections from her book *On Leaving Bai Di Cheng* (1993).

A note on romanization, the rendering of Chinese words into the Western lphabet, is in order. And a messier situation could hardly be imagined. Several ystems–each defective in some particulars–have been invented to handle this roblem, and two of them are in wide use. The first was developed in the nineenth century by two Englishmen: diplomat and linguist Thomas Wade and cholar Herbert Giles. Displite its imperfections, the Wade-Giles system was the irst to come into standard use and it remained the standard until two decades ago.

The other system has been adopted as official by the present government in Beijing and has become increasingly common, particularly in writing about conemporary China, This system, called *pinyin*, is better than Wade-Giles in some egards, worse in others.

Wade-Giles and *pinyin* exist side by side, and each author must decide how to andle the romanization problem. At the University of Californian in the 1940s I vas trained to use Wade-Giles, but in this work effort has been made to use the nore recent *pinyin*. There are a number of Wade-Giles transliterations that have ontinued their popular usages, e.g., *Tao* (the word for one of China's religions) nstead of *Dao*, as in *pinyin; ba kua* ("eight trigrams") or *kua* (hexagram), instead of *gua*, as in *pinyin*.

Current rendering in *pinyin* of the name of this, the world's third largest river, s "Yangzi." For centuries it was written "Yangtze." The Chinese call it 'Changjiang" (Long River).

Chinese words and phrases have been written in italics followed by English transation in parenthesis. Names of Chinese persons and places, instead of being italiized, have been written with the first letter in caps. In some instances, for clarity, ollowing the Chinese word given in *pinyin* in parenthesis the Wade-Guiles rendering is given.

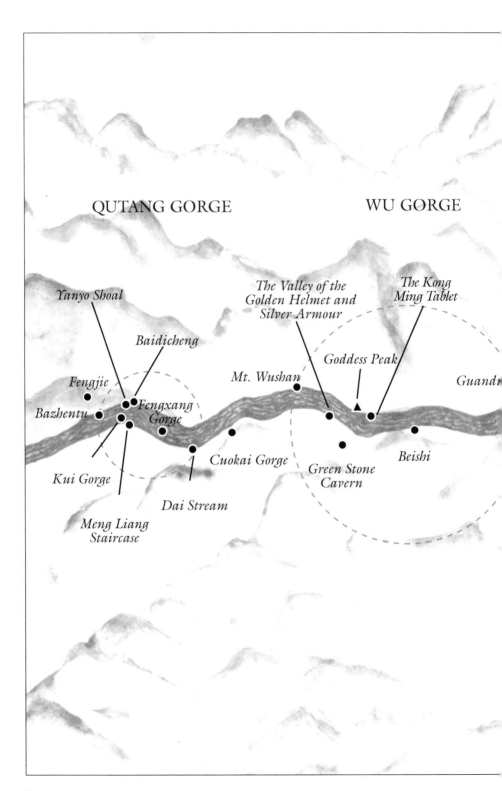

QUTANG GORGE

WU GORGE

Yanyo Shoal

The Valley of the
Golden Helmet and
Silver Armour

The Kong
Ming Tablet

Baidicheng

Goddess Peak

Fengjie

Mt. Wushan

Guand

Bazhentu

Fengxang
Gorge

Kui Gorge

Cuokai Gorge

Green Stone
Cavern

Beishi

Dai Stream

Meng Liang
Staircase

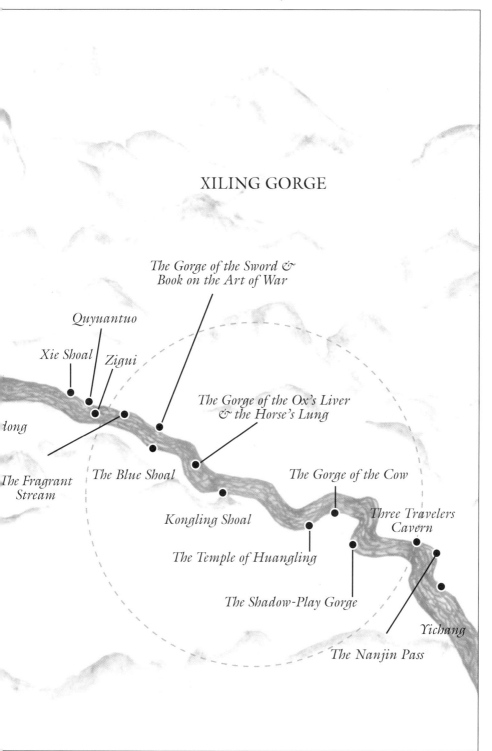

XILING GORGE

The Gorge of the Sword &
Book on the Art of War

Quyuantuo

Xie Shoal  Zigui

The Gorge of the Ox's Liver
& the Horse's Lung

dong

The Fragrant
Stream

The Blue Shoal

The Gorge of the Cow

Kongling Shoal

Three Travelers
Cavern

The Temple of Huangling

The Shadow-Play Gorge

Yichang

The Nanjin Pass

# Introduction

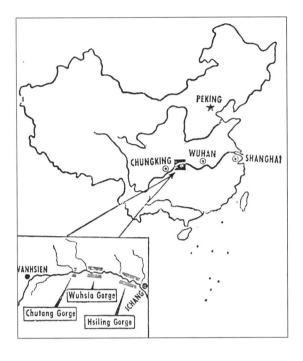

Winding for thousands of miles through the heart of China, the Yangzi River flows from mountain heights through gorge-encased rapids and past the dwellings of more than 400 million people. The Chinese appropriately call it Changjiang, or Long River, since "uncoiled" it would extend nearly 4,000 miles.

Geologists estimate it came into being 45 million years ago in the collision of India's Himalayan plate with the Eurasian continent. The event was so momentous that the river's formation was a mere episode. With its start in the glacial marshlands of the 20,000' high Tibetan plateaus the steadily enlarging stream flows south to the city of I Ping, then northeast to Chongqing, and east into its celebrated Three Gorges.

Midway along its course these gorges have been the river's throbbing heart. For 125 miles the river bores through China's Central Mountain Belt and cuts a series of narrow chasms that crowd the flow to a thread. Through the somber limestone walls rush snowmelt from the Qinghai-Tibetan deep-freeze glaciers 1,800 miles to the west and water from some 200 tributaries.

Bursting loose from its rock-bound ravines west of the city of Yichang, the Yangzi spreads out to become over a mile wide and pours into the vast Jinghan Plain. After coursing another 1,800 miles, gathering other rivers and lakes along its way and surging past many of China's largest cities, the river eventually sweeps by the great metropolis of Shanghai and empties, a 75-mile-wide mouth, into the China Sea.

Outside China the Yangzi is probably the least well understood of the great rivers of the world. Not so in China. The Long River's amazing parts read together and in a sequence build up a fascinating and multi-faceted picture. This, the world's third largest river, pours on and on as a tremendous physical fact. The Long River's trillion upon trillion water molecules–polluted, yet puri-ied by the sun–accumulate, flow and gain mighty force and significance. Hard-bitten boatmen, on 500-foot-long bamboo rafts or in 100-foot cargo junks, stroke long oars feverishly against the river's rushing current. The river sweeps away mere mortals, but also lifts them with magnificent panoramas.

The majesty and mystery of this great waterway have cast a brooding spell over Chinese life and legend. Recent archeological findings in the area suggest that the Three Gorges region was the second cradle of ancient Chinese civization. The Three Gorges have long been an important strategic area, the site of events of great historic interest. Dramatic narratives about the Yangtze extend back for millennia–records of disastrous floods, failures to dam and dike its rush to the sea and of numerous battles and kingdoms won and lost on its banks.

The Three Gorges enjoy the reputation of being a world-famous art gallery, providing inexhaustible source material for poets, dramatists and historians. Men of letters and famous calligraphers have frequented the region since earliest times. Many forms of classical poetry and drama have found expression in verse and tragedy about this region. To mention the *San Xia* (Three Gorges) is to evoke awe in the Chinese. The myths associated with the gorges are compared with those of the Yellow, Min and others of China's great rivers. These epics are cultural DNA, the unconscious programs that influence the way many Chinese see "reality" and respond to it. Or in computer terms, the gorges for millennia have been the software that took Chinese on adventures through their dangerous heartland labyrinth.

For 4,000 years the gorges' treacherous channels made the interchange difficult between the rich and populous Sichuan province in the west and the lush and more populous Yangtze Valley to the east. These three clusters of chasms and rapids, known individually as *Xiling*, *Wuxia* and *Qutang* are remembered in connection with ferocious battles between brothers 2,500 years ago during the tumultuous Warring States period. Moderns recall the terrible 1932-45 years of Japanese warfare when the gorges served as a barrier to the enemy's farther westward invasion.

Venturing into the funnel-like gorges, the ancient Chinese claimed, is like entering "the dragon's mouth." Precarious and awesome, hidden in the caverns of inaccessible mountains or finally uncoiled in the depths of the sea, this Chinese dragon unpredictably breaks forth into a torrent of activity. He unfolds himself in the storm clouds and washes his mane in the blackness of seething whirlpools. His claws are bursts of lightning and his scales glisten in the bark of rain-swept pine trees. His voice is heard in wind howling through chasms scattering the forest's withered leaves and so quickening a new spring.

Though dangerous, entering the dragon's mouth also bestows rewards. This "dragon" embodies the life-force–powerful, dynamic, changing. Entering his mouth invokes the quest for the meaning of life. Chinese associate the gorges with what James Joyce called "the grave and constant" of life and death, human suffering and endurance. Risking the Changjiang's gorges entails a struggle for survival, which teaches strength and goodness. Travelers become aware of the principal theme of classical mythology. It's the realization, as Joseph Campbell wrote, that, "The secret cause of all suffering is mortality itself, which is the prime condition of life. It cannot be denied if life is to be affirmed." I viewed my journey into the gorges as a metaphor of the human psyche's yearning for a centeredness and depth beyond the flux of existence.

My first experience of this river came at the end of World War I when I was only three years old and my parents held me on the rail of a Japanese passenger ship inbound from Seattle. At the wide mouth, with its shores still unseen, the copper-colored river poured into the blue-green of the China Sea east of Shanghai. My parents claimed that, young as I was, I asked: "Where does it come from and where is it going so fast?" Mine has been a life-long uncovering of an answer to that question.

In subsequent years I listened to guests in the South China home of Shantou (Swatow) where I was raised, tell of the awesome bottleneck gorges of the Yangtze River. They sketched images of scenic magnificence rivaling that of the Grand Canyon and described the obstacles and perils as those equal to the hardships of negotiating the Upper Nile. Like the awesome land of Oz, the far-away Yangtze gorges rang bells in my boyhood fancy. The intrepid 19th century entrepreneurs, envoys and Christian missionaries who surmounted the perils of the gorges and reached the remote western province of Sichuan were heroes to me as a young boy.

The Long River's gorges became more real and personal at age 14. This was when I went on camping trips with a resolute international scout troop in Shanghai. Around campfires in bamboo forests beside rice fields we shared stories more amazing than fiction about our fathers' real-life adventures. As the sons of missionaries working in different parts of China, we eagerly told of the hair-raising exploits of our extraordinary fathers. One patrol leader's father had survived being swept away by a flash flood in a remote mountain area and a subsequent plunge over a 100-foot waterfall. Another's father had been captured by bandits and held ransom for months. And still another's had been mauled by a wounded animal while hunting the rare blue tiger in the Fujian mountains. I told of my civil engineer father, turned Y.M.C.A. Secretary, who introduced showers to the port city where he was stationed and at one time saved a Chinese general's life by warning him of a plot to poison him at a banquet.

Reports by Dick Service, our senior patrol leader, served as the *piece de resistance*. He told of his adventures making it through the awesome Yangtze gorges on his way upriver to his home city of Chongqing (Chungking), where his parents, like my own, were Y.M.C.A. fraternal workers. His stories about treacherous rapids, dizzying whirlpools, shadowy cliffs with chiseled-out paths for low-bending trackers, capsized junks, wrecked launches and drowning passengers held us spellbound. His adventures in the dragon's mouth had our adolescent imaginations churning. We identified with the boatmen and trackers in their struggle to survive against the river demons. His having been in the vortex of such hazards added luster to his stature as our mentor and stirred us to hope someday to make that same journey.

We older scouts embellished these stories and passed them on to the tenderfoot recruits. These accounts became sacrosanct–part of the treasured mythology of our troop. We were venturesome adolescents, our dreams were aroused as we saw in our mind's eyes the river's long flow from the mysterious Tibetan mountains all the way to the China Sea. We connected stories about mastering the gorges with earning merit badges and getting ready to compete with the French, Italian, British and White Russian scout troops at the jamborees.

Dreams of venturing into perilous gorges became part of the troop's ethos: myths about who we were, where we came from, where we were going, how we should live and believe. With these myths we celebrated values personified in the pantheon of our heroes. These brave persons who battled waters and survived rushing through ominous abysses strengthened my sense of identity and became etched in my memory.

Sixteen years passed, and other experiences crowded out thoughts about the Long River. The year after our last Shanghai scout camp-out, I returned to the United States, via the trans-Siberian railway and Europe, and an Atlantic Ocean crossing. The last two years of high school followed, then four in college. Two further years passed while I worked at the Philadelphia West Branch Y.M.C.A. as Boys and Young Mens Secretary I moved to New York City to take up graduate studies at Union Theological Seminary. There, under world-class professors such as Reinhold Niebuhr, Paul Tillich, Harry Emerson Fosdick and others I was led on journeys in the great rivers of Western philosophical, theological and Biblical experiences. At the same time, fieldwork experiences in Manhattan's Lower East Side and the Bronx's Throggs Neck section plunged me into the turbulence of New York City's slums. My concern for the disadvantaged became etched by what I saw of the exploitation of absentee landlords, abject poverty, spreading crime, widespread alcoholism, and family disorganization.

In the summer of 1940, by extending the vacation of my last graduate work year to five months, I was able to return to China as a student envoy. As the war in the Pacific neared, I made my way through Japan, Korea, Manchuria and Eastern China. I then sailed on a British Jardine Matheson coastal ship to Haiphong in Indo-China (Vietnam). From there I traveled by rail to Hanoi and west to Lao Cai, that then was the back door to "free China." After reaching Kunming, the busy Chinese terminal of the Burma Road, I flew 500 miles to Chongqing, the war-time capital. We landed on an exposed sandbar in the middle of the Upper Yangtze.

That summer (1940), the city was bombed almost daily by the Japanese planes based at Yichang. Much time was spent seeking caves that served as air-raid shelters. Afterwards, came tasks of helping with casualties and comforting their relatives and friends at the hospital. I had no chance to travel the Long River from Chongqing to the east. References to the formidable gorges 250 miles downriver were not of traveling there, but of gratitude for their treacherous shoals and rocks that stopped the westward advance of the Japanese.

I was fortunate to catch a DC-3 plane connections for a round-trip to Lanzhou in the northwestern province of Kansu, then southeast to Kueilin, and back to the coast in Hong Kong. There I caught a coastal ship headed 600 miles north to Shanghai. With only U.S. $200 left, my prospect for getting back to New York looked bleak. I took my predicament to Eddie Wise, who ten years before had been my Sunday School teacher at the Shanghai Community Church and who now was the American President Lines manager. He waived the ruling that forbade Caucasians from traveling 3rd class and sold me a trans-Pacific ticket for $135. This enabled me to make it back to New York City by the first week in October (1940), I was exhausted, out of money, and having missed the first two weeks of fall classes.

Such a life time of incredible experiences I had gained! Twenty years before trans-continental and trans-Ocean plane routes were established, by train and ship I had crossed west and east over the North American continent and the Pacific Ocean. Traveling 40,000 miles, I had visited universities and churches in Japan, Korea, Occupied China, Indo-China, and Free China. Now (in October. 1940) I was glad to be starting my concluding year at the seminary.

It was a full six years before I had further contact with the Long River. In the spring of 1941 upon graduating, I moved to Chevy Chase, M.D., a Washington, D.C. suburb, to serve a Presbyterian Church as an associate pastor. In the fall of 1943, commissioned under the Presbyterian Board of Overseas Missions, I was sent to the University of California in Berkeley for Chinese language study. By the time World War II ended I had completed two-and-a-half years of intensive courses in written and spoken Chinese and special work on Far Eastern History. In March of 1946 I secured passage on the "Lane Victory" out of Los Angeles bound for Shanghai.

Arriving in China, after a seventeen-day trans-Pacific passage, I was assigned to Nanjing, the historic Yangtze River city, 200 miles inland from Shanghai. The capital of the recently returned Nationalist government, it also was a critical center for China's extensive reconstruction and relief organizations. A strategic political hub, Nanjing also was an important transportation entrepot. The rail head for goods and people from Shanghai, the city served as a key transshipping center for the large volume of material, communications and people headed west into the entire Yangtze Valley, especially the three key provinces of Jiangsu, Jingsi, and Anhui. A busy and burgeoning center, the city was also the home of three of China's first-rank universities and a prestigious Protestant seminary.

In the spring of 1946 Nanjing struggled with enormous tasks, including healing those who had endured Japanese occupation, assimilating the returning officials and their agencies back into the community and absorbing the swelling number of foreign embassies. Increasing influxes of famine and flood refugees further taxed housing, transportation and other municipal resources. Tensions mounted because the exhausted ruling Nationalists were increasingly pressured by the fast-growing Communist military and political forces.

Schools and universities in which I faced each of these overall hardships had additionally their own special difficulties. Students and faculties lived in gutted dormitories, ate reduced fare and studied in unheated and depleted libraries. Instructors and students also suffered civil rights violations and abuses at the hands of reactionary governmental agencies, escalating inflation, malnutrition, loss of loved ones.

The city was the crossroads of international as well as national leaders. In the spring of 1946, for instance, President Truman's special envoy, General George Marshall, was in the city. Since the United States had been the dominant ally in forces defeating the Japanese, Americans with the Military Advisory Group's 1,500 personnel made up the largest contingent of Westerners in the city. Others from the States included United Nations relief and reconstruction workers, business representatives and educational, medical and evangelistic missionaries.

American Army Air Force personnel stationed in Nanjing as advisors to the hard-pressed Guomindang military were especially in evidence. Their fliers frequently flew diplomatic and reconnaissance missions along the Long River. Working as a volunteer on a community refugee relief project with one of these pilots, Major McGinnis, I found he had kindred interest in the Yangtze Gorges. After learning of them in a college geography class he had been collecting information about them ever since. He had long been intrigued by their geology and associated history. He and I talked about wanting to explore for ourselves this part of China. We wanted to touch the heart of that section of the Long River, savor the scenic beauties, explore the historical sites, get closer to Hubei and Sichuan provinces' commoners, and look in on Catholic and Protestant missions in that area.

Our imaginings became a real possibility when another American pilot asked my friend, the major, to fly to Yichang, the city nearest the gorges' eastern entrance. Assigned to inspect former Japanese facilities and contact local Chinese reconnaissance teams, the pilot would remain in Yichang 20 days. The major accepted the invitation and asked if I would join them. With both our spouses back in the United States and both of us on leave, the major and I saw this as the opportunity to venture into the famed Dragon's Mouth.

The major proposed that we arrange to travel the gorges via river junk, in the centuries-old style. It was a manner few Westerners attempted any longer. Faster and safer is the three-day transit by one of the tough, shallow draft iron river steamers, or the three-hour, once-a-week air flight. The hazards and hardship of the ancient journey by junk, instead of deterring us, whetted our appetites for adventures. So it was that 16 years after my senior patrol leader had aroused my interest in the gorges, I was making plans to see them for myself.

By good fortune, we persuaded a young Chinese university instructor, Wang Shi, to join our adventure and serve as consultant and interpreter. A good looking fellow, with a full head of jet black hair and an open and engaging mien, he had been an actor before his rigorous academic work had become so demanding. A versatile young man, his interests included martial arts. Although not clubby, he was a fun-loving person who had many friends. His aristocratic inclinations, some of his friends said, at times made him seem aloof. Senior faculty members in his political science department considered him a bright and promising scholar. They appreciated that though from an upper class and respected gentry family, he was a strong advocate of peasants' and workers' rights. His colleagues reported that he was outgoing, assertive, and an insistent reformer. One of his colleagues, reported wryly, "Wang Shi is not one who can easily say he made a mistake." Another mentioned that he was the sort of man who said, "If it was not a challenge, why do it?"

An added bonus for us lay in the fact that, as a native of the upper river region, Wang Shi was familiar with Hubei and Sichuan, the two western provinces linked by the gorges. We counted it a good omen that Wang Shi agreed to join our expedition.

The major gathered reports from Air Force intelligence officers and I tracked down English-language travel reports of British and American missionaries, businessmen and consular officials. Most were of late 19th century explorers, with only a few in recent decades. The early accounts were rambling, but revealed how the gorges' challenges and perils cast a mysterious spell over passengers and boatmen alike. Articles from Chinese encyclopedias and annals Wang Shi dug out in the university library helped us gain background information we needed. Briefs he made from Tang and Sung dynasty poets and Yuan (Mongol) dramatists prepared us for the aura of mystery we were to experience.

Travelers' struggles in the gorges seemed to personify the conflict of a cosmic struggle between Heaven and Earth, between forces that create and those that destroy. These myths provide a world picture that explains why things are as they are, and contribute a sense of sanctity for their social order. These Yangtze gorges sagas try to answer life's imponderables: Where did I come from? Why is there something rather than nothing? Why is there evil and suffering in the world? What happens to me when I die? What are my duties? What is taboo? What is the purpose of my life? Who are the heroes and hero-nes? We found the same tendency to develop a moral/mythical landscape that gave their experiences larger than ordinary meaning even with recent travelers into the gorges.

Experienced Long River travelers were encouraging. They promised us a great adventure. They assured us we'd see countless historical sites that had inspired the poetry, myths, and dramas dear to Chinese. Some even promised we'd find treasured analogies, voiced millennia ago by Confucius, Lao Tze, Mencius, Ch'uang Tze and other Chinese sages.

Skeptical kibitzers, trying to deter us, raised caveats. This wild section of the Long River, they warned, had submerged rocks, treacherous rapids, cutthroat

bandits, epidemic pollutants and other hazards that could wipe out foreign travelers in a flash. They reminded us of the folly of trusting our safety to erratic and hijacking boatmen. We listened and thought, perhaps in denial, that those who venture into such inner and outer realms possessed a thread of Ariadne assuring connections with their known world and promising a way back. We held to our decision to risk the journey, figuring that the river's dangers would quicken us and possibly even shed light on some of our on-going inner struggles!

In these post-war months we were largely on our own in making the arrangements. The Chinese maps of the Long River's mid-section were far from those produced by the American Automobile Association. We found general agreement on the existence of three main clusters of the gorges–*Xilingxia*, *Wuxia*, and *Fengxia* or *Qutangxia*. The recurrent designations of intermittent chasms included: (1) Yellow Cat, (2) Lampshine, (3) Ox Liver and Horse Lungs, (4) Mitan, (5) Iron Coffin, (6)Witches Mountain, (7) Bellows Gorge, and (8) Gorge of the Eight Cliffs. Curiously, the mountain range in which they are located, in characteristic Chinese fashion, is not named.

Even the most recent maps, however, were confusing. Ancient settlements that no longer existed were indicated, while other long-settled centers were not shown. These inaccuracies made it difficult to locate the region's towns and monuments, also the channels and hazards travelers had told us about. We tried, nevertheless, to to identify the region connected with the battles between brothers 2500 years ago during the Warring States period and the mountains, valleys and glens that sparked ancient Chinese myths.

Finding out who were the key persons in each mission station along the way was more difficult than we anticipated, because of turnovers and furloughs of missionary personnel. Notifying the ones we identified took much doing. The major and I, impatient Americans in a hurry, were overly optimistic about being able to arrange a tight schedule. Against the odds we calculated that we could make the trip to and from Wanxian, the western end of the gorges, in 20 days which was our deadline to be back at Yichang to rendezvous with the other pilot for our return flight to Nanjing. To minimize delays–the ritual of hiring crews and provisioning a junk–we telegraphed Yichang, asking friends to begin hiring a junk and crew.

In conferring about our travel plans it was fortunate that from the beginning the three of us were simpatico. From our start Wang Shi helped greatly with his innovative and practical suggestions. He did not allow our petty questions about details bother him. In his no-nonsense manner he responded to our lingering doubts by assuring us, "You've already decided on this venture. In a few more days we will be doing it together. The time for questioning its feasibility has passed." We counted it a good omen that Wang Shi agreed to join our expedition.

Wang Shi, along with interest in Chinese history and philosophy, was much concerned with China's urgent need to modernize. This priority led him to locate reports on proposed projects to exploit the hydroelectric potential of the gorges. Transportation specialists and engineers saw the area as ripe for extensive development. Shipping companies recognized that if the shoals and rapids were cleared with dynamite, this stretch of the Long River could be transformed from a perilous bottleneck to an important east-west artery. Conservationists proposed expanded flood-control undertakings and an extensive irrigation network. Engineers pointed out that almost half the river's volume collects from above the Gorges, the 360-mile mid-section, between Chongqing and Yichang, and in this stretch there is a drop of almost 400 feet. Also, in many parts of the gorges the rock cliffs practically close in on one another, narrowing the space between them. Hydroelectric engineers, mouths watering at the prospects of the enormous potential for power, had already prepared grandiose plans, including blueprints for massive dams with multiple generators and large locks.

Wang Shi was enthusiastic about the possibilities of supplying populous Hubei and Sichuan provinces with electricity and about transforming the gorges from a bottleneck to a key thoroughfare to West China. He took a dim view of contemporary conservatives who invoked the reactionary counsel of Lao Tze (6th century B.C.):

> *For the world is a divine vessel:*
> *It cannot be shaped;*
> *Nor can it be insisted upon.*
> *He who shapes it damages it;*
> *He who insists upon it loses it.*

Though he railed against reactionaries that might try to impede massive beneficial projects, realist that he was, he was skeptical about the government's capacity to carry out such efforts. Problems of engineering and financing, he said, the Chinese could solve. But solving the problems of corruption, malfeasance and lack of unity was questionable. He commented that ancient Chinese philosophers advocated a preference for *"yi"* (righteousness) over *"li"* (profit), which today would mean public versus private profit. Righteousness, he said, refers to an appropriate, right, correct, suitable moral conception–all of which today is in short supply.

Wang Shi told us later he intuited that the major and I had more on our agendas than simply taking an unusual trip. He was right.

Personally, I was on assignment to assess upriver Catholic and Protestant church workers, members, and programs of missions. More than mere travel, I was to explore current strengths of upriver Chinese churches. I was to note the ways in which Christians were responding to China's post-war problems. I was to note the liturgies used, Bible groups organized, church school programs, new members classes, pastoral training programs, and other ecclesiastic work. Also I was to seek out the kinds of support groups and other reinforcements for renewal that had been developed, and the expanded community services they were engaged in. We wanted to find out what affect these institutions' efforts were having on Chinese farmers, townspeople, workers and families. I was asked to be alert to nuances such as the cultural and faith interactions between foreign missionaries and their Chinese co-workers and neighbors.

In this adventure we might even find a metaphor for the journey through life. The symbolic representation could offer fresh ways of thinking about life's purpose and provide a *via analogia* for considering the 'ground of existence.' In journeying, as T.S. Eliot's line puts it, "We shall not cease from exploration."

As to continued exploration, more was to come four decades later. In 1982, 1984 and 1991 the continuing search took me back into the gorges. I was to find how the People's Republic of China had effected momentous changes in the area, realizing some of Wang Shi's dreams of modernization. By far the greatest change in the Three Gorges region was signaled in April 1992 when China's National People's Congress (NPC) gave the go-ahead to dam the Xiling Gorge. The gorges which have inspired poets and artists over the centuries and attracted countless ogling tourists, will be radically altered in the building of the world's biggest hydroelectric and navigational locks project. Some of these changes will be described in the last chapter.

We recognized that this adventure promised many East-West cultural shocks for which we Westerners would need flexibility and patience. The major and I already knew the essentials for foreigners to live tolerably in China. Friends urged us to remember to hold in abeyance our Westerners' ways of thinking in order to learn about Chinese ways. This reminder suited us well: since an important concern of ours was to connect with Chinese people. We hoped to touch ordinary people's sense of being–their reactions in life's ebb and flow. We anticipated making new discoveries as we rubbed shoulders with Chinese common folk–the *laobaixing*.

We resolved to "hang loose," setting aside preconceptions. We resolved to stay alert to Chinese patterns of behaving, thinking and feeling. Developing a "bifocal approach," looking at both facts and meanings, we'd note the boatmen's and villagers' behavior, thinking and feelings. We'd be on the lookout for metaphors and myths that sparked the crew and people we would meet.

As our packs began to bulge with toothpaste, soap powder, insect repellent and toilet paper, Wang Shi questioned the advisability of weighing ourselves down with such amenities. Most of our Western accouterments were inimical to conditions aboard the gorges' river junks. The chasms we passed through might be spacious, but not in the 10' x 10' passenger area we three would share for 20 days. We had to prepare for the sardine-can existence. We'd better be ready to be squeezed in with unbathed/garlic-smelling oarsmen and trackers.

# Yichang Mission Hostel's Caveats And Counsel

*Yichang's River Front, 1946*

An ancient pylon-like pagoda on the Yichang riverbank was a pivot for our Army twin-motored plane circling the city. We had a spectacular view of the two mile wide Yangtze River sweeping inexorably eastward. On the south bank, a strange pyramidal hill rose from the Jianghan Plain. The ancient walled city with new settlements mushrooming outside each of its gates, spread asymmetrically over the north bank. Far away, towering on the western horizon, we caught glimpses of the palisades guarding the east entrance to the gorges.

Completing a giant circle, we landed where, less than a year before, Japanese Zeros and bombers had taken off to rain terror on China's interior cities. The enormous airfield, set in a plain of rice paddies, appeared deserted. The once-proud bastion of Hirohito's crack squadrons now was but a monument to defeat, with empty hangers and dilapidated buildings. With no passenger center and no evidence of the city in sight, we wondered if we were anywhere close to Yichang.

A small truck emerged from the orange grove adjoining the field and stopped near us. The driver loaded our gear, buckled us in, and quickly had us bouncing along the potholed cobblestone highway to Yichang. His pall-mell pace never slowed, even as we reached the outlying villages. As the jeep careened, we struggled with the fact that only four hours before we had been 800 miles down river in Nanjing.

The closer we came to the city the more the country road became choked with people, chickens, pigs, carts, and bicycles. Within sight of the city wall, the country roads opened to a wider and smoother riverside boulevard that led to the Bund. At close range what appeared from a distance to be a foreboding river bastion became a lively urban center. The city exploded from its sedate and ancient walls. The western style buildings clustered at the river's edge near the South Gate bore the marks of 19th-century British colonial architects.

Midway on the Bund we reached the broad central flight of stone stairs, astir with bucket carriers splashing water and slops, burdened coolies and pushy pedestrians. At the base, a series of pontoon docks served as the mooring for rows of junks and other craft stretched in an unending chain along the river's edge. Resembling a logjam, they lay two, three and four deep. Hundreds of Sichuan-built junks, with their high-varnished cypress woodwork and high-castled sterns, and an array of craft, looking "like the teeth of a comb," as the Chinese say, made a spectacular display.

Steamers anchored in midstream were surrounded by lighters transferring cargo to the shore. Wide cement slips with embedded iron tracks led from the pontoons at the water line up to warehouses on the Bund. The river margins here are not wild and rocky, as we would see upstream, but were lined with concrete levees.

During the late 19th century, the imperial Custom House had dominated the row of Western-styled offices and residences. At either end of the Bund were small, plain, box-shaped shops and houses clinging to steep hillsides, grayed by coal dust. These crate-like structures lost their modesty in the winter when the river level dropped, revealing their naked 50-foot piers. They were separated by a few long staircases, or narrow-gauge cable car tracks reaching up from the river. Farther along the western river edge, smoke billowed from the reconstructed furnaces of the yards of the rejuvenated Ming Sung iron and ship works.

The recently built-up area between the river and the walled city bulged with colorful store-front kitchens, small brass and tin works, carpenters' sheds and retail shops. Sidewalk stalls served roasted chestnuts, noodles and flatbread. Narrow alleys reached out toward the crowded living quarters which mushroomed to the rear. Everywhere clusters of men and women, boys and girls swarmed about, eating, buying, talking and working.

This six-lane thoroughfare bore the heavy traffic moving toward the South Gate. Our driver laid on his horn to clear a way past pedestrians and cyclists peddling in self-absorbed slow motion. Approaching the dilapidated 600 year-old wall, we could see how it had been cut in many places to accommodate modern traffic. The tower's superstructure, however, had been rebuilt and the massive brass-studded doors were in tact.

In 1946, with a population of over 100,000, Yichang was the largest center between the tri-city metropolis of Wuhan to the east and Chongqing to the west. The number of Western residents that year was only a fraction of what it had been before the war. The present number included British, Americans, French, Belgians and a few Russians. They were consular and customs officials, business persons, and Catholic and Protestant missionaries.

Once inside the city we were driven northward through a maze of still bumpy avenues. Going through the North Gate we passed the walled compounds of both of the Scotch Church Mission and the Swedish Missionary Society. We could see the foreign-styled residences, schools, and churches. In the 19th century these properties on alleys outside the walled city, were the only places Yichang authorities allowed missions to get started.

Farther on, still outside the city, we saw the extensive compound of the Catholic Mission set atop a beautiful knoll. Before we reached the hill we turned into the China Inland Mission's hostel, where Wang Shi and I lodged. The two pilots were driven on to a nearby officers' residence. Friends at the C.I.M. hostel welcomed us and asked their accommodating cook to serve us a late lunch.

We were relieved to find that Mr. Chen Yu, the mission's administrator, had engaged a river junk for us. He also had arranged to have Robert Thompson, an English-born, third-term American missionary, travel with us. Thompson's destination, farther inland in Sichuan, would take him beyond our turn-around city of Wanxian. Thompson, he told us, was an experienced upper river traveler, and more important he had "good face" with the *lao-ban* (skipper) of our chartered junk.

Mr. Chen took us into the dining room, where he introduced Thompson. His friendly, straight forward and good-humored manner was engaging. The easy confidence he shared was reassuring to Wang Shi and me—another good omen for our trip.

Gregory Studd, one of the mission's younger evangelists, hosted us at lunch. Boyish and reserved in appearance and with his Yorkshire brogue he reminded us of what we had heard about the 19th-century British origins of his mission.

"I'm tolerant of Americans," He commented, wryly. "I had to be during the year I studied in the United States."

"How did you three get together?" Studd asked, wasting no time finding out about us 'down river threesome,' as he called us. We in turn, found that he was a Baptist from the Midlands and had been a cricket player in college. One of our other hosts added proudly that Gregory was the grandson of Charles Studd, one of the celebrated seven "Cambridge converts." The famous grandfather was part of the fervent and dedicated evangelicals who, in the 1880's and 90s, won many volunteers and enlistments for the C.I.M. on both sides of the Atlantic.

We sat forward in our chairs when we found that two months ago Studd had made the trip through the gorges to Wanxian and return.

"Traveling in these parts is never a string of pearls," he said. "In picturesque ravines you may be treated to sweetly scented orange and peach blossoms. But more often there're threatening rocks and dangerous rapids, delays and disappointments."

"First off," he continued, "can you loosen your tight schedule? In counting on a twenty-day round trip you're not allowing for the many unexpected happenings that always occur between here and Wanxian. . .Our experience has taught us the up-and-return trip often takes double the time we plan. This section of the Long River is notorious for its serious hazards, contrary winds, treacherous currents, balky crew, long waits in towing-lines, junk crashes, obstinate officials and river bandits."

"Second," Studd continued, "Do you have plenty repellent–to combat bedbugs and foul odors? Also, how're your nerves?'. . .The sting of bedbugs and the consumptive coughs of the emaciated crew, are minor compared with the terrors of the river when it is rampaging. Even with steady nerves, split-second reactions and years of experience, the best of crews can be undone when the river is on a rampage. The Long River is merciless. Bleached bones piled like a white pagoda on the north bank of the Hsintang Gorge reminds the living of the dead claimed by the fateful 'dragon's mouth passage.'. . ."

"Good afternoon and welcome to our Yichang hostel," interrupted a heavy-set distinguished-looking gentlemen in his late fifties. "I'm Abraham Jones, and which one of you is Cowles, the Presbyterian from Nanjing who wrote me?"

"Abraham is this mission's indispensable senior missionary," Studd explained. "His salt-and-pepper hair and pointed beard give him a severe appearance and his loyal fundamentalism lead some to consider him austere. But he's a warm-hearted Midwesterner–genial and open as the Kansas plains. Just back from furlough, he's beginning his fourth term with us. He outranks and outruns us all. Amazing person! He keeps us happy while keeping our noses to the grindstone!"

Abraham addressed me with a mischievous twinkle in his deep-sunken eyes: "As for you, Cowles, in the first months of your first term and a reputed East Coast liberal, I've anticipated trouble with you. But in my 30 years in these parts, I've seen all sorts of travelers. You don't have horns and a tail, so we should get along."

Brother Jones, as he asked us to call him, reminisced briefly about his Kansas origins. Before long, however, he got around to our trip into the gorges and his skepticism regarding our overly optimistic plans.

"You remind me," he said bemused, "of how my Missouri grandfather Ebenezer felt in the 19th century when he saw starry-eyed Easterners rolling into St. Joseph, expecting a smooth trek across the plains and Rockies. Upriver junks bear some resemblance to the idealized 19th-century prairie schooners. On the Long River's gorges, you won't meet menacing Indians, but you'll be savaged by whirlpools, rapids, dysentery and bandits."

Others among our new friends told of the boatmen's drawn-out starting rituals. The first day, the captain bargains about money for supplies and crew; the second day, food and supplies are bought and the crew is hired; the third day, the crew's debts are paid; the fourth day is spent in celebration; the fifth day is for visiting shrines to propitiate angry river gods; the sixth day, customs experts inspect the bamboo tracking cable.

Angela Hubbard, an older single woman, maneuvered to ease Abraham's and Gregory's discouragements. Changing the subject she asked what we thought of Yichang's distinctive Pyramid Hill–the incongruous triangular mountain on the river's south bank. Science teacher that she was, she suggested that in reality it was a drumlin, a pile of rock and sediment thrust up by glaciers as they ground their way through this area eons ago.

Not so, however, according to local geomancers, she explained. To them, for centuries, the strange Hill with its peculiar position and form presented a fearful nemesis. Diviners spread the popular suspicion that some ancient ruler had interfered with the correct *fen xui*, the mysterious balance of earthly and heavenly forces. Much of the populace feared this miscarriage of nature and held that it bore ill for the city's prosperity. In the past, priests routinely offered elaborate prayers to allay the divine fury incarnated in this grotesque angular mountain.

Chen Yu, the animated veteran business manager, came in as we were finishing lunch. A bundle of smiles and energy, he announced that he was ready to escort us for the afternoon to show us the city. A native of Hubei province and a 20-year resident of Yichang, he proved an information-packed guide.

"Our city," Chen began, "has a propitious name: '*Yi*' means 'proper,' 'fit,' or 'right.' And '*Chang*' means 'prosperous,' 'shining,' or 'good.'. . . It's questionable whether we're 'right' and 'shining.' But we are working on being 'proper' and 'prosperous.' . . . "

"The city's major industries," he explained, "are chemical, pharmaceutical and textile manufacturing. The surrounding area is famous for tangerines, porcelain, black tea and mushrooms. But before seeing these and other sights, let's first visit the mission's schools before the students are finished for the day."

School was serious and intense. Classes started at 7:30 a.m. and continued until 4:30 p.m. Choruses of recited lessons and exuberant play at recess made for a noisy environment. Elementary school boys and girls, unaccustomed to seeing foreigners, stopped in their tracks to look us over as we entered the yard. Soon recess games were disrupted as more and more curious pupils gathered around us. The children jumped, skipped, laughed and cheered at the words of greeting we offered.

Classes were in loud progress next door in the delapidated central building of the middle school. Geography, appropriately, was the subject of the class we squeezed into. Several students who were squatting on the floor with their open textbooks accommodatingly moved forward into the aisle to give us standing room in the back. The redoubtable woman teacher tried valiantly to continue the lesson despite the commotion we created. Soon she asked us to speak about the afternoon's lesson–northern Africa. Students, however, were more interested in America and Americans. Hands went up raising questions about the United States: Where did each of us live? What did we eat? What sort of houses did we live in? What sort of schools did our children attend? What were our salaries?

Li Fang-shih, assistant middle-school principal, while escorting us across the grounds, described some of the difficult conditions his staff confronted. His descriptions were less a litany of complaints, and more an assessment of the herculean tasks these school leaders faced. The problems included: scarcity of trained workers, insufficient funds to meet payroll, problems transporting pupils to schools and the workers to satellite centers. Post war months present uncertainties and organizational break downs, political and economic unrest, loss of key supportive board members and administrative officers who fled west during the war and never returned.

"Repeatedly we're frustrated and often exhausted," put in the ten-year veteran teacher accompanying us. "Teaching has never been easy. And, though it's long been one of China's most honored professions, teachers have never been well-paid. But we're not discouraged. Amid the troubles and confusions there are yet satisfactions, especially the grateful response of appreciative students."

The teachers' reports were cut short to make way at the big entry gates for the children pouring through on their way home.

At the high school, short of time, we did not visit a classroom. We were fortunate, however, to catch visits with three instructors and Mr. Liu, the resolute middle-aged principal. Praising his staff's fortitude and flexibility during the Japanese occupation, he told amazing stories of the teachers' innovative making the most of very little.

"You'll see the same hardships in schools and colleges all over China," Wang Shi reacted, as we walked toward the high school. "China's entire educational system has similar hardships: serious overcrowding, lack of teaching materials, buildings in disrepair, over-worked and worn out teachers. . .I'd like to ship half my college graduating class here to Yichang to help out."

Out on the busy avenue again, Mr. Chen resumed his spiel about the city. He described historic spots in the nearby hills. He explained that he would now take us to Sanyouping (Three Travelers Cave), a favorite spot in the hills outside the West Gate.

En route to the caves, Mr. Chen sketched the Japanese bombardment, capture and occupation of the city. He told of the fateful events of 1939, with the Japanese advancing relentlessly up the river, headed inevitably toward Yichang. The capture of Hankow, 400 miles down river, had meant that no other large city lay between the enemy and Yichang.

The possibility of transporting even a fraction of the crucial supplies to Chongqing, the war-time capital, 300 miles upriver, had appeared hopeless. The vital war materiel that had poured into Yichang from all parts of China seemed doomed to fall into enemy hands. But a superhuman effort by the Ming Sung yards had surpassed all expectations in building enough ships to evacuate tons of crucial supplies. Chen became animated as he recalled the feat of what he called the "heroic plant."

In those despairing weeks during 1939, the Free China government called upon Lu Tso-fu, head of the Ming Sung Company, to organize a fleet of ships to move as many of the supplies as possible upriver in a race against both the Japanese Army and the fast-approaching July flood waters. In addition to the nearly impossible logistic task, Lu was besieged by bribing entrepreneurs frantic to move their particular cargoes piled on the docks. Nevertheless, amid the confusion of conflicting demands and criticisms, he devised and enforced a firm system of priorities.

Manager Lu radioed all available ships to report to the Ming Sung yards. Hasty repairs were completed on three disabled steamers, and five more ships were salvaged and rebuilt. With fuel-oil supplies gone, one diesel-engined ship had to be converted to steam power. Too short to permit the installation of a steam engine, the ship was hauled ashore with skids and hand winches, cut apart amidship and lengthened by 40 feet. A boiler was reclaimed from a sunken ship and reinforced with scarce supplies of plate and tubing. The four steel-hulled and thirteen wooden ships under construction were rushed to completion. When the Japanese started bombing, much of this innovative improvisation had to be carried on in caves excavated from the riverbank's solid rock.

To move 20 and 30-ton loads, he had available only a few trucks and a few decrepit cranes. So he organized coolies into large work crews. Around the clock these teams of humans shouldered and moved freight. Day and night the chant of workers and stevedores rang out. Machines, boxes, bales, parts and supplies were carried aboard, ship after ship, by the tens of tons. Most of these loads were moved on the shoulders of two, four, ten or twenty sure-footed coolies, picking their way down slippery banks and across narrow gangways with their rhythmic swaying bamboo poles. Day after day the steamers battled the rapids to reach upriver ports with their essential cargo. The mountains of machines at Yichang grew smaller, until 42 days after Mr. Lu had arrived, the last machine was loaded. The impossible transport job was accomplished! When the Japanese marched into Yichang they found the city's wharves and warehouses empty.

"Now, seven years later, the heroic Ming Sung yards are comparatively quiet." Mr. Chen added, concluding the city tour he had escorted so enthusiastically "But Yichang still shows signs of its stubborn stand against the enemy. You still see pill boxes, barricades, trenches and pock-marked walls."

Reaching *Sanyouping*, we found the caves tucked into the hills situated in a beautiful fruit grove overlooking the river. Nearby was an historic pavilion and a new giant Buddha. They had been built to mark the entrance to the most dangerous of the gorges, the Xiling. A statue of the Three Kingdom's, general Zhang Fei looked out toward the water.

Mr. Chen told us that Chinese scholars have divided the poems of the Three Gorges into three kinds: descriptions of nature with political meaning, human history and poems in praise of particular places. An illustration of poems that describe the natural wonders of the Gorges to serve political purposes, he said, is Bai Juyi's poem entitled, 'The Entrance of Three Travelers Cave.' "This scenery is wonderful," Wrote Bai Juyi, but he used the 'poetic soul' of the mountains and rivers to express his despair and the bitterness of his lot. Even on sighting the Xiling Gorge, the poet moodily wrote, "If you want to know how great my worry is, well, it is higher than Yanyudui (Goosetail Rock)."

The second type, Mr. Chen explained as we drove back to the city, are poems that describe the history of human activities and of civilizations, or disseminate scientific knowledge, history, geography, politics, military lore, local customs and specialities, hydrology and shipping, and the weather. . .The third style are poems that sing the praises of scenic spots and historic sites along the Three Gorges, using them to express patriotic feelings.

We stopped at a dingy wayside inn in a tiny village. Clusters of noisy children and raucous carriers were gathered around the several stalls crowding out into the narrow country road. From inside, however, we could hear the graceful and heart-stirring sound of classical Chinese music. It was so sweet we couldn't help pursuing the source.

We found a group of young musicians performing with ancient musical instruments from archeological excavations with such exotic names as 'Bianzhong', 'Bianquin,' 'Fangzian,' 'Yun' zithers and inverted bells. We became absorbed as they plucked the zither strings, struck the chimes, and rang the bronze bells. We wanted to spend the rest of the afternoon in that intoxicating place! Instead we returned for supper back at the Hostel.

Later, around the dinner table, Gregory and Angela told us more about Yichang. They described the life of Westerners during these months following the close of World War II. Winter evenings, they said, were long and dull, summers were hot and mosquito-infested. The old hands had long ago explored the intellectual depths and shallows of their neighbors and so knew their colleagues' thoughts and feelings. Mental and social capabilities of newcomers were quickly assessed. The arrival of a stranger, the weekly mail boat and the changes of the customs or consular staffs were the chief varieties of life.

Gregory Studd took advantage of the moment to acknowledge his respect and admiration for Angela Hubbard's long and remarkable contribution to the Yichang mission. Angela, originally from a small Illinois town, was serving her third term at Yichang. From a large rural family, she had worked her way through college by substitute teaching. After her Commencement she arranged also to graduate from obligations to an ailing mother and younger siblings. She took steps to go abroad as a teacher or nurse. As a candidate for service in China, she could well have written that her motive included, "The desire to live a holy life and to help others to do the same."

This resolve cut her off from the familiar and from the likelihood of meeting an eligible male. Her difficult commitment amounted to entering a Catholic order. She loved families and often wished she had married and had children. Angela, however, had found that her work with hundreds of Chinese youngsters had become a delight instead of a burden and fully as significant as the teaching she might have done in a one-room country school in rural America.

After vespers, missionaries gathered on the screened-in porch. Glasses of ginger ale or cups of tea in hand, they had their "happy hour." Relaxing in creaky rattan chairs, they shared bits about the day's events and people. As Abraham Jones loosened up, his colleagues relaxed and became more revealing about what had brought them to this distant inland station.

In the illuminating hour that followed, instead of more details about the Long River's gorges, personal interest gems were shared. The major, Wang Shi and I gained unique cameos of heroic people working to innovate in this mission outpost.

"As to my Midlands English," Greggory Studd said, responding wryly to my acknowledgment of his Yorkshire brogue, "it reminds the Yankees here that it was an Englishman, Hudson Taylor, who started the C.I.M. back in the 19th century! In this century English leadership continued, but increasingly the new workers came from North America and Western Europe.

From its beginnings, the mission tried to get beyond its 'foreignness' and stress its 'China-centeredness,' in language, organization and practice. Effort was made to train Chinese pastors and teachers to eventually take over the mission's educational, medical and pastoral functions.

"We are grateful to have Mr. Studd," interrupted Abraham. "He keeps us on our mettle in more ways than speaking correct English. Even though the rest of us Westerners now outnumber our English colleagues, we benefit from his encouragement–not only to speak correct Midlands English. He boosts our spirits and his unwavering emphasis on evangelism and the mission's 'China-centeredness' keeps us all on our toes."

"I remember my father," Abraham continued, "who was a C.I.M. missionary before me, telling me how he began as a starry-eyed young missionary, at the turn of the century. He said he focused on 'rescuing heathens from hell.' Before long, he found it was the heathens who rescued the foreigners from their hell. At first he insisted on prospective converts 'surrendering their individual wills to God and Christ,' only to find that they hadn't the slightest conception of Christ and less of an idea about what sort of a God he was talking about."

As we began to get acquainted with Abraham Jones we found a remarkable veteran and not at all the austere and stuffy person we first considered him to be. His heritage was as fascinating as it was unique. He had inherited his Kansas father's iron will and dedicated devotion to the China missionary enterprise. As a son of the mission field he had seen other missionaries, who had not died, often despair and return home in anger that the charity they had given had not been accepted. The senior Abrahams persisted in serving at the interior mission station where they were assigned at the turn of the century. When Abraham's mother, an equally intense C.I.M. devotee, died in childbirth, father Abraham remained in China and carried on as a single parent.

Years later, when the young Abraham, decided to follow in his father's footsteps, the mission's examining committee had more stringent requirements for 20th century recruits. The son, with a more thorough education and good health, was readily accepted and sent out to China to begin his missionary career in 1916. Being raised in China, his Chinese language was flawless and he intuited naturally the nuances of how Chinese thought and felt. Furthermore, he knew the poignancy and suffering of missionary life.

The times in China were dark in 1916. Convulsed in the years following the overthrow of the 267 year-old Manchu dynasty, the troubled country was entering the era of rapacious warlords. Even though the United States had not yet become drawn into that World War I. European nations were into their second horrible year of tearing each other apart. English and French missionaries in Chinese cities looked daggers at German missionaries. China was sending coolies to Flanders to help dig trenches and was itself in unbelievable turmoil.

Abraham the younger's first assignment was to a small and isolated Sichuan station, 200 miles northwest of Yichang. Working under the supervision of a Chinese evangelist and a veteran English missionary, he preached, taught Bible classes and traveled to homes, carrying on first aid work in outlying villages. Each week day he spent two to three hours with his tutor, reading and writing Chinese. During this term, he and his wife had two children. The youngest, "an exuberant two-year-old blond angel," as Abraham spoke of her, died during a typhus epidemic.

At the end of a four-year stint the family returned to the States on furlough. Back in Chicago, he took refresher courses and deepened his evangelical convictions at the Moody Bible Institute.

Returning to China within the year (1921), he was transferred to the larger mission of Yichang. For a few months the mission met less antagonism from Chinese officials and less hostility from the populace. Evangelistic work expanded in the burgeoning river-port with its productive outlying rural feeder areas. Christian workers were heartened.

By 1922, however, the Chinese hopes that the overthrow of the imperial regime would lead to a new democratic and powerful China able to deal effectively with her own problems were further dashed. The country's newly (1921) organized Communist Party began to be a factor in the lethal national mix. Political-military rivalry under "war-lords" divided the country into contending territories and imposed the indiscriminate conscription of their youth. A series of floods, crop failures, and famines compounded the worsening economic, political and military conditions. Commoners' uncertainties and hardships increased.

By 1927 anti-foreign feelings escalated. Angry mobs accumulated in cities and demonstrated for an end to Western imperialism. The missionaries were charged with being in league with the foreign capitalists. The demand was to "run all foreigners out!" With nationalism and patriotism becoming more ascendant, attacks on Christianity and Christians were intensified.

In the same year (1927) Central China was enmeshed in the grinding and cataclysmic throes of Chiang Kai-shek's and his coalition of Southern warlords' northern campaign.' In Shanghai thousands of Chinese Communists were machine gunned down by Nationalists in their ruthless drive to gain control of the Yangtze Valley. The Nationalists' success brought the end of the denouement of the turbulent "war-lord" days but did not bring an end to political and economic insecurities. Old problems remained unsolved and new difficulties emerged.

Following its victory the fledgling Nationalist government established comparably stable social and economic conditions within cities and succeeded in pacifying wide areas of the country side. In this short lull anti-Christian opposition lessened.

Foreign missions and Chinese churches were allowed and even encouraged to provide educational and health services for the people, albeit in the midst of continued social disorder. In these years (1929-31) 7,675 foreign missionaries served in China–a peak that has never been surpassed.

Within only a few years Japanese armies, having invaded China's northeastern or Manchurian provinces two years before (1931), pressed down to Peking and threatened Shantung province. They bombed and captured Shanghai and other coastal centers. The foes pushed up the Yangtze River toward Nanking. After mercilessly raping that capital city and murdering 300,000 of the populace, the Japanese army pressed west. Soon their forces were threatening Hankow, the next large city east of Yichang. By 1934 the attack on and fall of Yichang was imminent.

Abraham with his wife and two young children moved up river, first to Wanxian and then further west. He worked with rural pastors surrounding a center 80 miles east of Chongqing. In 1940 physicians in Chongqing insisted that, for their health and safety, his wife and children should return to the United States. This involved a long and hazardous journey. They traveled by boat up the river, and then by bus southwest to Kunming. From there, again by bus, they took the Burma Road to Rangoon, where they caught a ship for the long voyage back to the States. Before Abraham himself could exit and join them in the States, Pearl Harbor occurred and he was marooned in the small Sichuan station for the duration.

"In addition to widespread destruction and terrible loss of life, the Japanese war years (1941-44) brought severe economic instability and political disorder," Abraham explained. "Refugee churches in the west were swamped with inquirers. The increase was gratifying, but not without a host of new difficulties. We had to learn, for example, to seek out people's motives for becoming Christians. When we failed to do this, many of those received were found to have no real concern for Christ's work. Much additional work went into disciplining their faltering commitment and backsliding into opium-smoking, gambling, dishonesty, or heavy debts for extravagant weddings or funerals. Working with the unredeemed was hard; trying to service the unredeemable was impossible. Missionaries and Chinese colleagues alike often worked 16 hours a day. Exhaustion and frustration brought on frequent burn-outs."

"After V-E day (April 1945)," Abraham continued, "I squeezed into an overcrowded rickety bus and survived a five-day hair-raising ride over 350 miles across mountains to Kunming. From there I caught a convoy down the Burma Road and eventually got back to the States for another furlough."

Three months ago (1946) and 30 years after his start, he had returned to China. He was glad to be back in Yichang. This term, his fourth, offered both promise and difficulties. Though peace was welcome, many of the same problems his father before him had struggled with remained. Now they were magnified and their solutions more complex. Civil war was heating up, even as the enormous tasks of reconstruction were everywhere apparent. Christian workers, more than ever needed flexibility and decisiveness amid the period's confusions and changes. What's more, he missed his family, since he had not been able to bring them with him this time.

"It's heartening," Abraham reported, "To see how Chinese Christian pastors, teachers and lay leaders are facing the many old and new tasks before them. Significant positive things are occurring. Within the new openness of spirit we are experiencing, Chinese church leaders and missionaries alike are rethinking what work and emphases are 'essential'.

Many Chinese Christians have caught the vision of Chinese propagating the faith (evangelizing) in all parts of China. Chinese Christians increasingly form their own spiritual, moral and conceptual relationship to God in Christ. More are developing their own sense of how the 'old life' can be changed into the 'new.' They know they must state their faith in Chinese idioms, images and deeds to make them meaningful to their neighbors.

"We missionaries have had to become more flexible. Rigid and doctrinaire approaches hinder instead of help communicate our message. Rivalries and fragmentation in the Christian witness are disastrous. The old system of fragmented Protestantism needed to come to an end. We are all bound in one bundle; we advance together or we fail together. Every denomination's 'China mission' confronts conditions demanding change. All face reconstruction's costs and extent, renewed Chinese nationalism, the reality of a strengthened indigenous Chinese church, reduced funds and personnel from sending churches.

"The critical task, however, no longer can be how to advance the missionary enterprise, but must be how to strengthen the Chinese church. The key questions are: how is the Chinese church to become self supporting, self governing, self propagating, and more accepted and influential within Chinese society.

"Many of our current Chinese pastors and leaders, though depleted in numbers, are young and an increasing number are women. Liberated now, they have become more aggressive and more determined to develop a new vocabulary, new forms and new approaches appropriate for the new day. Millennia old folk religions cause difficulties, as does the tight family system that often limits its members' freedom to hear and respond to the gospel."

Abraham sat back, spent but satisfied. In a moment he concluded, "It has helped me to review the years with you. Thank you for listening."

"Brother Abraham," coaxed Angela, again guiding the conversation into lighter considerations, "you've been back from your leave in the States for months now, but you've told us little about how you found the hamlet that was your family's hometown."

"In faded towns of central Kansas," Abraham ruminated, "ghosts and live inhabitants sleep squared to the world, neatly, like accountant's figures!. . . How's that for a start?"

"When you return to your boyhood town and county," he added, "you find it wasn't the town or county you longed for–it was your boyhood."

Pausing, he concluded, "It's taken a lot of living to become aware of where I had come from. For years I missed developing my personal identity and allowing myself to be my own person. In time I've come to appreciate the distinctiveness of my heritage. Now I'm glad to be back to my other hometown, Yichang, here on the Jianghan Plain!"

# Renewing Old City Served By Vibrant Mission

*Mission School, Yichang*

Early the next morning, gear in hand, the major, Wang Shi, Thompson and I were at the administrator's office looking forward to a before-noon shipping out to the gorges. We found Mr. Chen gone. His associate, Mr. Liu, greeted us with the word that the *lao ban* (skipper) wanted two more days to complete outfitting and provisioning his junk.

Liu explained that Mr. Chen, anxious to not lose 'face' with us special Nanjing travelers, was now at the river edge trying to arrange an earlier departure. The skipper, in turn, does not want to lose 'face' with his friend Mr. Chen.

The major's and my eyes met, remembering the delays Gregory Studd and the others told us about the day before! Our readiness was futile–no match against the forces of delay.

Well aware of our impatience and undisguised irritation, Mr. Liu reassured us that the delay provided the opportunity for us to see a number of places not seen yesterday. At the large new city market we could see farmers from four surrounding counties display all sorts of the region's fruits, vegetables, and meats. Then we could see craftsmen at the North Gate and in the adjoining shops

Hubei artifacts, Sichuan silks and brocades, and Tibetan tapestries and jewelry–all of which make excellent gifts. After some shopping we could visit the Catholic center. "It's the city's oldest mission," concluded Mr. Liu, "and a most worthy establishment, and one my great grandfather 85 years ago helped start."

We sensed that Mr. Liu, proud of his native city and now a part-time high school history teacher, had a vested interest in the tour he proposed. Tensions would be compounded if we made Mr. Liu lose 'face' by declining the tour he suggested. The major, a committed Catholic, welcomed the suggestion. Realizing we could do nothing further to hurry our departure, we accepted Mr. Liu's alternative. Wang Shi agreed to accompany us.

In the hired horse-drawn carriage we were to ride in, the pair of facing seats placed us as a fixed audience for Mr. Liu to tell us about the city. First he briefed us about the unusual regional market we were to see. He explained about the conflicting sectional claims of different counties (xian) and of the other problems that had to be overcome in completing the project. Soon, like all travelers, we were walking from one intriguing stall to another in the enormous market.

Back in the carriage, headed for the North Gate, our knowledgeable and enthusiastic host described the diverse craft workers we were about to see. He praised Yichang's printers, tinsmiths, tailors, embroiderers, pewter and cabinet makers. Mr. Liu had briefed us well and helped us understand and appreciate the array of variegated displays and products. Wang Shi, champion of the common folk, approved of how Mr. Liu called to our attention the craftsmen's diligence, skill and ingenuity.

Finishing the market and craft shops visits, Mr. Liu regaling us with jokes and local anecdotes. He shared accounts of life for citizens like himself in Yichang during these post-war days.

"Restrictions and uncertainties of the painful occupation years were difficult to accept," he said. "But when the weight of these negatives were lifted, we found we had learned bad habits: defensiveness and dependence, resistance and procrastination. Present conditions require different strategies from both pre-war and war years. We can't slip back ten years to how it was before the war. Yet, that's what we find easiest to do.

Approaching the Catholic Mission Mr. Liu, history teacher that he was, told us about the Catholic center's beginnings.

One of the Society for the Propagation of the Faith's most westerly outposts, this mission had a rocky beginning. The first two priests, one French and the other Belgian, reached Yichang in the mid 1850's. They arrived at an unpropitious time. In this central area of China the wounds of the devastating Taiping rebellion were not healed. Widespread resentment of foreigners had followed the humiliations inflicted by the Britain-instigated Opium Wars

1840's). Rancor against foreigners, and particularly missionaries, was intense and unrelenting.

Month after month the priests' negotiations for permission to hold public meetings were fruitless. They and their handful of converts frequently met with persecution. Xenophobic officials had imposed a three-year delay before the worshipers were permitted to locate temporarily on a marginal plot outside the city. After procuring the land another three years elapsed negotiating building permits. All the while, the missionaries were surrounded with malicious rumors, vandalism, personal abuse, ostracism and periodic attacks from rowdies instigated by suspicious gentry.

The first breakthrough came when officials finally granted permission to the missionaries to start a kindergarten. The next break came three years later when permission came to establish a primary school. In 1865 a middle school followed. It was in this development that Mr. Liu's ancestor, as one of the deciding gentry, had been instrumental in helping to start the mission.

By 1870 competition from the now arriving Protestants challenged the mission's brothers and sisters. The Protestants' conditions for participation were less stringent and they did not demand financial recompense for losses incurred by the Chinese rioters. Also they welcomed all into their schools, clinics and worship services.

Catholics, in contrast, aroused resentment and resistance against certain membership conditions, such as: (1) placing the Roman hierarchy on a level higher than the ruling mandarins; (2) exclusion of "heathens" from sanctuaries during the celebration of Mass; and, (3) the secrecy which attended the administration of the last rites, a restriction obnoxious to many Chinese who did not consider it important to respect individuals' privacy.

Throughout China, persecutions, riots and general unrest plagued missionaries. One of the most serious incidents was the so-called Tientsin massacre of 1870, in which a mob destroyed an orphanage and the adjoining church and killed the French consul and several other French men and women, including ten sisters and one priest. Widespread riots also erupted in the Yangtze Valley east of Yichang in 1890 and 1891. This time, Protestants had been the chief victims. When foreign governments took up the cause of their nationals, another round of violence occurred. Great resentment flared, for example, over the heavy indemnity the French extracted for damages in the Tientsin killings.

In the 1870's and '80s the facilities and trained personnel of both Protestant and Catholic missions were limited. Both were hard pressed to provide humanitarian services. One particularly needed service was the care for the emaciated babies abandoned at the mission gate. Such a service, however, was difficult to establish and maintain. But once begun, the missions proved themselves to be efficient administrators. One 50-year-old orphanage we visited, designed to accommodate 200, that year housed 400 abandoned children. Each child received loving care from the Belgian and Chinese sisters.

As the populace came to see and appreciate the visible benefits of the churchs' schools, clinics, orphanages and humanitarian services, the gentry's antagonism was blunted. In the '80s popular resistance was further eased because of the assistance missionaries gave to litigants by contacting the French envoys in Beijing to exert pressure on local magistrates.

Over the years the mission was fortunate to be directed by a succession of far-sighted leaders. They extended its ecclesiastical and educational work, despite the perennial problem of overloading a perilously depleted staff of foreign and Chinese clergy. Through its health services three clinics and a 50-bed hospital were established. For years these mission units provided the only modern medical services within a 150-mile radius. Throughout the last fifty years long lines of patients have crowded these centers seven days a week.

Upon reaching the mission we were greeted by the administrator, Mr. Liang, a close friend of Mr. Liu. Mr. Liang introduced us to the the distinguished looking and winsome mannered middle-aged sister, dressed in Chinese habit, who had stopped in the office.

"This is Sister Catherine, originally from Louvaine," he said, "but, having served two eight-year terms, and now is beginning her third, she's an Yichang veteran." And turning to the younger Belgian 'brothers' coming in the door, Mr. Liang said, "Let me present these two enthusiastic newcomers who have arrived from Europe in recent months. They're absorbed in language study and already are helping with our parish work and in the clinics."

In passing the mission hospital with its lines of waiting patients spilling over into the courtyard, Mr.Liang told us of the expanded health services which now included this 95-bed facility and four out-patient clinics. He explained that modern surgical and pharmaceutical supplies were limited. The staff, then only one-third its usual strength, was serving the needs of the people as best it could. The medical staff–two Western-trained Chinese physicians, one sister who was the charge nurse and three Chinese assistants–continually was on the verge of exhaustion.

At present the veteran Bishop, who held the mission together during the Japanese occupation, was on furlough in France. Father Henri, his associate, now in charge, was an impressive-looking elderly man, with thick, iron-gray hair and a well-trimmed mustache. As he walked over to greet us, children ran up to him, kissed his hands and hung on his robe and older parishioners asked for his blessings.

Scheduled to celebrate mass in a few minutes, he asked us to join the worship. The major, Thompson and I accepted the invitation. Wang Shi, who had never attended a mass, hesitated at first, then agreed. The Chinese liturgy was not easy to follow, but the chants and plainsong carried us through the sequences. Father Henri, garbed in a black Chinese robe with a surplice and multicolored stole, provided an commanding presence. His humble manner of celebrating the sacrament invited an awareness of the divine.

A respectful mumble of assent went up from the congregation when Father Henri, in his prayer, gave thanks for 'the long procession of believing ancestors.' "Our good works," the father proclaimed in his brief and practical homily, "fail unless they're centered on what is understood as God's will. We his children are cast in His image, but in our willfulness we often go astray. Our patient God is trying to show us His Will and help us correct our imperfections." The simplicity and solemnity of the mass and the visible evidence of reverence of the worshipers proved quieting.

After Mass Wang Shi was quick to approach the officiant, asking, "Father Henri, you believe Jesus' body and blood entered the bread and wine you served?"

"Yes," the father replied, "It's a tested Catholic belief."

"But," Wang pressed, "isn't it shaky to rest one's practices simply on traditional ideas?"

"True," Father Henri affirmed. "Motivation for religious observances should be more than routine or habit only. The roots of this act run deep in church history, sacred scriptures and in the lives of believers. And, as I act on my belief about it, it is proven to me. Whether or not a worshiper accepts the miracle of Christ entering the physical elements, the important thing is that we do this in *remembrance* of Jesus and as a seal of our being bound together through Him."

Wang Shi wasn't convinced, but voiced a question about another matter that had concerned him, "Is your kneeling an expected kowtow?"

"No, it's neither 'expected' nor like the civil act of 'kowtow'," Father Henri responded, "It's a sign of respect. You, as an advocate of the people, should approve it for its democratizing value and the way it promotes participation of the people. 'Liturgy' literally means 'the work of the people,' or 'making God visible and alive to the worshipers.' You say in Chinese *nien ging*, 'remember the sacred,' or *dao gao wen*, 'pray genuinely.' Deeper than postures or mouthing words, kneeling is a reminder that God is great and near. By kneeling I also remember I am a part of a community and I am not alone. And as worshipers we come not as protesters to claim our rights, but as sinners to confess our wrongs and imperfections."

"When your people call you 'Father,' " Wang Shi persisted, "Do you consider your parishioners untutored children?"

"Yes, and no," Father Henri answered. "The fact is that many are untutored children. They need teaching and parenting in the Christian faith. But this gives me no right to look down on them or in any way to be condescending toward them. St. Paul talked of giving milk to new believers. The fullness of the Christian faith is often far beyond the experience of my hearers. Appreiciating the level of their understanding, and never belittling them, I try to translate my convictions to listeners in ways they can grasp. . .My new friend we need to talk much more about these important questions you raise."

In an adjoining office, Father Henri found Father François and introduced him saying, "This young-looking brother has served us three terms and is our best one to show and tell you about the mission's work and life."

Father François' strong handshake, friendly voice and mischievous twinkle in his eye, put us at ease and drew us to him.

In his attire, the way he walked and his gestures, Father François looked Chinese and the humble Franciscan that he was. He illustrated how "siniciza tion" often occurred with those who serve many years in China in those times. Being immersed in the yang and yin of Chinese life exerts a leveling process on foreigners.

First, he wanted us to meet workers in the offices around the courtyard. Making the rounds he enthusiastically described the mission's evangelistic educational and humanitarian works. In addition to Sunday worship, there were regular Bible study groups and catechism classes. Special services were offered for the sick, orphans, elderlies and dispossessed. Chapels, schools and clinics were centered in the city; satellites, or "sister centers," had been established in outlying villages and towns, as far as 100 miles away.

Father François became more animated as he found in us an appreciative audience. He soon slipped from talk of programs and activities to his and his colleagues frustrations over the immensity of the mission's tasks. "We speak of the good news, and to the multitudes it is neither news nor particularly good. It's the old, old-story of what happened two thousand years ago. All our programs, services and personal witnesses are but a drop in the bucket compared with the peoples' needs and insecurities. It's discouraging to see how limited is the church's influence and outreach, but it's reassuring to find that the word and influence of the Almighty somehow continues to get through despite our human limitations."

"In other years," he explained, "church leaders sought a 'soul count' of converts, now the emphasis focuses on 'growth.' But we do not see enough growth in depth of understanding and change in lives. The work is intangible, hard to measure."

"That 'intangibleness' of your work and your faith," Wang Shi broke in, "raises the question for me: why and how does it happens that Chinese, practical by nature as they are, become Catholics."

"It's interesting that the 'spiritual' aspects of Catholicism are not stumbling blocks for the average Chinese," The priest answered, you know better than I how commoners live in a world of spirits inherited from their long history of folk religions with many gods. The powerful ethical appeal of Christianity is one of the strongest attractions of Christianity. To accept Christ as Lord of one's life demands a leap of faith. But that doesn't mean such a commitment is unreal or impractical."

"Strong pulls of traditions and family ties sustain Chinese," the Father continued. "If the wrench from those customs and relationships is too painful, the inquirer may back off. Many Chinese are surrounded by social hostility when they show interest in Christianity. Often they have to overcome a powerful cultural opposition not known to Westerners. A large number of our converts have not had the benefit of education and access to modern ideas. The comparatively few Chinese college graduates must sort through Taoism, Buddhism and Confucianism and reconcile nihilism, scientism, Marxism and other 20th century 'isms' in order to embrace Catholicism."

"During the Japanese occupation," the father explained, "Chinese church workers and Western missionaries in their faithfulness gained a positive reputation for their unselfish good works. But their service demanded great flexibility and faithfulness. These same qualities are needed now in these post-war months.

"Japanese oppression is over," he observed, "but China's perennial problems of poverty, disease, illiteracy, and unresponsive bureaucracy remain. Farmers continue to be extorted by bandits, ground down by absentee gentry, wiped out by repeated floods and famine. Political leaders, headed into uncharted territory are overwhelmed with the magnitude of reconstruction. The much needed 'social reconstruction' is talked about but not worked on. Run-away inflation compounds these long-standing political and social ills.

"In a time of such instability the mission's task is difficult," Father Francois explained. "Time-consuming catch-up tasks soak up workers' energies and resources. Damaged buildings need repairs, disrupted programs and services require reevaluation and possible restoration. Experienced personnel and adequate funds and supplies are limited. To survive amid the current contending "powers and principalities"–Guomindang, Communists, bandits and guerrillas–requires what our bishop describes as a 'delicate responsible neutrality'.

As to the mission's ministries the Father was encouraged with having more licentiates and priests than before the war. But in recent years the mission hasn't made enough impact on young intellectuals or on the second-and third-generation Chinese Catholic families, who in the past were the strongest sources of an indigenous clergy. Since many Chinese clergy and lay leaders who refugeed west have not returned, more churches are left without guidance; the number that remained are still too few to man each congregation. We have had to begin crash training programs to prepare our priest-recruits to fill the many vacancies.

"Here we are at my humble apartment," the father said, ushering us in with oriental-style apologies and gestures. The small outer room that doubled for a study and living room was spartanly furnished with a narrow desk, a few books and a tiny altar. He urged us to sit on the stools he pulled into a circle.

The major's noting the portraits propped on mantle unleashed a flood of feelings in Father Francois as he identified each one: "That's my mother, that's my father, and those are my sisters. They all live near each other in Bruges."

"Serving in Yichang so many years," the major observed, "and so far away from those loved ones pictured there must, over the years, have been quite a personal sacrifice."

"Often I remember Belgium, my family, my university and my seminary," he said. "But now China is my home."

He then provided glimpses into his times of loneliness and struggles with the ingratitude he occasionally encountered. Surrounding him were dark and filthy rooms, plain and sometimes unclean food served with chopsticks mouthed by consumptive brethren, foul-smelling sewers down the middle of the streets, unceasing noisy talk in a foreign tongue, pentatonic scaled music, often squeaky or clashing, the crowds' unceasing reaching for help, people taking advantage of the priest's largess, frequent ingratitude, insensitivity to an individual's need for privacy, and the lack of physical intimacy.

"Yes, human that I am," Francois admitted, "I of course have my troubling moments. In those times the love and concern my classmates and family send strengthen me."

Noticing a violin hanging on the wall, Wang Shi asked if the father would give us the pleasure of his playing.

Father François picked up the instrument, as if returning to a long-neglected friend. Putting it to his shoulder he began playing two Belgian folk melodies, then the hymn, "Rock of Ages, Cleft for Me."

Interrupted by the servant entering with a large tea pot and cups, the father set the instrument down. Proposing a toast of wine from a local vineyard, he said, "This is to warm our hearts and seal our time together." Thompson, staunch Puritan that he was, raised his cup of tea and shared in the toast.

"As to how Chinese feel about Protestant and Catholic missionaries," Father François estimated, "generally, both branches of Christianity are accepted. Some people, we are told, are attracted to Catholic faith by what they see of priests' and sisters' lives. Our clergy live next door to the churches and are called on often to answer the needs of their flocks. Protestant missionaries, however, have tended to live in larger houses and often have more amenities. Protestant missionaries, having their families with them, may be shielded from some of the emergency requests of parishioners. Protestant clergy, with their wives and children, provide worthy models for Chinese, who greatly prize the family."

"What of your taking on Chinese ways, manners and attire?" asked the major, picking up the impression Father Francois made on us initially.

"Brothers and sisters of our order," Francois explained, "years ago decided they should follow Chinese customs as much as possible. They reasoned that this was called for since they taught and preached about peoples' equality before God and their common goal of being 'at one with Christ.' Wearing Chinese clothes, speaking Chinese and adopting Chinese manners demonstrates our desire to be on equal terms with our Chinese brothers and sisters."

Talking about 'accommodation', Father Francois suggested, "it means building bridges, Chinese to Westerners and Westerners to Chinese. Here in China it is not so much my learning that counts, but giving water to parched lips and food for empty stomachs and healing for broken bodies. What counts is the genuine expression of the spirit of Christ.

"As to Western missionaries' 'accommodation,'" Wang Shi interrupted, "since they are foreigners, Westerners will always remain limited in how much they can 'accommodate.' One of the obstacles to winning the country to Christianity is not Chinese 'clinging to some pagan creed, but Chinese' tolerance. The Chinese feel unwilling to grant Christianity the exclusive title to belief which to Europeans and Americans seems natural."

"Yes, differences do exist," the Father said. "The benefit of having higher salaries may impair Westerners' rapport with Chinese co-workers. Chinese clergy usually live more modestly and are closer to the impoverished commoners. For this reason, the Franciscans, 80 miles down river from us at Yangxi (Jiangling), take their vow of poverty more seriously than we do."

"Why and how Protestant missionaries choose to live," Thompson added, "Is usually based on considerations of health, child rearing and the desire to offer a model of an alternative family life."

"All right," Wang Shi replied, "I can see the importance of keeping healthy and creating a home where children can be brought up in ways of their homeland. But, let me tell you how this looks through Chinese eyes. The 'reasons' for keeping a higher standard of living than Chinese pastors are often seen as protective and rationalizing actions."

"Important point," Thompson responded. "Though the missionaries' life may be justified, we Westerners need to check ourselves lest we raise barriers between ourselves and our Chinese co-workers."

"Yes," the Father assented, "the Chinese are not the only people who build walls to keep the barbarians out. In our provincialism and nationalism we all build protective walls. God is against such wall-building. Nineteenth century missionaries entered China with the protection of Western warships. As long as they were seen by the populace as backed by military power Western missionaries efforts to proclaim the peace of Christ was a mockery."

"This conversation stirs up strong reactions inside me," put in Wang Shi. "Much of what I am hearing about 'accommodation' is surface stuff only. It's good that you struggle with mastering Chinese language, adopting the Mandarin cassock, using more vernacular instead of Latin in the mass, developing a lifestyle that is close to that of your Chinese brothers and sisters. But outside missionaries' walled compounds, a revolution is going on, and many powerful forces are demanding a new China. In the new China a fragmented church won't be able to make it. Were all churches to unite in a national Chinese Christian church and there arose the question of the loyalty to church or Chinese patriotism, in China today, patriotism will win out!"

A very sensitive nerve had been touched. Courteous chit-chat was no longer sufficient.

"You are a wise and bold young man," Father François, interrupted, "and I thank you for your frankness. I miss being able to converse with knowledgeable and concerned persons like you. You have touched issues that have kindled many fires within me!"

"When, as a licentiate in England, I was preparing, to come to China," Father François reminisced, "one of my professors called to my attention the lines from T.S. Eliot's 'Waste Land':"

> *Here were decent godless people:*
> *Their only monument the asphalt road*
> *And a thousand lost golf balls.*

"The professor suggested that in China I'd be meeting millions of 'decent godless people' and added that at least the monuments of the Chinese would be more than 'asphalt roads' and 'golf balls.' He said that often we churchmen would have more trouble from pious bigots than from militant Marxists. With Marxists you know what you are up against. My mentor said our despair serves 20th-century Westerners by making us see our need for grace. We need it more because our knowledge and technical achievements make pride in our power more perverse and destructive."

"For the individual," Father François concluded, "any false confidence a person clings to will make him less receptive to salvation through Christ. For society, as Mr. Wang says, the ignoring of injustices is gross negligence for those of us who have Christian convictions. We Christians are culpable for doing so little to correct social injustice. The root causes of the injustices that occasioned the need for humanitarian services have been ignored."

Pouring another round of tea, the Father sat down again and slipped into a pensive mood. His 'rusty English' had been taxed to the limits. Yes, he seemed spent from the exercising the opportunity to voice his feelings. In this pause his thoughts seemed to be sweeping across the 24-year-stewardship of the energies, talents and commitment he had given the mission.

How does a person cope with such an array of experiences contrary to those in which he was nurtured? This new friend had shared with us that he struggled periodically with bouts of loneliness. Like other Western priests and sisters, severing home ties, being separated from friends and living month after month half way around the earth must have accentuated the need for genuine intimacy. Father François lived in the midst of crowds, but had communion with very few.

Father Francois' wistful expression enveloped us with silence. Though smiling, we sensed a ruefulness. In revealing a bit of the shadow aspect of his life with us, he had gained relief and reassurance. Like Francis of Assisi, he was without pretensions of glory or designs for power. His sincere dedication to his flock and his faith sustained and empowered him. He was confident that God was his keeper. He transposed his loneliness into a surety that no experience would be able to "separate him from the love of God through Christ." In this assurance Father François found strength and meaning through a life of service to others.

He was our brother who intuited his fellows' miseries and aspirations, foibles and nobility. He took seriously his calling to be a faithful sharer of light, though he had admitted that his optimism and hope often wore thin. In this pause it seemed he was about to confess: "But for the sustaining power of God, I'd go home—or go mad!"

Breaking the silence, Father François said, "Forgive my personal references and for going on so long. I find little opportunity to talk about matters of the heart. You have been patient listeners. You must go, but allow me to venture a few parting words about your journey into the gorges."

"I have always wanted to make the trip you are about to take. I hear there are impressive sights and treacherous waters. In the cramped quarters you'll have no toilets, but quite a few bedbugs and roaches. I entrust you into the hands of skilled boatmen–tributes to China's amazing and resourceful ordinary people–the *lao bai xing*."

"Blessings on you!" he said, raising both hands. "May God's guiding presence go with you."

# CHAPTER THREE

# First Night Aboard The Junk: And Yet Another Delay

*Junkmen At Ease      Original by Bird Bishop, 1898 Photo enhanced by Helen Houser*

Mr. Chen, the mission business manager, had hurried the skipper to an earlier departure. Our new friends at the hostel congratulated us for being able to begin westward without further delay and we in turn were grateful for their coaching and reenforcements. Their introductions to Mr. Chen, Mr. Liu and the Chinese teachers helped to acquaint us with this important up-river port. The major and I felt doubly encouraged by Wang Shi who had proven himself amiable and flexible and by the fortunate addition of the experienced and good-natured Thompson.

At the Bund, when we located the mooring, we paused at the upper landing. The sun on that sparkling afternoon caught the river at an angle that transformed the waters from their usual hostile muddinesss into an inviting gold.

Looking toward the waterline, we saw row upon row of the upper river junks of all sizes. From this perspective they looked like low-slung, elongated highway big-rigs. Taking stock of the unending lineup of the larger vessels, we noted that most were of the *ma-yang-tze* class of junks. They shared the characteristics of low square bows and high angular sterns. Their tall masts were placed forward on a hull shaped, as the Chinese say, "like the head of a snake and the body of a tortoise."

Designed millennia ago in the neighboring province of Hunan, now most of the junks were built at Wanxian, where its hills were noted for their sturdy cypress trees and its docks for their skilled builders. Built as cargo ships and houseboats, they measured from 80 to 125 feet in length and 12 to 15 feet in beam, with a displacement of 50 tons and more. Instead of for speed and grace, these behemoth junks were built for the sturdiness and maneuverability required to survive the river's battering and treacherous currents. There were few fancy frills on these large junks, but they were well built to do their job. Nothing is wasted on appearances–except perhaps the ornate sterns. "Ours, for example, is like that," Wang Shi said, pointing to the junk backed into the mooring alongside. "It has square windows of ground oyster shell, rice paper and pieces of stained glass. The frames and surrounding beams are painted with colored designs."

Some junk designs were said to accentuate differing shapes for other reasons, such as to evade transit tolls. Despite their inelegant appearance and their reduced space for loads, these junks were much prized for the profit they could bring to their owners engaged in trade through the Three Gorges.

Getting aboard the junk entailed a precarious balancing act. Each wobbly step on the slippery planks threatened a plunge into the current.

The hard-faced man on deck who met us identified himself as the *lao ban* (skipper). Turning to the gaunt and inhospitable woman to his right, he said curtly, "That's my wife." She gave us a glance and went right on barking epithets toward the crewmen. It was clear that even a Thames or a Rhine bargeman would take notice of her.

Pointing with his elbow to the tall, athletic and handsome young man at his right the skipper commented, "That's my Number One, the *tai-gong* (first officer), who, with a congenial sense of pride, began to orient us to the *wu ban*."

Like most of their class, the friendly *tai gong* began, it was built upriver in Wanxian. "The planking," he explained, "was over three inches thick and the outside of the hulls were stained with lemon-yellow pigment and rubbed with a durable native tung oil."

He pointed out the bulkheads that made 12 watertight compartments. The upper deck, aft, provided space for the helmsman who controlled the ten-foot-long tiller and was protected by a permanent curved matting covering. The cabin located behind was occupied by the skipper and his family. The elevated stern section with its brightly painted transom also was practical in providing space to mount the *wu ban's* big 'A-shaped' rudder that improves handling and steering.

Looking toward the huge 3½ inch thick, braided, bamboo coils on either side of the enormous mast, the *tai gong* explained, "those are the tow-lines."

The sail was furled around the long boom which was better than head-high, so the crewmen could work underneath. The sail was a typical Chinese one, quare or trapezoidal lug sail, with a portion, the "luff," forward of the mast o help balance the larger part. After its shape, the most visible characteristic of he Chinese sail is the several battens, stiffeners of bamboo running parallel to he bottom of the sail. Smiling, the *tai gong* commented, "You know it's said hat a typical Chinese sail is one-half sail, one-quarter patches, and one-quarter noles." Waving in the direction of the crew at their various stations, he explained the compliment would be 60 or 75: 24 oarsmen, 18 sweepsmen, up o 24 trackers, the cook and the *lao ban* with his family.

Chinese oars are pushed from a standing position, unlike Western oars vhich are pulled from a sitting position. Along with the sail when there's a wind, our *wu ban* would be propelled by a rowing crew of 16 or 20, half working each side. The junk also has sweeps, called *yulows*, fore and midship which extend toward the stern. They are wide sculling or oscillating oars that the weepsmen move back and forth and feather the blade at the end of each stroke by a quick pull on the rope attaching it to the deck. The sweepsmen doubled as either rowers or trackers.

From the mast to the bow was space for a pair of oarsmen, the sweepsmen and our corp of trackers. The 20-foot section aft of the mast served as the area for other oarsmen. Aft of that space, in a tiny 9' x 9' hold, was the galley, presided over by the cleaver-wielding and lantern-jawed cook.

As to toilets? It was understood that such facilities were ashore, or over the gunwales.

Gesturing to the 12' x 10' covering aft of the galley and in front of the helmsman's platform, the *tai gong* said, "That's you passengers' place."

"More than cozy, it's going to be snug," Thompson commented as we laid down our scant baggage. . .We needed no reminder that we were not on a luxury cruise.

Before sundown bowmen cast off the forward lines, pulled up the mooring takes in the stern and poled into the main stream. Once away from the tangle of Yichang's junks, 12 oarsmen, manning six oars on both sides, began stroking against the current. A pair of sweepsmen hoisted the sail to catch what little breeze there was.

As we made headway against the current we noted with surprise that instead of heading west, we were pointed for the south bank. The first officer, at the tiller on the aft deck, explained that the skipper had stayed ashore to get the required sealed transit permit. We would lay over for the night and the skipper would be aboard by daybreak and early we would head for the gorges.

Though without formal rank, each boatman had his place and function. First came the *lao ban*, or skipper, who sometimes was referred to as *lao da*, honored big person upon whose decisions the rest of our lives depended. In addition to his navigational expertise, he needed to be a deft entrepreneur, since he was part owner of the junk, negotiator for cargo, booker of passengers, supervisor of the cook's purchases and cuisine, and the responsible steersman. He bargained for extra trackers, paid wages and haggled with tax collectors, passengers, freight agents, soldiers and bandits.

Second in command was the *tai gong* or first officer. He was both executive officer or crew foreman and navigator-pilot. He often doubled as the chief bowsweep operator. Eyes fixed on the perils ahead when the junk was moving, he never left the great bowsweep except for meals. The cook was something of a second officer, an assignment that required minimal supervisory or navigational skills and maximal ability to satisfy the crews' stomachs. After the cook came the sweepmen, then the oarsmen and trackers.

Within 30 minutes, we had reached a quiet stretch along the south bank. The bowmen rammed long poles fore and aft into the mud to moor in line with a fleet of other waiting junks. In short order the cook began dishing out bowls of rice and white cabbage.

Squatting on their haunches or perched on the gunwales, some of the crew puffed cigarettes, while others smoked pipes. All chattered incessantly. As the sun set, the crew bent bamboo slats from gunwale to gunwale and unrolled mats over the hoops as a covering. Elbow to elbow with one another, every movement was a community affair and communication was unavoidable. By squirming and wedging between one another, they found enough spaces for themselves.

Primal images of the gorges, stirred by my adolescent scouting friend, were taking on substance. Why worry over further delays, I thought, when the swirling river sweeping past and the squeeze of humanity on the junk commanded attention?

Thompson, accustomed to the men's up river dialect, was in perpetual conversation with one or several of the crew. Their local dialect, often slurred, was difficult for me to follow, so I missed half the banter. Their understanding of what we said, in turn, was blocked at first by their provincial and xenophobic assumption that foreigners are beyond comprehension. They responded, however, to the slightest overture and humorous turn of phrase.

We were far from noiseless at our anchorage. Above the buzz of our crew's jabbering, we occasionally heard the piercing wails from the stern cabin of the skipper's youngest grandchild, the five-year-old *xiao mei mei*, or boat infant. The crews of boats in the flotilla around us were as restless and talkative as ours. Some gambled, while others sipped tea, played the numbers or strummed on squeaky bamboo fiddles. As the hours passed, the merry-making escalated.

The laughter and outbursts of song and story diverted our attention from the discomfort of the narrow plank that was our seat and blunted our American eagerness to get going toward the gorges. Perched on the aft deck, we absorbed the historic rhythms of the Long River's boatmen. In these first few hours aboard the junk, we were already on our way. Sidelined as captive observers, we had no alternative but to listen, learn and try to appreciate.

River, sky, *wu ban* and rough-hewn men wrapped us in the natural order of things. In time the excited temper of the mounting commotion distracted us from our squeezed-in discomfort. The experience of the crew's fellowship laid waste our grandiose ideas about improving cross-cultural relations, developing humanitarian projects and winning converts. Instead of seminars on Chinese culture, the major, Thompson and I would live lessons in the 3,000 year old manners of the boatmen.

Whatever experiences the gorges might give us, we already were gaining a respect for the crew's raw humanity. These oarsmen and trackers were penniless and tattered, smelly and sweaty, belching and snoring, given to terrible exertion, followed by loafing. Day after day they lived on life's margins, overcoming great difficulties and dangers. Though they often teetered on the edge of death, they talked little of their fears and insecurities. I counted these Ulysses of the Long River among the treasures of the gorges.

Thompson, tall, sandy-haired, in his mid-forties and originally from a large midwestern farm family, met each new day hoping for surprises. A man of unshakable faith, he nevertheless was acutely sensitive to the fact that his convictions were not shared by everyone. With him you knew where he stood, and you also knew that he was open and interested in you.

The major also was just over 6' tall, and though in his early '40s, with his salt-and-pepper hair, looked older. His 32 missions over Europe had not only grayed his hair but wrinkled his brow and sobered his manner. Raised in a small Atlantic coastal community, he had taken his engineering training at a prestigious eastern university. He had enlisted in the Army Air Force prior to Pearl Harbor. When our Base chaplain introduced him to me he seemed a bit aloof, with much on his mind. As I got to know him better I found I was wrong about the aloofness, but right about his surplus of interests and concerns. Though intuitive like Thompson, the major tended to be more calculating and deliberate. He was used to having a crew and squadron under his command, but person-to-person he was tolerant. He and his wife back in Pennsylvania had a son and two daughters.

As for me, I was six-foot tall, with a head of blond hair and roaming brown eyes. Slender and athletic in build, I was a bundle of energy. And, as I had told Abraham the night before, I was a 'work-ethics' Calvinist–always busy with a variety of projects. I looked younger than my 31 years, but from the places I'd been and things I'd done I was often taken to be older.

Asked for more about myself, I explained I was born in Kentucky to southern parents. With two brothers I was raised in Swatow, South China and for two years was in boarding school at Shanghai. Returning with my family at age 15 I completed high school in New York. After graduating from an Ivy League college near Philadelphia I went on to a prominent graduate school in New York City.

"I do know," the major added, "Cowles is the oldest of three brothers. So, being first born, he's supposed to respect law and order and understand the importance of power and authority. However that may be, he's a cosmopolitan who's always enthusiastic and with a zest for action. Over the weeks, working together on community projects, I've found him cooperative, reasonable and dedicated. He'll have to tell us how he got this way."

Taking the major seriously, I said, "What cooperativeness I have comes from my people-loving parents. Both being Southerners and respectful of Confucian 'reciprocity', courtesy was important for them. Saying 'please' and 'thank you' were always more than protocol. Golden phrases of concern for people needed to be more than flattering–they had to be genuine."

"Being seen as a cosmopolitan is a compliment. Racial prejudice, according to most of my Southern kinfolk, was an indisputable fact of life. Not so with my father and mother who looked at all people as created in God's image. My brother and I were to remember that Jesus was an Oriental and that living in China we were guests of a different race. Other races were to be appreciated and respected, never looked down upon. Many of my brother's and my childhood playmates were Chinese. Others were Japanese, Russian, German, British, French and even a few American Baptist."

"And we were given frequent reminders that victimization of the poor was wrong. The ghastly slaughters of World War I were always referred to as evils. This led me to join groups that worked for justice and peace."

"What reasonableness I have was acquired with difficulty. College courses, especially in science, drilled me in rational thought. But how much more I needed to learn and master! That humbling lesson is with me now as I think of my limited grasp of the Chinese language. Superficially fluent in conversational Mandarin, my vocabulary is scarcely 3,000 characters. An 'educated' person requires at least 6,000 and my worn Matthews Chinese-English Dictionary lists more than 30,000 characters."

"As to being energetic, yes I have a full schedule and often am in a hurry. Also, present tasks and events usually are so interesting that I rarely have time to look back. One exception is that I look back over my shoulders toward mentors I admire. The imprint of parents, respected professors and supervisors made a strong guiding gestalt for me."

"As to being 'naive,' perhaps I am. Before college I fantasied myself an adventurer and romanticist. Regarding evil, for example, I'm unrealistic. The situation in which I was raised was a tiny sanitized island surrounded with a sea f misery. Shielded in our compound by 9-foot-high walls, and with the U.S. Navy ship "Ashville" anchored in the harbor, I was always safe. Yet all around was a sea of lethal diseases: leprosy, the plague, tuberculosis, typhus and cholera. The surrounding neighborhood was rife with poverty, slavery, murder, kidnaping, extortion, rape and infanticide. Protected from evil, I nonetheless felt surrounded by it and helpless before it. It was as if I could extol the loveliness of the rose garden but had better not explore the source of compost. Our family withdrew to our own special agenda, and fancied that our intentions and motives were the purest imaginable."

"Enough about me. Let's review about our special instructor, Wang Shi."

Of medium height (5' 10"), Wang Shi was tall for an upper Yangtze man. He looked like a man in his late '20s, but claimed to be 32. Slender, strongly built, he talked expressively with his hands, shoulders and sparkling eyes. Handsome, with close-cropped hair and delicately formed cheek, he nonetheless had the appearance of someone to be reckoned with. His simple wardrobe consisted of two changes of clothing, and his personal kit consisted of a tooth brush, comb, piece of soap, safety razor, and tiny vial of cologne. But with his Western-style trousers held tight by a 28" belt, plain loose-fitting shirt and pair of canvas shoes, he always managed to look immaculate.

His parents, both college graduates and professionals, had five children of whom he was the third. Being a 'later born,' we assumed he continually sought ways to surpass his older siblings and that he didn't endure for long the strict leadership of others. Although reluctant to talk much about his parents and siblings, he let it be known they were dear to him and he wanted to be a faithful son and brother. He had great admiration for his father. He once told us, "My father was very intelligent, accomplished and had a strong sense of 'rectitude' (li). But he was uninterested in promoting himself and gaining power. He is the example I have followed all my life." In one of his more pensive moments he said of his mother, "My mother was intense, sensitive and caring. I've wanted to repay her for her loving nurture."

He told us he was married to a school teacher and that they had a three-year-old son.

His college education made him an intellectual, his ability to speak English was atypical but characteristic of a fast-growing group of college graduates. He was a member of a respected, privileged elite, who held–or was destined to hold–positions of responsibility. In many ways he reflected the emerging China. Though to a degree reserved, he was by no means shy. When he spoke he expected a response. He had a refined, balanced outlook and judgment, a winning self confidence and a sense of humor, though he did not smile often. He usually seemed intent on unraveling the secrets within the project, person or situation at hand. His focus was aimed, not at confrontation, but at uncovering the 'truth.' When he was sure his facts were 'solid,' as he would say, he was unshakable in his views.

In the last two days, particularly at the C.I.M. hostel and with the brother at the Catholic mission, Wang Shi's ways of interacting had come to the fore. I recalled his unfinished conversation with Father Francois about 'accommodation.' I sensed Wang Shi not only had more to say, but was trying to ferret out an underlying truth. My intuition was on the mark.

"One of my professor friends in Nanjing decided to become a Christian," Wang Shi said. "After he was baptized, he told me it was difficult for him to accept Jesus as his 'personal savior' and 'only Son of God.' He explained that his family was Buddhist and, as a Chinese, he had absorbed Confucian thinking. It was not easy, he said, to commit himself to Jesus. My friend continued struggling to accept the Christian faith and to see how Jesus' ideas and teachings apply to China's ongoing revolution."

We three Westerners caught the importance of his insights. We also were made aware of Wang Shi's directness, persistence and courage. More than this, we came to realize the importance of according him more "face!" He deserved more appreciation of his unique identity than we had shown him.

I suggested, "We from the West have a lot of learning to do. We must try to see the enormity of China's continuing revolution. We must become more sensitive to the ways individuals and social institutions were disrupted and now are struggling to develop new structures. It's not enough to point out that these painful upheavals in China are related to radical, world-wide change. We need to help open international 'change agents' and link them with Chinese working for change."

Forty-eight hours before we had hardly known one another. In the last two days, we'd become bonded. Wang Shi, with one of his knowing smiles, commented, "Your ancestors may have been German, Scotch and Welsh, but you're typical Americans: honest, straight-forward and enthusiastic–my favorite type of people."

Wedging himself between Wang Shi and me, the first officer *(tai gong)* invited response with his friendly *"ni hao"* (hello).

The major, an inveterate questioner, quizzed him about his parents, his boyhood and his schooling. Did he have a wife? How about children?

The *tai gong* leaned back and with a smile said, "You want to know everything about me, all at once?"

We learned that he was born and raised in a small country town north of Wuhan, 350 miles downriver. His parents were poor tenant farmers, barely eked out a living with him, his two brothers and three sisters. He had completed only five years of school. This surprised us, for in his speech and manner, he showed understanding and curiosity associated with education.

Uneasy talking about himself, the first officer started questioning the major about his boyhood and his army service. Before long he turned to ask about Thompson's early life in England and his growing up in America.

An outburst of curses from the sweepmen interrupted us. Rising to quiet the ruckus, the first officer explained, "They are throwing coins, hoping to get favorable numbers for a hexagram."

Thompson told us their game was based on the heads-or-tails readings they got by casting three coins. The readings referred them to a hexagram–six lines, some full and some broken, which portended events in the invisible world, recorded in the enigmatic classic the *I Ching*, or Book of Changes.

Wang Shi said his current graduate students were skeptical about the resurgence of attention to the ancient classics, especially the unscientific *I Ching*. He conceded, however, that going to the *I Ching* was more substantial than an occult going to the ouija board or the yarrow cards and sticks. And none other than the esteemed modern thinker Kuo Mo-Jo, in a recent lecture at the university, had recommended exploring the *I Ching* for new alternatives needed by China.

"This ancient book's reasoning may not satisfy Cartesian causality," he said, "but the recordings rest on the accumulation of long-tested Chinese wisdom. Read in context, its advice can be more shattering than the advice of the astrologer, palmist, crystal-ball gazer or tea-leaf reader. Those who go to the *I Ching* looking for magic may find in it terrifying accuracy."

The first officer reported that several men found ominous indications in the hexagram they drew. To them, line one read: "He appears wishing to advance, but finds himself kept back," while line two predicted: "Shows its subject with the appearance of advancing, and yet of being sorrowful." Line four was associated with: "However firm and correct he may be, there will be occasion for regret."

In contrast, others argued for an optimistic interpretation because of the phrases: "There will be good fortune," "blessings will be received" and "to advance will be fortunate, and in every way advantageous."

Conversation about hexagram number 35, increased. Referring both to natural and human phenomena the preamble suggests:

> . . . , *image of progress,*
> *Remorse disappears,*
> *Take not gain and loss to heart.*
> *Thus the superior man himself*
> *Brightens his brilliant virtue.*

"Progress," Wang Shi explained, "is seen in natural forces pushing upward. as in the changing seasons and in the way living things develop. *Chin* includes the idea of inner growth as individuals move from immaturity to maturity. Progress occurs in society as its people move from dependency to independence."

"Wait a minute," I interrupted. "We started with the sweepmen's outburst then switched to talk of the hexagram *chin*. Let's go back to the crew's arguing up bow. What do they see as the omens for our trip's success or failure?"

"The answer was what they call a 'yes but' answer–indecisive," Wang Shi said with one of his knowing smiles. "The more ambiguous the answer, the more there is to argue about. Let's try our own throw with Lao Ma's coins."

Our draw was the number 32, *heng*, or duration. The commentary read "Duration,. . .where movement is not worn down by hindrances and where firmness and unity of character are won. . .Perseverance can further and deepen personality." The *I Ching* says:

> . . . *The image of duration,*
> *Thus the superior man stands firm*
> *And does not change his direction."*

"Oh, come on!" interrupted the major, grinning from ear to ear. "That's close to being either gobbledygook or simple tautology. The *heng* hexagram sounds like saying two plus two equals four, or simply what was just was, and what will be will be. But, you know me, I'll accept strange meanings if they're rational."

"*Heng* can't be easily dismissed," Wang Shi chuckled. "It's about nature's unswerving regularity, such as movement of the heavenly bodies, the rolling of thunder, the blowing of the wind. . .It also has to do with the continuum that holds opposites together. Everywhere we see the interaction of opposites. We find yin and yang, dark and light, the female, and the outgoing life stream of seed, the male; the light and active spirits, *shen*, over against the dark and ominous spirits, *guei*."

"Duration within the flux of natural events," added Thompson, "is the *Dao* (Tao) or Way. It correspond to the Greeks' Logos, the eternal law in nature and societies. Confucius said, 'Everything flows on and on like the river, without pause, day and night.'"

"Duration," Wang Shir added, "helps people become self-contained and self-renewing. A Chinese proverb says, 'A durable person takes responsibility and becomes far-sighted.' Having a 'long view' gives individuals a sense of destiny. The paragon, or 'superior person,' endures by being a 'listening subject who changes his ways to flow with the forces of the cosmos.'"

"Duration also has a social dimension," I suggested. "Patient staying power, for instance, helps groups become unified. In listening to one another, we develop durability as we become responsive in our community."

"Good fortune or misfortune, humiliation or remorse depends on a person's judgment," Wang Shi said. "Making accurate value judgments is crucial. Confucius speaks of people arriving at judgments as 'clothing the images in decisive actions,' or 'putting ideas and virtues into deeds and words.'"

Wang Shi and the major stood up and stepped toward the galley. This gave the rest of us room to stretch. With little prospect for quiet, we passengers resumed our cross-legged sitting on the deck that was our quarters. As the night chill crept up from the river, we were glad to warm our hands about a charcoal brazier.

"I'll accept," Thompson continued, "the hexagram's directive to be aware of what the river's flow was, is and will be. In the split second a moment ago, it was up and ahead of us, but even as we talk, it's flown past us. In the present, right now, the ever-changing river surrounds and buoys us up. As it flows, always rushing to the sea, the river gives us fleeting glimpses of new opportunities."

Wang Shi returned to our conversational circle with thoughts churning. As usual, he wanted to get down to priorities. "In these reconstruction days," he started, "we need to be less occupied with 'omens' and the *I Ching* and more concerned with innovative programs for a new China."

"The *I Ching's* idea of duration," Thompson surprised us, "makes sense to me. I see a connection, Scotch Presbyterian that I am, with my belief in predestination! It's not too far-fetched to claim that it's more than accident that we four passengers, who days ago had never heard of the other, are sitting on a junk in the moonlight offshore from Yichang, talking about the *I Ching*."

The *tai gong* and Wang Shi held a short dialogue in Chinese about how to explain the *I Ching*.

The gist of what they were saying echoed what the psychiatrist Carl Jung wrote about the book, "Its predictions are eerily linked to actual occurrences, not causally in the Western rational sense, but more 'acausally' related in the Eastern metaphysical sense of being parts of a cosmic design that lies beyond the reach of science but is partially accessible to the unconscious of the person casting the coins or the yarrow sticks."

"The *I Ching*, according to Jung," I suggested, "rests on the 'principle of synchronicity.' The images found in the hexagrams are indicators of the essential situation prevailing at the moment. This is intended, not as anti-reason, but as an effort to interpret a complete image of heaven and earth, a microcosm of all possible relationships. New scientific observations show that the chance that figures in natural processes is so common that under natural circumstance. events conforming to special laws are almost an exception. This observation led Jung to stress the importance of durable myths and patterns of behavior by which people live, which he called 'archetypes.'"

"I'll have to think more about 'archetypes,'" the major responded. "But immediately I see time as an element of duration. Time, as duration, is espe cially important for flyers. Getting to a chosen destination depends on calcu lating accurately time as well as space. In navigation we see time as universal like your description of *heng*. Fliers operate on the basis that time is a constant We navigate by accepting Newton's theory that time is real, flowing uniform ly. We count on time ticking off in a straight line, going from T1 to T2 to T3 and so on.

"The linear view of time has its limits," he noted. Thinking of time as an assembly line doesn't cover many other aspects of life. Newton, for instance recognized that 'time is aloof, keeping its own independence.' This view of time's 'aloofness' explains how it fosters alienation. In an individual's life, as in history, we find more than straight-line or one-dimensional time."

"Interesting point," I said. "When people venture from the usual straight flow of events and try a new course, significant breakthroughs occur. Creative things often happen. These turns away from ordinary paths provide the condi tions in which protest against the status quo is possible. Tragedy occurs when this opportunity is not taken or is cut off. Then the rate of oppression mounts former visions prove illusory and hopes are dashed."

"I like what you said about times of protest," put in Wang Shi. "You were about to say more . . ."

"Yes," the major continued, "another side of duration implies keeping on course, which requires balance. Pilots rely on a gyroscopic compasses to keep on course. The spinning gyroscope balances opposites, compensating the changing forces of wind, altitude and direction. People, like a plane, need a bal ancing inner guiding system."

"True," I affirmed. "Mental health depends on persons having such an inner guidance system. Harry Guntrip, an English psychiatrist, reports that when patients are about to fall into a psychotic episode, their 'durable inner center' no longer holds. Their confusions and conflicts spin out of control Losing their 'durability' or emotional balance signals regression. Thought become unrealistic and behavior asocial."

Suddenly our bowmen shouted an alarm that drowned out our conversa tion.

We looked upriver and saw the outlines of a large junk bearing down on us Moored ten or so boat lengths upstream, it had broken loose from its holding stakes. Before we could brace ourselves, the impact came. The starboard side of the out-of-control junk crashed our bow on the port side. Our mooring stakes were jerked back, but held. The colliding junk spun around, slamming its stern into our midsection. As it swept past, its crew, manning four pairs of oars, rowed frantically, trying to get the craft under control before it collided with other junks in the flotilla.

The skipper's wife shrieked over the crew's curses and shouts.

The *tai gong* kept his cool. "In this current, mooring stakes must be sunk deep," he explained. "The river's rush to the sea is like the force of death."

Surveying the bow and checking his crew for injuries, he reported that we were fortunate. The row of old tires lashed to the bow cushioned the collision. Our *wu ban* was not damaged. Two bowmen had been bruised when the impact threw them against the capstan. Others of the crew, rolled up in blankets, had cushioned each other from harm.

We nestled into our bedrolls and squeezed into our 12' x 10' accommodation to sleep under the starlit sky. We imaged those at the missions and the schools, impressions on boarding the junk, the surging waters, sunset on the Long River, the bowmen's fracas, puzzling over the hexagram's ambiguities and the collision! These beginnings differed from our expectations, but not a single happening did we wish to part with or change.

And now, we four–engineer-pilot, Chinese intellectual-activist, Calvinist-evangelist and missionary-teacher–compacted into our cramped rectangle not much larger than a king-size bed, were challenged to sleep. Our crowded minds and the crewmen's snoring made it difficult to "go gently into that good night" beneath the stars.

CHAPTER FOUR

# The Yichang Gorge Beckons

*Palisades, Xiling Gorge Entrance*      © *Helen Houser*

At sun-up the next morning, following our rice gruel and pickled vegetables, the expected early start did not happen. Our exasperation mounted as hour after hour gave no sign of the skipper and no explanations about the delay. We were not alone in our irritation. The skipper's wife's tightened jaw and explosive silence let us know that she was, as the Chinese say, "spitting angry." The stoical cook, on the other hand, wondered why the major and I were so fretful over the unavoidable. Shrugging his shoulders, he said, *"Mei you fa zi,"* (nothing can be done about it). His smile and evasive manner aroused our suspicion that this delay might be tangled in some scheme he was privy to.

The crew remained irritatingly unperturbed, taking the delay as a matter of course. Not bothered that precious hours were being wasted, some perched on the gunwales, talking and joking. Occasionally a crossfire of verbal jibes broke out between them. A few napped, while others smoked their pipes, picked lice or played the numbers. They welcomed any delay that gave them time for *xiu xi*, rest and a break.

"Damn this lack of concern for time, Daoist (Taoist) stoicism, or whatever!" the major blurted out. "Americans may waste things, but these people waste time."

Thompson added, "What we Westerners take as Chinese apathy concerning time has evolved over the centuries as a pragmatic cultural response to the conditions of their lives. Chinese patience is as unique as Chinese blue porcelain."

"To survive, Chinese have to learn patience," Wang Shi added in agreement. "Our parents teach patience as a virtue. One of our proverbs says, 'A person who cannot tolerate small ills can never accomplish great things.'" Westerners, so often rushing about are compulsive about time. Chinese are not indifferent to time, but they feel 'why worry over situations you can't change.' Also, waiting frequently is a way to save our skin. Chinese take a pragmatic approach to time as the English take to umbrellas, because the political weather usually looks a little cloudy. Venturing too far out alone risks getting drenched. For example, meddling in matters that are the responsibilities of those in authority and beyond one's own control may bring you trouble and anxiety."

"Chinese patience," Thompson added, "frequently is an adjustment to economic and social conditions. It takes patience to live within chronic pressures of impoverishment, overpopulation and the complicated obligations to large extended families. These insistent economic and social problems restrict expressions of individualism and call for patience."

"Chinese protect themselves and close associates," Thompson explained, "with webs of doing the 'propitious.' The proper etiquette for particular persons and situations is learned early. Friction is minimized when persons fulfill *gui jiu*, or ceremonial procedures. Our skipper, for example, may be detained tending to matters of protocol that require their particular rhythm, over which he has little control."

"True, the 3,000-year-old emphasis on 'propriety' lives on," Wang Shi responded. "The *Li Chi*, or Book of Rites, one of the five classics, stresses the observance of proper rituals even in the humblest of interchanges. Individual expression that ignores social rules of propriety disturbs social harmony. Propriety is raised to the level of a moral principle. Time schedules must accommodate the convenience of the other person. Prearranged and arbitrary appointments may threaten others. In these times, however, changes are coming."

Our ruminations about time and patience were cut short by rumblings among the bowmen.. The first officer hurried past the oarsmen midship to reach the poop deck. Taking hold of the tiller, he ordered, *"Tso la,"* (let's move). The oars splashed into the river. The junk headed upstream but soon veered toward the north bank where three lashed-together boats made an auxiliary landing. As we neared the landing we saw our long awaited skipper talking with two other junk captains.

Our skipper nonchalantly stepped aboard and began barking orders. His show of authority quieted the complaining oarsmen, but did not calm his stormy wife. Letting her rave, he gave us passengers a perfunctory greeting and directed muffled words toward the cook. Taking over of the tiller, he commanded the rowers to pull harder and the bowmen to get the pairs of long yulows in motion to pull toward the gorges' portal.

Off our stern, an upriver motor-powered ship, more than twice the length of our junk, was gaining on us. It was one of a growing number of shallow draft steel-hulled ships that ran the gorges at this season. Introduced by the British after World War I to increase trade and influence, this particular ship was one of the vintage models. Not as trim and efficient as the vessels that ply the Rhine, the Thames or the Hudson, it nevertheless harbingered the future, promising to replace coolie power.

Holding fast to the heaving tiller as the motor ship's wake buffeted our rudder the captain widened his footing to keep his balance. As the junk rolled with churning waves, he shouted to the rowers for greater exertion. Disdaining the intruding sign of "progress," he cursed, "Every year, there are more of those motor vessels and fewer of our ancestors' *wu ban*."

As the ship moved past a hundred yards to our port side, we saw its narrow-beam, double-decked, sharp bow and heard its thumping diesel motors. The towering captain stood motionless, eyes straight ahead, anticipating the seriousness of navigating the gorges. On the starboard, the young chief officer looked grave and nervous. On the port side stood the river pilot, his face the color of Ming ivory, impassive, immobile except for his right forefinger, which pointed directions. In the background, the mate was at the wheel. No one spoke. The only sounds were of swirling water and panting engines.

"Yes, that's an easier and faster way into the gorges," Thompson commented. "These modern vessels offer greater safety and more cargo and passenger space. But there's a trade off: they provide less time for sight-seeing. Aboard those ships you miss a close look at the bewitching temples, pagodas and storied landmarks. Traveling in this time-honored junk we'll have more adventures."

Our junk pushed through a drifting fog past a series of pyramidal peaks forming the menacing fangs of the Tiger's Tooth east of Xiling Gorge's entrance. The movement of the earth's crust and nature's weathering have twisted the boulders into grotesque shapes, creating the Potted Landscape of the region. The channel narrowed from its mile width to 1,200 yards, then 1,000. The lofty jagged cliffs, outlined menacingly whrough the mist, appeared ready to push us away. Stroke by hard stroke, however, the oarsmen kept pulling toward the palisades.

About noon, when the fog lifted, the first officer called from the bow, *"Yole Tonglingxia"* (We've got the Eastern Gate). We began to see the magnitude of how the Xiling Gorge pierces China's Great Central Mountain Range. Entering the portal's twin promontories, the massive limestone cliffs seemed ready to close in and consume us.

Mists rose and fell, often enveloping us in a haze, then suddenly clearing to highlight peaks, precipices, coves and shoals. The strange-appearing boulders and rock faces were identified with books on the art of war, double-edged swords, a man leading an ox and even a monk hanging by his feet. At the point where the river makes a right angle turn, we were told this ravine was known as The Shadow-Play Gorge.

The channel turned left in a giant horseshoe bend. We passed the Gorge of the Cow, more euphemistically called Yellow Ox, or Yellow Cat Gorge. The shape and shine of the crouching rocks make either name appropriate. Not quite halfway through, on the right bank, was the water-worn Dragon's Cave, reputed to run inland for miles. Within its mouth was the limestone rock dragon guarding his lair.

Twelve centuries ago, this imposing gateway inspired Li Tai-po, a revered Tang dynasty poet, to write:

> *Three dawns shine upon the Yellow Ox,*
> *Three sunsets—and we go so slowly.*
> *Three dawns—again three sunsets—*
> *And we do not notice that our hair is white as silk.*

Progress through the Yellow Ox Gorge didn't take three days, nor did the experience whiten our hair. In this first of the three sections of the Yichang Gorge, however, we found ourselves drawn through an eerie tunnel. The occasional sun rays that penetrated the gloom reflected spectral images off the cliffs.

The narrowing passage hastened the current, slowing our upward movement. By hugging the north shore, we found a deeper channel where the current was slower, but in the lee of the cliffs we had less wind for our sails. A heavier load was put on our rowers. With their bare feet braced against the cross boards, they bent low coming toward us, then dipped the blades far back, with legs tight, stomach and arm muscles bulging, and faces drawn. With each forward stroke they gave a plaintive call which was answered on the back stroke with a chorus. With all their effort we seemed barely to inch against the river's thrust.

A mile farther, where the river's course straightens toward the west again, our *wu ban* burst into the Lampshine section of the Xiling Gorge. Dead ahead, in the hills on the left bank, was Huangling Temple. With our eyes riveted on our oarsmen maneuvering the vessel around the bend, we didn't give the

*Hualing Temple and Xiling Gorge Riverscape*        *Courtesy Hsiao Pi-yu*

ancient site the attention it deserved. Our visibility within the dark canyon shifted from bright to grim and back again as mists rose, fell, lifted and clouded again. When the clouds parted, the sun set the north cliff ablaze in sharp contrast to the ominous dark south wall.

As we emerged from the haze, nooks and crannies in the walls were illuminated and the jagged peaks piercing the clouds were set aglow. The profusion of flowers Thompson and I spotted in these kaleidoscopic scenes defied our attempts to identify them.

The oarsmen's labored strokes brought us around an awesome set of weathered granite towers. Their doleful work chorus subsided into a brighter melody celebrating the *wu ban*'s successful escape from the portal's clutches.

By bringing the *wu ban* through the first section of the Xiling Gorge–the great Eastern Gate, the Dragon's Cave, Yellow Ox and Lampshine Chasms–the skipper had regained "face." He had taken the vessel successfully through the first series of rapids and his wife had exhausted her spleen at him. His dour mien relaxed and his tongue loosened. He was ready to voice his feelings about the gorges. He called the lead oarsman to take the tiller and stepped from the poop deck to our passenger section.

"When mountain streams pour into the Great River," he said, "all becomes *luan qi ba zao* (all at sevens and eights–confused)."

Gazing into the splendor, he surprised us with his sentiment: "It's *mei li* (beautiful) and *qu chiu* (humbling). . .Every time I come through these gorges, I feel like the first explorer."

Pausing, as if he'd surprised himself, this rough-and-ready commoner seemed trying to define the immensity of the scene.

"My younger brother is an artist," the first officer said, responding to the skipper's feeling. "Once, when he came on this trip with me, my brother told of how deep canyons, jagged cliffs, pine trees, rolling clouds, mountain mists and waterfalls excite him. They make him want to paint on the spot. He visited the famous mountains Huangshan in Anhui and Omeishan in Sichuan to make paintings. To paint such scenes, he says, you must be in harmony with nature."

"Yes, appreciation of nature," broke in Wang Shi, moving to the gunwale to get a better view of the cataract we were passing, "tells us about who we are. An outer landscape often points us toward our inner self. The material world influences our destiny in more ways than we usually realize."

"You talk like my brother," the first officer continued. "He says the painter reminds people of some piece of the physical world or some behavior or experience they like. He says in his paintings he shares his own chasing after some feeling he likes."

The skipper, impervious to our conversation, barged in, "My wife tells me last night you were much interested in the bowmen throwing numbers. It's an old pastime for the common folk. In uncertain times people look to hexagrams for hope."

Before we could respond, the skipper threw down three worn coins. The throw gave the number "55"–*fang*, suggesting progress and development, which prompted him to exclaim: *"Ai ya! Hao!* (good omen!)."

From his pocket he drew out a dog-eared commentary and showed us the writing about the hexagram *fang*. Its three broken and three solid lines suggest the sun and the moon's waxing and waning. Associated are points of ancient wisdom:

> *Brilliance is joined with movement, making for abundance.*
> *Its waning follows, so treasure it while it lasts.*
> *Confidence, progress and development increase—good fortune!*
> *There's no occasion to be anxious over a change.*
> *Pride arouses resentment; humility induces friendliness.*

Withdrawing from our circle as abruptly as he had appeared, the skipper stepped back to take over the tiller, leaving Wang Shi and the *tai gong* to pick up the sequence.

"Traditionally," Wang Shi explained, "the hexagrams were used in divination to foretell events, reveal occult knowledge or reinforce inspired guesses.

This motive persists with the uneducated commoners. The interest of the *lao ban,* like that of many people, is to find in the *I Ching* reassurance and security. They have confidence that its wisdom gives recommendations for charting present and future action."

"Whether the hexagram's lines are broken or unbroken," the *tai gong* suggested, "tells us certain important things about where and how you stand at any given moment. It pictures, for example, yin as the unbroken line and yang the broken line."

"The hexagrams' wisdom has many angles," Wang Shi agreed. The unbroken and broken lines carry the old idea of complementary qualities that make up all things: positive and negative, female and male, right and wrong, here and there, now and then, down and up. Each moment fits into the order of nature, linking persons to the cosmic workings of yin and yang.

"It's not only 'all things,' or 'being,'" Wang Shi added, "but 'becoming' that Chinese philosophers look for in the hexagrams. Confucius, for instance, valued the hexagrams because they suggested a range of meanings without prescribing any–a position that exasperates Westerners who demand logic.

"The average Chinese, wanting to appear wise, is not above figuring that if the sages saw so much wisdom in the hexagrams, perhaps people should try to understand the hexagrams' importance for them personally. The hexagrams also have a balancing power. The various combinations of lines suggest holding opposite meanings together. One meaning stems from the emotional reaction of the individual perceiver, the other meaning comes from explanations given in well-defined rules set by cultural values."

A bowman's shrill warning shout, *Kongling xia lai le,* cut short our talk of nature's magnificence and the wisdom of the *I Ching.*

Trembling and with much gesticulating, the agitated cook pointed ahead to a cluster of ominous boulders midway in the Xiling's Channel. "At those Deer Horn Rocks few escape without property damage, loss and brushes with death," the cook said.

This series of enormous rocks block the channel's center and divide the river into two dangerous narrow channels, creating "the Gate to Hell." The midstream rock barriers and the shoreline's shifting silt combine to make the south passage impossible and the other unpredictable. The swift current through these banks is treacherous, with menacing whirlpools, eddies, and cross currents. The flow is influenced by the varying width and depth of the water level and by the river's underlying ridges and troughs. All this may lead to a sudden wash-out of the silt which forms a moving body of quicksand so dangerous that boats tie up to the bank when "the sands are on the move." In the '30s this Charybdis and Scylla-like cauldron had claimed dozens of steamers and countless junks. These conditions make the Kongling run one of the most danger-us of the Three Gorges. It was the section of the river blockaded in 1939 to halt the Japanese advance.

About the Kongling's perils the Sichuan poet Tu Fu composed an epic sonnet:

> When we passed the Deer's Horn Rocks, we were
> assuredly passing through danger.
> How is it possible not to change color when
> crossing these evil rapids?
> To sleep on the high pillow would show that one was
> unduly confident, and regarded one's person trivially.
> Books of poems and histories were all overturned
> and thrown into disorder;
> Of things packed in bags—half were wet, and crushed.
> On the precipice of life, we looked down giddy and anxious;
> At any instant we might be in a desperate situation.

Our anxiety was accentuated by Thompson's accounts of a British civil service agent whose boat disappeared from under him in this channel; and then, of a missionary, at the turn of the century, who aboard a junk carrying his wife's coffin downriver, had his boat dashed to splinters, sending the coffin on a solitary voyage. Many others, he added, if they survived, reached their destination *sans* possessions.

The skipper at the tiller tightened his grip, the first officer at the bow sharpened his focus on the narrowing channel, and the crew was on the alert. All watched tensely the *wu ban's* approach to the dreaded Kongling (Deer Horn Rocks). Since it was "low water," the outlines of the treacherous shifting sandbars could be seen. Then, midstream, we saw the black sawtooth boulder, crouched as if waiting to pounce on some wayward *wu ban*.

Fortunately wind and current were optimum for making the upriver passage. The oarsmen pulled to the left of the sandbar and to the right past the rocks. Pulling past the hazard, the trackers' chants became a requiem that was answered by a chorus from the stroking oarsmen. Though the crew negotiated the maneuver without mishap, we still gained respect for this grand gorges' perils and were glad that they were at least spaced out.

Rounding a large outcropping, we cleared the fierce mile-long turbulence in which our crew and trackers had struggled for almost an hour. The *tai gong* left his vigil at the bow and took off his pilot jacket. Returning to midship, he commented, "Pulling through the Kongling passage safely is a big relief!"

With the Kongling Rocks behind us, we entered a wider, calmer stretch of river which eased the drag for the oarsmen. Westbound junks like ours kept as close to shore as possible on the side most unencumbered with submerged rocks and easiest on the trackers–a combination that often proved elusive When the wind died down, the work of oarsmen and trackers became more grueling. Their load was lessened when gusts of wind filled our sails and treated us to the low music of the river parting under our prow.

The relief was brief. We soon entered a constricted gorge with another set of rapids. Again we heard the oars' creaking and sweeps' swishing.

In a matter of minutes we approached Zigzag Reaches Rapids. Our anxiety over the this portion of whitewater was somewhat distracted by the cook's simultaneous urgings to take note of the grotesque projections on the south wall–a veritable Rohrschach in stone.

The channel widened and brought us into the awesome *Niu Kan*, or Ox's Liver and Horse's Lung chasm. The high perpendicular walls limited the horizon to the hills above. The sun cast slanting rays into the depths and was prismed by the spray into rainbows.

The jumbled rocks three hundred feet from the water appeared as the body parts of animals. We were told we were in the Ox-liver and Horse-lung section of the Xiling. We struggled to spot the "liver" and "lung" while the cook pointed out the semblance of a human face, known as the Clown of the Yangtze. Simultaneously the eager guide wanted us to notice on the south bank the hoary Zhao Jun Memorial, believed to be associated with the ancient Ba-Shu people.

Wang Shi briefed us about the Ba-Shu people who occupied this region during the middle and late years of the Warring States Period (c. 300 to 150 B.C.). The Ba-Shu had been defeated by the Han. Few Ba-Shu sites have been excavated, so most of what is known of their culture comes from legends, the best-known telling of Lin Jun and the five clans. In triumphing over contenders for leadership of the people he was named Lin (Lord or Chief) Jun. After his death, it is said that he turned into a white tiger. The *Hou Han Shu* (Book of the Ba-Shu) records that this ancient people sacrificed human beings to white tigers they believed to be reincarnations of their founder, Lin Jun.

The afternoon brought us a sky of rich blue, soft streaked with veins of mist. It seemed alive, as if it were one huge, perfect, overarching petal of the universe. The mountains on either side of the river issued red and purple, then black and green, against the blue. Myriad shapes formed a mystery of infinite variety. Smoke rose in pale blue shafts from small thatched-roof houses set high on the ramparts Here and there a cherry or plum tree stood clothed in full blossom. A white pagoda, like a hand-carved piece of ivory, sat on top of the highest promontory.

Cracks in the walls grew maidenhair fern and narrow ledges sported purple primroses. Streams tumbled over rock tables etched by water and wind into shrines with pillared fronts. In these formations we saw the semblances of gos-

;iping women, rollicking children and tottering elderlies.

Wherever the cliffs became less vertical or broke into rock ledges, mankind ntruded with unbelievable structures. On minuscule platforms, tiny houses ıad been built, their backs burrowed into the rock and their fronts cantilevered over the edge.

Children were protected from tumbling into the watery depths below with halters and rope fastened to posts. One level down from these deep-eaved shanties were minute plots of ground cultivated by owners who lowered themselves with ropes. Each of these tiny habitations seemed ready to plunge into the river. Tucked within the natural rock sculptures, these brown-roofed villages accented the scattering of orange and pomegranate trees. Wherever a ten-by-ten-foot plot was available, we could see green shoots of young wheat or rice. These clumps of trees and houses seemed lost against a rising mountain. Others were bisected by gullies that cradled mountain streams.

Coming to a calmer section of the Xiling, the major surprised us when he drew from his pocket a package of miniature yarrow sticks, bought at the market in Yichang. With gusto he spilled them on the boards where we were sitting.

The hexagram 29, *Kan*, was indicated. "That's the Abysmal Water image," Wang Shi told us. "It suggests life, like a mighty river surging toward the ocean, demands that people learn to flow with history. Superior persons meet the inevitable dangers that occur with skill and persistence. Facing every vicissitude they remain true to self and cooperative with others. Following this brings success; failing or denying this plunges the person into the abyss."

"More than mere platitudes," Wang Shi suggested, "these words guide people to meet life's changes and hazards. Wise action stems less from following rules and more from the character a person has developed. In life's currents, realities must be assessed and dealt with deliberately and steadily. The reference is to those who are purposeful and caring for self and others."

"In the West," the major replied thoughtfully, "we talk of the Protean person—one who is adequate, poised, ready to take on new roles, adaptable and accommodating. Such a person, confident in his or her goals, keeps ahead of the current, keeps control of self and thus teaches by example."

"The river is an abyss for the Chinese," Wang Shi added. "'Forward and backward, abyss upon abyss,' as the saying goes. The implication is that every movement may lead to danger. The worst peril strikes when persons don't keep ahead of life's flow—they surrender their initiative and lose the 'right way.' People must exercise their freedom responsibly, else they remain tangled in their mistakes and failures. In life, as in journeying, realistic stock must be made of rocks and shoals, eddies and whirlpools. From nature comes important analogies for individuals and their relations with others."

"These sober counsels of the Book of Changes," the major commented "may have been relevant to Chinese societies 2,500 ago. But we, in the twentieth century, don't want to live by chance or the throw of yarrow sticks. I'll grant, however, there are analogies for life in natural processes. Also I see how the idea of abyss suggests elements of existential thought that press us to seek the ground of existence."

"Yes," Thompson observed, "this concern reaches for a theology based on being and existence. It is the concern Pascal must have had when he said 'There is an infinite abyss in persons that can only be filled by God himself.' A verse in the 130th Psalm says, 'Out of the depths I cry unto Thee, O Lord!' In other words, out of the abyss thoughts, feelings and yearnings reach out for a response from the Almighty. Also, from the abyss of our deepest selves we cry out–like Wesley–for guidance and grace to start on the path to perfection."

"The idea of persons having an abyss that God fills," Wang Shi reacted, "is one I've not thought of. Chinese don't think of people being split psychologically by an abyss. We recognize people can be divided by deceitful rationalizations. Some commoners believe in malignant spirits that invade and divide people. Facing facts and holding to a sense of purpose keeps people from falling into the abyss.

"A crystal," I ventured, "provides an illustration of psychological representations. Its axial system determines the crystalline formation in the saturated solution, without itself possessing a material existence. So it is with people's archetypes. Struggling with/in this great river presents a range of archetypal images. The river with its high walls, the gorges' grand vistas, and the boatmen's courage present more than water, cliffs and human effort. Nature's beauty was more than mere pretty scenes. It reminds us of what Carl Jung described as the Collective experience of humanity. Represented in 'archetypes' within the collective unconscious, it contains thought modes and reaction patterns that are typical in all humanity."

A bowman shouted back, "*Da Tan lai le* (big rapids coming up!)" This hard fact cut short our philosophizing.

The skipper at the tiller and the *tai gong* at the bow, the *wu ban* was steered toward a wide cove on the south bank where we would dock for the night and the next morning enlist reinforcements for our limited band of trackers.

Mean while, as we began to hear the roar of waters crashing over rocks in the narrow channel ahead, the cook started telling us about the Da tan. we would negotiate on the morrow. Its alternate name is Xin Tan (new rapids since it was formed only three centuries ago, by an enormous landslide Because of the notorious toll in lives it has taken, it is sometimes called Empty Boat Rapids.

The Xin Tan's first section was considered especially perilous when the waters were high. The second section, the Kuadong, though shorter, would be rougher. He warned us, that "the smallest pilot error in judgment, any slowing of the sweeps, a towline breaking or unnoticed submerged rocks could spell oblivion in the yellow-copper river."

"Look over there!" he said, pointing to the cusp of the cove, on the edge of the white water. The crews of two shipwrecked junks were camped onshore under mats pulled from their boats. Clothes, cotton goods and other salvaged cargo spread on bushes were drying in the sun. Tops of masts just below the water reminded would-be voyagers of junks that had not cleared the rocks.

"As we go up," the cook added in a lugubrious tone, "we'll probably see battered skeletons of junks on the rocks and corpses floating downriver."

Once the junk was moored, the crew crowded the galley for second-rate rice mixed with cabbage and a treat–bits of pork fried in sesame oil. We passengers ate with the *lao ban's* family and the *tai gong*. The oarsmen, bowmen and trackers squatted around the midship hatch.

As always, the meal was fast and furious. The men balanced their bowls on the fingertips of their left hands, close under their chins. Into mouths open wide they shovelled food with lightning-quick chopsticks. They stuffed their cheeks and began again. As if in competition, they left no time for mastication–much less for the pleasure of taste. In less than five minutes, bowls and cheeks were empty. They avoided drinking cold water, always taking boiling water or water in which the rice had been cooked.

The men washed their bowls in the river and squatted on the gunwales with their pipes, content to chatter as they watched the moon rise over the slopes to the east. Onshore between two large willow trees they built a fire. The genial *tai gong* invited us to join the circle of crackling flames. While we talked of the beauty around us, the cook, now in a jovial mood, threw three ancient coins on the sand until he had the evening's hexagram.

When he called out the number 27, the ideograph *"I,"* we were suspicious that he had stacked the find, because this hexagram meant "the corners of the mouth" or "providing nourishment." The cook drew the hexagram with his finger in the sand: unbroken lines at the top and bottom and four sets of broken lines between. "The image is the mouth," he said. "Upper part stands still, lower moves up."

Wang Shi obliged by reading from the commentary:

> *"At the foot of the mountain, hunger.*
> *Pay heed to the providing of nourishment*
> *And to what a man seeks to fill his own mouth with.*
> *The superior man is careful of his words*
> *And temperate in eating and drinking."*

"In other words," he explained, "man is dependent on nourishment both for self and others. Also, heaven and earth provide nourishment for all people. Mencius, for instance, said that 'when God comes forth as thunder in the mountain, all things are completed.'"

"*A Ya*," the first officer interrupted. "I hope as we journey 'all things will be completed' well," revealing his concerns about the dangers ahead. "The two sections of the Xiling Gorge we passed through today, though rough, are short. Up ahead the Niugan is three miles long, the Mitan four, the Wushan about 20 miles, and after that the Fengxien is about four. Each has its particular hazards. In between the rapids are *hun li hai* (very wild). What we have ahead will not be easy."

"The *tai gong* is thinking about more than only physical danger ahead," Wang Shi added. "In talking with me this morning he expressed the Chinese feeling about the symbolic meaning of traveling these gorges. It's not only the dangers ahead, but the meaning of the journey, that is important. He feels that our small purposes, like this trip, must relate to a sense of direction and purpose in our lives. If we see no meaning and no connections with the flow of our history, we are without courage when tragedy strikes. Seeing an ultimate significance for our lives gives small day-by-day happenings meaning."

The "small meanings" surrounding us at the moment were the intimate cove, the willow trees, the boatmens' jabbering and their squeaky fiddles. The simple setting promised a mellow evening.

"It's very Chinese," Thompson mused, scanning the cliffs hemming us in. "The gorges' austere beauty and awesomeness–particularly at twilight–triggered the imaginative reactions of Chinese poets, novelists, dramatists and historians. Journeying through the gorges is like entering the bloodstream of Chinese life. Struggling up the river you touch the heart of China."

"Artistic sensitivity is a pervasive Chinese quality. You see it in the design of the commonest utensil, shop signs, calligraphy, the rhythmic movements of cart pullers, the masks and costumes of a Peking opera. China's political and spiritual discords are crushing, but her artistic sense of a unifying harmony provides a saving grace."

"More than a 'sense of unifying harmony,' however," the major said, "is required to build a dam in these parts."

"As a scientist, I see the river and these cliffs in terms of their mass, acceleration, physical composition and relations. The natural order is discoverable by sensory experience, but it's less for artistic appreciation and more to manipulate and utilize the material. In scientific inquiry we approach nature with precise observation. Engineers are trained to observe objectively, measure, see connections and make hypotheses. This approach gives us some control of exterior forces and enables us to manipulate them for human purposes."

"Dam builders," the major continued in his detailed and practical way, "have to measure and calculate the composition of these rock cliffs, determine how they behave under different conditions, prepare plans, hire work crews, gather supplies, set completion dates. They are concerned less with the magnificence of a promontory and more with the silt content at its base.

"From my angle," he said, after giving Wang Shi time to translate to the attentive *tai gong*, "nature is a realm of objects, like that pagoda up there or our junk here. To create and control these objects we need more than intuition or guesswork.

"Granted," Thompson said, "the scientist's job is different from that of the artist. Engineers must explain existence in terms of natural relations discovered by empirical inquiry. They must find hard facts and causes within the world."

"Surely," I put in, "these differing approaches to nature supplement rather than exclude one another. The first officer's artistic approach, the major's empirical and Thompson's way of faith raise essential questions in different realms. The religious person needs the scientist's approach to the intelligible world and also the artist's appreciation of the universe. And the modern intellectual and artist do not have to relinquish assurances of religious experience in affirming modern knowledge."

"True, I've found the way of faith provides a foundational approach for dealing with the world," Thompson affirmed assuredly. "My faith tells me this canyon and river were created according to God's Plan. My faith finds a supernatural cause beyond all finite causes. The religious idea of a transcendent Creator makes possible, rather than hinders, scientific understanding. It gives a deeper awareness of nature's artistic harmonies. My religious conviction ties together these approaches. I'm convinced that to be spiritual is to have a more intense awareness of what surpasses ordinary life."

"We live in a time," I noted, "as Father Francois said the other day, when the assumed meanings of life are threatened. For many moderns, traditional values have collapsed. We feel uneasy and uncertain as new and lesser meanings spring from forces beyond our control and crowd out old meanings that long have steadied us. The resulting sense of meaninglessness is not alleviated by either scientific methods or artistic appreciation."

"Yet occasionally, some unexpected event may strike scientists or artists with a numbing sense of the meaninglessness of existence. Suddenly they experience the anguish of sinking into a life devoid of a solid bottom. It takes commitment to something ultimately important, such as a sense of coherence within historical destiny, to give meaning to life. A strong belief in God gives life meaning. This conviction provides confidence that our life is moving toward the realization of larger goals, including doing God's will. The contingent meanings in our lives, then, point beyond ourselves to God as the fount of all meaning."

After Wang Shi explained the drift of the conversation to him, the *tai gong* nodded and smiled. Like us all, he was saturated with "thoughts too deep for words," so he stood up, stretched and responded, "We'd better get some sleep. Tomorrow will be a difficult and long day."

Fog hung like lace from the pines and willows which dotted the cove. Clusters of boatmen huddled on their mats, squirming to stay covered under their tattered blankets. The flickering fires cast shadows of their forms against the bushes. As the embers of the fires dulled, darkness settled. Picking our way up the slippery gangplank, we could hear the Long River's waters crashing on the rocks along the shore.

The memories of this day long remained deeply etched. It was a day crowded with images of angry waters, boats buffeted by the winds and current, and forlorn, majestic shorelines. The morning had begun badly with the skipper's delay, yet at last we had started into the gorges!

Excitement had come as we passed through the Dong Ling Xia (the great Estern Portals). There had followed the grueling pull for the oarsmen, the punishing haul for the trackers. Dependent on the crew's strength and skill, we passengers had been plunged into terror by the convulsions of the rapids. The kaleidoscopic whirl of feeling, thought and faith flashed against the starless night. The day's end came with the circle around the embers. The tai gong's interpretation of the voyage into the gorges as part of life's journey and the round of exchanges about the artistic, scientific and spiritual ways of coping with the world stretched our perspectives.

At Lao-min-tzi cove mooring we were denied our needed good night's rest amid the snores and groans of the crew. They twitched and jerked like dogs beside a hearth. Bedrolls did little to ease the hard floorboards under us. The air was chilly and damp. Crawling insects came to feed on us from the hard-sinewed oarsmen, whose sleeping mats lay around us. Knowing some had scabby arms and ugly leg sores, I itched continually, half-believing myself infected with ringworm, impetigo and white fungus. Then, before dawn, the wild choruses of crews on the great cargo junks surging downstream pounded panic into our nightmares.

# Through The Xiling's Gates Of Hell

*Tracker's Shanties*

Before dawn, 15 feet aft of us, *Lao Ma*, the skipper's explosive wife, erupt-ed in a tirade against her husband that escalated into a nose-to-nose show-down. Frightened little granddaughter, *Xiao mei mei*, began to wail and her 8-month-pregnant mother tried to quiet both her and the battling parents. The cook from the galley six feet in front of us muttered invectives over the trou-ble he was having starting the charcoal braziers. His efforts at fanning blew an asphyxiating blue smoke into our faces. The crew, from midship to bow, were out of sorts and anxious in anticipation of the perils which lay ahead.

Packed so tightly in our bedrolls we had to take turns extricating ourselves. This morning it was my turn to be first, the major and Wang Shi next, and Thompson last. Then to give ourselves room to stand and put on our trousers, we had to roll back the mud-encrusted matting over the arched stays above us. Crew members were intrigued with the rubric of our foreigners' way of dress-ing: putting on trousers right leg first, and shirt right arm first.

*Lao Ma* (Mrs. *Lao ban*), was irritated at the pushy and quarrelsome oarsmen and bowmen who crowded around the galley and at the cook for not filling the passengers' bowls first. In a scathing outburst she cursed the crew and the cook. Not to be intimidated, the cook slapped his big cleaver on the hatch in a gesture to get her to mind her own business. He filled our bowls with rice, sprinkled them with slivers of dried fish and pickles, and as a bonus broke a raw egg over the serving.

Seated on the gunwales like the oarsmen, Thompson explained the crew's irritability was par for the morning when they were headed for the dreaded *Xintan* (Empty Boat Rapids).

Trackers were clamoring around our mooring, eager to be hired. Each group had its spokesman who vied with the others to have their particular band chosen. The skipper desultorily began dickering for 50 reinforcements. The crowd rose in an uproar, yelling: "*Bu gou, bu gou!* (Not enough, not enough!)." The adamant foremen were disgusted. They argued that for our large *wu ban* in the current's present speed at least an additional 100 were needed. They cupped their hands behind their ears, looked in the direction of the roar from the *Xintan*, pointed to the red-sailed lifeboats and repeated, "More fast water and worse rock piles mean harder and riskier pulling."

The skipper's words and manner stirred increasing discord and when his loud-mouthed wife entered the negotiations all hell broke loose. With cool defiance, the skipper walked back to his sanctum on the poop deck and left the *tai gong* ashore to continue the bargaining. Egged on by their agents, the trackers became noisier and more demanding. Their insolent mood flared and issued in abusive words and threatening gestures. "You stingy bastards!" they shouted. "You care only to save a few coppers and nothing for us who can be dragged to our death in the rapids!"

The more vociferous of the leaders took the new tact of trying to enlist the help of Thompson, standing at the bow trying to calm the storm. The foremen asked him to persuade the "tight-wad S.O.B. *lao ban*" to hire enough trackers. When Thompson hesitated, the angry foreman mistook his quiet self-control for foreign arrogance and cursed him. Some resolution to the impasse seemed possible when the *tai gong* upped the number to be hired to 75.

Voicing a final explosion of disdain, the foremen quit the negotiations, refusing to talk further, either with the *tai gong* or the foreigner, much less the *lao ban*. Whereupon the *lao ban* offered to hire 5 more trackers. The agitators, still cursing, turned away, saying they would wait until their lead foreman returned with the cook, who had disappeared up the path past the trackers' encampment. As the trackers cooled their tempers, we braced ourselves for more delay.

In a surprisingly short time, the cook came down the path carrying an enormous, kicking rooster. With stilted pace, the cook and the trackers' foreman approached our *wu ban* like a priest and an acolyte. Theirs was an air of grotesque stateliness, as if stalking something elusive. With a flourish, the cook drew a knife from the cord that held up his trousers and passed it to the foreman, who took a stance like that of a mighty king in the Peking opera. With aplomb, he slit the crimson throat of the cock. Together they aimed the pulsating spurts of blood at the beam across the junk's fish-head bow. When the spurting was exhausted, they plucked feathers from the expiring rooster and smeared them into the blood on the bow timber.

This propitiation by their leader quieted the irritable trackers and our anxious crew. They became cooperative, agreed to the larger number of trackers and pay offered by the *lao ban*. The two chosen trackers groups, totaling 80 men in all, were an assortment of rowdy rag-tails. Their tall foreman must have been picked less for his friendliness and more for his broad shoulders and determined jaw. He explained his strategy: his men must pull at the head of the towline, a safer location for the haulers, since the farther back they were, the easier they were to be whip-lashed from the trail into the river. Called the *dai wan di*, he was dressed in a less- ragged and less-faded blue coat than his impoverished pullers. He declared his combined teams of trackers were ready to depart for the rapids.

Aboard our *wu ban* the cook continued raising our anxiety about the *Xintan* Rapids. Describing the river as a dragon on a rampage, with claws reaching out to claim people's souls, he added, "we in the *wu ban* must defy the river spirits' fatal drag. Even though the crew made offerings and vows at Yichang temples and we smeared the sacrificial chicken's blood over the bow and sweeps, these propitiations may not be enough when the river gods are angry!"

Sensing our mounting anxiety as we listened to the ominous roar of the *Datan* (Big Rapids), the man tried to calm us with diversionary observations: "Those lifeboats up there are ready for us. See how smart-looking, turbaned crews steer their junks in and out of the eddies and dodge around the rocks!"

We caught sight, for the first time, of two sturdy lifeboats with red-and-white striped sails. With large sails and powerful rowers, they crisscrossed the river upstream from our mooring. Tough river worthy craft, they were manned by seasoned specialists. Called "mercy boats," their sails were inscribed with Chinese ideographs. They warned of special dangers around the rapids, where most of mishaps occurred.

Then, looking toward the shore, the cook stuck out his chin, pointing toward the approaching skipper, who was escorting a man he treated as a dignitary. "*Lai la,* (he's coming)," the cook said, "there's the river pilot the skipper engaged. Now there'll be two responsible for steering us through the Dragon's Mouth."

"Named *Wang-si*, or Wang the Fourth," the cook added. "His great-grandfather, grandfather and father had all been respected river pilots. Like many of them, he's Sichuanese–short, stocky and sure of himself."

Bold of stride and garbed in a distinctive black jacket, the man looked expert. Walking up the wobbly gangplanks, he eyed with approval the *wu ban'* bow which bore smears of the sacrificial rooster's blood and feathers. His initial act was to stand on the bow and propitiate the river deities. He used the words written on the flag he waved: "Powers of water, give a lucky star for the journey."

Not to be left out of a ritual, the cook threw handfuls of rice over the gunwales.

Making his way aft, the pilot conferred with the skipper and first officer. Moving to the midship, he gave directions to the crew.

Vessels were required to take their turn going up these rapids, ours was eleventh. The major and I, to minimize further delays, offered the skipper a bonus if he could arrange to get towed before noon. The incentive worked, however, it would still be two hours before we could pull away from our mooring. The first officer suggested we take some time ashore.

Led by Wang Shi, we walked past the fire circle we had enjoyed the night before toward the ghetto where hundreds of transient *ku lis* (coolies) were gathered. Refugees from rural areas in neighboring provinces, they had fled famines and floods, migrating to the river on the chance of eking out an existence during the navigation season. On the river's shores, they squeezed into holes bounded by hooped bamboo stays and covered with straw matting, leaving them vulnerable to being swept away by the slightest rise of the river.

"*K'u* means 'bitterness' and *li* is 'work'," Wang Shi explained, "and theirs is indeed bitter work." (The common belief is that the term originated in India.)

"These trackers have dropped through the cracks of society," he continued with concern. "Most of them are fourth, fifth or sixth sons of families that are already below the poverty line. Sometimes they are pushed out by fathers or older brothers who consider them uncompliant. But, more often, their families, farmers for the most part, have no more space and food for them. Turned out by their families, they also become uprooted from their villages. They become marginal people who lead a precarious existence and die early. Viewed as expendable, they are used and abused for what their muscles can lift, carry and pull. It is as if they were born only to haul burdens, pull oars, man *yulows* and tow cables."

"There are so many of these unfortunate people," Wang Shi said angrily. "They are economic and social exiles. They slip below the general population we call the *laobaixing* ('the old one hundred names'). Losing their kinship they lose their surnames and become nameless, known only by their function.

Losing their solidarity with their community, they lose their identity and any semblance of security."

Their mat-shed hovels seemed more like dog kennels. The sights and smells of degradation and misery swept over us like a tidal wave. Nurtured in the ambience of Western suburbs, trained in the ivied walls of academia, immersed in secure urban sophistication, we had never experienced hunger for more than a few hours, let alone the struggle to survive in such submarginal conditions. Wang Shi winced and stayed close to the three of us foreigners as we passed one after another tumbled-down mat shelter.

Totally dependent for their livelihood on servicing junks as extras, they were even poorer than the lowly rag-tag beggars who panhandled around the moorings. Filthy and ragged trackers readied themselves in hopes of being among the few who would be chosen for a team of pullers. Their women tended fires over which they warmed burnt rice and spoiling meat, flecked with fly eggs, in tin-can pots. A few, with half empty bowls, squatted outside their hovels. Behind the dilapidated shacks, men were relieving themselves.

Beside them were others who washed their faces in communal buckets of river water. These would-be trackers were tattered and dust-caked. They were too undernourished to be sturdy, too marginal to qualify for more secure employment. Some heaved excruciatingly with consumptive coughing and others, who were stretched out, seemed dying in pallid strips like sprayed weeds. Others milled around as if they had nothing to do, nowhere to go. Speculation about life's meaning was the least of their concerns.

Their survival on the edge was not pretty. Revulsion, even from family members, went with devotion. So painful and fearful was it to touch one another that at close quarters, it was hard to distinguish love from hatred. Wrung out with pity, or cursing, people shared their rice even though each day tens died of disease and malnourishment. It was out of the question for any one of them to speculate on life's vanity or its meaninglessness.

Yet there was solidarity in their destitution. Like any other group of people, these human cast-offs, too, had their own routines and manners. Theirs was a strong present-time orientation. Ideas about achieving or planning for the future were unthinkable. Depended on chance and fate, they had no way to defer to even a meager gratification. Their resignation and fatalism rendered them gullible to suggestions for improvement and vulnerable to being further taken advantage of and impoverished.

Their curiosity was greatly stirred, however, at that morning hour, by the sight of three light-haired foreigners. Our contrasting clothing and mannerisms were more than interesting; it was entertaining. Eyes were riveted on us. Childlike, they rubber-necked, pressed closer and tried to touch us to feel whether we were real. Women and children surrounded us and asked Wang Shi who we were and where we were from.

Reassured by their intense attention, we were numbed by their appalling circumstances. To see, hear, smell and touch these eager but so destitute refugees was very humbling. We Westerners, used to our machines and technologies, had too little sensitivity for the back-and-spirit-breaking toil that was the daily fare of these people. With stomachs always empty and outlooks always hopeless, their existence was hard to comprehend.

It was reassuring to receive their smiles and nods of approval, by which they tried to share their humanity with us. How could we reciprocate and share ourselves? We found it difficult, but, nevertheless, we tried. Incredulous and delighted when Thompson and I spoke Chinese, they were perplexed by our Mandarin that differed from their own garbled dialect. Seeing this puzzlement, we mixed our comments with animated gestures. Although they didn't understand some of our words, they echoed our friendliness.

When we headed back to the junk, we were like four Pied Pipers trailed by crowds unwilling to let us go. Reaching the junk, we found Lao Liu, the lead oarsman, standing at the bow. With a commanding presence, he dispersed the crowds we had gathered. With his strong gnarled hands, he pushed the people back and ordered them to let us make it up the gangway.

Pointing to the diminutive young bowmen at the head of the gangway, the swarthy oarsman said: "*Xiao Liu* (Little Liu) there is my nephew. He'll take you back to your section."

The youth was enveloped in an oversized garment, giving him the look of a fragile adolescent wrapped in a strong man's coat. Combining bruised innocence with clownishness the bright young fellow represented the unfinished, undefined manhood that carries with it no responsibility. But the young man's intelligent face was noticeably a step above those in the crowd of miserables we had just left ashore.

Shaken, we asked ourselves: "What conditions of history, what structure of society had brought these people into such deprived niches? Had they no alternatives? No other way to put food in their stomachs or find adequate shelter and clothing? Considering our affluence, we were ashamed and guilt-ridden for the inequity. "

Such poverty grinds humans down, breaks the spirits of the bravest. A few, with daring and enterprise, may rise above these conditions, but for the majority, their poverty produced ingrained habits resistant to change. As they became accustomed to their lot, they doomed themselves to the lot of Dante's ferryman who knew only the river crossing to Hades.

To see, hear and smell these eager but destitute crowds was profoundly unsettling. It was hard for us to comprehend the reasons for their dehumanation. We reached for deeper dimensions of compassion.

When our turn came to start into the *Xintan* the sweepmen loosened our mooring ropes and started poling away from shore. Six of the trackers who had been bargaining with the carriers scrambled aboard, joking with the oarsmen. The long yulows, instead of tucked astern, were aimed forward to enhance steering.

High on the north-shore bluff, we could see the hanging village of *Xintan*. The shop-lined alleys were so steep they were paved with stone stairs. The skipper told us that most of the houses had been built from the wreckage of junks. Added to the tiny, overhanging shacks, little shrines and a red-walled temple peeked from hillside glens. As we came closer to the Big Shoals, the greenery and signs of humanity gave way to a towering canyon wall that narrowed the river into savage waters.

Sight of a pair of red lifeboats with striped sails signaled our approach to the *Xin Tan* (New Rapids) or *Da Tan* (Big Rapids). More warnings were given by the cook. Having described the river as a "dragon on a rampage, with claws reaching out to claim souls," he added, "At this point, we in the wu ban must defy the river spirits' fatal drag. . .The crew's offerings and vows at Yichang temples and our smearing the sacrificial chicken's blood over the bow and sweeps may not be enough to appease the angry river gods!"

The crew's wisecracking stopped as we came into the current and barely inched along westward. Our oarsmen, reinforced with an extra pair, had to pull hard to cope with the eddies around one after another pile of contorted rocks barely covered by the spring rise of the river.

At the foot of the cliffs on which the village was perched, an outcropping of boulders provided a landing where the trackers we carried got off to join the 30 other hirelings who had been engaged.

Further delay came when the skipper, still out of sorts, decided to have a portion of the cargo portaged around the rapids. The skipper ordered the cook to take the shore path around the rapids with the junk's papers and money, as well as the less valuable "possessions"–his wife, pregnant daughter and *Xiao mei mei*. The t'ao lao (head tracker) and his band, now in better spirits, made a game of the unloading and bargaining for porters. We passengers were welcome to remain aboard or to walk ahead of the trackers on the tow-trail. We opted to take to take the tow trail to get a bird's eye view of the channel and to have the chance to be closer to the trackers as they labored on the tow-line.

When our *wu ban* was next in line to start into the *Xintan* we were given the chance to watch the ascent of the junk ahead. Larger and heavier than ours, it had a longer column of trackers, close to 135. All strained at their harnesses. The enormous vessel moved up slowly and at times seemed to slip back. Often it looked doubtful that the combined exertion of their trackers would budge the boat. We decided it was better not to watch.

The *tai gong* took his place at our bow. Dressed in a better-than-usual jacket, with sleeves folded back, he was poised and set, as befits a first officer, ready to do his part in guiding the vessel. The towline had been played out, and now the trackers in their harnesses began to take up the slack. The *tai gong* raised his arms, and the drummer at the mast pounded out the signal to advance for the trackers' leader on shore.

The thousand-foot-long, plaited bamboo towline had been uncoiled and passed over our *wu ban's* masthead. Our bowmen played it out or took up the slack as required. Since it was to haul our large junk through the especially demanding *Xin Tan*, it was the toughest hawser available. Onshore the ungainly line was stretched forward and the trackers hitched their bandolier cords to the thick bamboo cable. These slings were wound around the cable with a toggle or button so that the hitch could be thrown off and reconnected in moments. With bandoliers slung from the shoulder and waist, the half-naked coolie trackers took hold of the hawser. In pulling, picking their way over rocky towpaths, they often bent so low that they were practically on all fours.

Their lot was one of precarious drudgery. They crept to the cadence of the bowman's beating drum. With their almost imperceptible paces they exerted a constant pull that helped the boat inch upstream through gaps in reefs. A faulty cable, a slippery hitch or slowness of the steersman at a crucial moment could spell disaster. In split seconds trackers could be whipped off tow-path into the raging river. Junks could end upon a jagged reef or sweep out of control and crash into vessels moored below the rapids, waiting their turn to be hauled up.

Several naked men, perched on rocks, readied themselves to wade or swim in the wake of the towline, throwing it clear as they went. They performed daring feats, often risking their lives swimming to rescue an out-of-control junk.

The inboard end of the hawser at the deck was bound round the mast. At the tabernacle nearby, the drummer squatted on his haunches, drum between his knees. He beat an incessant tattoo with a pair of sticks, an "all's well" signal to the trackers. He instantly altered the beat to a sharp rat-tat, rat-tat when the slightest trouble occurred, signaling the trackers to slack or stop pulling.

The response from the long string of trackers onshore was a loud *chor, chor, chor,* (or "put your shoulder to it!"). With the play in their bandoliers, they swayed a little from the axis of the towline, while keeping a tight forward pull. Steps were short, and bodies stooped so low that hands often touched the ground.

Aft, on the raised platform, the helmsman-pilot grappled with the 10-foot long tiller. The skipper watched nearby. When any hitch occurred he rose to the occasion, raving and cursing–often returned to him by the gangers, who vent him one better. And if the crisis worsened, Mrs. *Lao Ban* was on hand to pour out more vitriol.

Headway was exasperatingly slow. The intense exertion of oarsmen on board and the trackers on their carved-out trail ashore wall was breathtaking to watch. The rocks between the sluices were barely visible. The skipper had to navigate through the channel where the angry copper waters churned. Next came a long, wedge-shaped tongue of fast water rushing through another narrow channel. The heavy towline, creaking and jerking, seemed an elongated umbilical cord.

I found following the towtrail more difficult than I had anticipated. We picked our way over the rocks for a half mile, then scrambled up the cliff onto the carved-out path. We found the lead tracker was like a friendly wolf at our heels.

The flexible rod he held was a sign of his authority. Often as much as 1,000 feet ahead of the junk, he served as look-out, though primarily his job was to see that the bamboo tow cable was pulled with full manpower and kept taut. Not a yelling, whip-cracking taskmaster, he moved up and down the column of haulers, coaxing and cajoling. His superior brawn and resolution were commanding. Occasionally, he even pulled at the head of the towline.

His remarkable repertoire of calls, chants and responses was unique. Each chasm or crisis seemed to have its own appropriate melody, which he led, thereby enhancing the *esprit de corps.*

The gouged-out towpath led up an incline. The trackers, still chanting, moved slowly with shorter steps. With increased effort, they kept their cadence. The rock-hewn tunnel was so confining that we Westerners had to duck our heads.

A crisis interrupted our labored ascent. In the first part of the rough waters an other junk, smaller and more maneuverable than ours attempted to pull ahead of ours. Its mast caught in our sagging hawser. The other junk, with its team of 90 trackers, was trying to swing its towline over our mast and pass us. An excruciating explosion of yells erupted from our rear-guard team. Blood-curdling shouts and epithets arose from our oarsmen, warning the intruding junk's crew to back off.

Livid, our *lao ban* shouted a stream of curses at the skipper of the trespassing vessel. When any new mishap threatened, he rose to the occasion, raving and cursing–often returned to him by the gangers, who went him one better. As the crisis worsened, Mrs. Lao Ban was on hand to vent her anger.

By means of the drummer, the alert first officer, signaled to our trackers to take up the slack in our hawser and clear the entanglement. The fast cadence on the drum meant "pull harder," Though the crashing waters often drowned out these cues. Auxiliary drums ashore rose above the rapids' pounding. The skipper and pilot at the helm conveyed their messages with flag signals. In seconds the amazing column on their precarious towpath took up the slack in the towline and the intruding junk's mast cleared and our cumbersome vessel pulled ahead of the would-be line-breaker.

A crescendo of drumbeats confirmed that we had reached the Dragon's Mouth, the most tumultuous section of the rapids. The trackers, oarsmen and sweepsmen kept our *wu ban* moving forward at a snail-pace.

Shortly, in addition to our continuing struggle with the *Xintan* rapids, another challenge struck. The lead tracker spotted upstream the large cargo junk that earlier had started ahead of us. Our *t'ai wan di* signaled that the big vessel was in serious trouble. Hauled by two hawsers with nearly 80 trackers on each cable, it was floundering.

In a split second, our lead tracker's chant became a shrill warning cry. Our tracker column halted and kept our cable taut. A cataclysmic din of drum-beating arose, gongs clanged and firecrackers exploded in an attempt to ward off evil water spirits.

The distressed junk's forward hawser stretched, frayed and snapped with a horrible crack, whipping five of the last coolies off the precipice into the waters below. The others in their column, like tipped dominoes, fell face down in a row. But they picked themselves up and scrambled back to reinforce those on the second hawser who were now pulling a double load.

From our vantage point the distressed trackers looked like quadrupeds. The wiry men seemed to tremble as they hung to the towline. The junk barely held, but the desperate column bent lower and persisted with hauling. We watched the crisis worsen as the imperiled junk's frozen trackers were trapped ahead of our blocked column.

Then the second hawser, lighter than the first, began to fray halfway down its length. Their lead tracker, seeing the inevitable, ordered his men to brace themselves for the break. As the second line snapped, the giant junk spun, tilted and lurched out of control downstream.

The stricken cargo vessel rushed toward our junk. Our lead tracker shouted for the trackers to back down. Simultaneously, in a remarkably coordinated maneuver, our oarsmen, bowmen and helmsmen veered our junk closer to shore. The other vessel swept toward us, but careened past, within a boat's length away. We caught our last glimpses of the desperate crew trying to bring the vessel under control. As it catapulted into a whirlpool, two lifeboats were ready.

With our hearts still in our throats, we looked for the five trackers who had been jerked off the cliff into the torrent. Miraculously, one's bandolier had caught in a tree. Our rear guardsmen joined the other junk's swimmers in rescuing the other four. As our junk continued inching upriver, we passed the rescued coolies, clustered on a large boulder, blanched and exhausted, looking like drowned cats.

Another column of trackers moved toward us, dragging their junk behind ours. Hardly missing a beat, our lead tracker sang our coolies forward again. Though awestruck at what we'd seen, the major, Thompson, Wang Shi and I could not pause to let our hearts catch up. The tracking team continued its steady pull, the rowers and sweepmen kept their pace, enabling skipper and pilot to steer the junk through the second and third section of the *Xintan* Rapids.

Rounding a bend, we came to the foot of the Pillar of Heaven promontory that appeared to leap from the water, rising nearly 2,000 feet. Other ramparts almost as high followed, hemming in with perpendicular cliffs the channel below us. Their summits, tufted with sprinkles of dark green pines, narrowed to focus on clouds turning golden in the afternoon sun. The walls were broken into buttresses and fantastic projections of splintered rock that cast deep shadows on the river below and made more difficult the struggles of trackers on the trail above. The towline had to be played out to its limit as the trackers made their way on the towing trail 150 feet above the river. Our trackers kept up their tortuous crawl along the cramped carved-from-granite towtrail, like goats making their way over boulders and across crevices, keeping the tow-line taut. Straining in their rhythmic heaving, they united in a throbbing, brawny chorus. The rising and falling of their plaintive work music reverberated through the gorge.

Below, we could see the *wu ban's* bowmen roll the forward-pointing yulows, waging a battle to keep the junk's bow at the correct steering angle.

As we left the towering cliffs and neared the end of this gorge, the trail descended to the shore. With a break in the limestone walls, the skipper steered the *wu ban* to a low shoreline rock shelf. This gave us, who had taken the land route, the chance to get back on board. 20 trackers were also taken on to reinforce our rowers who soon pulled the *wu ban* out into a smooth stretch above the *Xin Tan* Rapids.

Our time in calmer waters was short. Late in the afternoon we came to the turbulent Gua Dong. The *tai gong* persuaded the skipper to hire 15 more pullers. In minutes we were into another portion of angry water, called the Chasm of the Military Code and the Precious Blade. The *tai gong* said it was named for warriors who had defeated rapacious invaders. Wang Shi noted that it is also known as the Rice Granary Chasm since, long ago, an official hid his store of grain in a cave in the south cliff.

The dangerous point came midway up the section where sharp, black rocks pushed through the foam. Our anxiety was heightened as our column of pullers began to gain on those of the larger junk ahead of us. Our drummer eased his beat and slowed our trackers' pace. We had to share part of the agony of the hundreds of straining pullers in the two columns. Calls of the foremen, signals from the drums and the unceasing exertion of the laboring columns kept us aghast, moment after tension-filled moment. The combined effort of the crews and trackers left us awe-struck.

We passengers were too shaken to talk. Wang Shi commented, "As I worried whether the five trackers were rescued, I thought of what the 5th century philosopher Chuang Tze's (5th century B.C.) wrote after seeing a frightening junk accident 'The distinctions between life and death are obliterated upon grasping the vision of the One.'"

Wang Shi, sensed that the ancient reference hardly bridged the abyss of tragedies we had witnessed. He thought a minute and asked, "But how and when can we 'grasp' such a vision?"

As the shadows lengthened and the thin band of sky turned crimson, we cleared the last *Xiling* rapids. Gradually the high canyon walls eased into hills and we pulled into a broader stretch of river. Chocolate-yellow and streaks of green mixed in the flow. The cook pointed ahead to a ravine on the north bank, explaining that the green water was a tributary coming from the heights.

Ashore a few pines straggled up the barren rock. We watched the lengthening shadows in the valleys. The mountains seemed to have heaved themselves up, their strata almost perpendicular. Amid the limestone turrets and cathedral spires, we were intrigued with the sight of beautiful bridal falls pouring down from the crevices in the rock walls that continued to hem us in. The charm of the canyons compensated for the harrowing risks of the river. Bands of grey limestone alternated with red sandstone upended and curved, while along the water's edge spits and shingles of sand and gravel piled up. Arched bridges and tiled temples peeping from wooded ravines caused my mind to daydream of battling fire-breathing dragons and rescuing princes.

Scattered masses of ferns, slender-stemmed palms and bursts of red azaleas mingled with groves of golden bamboos. This was not the usual China with masses of people, quaint bridges, curled roofs and formal gardens. Here was a subtropical Chinese Switzerland–an intoxication, a dream.

The skipper steered the *wu ban* to shore so that the few trackers still on board could join those on the tow path. Once ashore they exploded with shouts of celebration: we'd triumphed over the *Xintan*. Like proud coaches, the pilot, lead tracker and first officer, congratulated the crew and trackers.

The *t'ai wan di's* (lead tracker) commanding presence and calm had been impressive. The major, with Thomson translating, conveyed his appreciation to the man, telling him he deserved the title of M.V.P–most valuable player–for is victory over the *Xintan* rapids.

"It was nothing; all in a day's work," the embarrassed tracker said. With that e took an extra bandolier from his belt and presented it to the major. Eager o explain his craft to the foreigner, he demonstrated how the sashes were tached by a cord with a large button on the end. This hitch, he explained, an be instantly thrown off with a twist of the wrist. He then pointed with his aton to the tow cable. "Larger in thickness than a strong man's arm," he said. The one we had today is among the best. It can withstand tensions up to ,000 kilos (Almost 10,000 pounds per square inch). The cable's knife-like dges score soft sandstone boulders and often cut trackers arms and shoulers."

He said one part of his column had riverside mat-shed shanties at the head f Mi Tan Gorge. Others he would take downriver to tow up another junk. heirs was a 12-hour day, risking their lives to drag heavy junks. Theirs were ights of only fitful rest, for even through the coldest nights, they slept outoors on plank beds or mats. They were a tough but short-lived lot.

"Talking about commoners is one thing," Wang Shi said. "Walking bareooted over rocks with them, like we did today, is something else! It's easy for ntellectuals to idealize the ordinary citizen; it's harder to walk beside them as ney labor."

"These ordinary people have a right to be more than expendable ones. hey are the stuff of our country. Regretably their ignorance and superstitions ck them in fear. From childhood on, they find it's useless to complain of their itter lot."

Consideration of the plight of these *lao bai xing* (commoners) was a subject Vang Shi could not let go. "Now that the Japanese war is ended is the time," e said vehemently, "to finish the 1911 Revolution. We must build the new China that Sun Yat-sen and the Wuchang martyrs fought for."

The skipper's shouts, "Time to move on!" cut short the young instructor's vords.

Hugging the north bank, our exhausted oarsmen pulled the junk toward Miao He, or Temple Rivulet, a nondescript village which despite its name howed no sign of a temple. This seemed hardly an auspicious place to land fter surviving the Xiling Gorge's final gauntlet.

We were relieved when the skipper at dusk steered the junk to the south ank and toward the more inviting Lao-min-tsi inlet that appeared to offer an nviting setting.

The pebbly cove sheltered the village of Nan-to on its western shore. erched on a promontory that jutted into the river was the town's celebrated even-storied pagoda. Not many of the towns visible from the gorges are big enough to warrant such a monument. It was built two centuries ago as "benevolence" for the town by a group of junk owners who had managed to survive until retirement. Tall, slender and stately, it emerged from a grove of orange and loquat trees. In the background was the 9,000-foot mountain, Jiu Chong Dian Shan (Nine Levels Reaching to Heaven Mountain).

The mooring toward which the *wu ban* was directed, called *Ju Yu fang* (Fish Gathering Cove), was at the confluence of a meandering stream. Approaching this mooring was an artful process. Our bowmen felt their way toward shore by thrusting down their long bamboo poles ahead of the bow. Coming in was more involved than throwing out an anchor and tightening ropes around deck cleats. Finding and claiming a slot often required negotiating with other skippers. Since a place was available and a stake remained on the bank, a bowmen jumped into the water with a line and made fast to the pole. Heavy rubber fenders, fore and aft, were positioned to prevent damage when bumping other junks.

After the bow slid to a stop at the wooded shore, the usual details were attended to quickly. The first officer and the bowmen cleared lines and swung the long black *yulows* back on the junk's afterdeck and lashed them to pegs midship. A pair of oarsmen turned the windlass to lower the huge brown sail. Performing these intricacies with a flare, the crew gave a finale to the day's voyage.

Walking down the two-board gangplank with us the skipper gave an approving nod, and commented, "Favorable winds, strong oarsmen, steady trackers, cooperative *tai wan di* and good fortune brought us through the Xiling Gorges." He couldn't say more, for the trackers and their foreman swarmed around him, clamoring for their pittance of pay.

This another "through the dragon's mouth" day, had severely tested the mettle of our crew–and with them, ourselves. Having pulled through the first and longest of the gorges, with its archetypal struggles, we gained confidence and hope. Boatmen and passengers needed to withdraw from the river's turbulence. We needed to silence the roar of the cataracts and allow ourselves to "be still, and know–" We were glad to reach this tranquil cove that promised a time and place for quieting.

# Qingfan's Restauranter, Philosophers And Monks

elen Houser '98

*Qingfan, an Idyllic Cove*

The miniature settlement where we found ourselves had the poetic and inviting name of Qingfan–Emerald Banner. Houses occupied both sides of a lush glen, but the west side, looking like an embossed cameo, attracted the greater attention. The two halves were linked harmoniously by the graceful arch of an ancient stone bridge. Up a deep ravine was a bridal falls and the valley was closed by the far away and lofty mountain, *Jui chong dian shan.*

The town had an air of prosperity and contentment about it. Its cliff-hanging houses on the western slope, built 400 feet above the river, balanced one atop the other. Its buildings sported graceful curving roofs and intricately-carved eaves. Colonnades arched over shops and eating places. Broad stone steps leading up from the river's edge provided the town's chief thoroughfare. The houses, shops and restaurants jutting out over the cliff suggested Verona, Italy.

A romantic place, it was worth the laborious ascent of 517 steps. The houses were surrounded with loquat, oranges and pomegranate trees, their dark foliage shimmering in the afternoon sun. Little wonder that many of the wealthier surviving junk owners had retired here!

We passengers were treating the first officer and cook to an evening mea ashore–the skipper and his wife had declined our invitation. We asked the coo to choose a restaurant. He led us to an entrance pungent with the smell c roasting chestnuts and barbecued pork.

Crowds, more curious than impolite, pressed the entrances and balconies t savor the rare sight of foreigners. Streams of eager people came from every where and pushed one another to get front-row views. All through the mea they squeezed around us, staring and asking questions. As we finished our las dish, our cook muttered under his breath, "We got only second-rate food. But he thanked the proprietor and entered a lengthy bargaining bout to bu five chickens and five dozen eggs.

Taking leave of the restaurant involved lengthy amenities: describing th graciousness of the hospitality extended us and the tastiness of our fare, an exchanging name cards.

The gregarious restaurateur insisted on accompanying us up the hill. He se a fast pace up the wide stone steps above the rows of shops. We must, he said reach the highest *tingzi* (pavilion) and the promontory capped by the seven storied pagoda before dark. From there, later, we could stop in the Dac Memorial Hall. Then, at the monastery on the other side of the hill, we coul catch the Buddhist monks at their vespers. He talked eagerly all the way up th hill, telling us of Qingfan's scenic and historic sites.

Reaching the top of the hill, our host pointed to the obelisk erected to th memory of Captain Plant, the adroit English seaman who had won the respec of the Chinese junk owners and had lived in a Chinese house near the pavilion The spot commanded a magnificent view. I had read about this vista in th dog-eared book, *Glimpses of the Yangtze Gorges,* written by the old captain i 1890. In lyrical words, the Britisher-turned-Chinese had written:

> *Below lies the rushing foaming rapids. . .Upstream the long defile of the precipitous P'ing Su Gorge stretches away in the distance. Downstream is the awesome Noggin Gorge running far into the Jiu-Wan-Ji or Nine-Cornered-Ravine. All around and almost overhead, snow-capped peaks. . .The gorges up and down stream are outlined sharply, their cliffs radiant with magnificent coloring when the sun is shining, or resembling some awesome passage leading to endless gloom when the day is overcast.*

The pavilion was being restored. Inside, the newly gilded plaques wer highlighted by the setting sun. Wang Shi was ecstatic to find that most of th engraved wall decorations memorialized Chuang Tzu, one of China's illustri ous thinkers and writers, and a favorite of his. Wang Shi scanned each plaqu as if he had found a special treasure.

"Only a few chapters of his works have been preserved," Wang Shi explained, "making his writings some of the rarest of the Chinese classics. And now the last sun of the day gives a special light on some of the most memorable sayings of this master."

Wang Shi translated the gold-foil inlaid ideographs. The words of the ancient sage echoed the emotional bangs and bumps of the day's struggle through the Niu Kan Chasm and the Datan (Xintan) Rapids

The first plaque we came to, written 2,400 years ago, had a contemporary ring:

> *We sail within a vast sphere, ever drifting in uncertainty, driven from end to end. When we think to attach ourselves to any point and to fasten to it, it wavers and leaves us. . .Nothing stays for us.*

Beside it was another plaque that spoke of the workings of the cosmos:

> *The spirit of the universe is subtle and informs all life. Things live and die and change their forms without knowing the root from which they come.*

Though weary from negotiating the day's perils, we were intrigued with the pavilion's uniqueness and stirred to inquire and listen. The ambience of this moonlit hill overlooking the river, heightened our awareness. We were captivated by this ancient sage's wisdom wrung from his struggle with life's turbulence. Searching the nature of being and the sources of knowledge, he had probed the depths of the human soul. Like Pascal, Chuang Tze began his search into the cause of life's turmoil because of despair. He had felt the pathos of human life—its fears, tragedies and transitory nature.

Lin Yu Tang, a 20th-century interpreter, observed that Chuang Tze, "penetrated the problems of reality, developed a theory of eternal flux governing transformations in the universe, and advocated letting people 'fulfill their nature.'" In his existential insistence and introspection, Chuang Tze was strikingly modern. His innovative and far-ranging philosophy challenged conventional Confucian thoughts and bureaucracies.

Chuang Tze's teacher and mentor, the immortal Lao Tze, lauded meekness, or "keeping to the female." In contrast, Chuang Tze was pithy, robust and joyously masculine. For Lao tze, for example, water was the symbol of both strength and softness. For Chuang Tze, water, even in its quiescence, was a paradoxical symbol of latent power—like the Long River. The delicate yet biting expressions of the brilliant disciple showed a reverence for all life. He combined a sharp intellect, great imagination and a gift for lucid expression.

Surviving passages show Chuang Tze was an idealist and mystic, an intellectual and also a man with a playful wit. He delighted in poking fun at the stuffy Confucian orthodoxy of his day. One wall in the Memorial Hall was devoted to plaques quoting the sage's description of his own work. With honesty and self-knowledge he had explained himself thus:

> . . .He gives free play to his spirit without restraint. He regards the
> world as hopelessly sunk in a muddle, unworthy to talk to Zhou (himself).
> . . .Above, his spirit wanders with the Creator, and below he makes friends
> with those who move from beginning to end and transcend life and death.

Other plaques highlighted the three classes of words he used, "serious," "ladle," and "allegory." "Serious words," describing truth and wisdom, he expressed in epigrams, such as:

> Our mind is finite, but knowledge is infinite. To pursue the infinite
> with our finite intelligence–Alas! What a dangerous occupation!

"Ladle words" poured out of his creative mind. In the best known of the "ladle words" he compared himself to a butterfly's dream of becoming human:

> I, Chuang Zhou, dreamed I was a butterfly, fluttering hither and thither. . .
> I was conscious only of my happiness as a butterfly, unaware that
> I was Chuang. Soon I awaked, and there I was, veritably myself again.
> Now I do not know whether I was then a man dreaming that I was a
> a butterfly, or whether I am now a butterfly dreaming that I am a man.

Chuang Tze used "Allegory words," in fables designed to drive home a point, or to lampoon the overly-serious "great people" of his day. An example is a parable showing the superiority of the invisible over the visible mechanisms of the universe:

> The gui (a mythical one-legged, hopping animal) envies the centipede, the
> centipede envies the snake, the snake envies the wind, the wind envies the mind.

The gui tells the centipede about getting around by hopping on one leg and asks, "How do you manage with so many legs?" In turn the centipede questions the snake about his superior mobility, and so on to the mind. Natural forces humble us. The wind, for instance, terrible tempest that it can be, forces us puny humans to acknowledge limitations. Chuang Tze concluded, "From many small defeats I achieve great victory. But achieving the greatest victory belongs to the master mind."

The three main areas of Chuang Tze's philosophy were also recorded on the wall plaques. First is his theory of knowledge, the impossibility of knowing the infinite through finite intelligence. Finite reasoning, he held, leads to one logical non sequitur after another. He thus chided the dialecticians, popular in his day, pointing out that "they can overcome men's words but cannot convince their minds." And he counseled, "Maintain the unity of your will. Do not listen with ears, but with the mind. Do not listen with the mind only, but with the *qi* (spirit)."

Second, Chuang Tze proferred both a concept of the relativity of standards and the equalizing of all things. All the strange and monstrous transformations seen in nature, he claimed, are "leveled together by Dao (Way); even a clod of earth does not lose the Way." He gave the illustration: "If a man sleeps in a damp place, he will have a pain in his loins, and half his body will be as if dead. But is it so with an eel?" Similarly: "human behavior is inescapably conditioned by the fact that life arises from death, and vice versa." So he recommended that we "take as our compass that we are something, but we are not everything."

The third area of Chuang Tze's thought, recorded on a long plaque, concerned the polarity of life and death as one of the ultimate opposites. "How do I know," he asked, "that love of life is not a delusion? Perhaps he who dreads death is as a child who is lost and doesn't know his way home." Or, "If we know that east and west are opposite, and yet that the one cannot be without the other, we know the due adjustment of the function of things." The opposites of right and wrong, for instance, must be accepted as distinct. Yet both, being rooted in Dao (Tao), are involved in endless change. "The corruptible," Chuang Tze said, "becomes mysterious life, and this mysterious life once more becomes corruptible." Chuang Tze proposed innovative moral guidelines for behavior. Instead of abolishing the distinctions of right and wrong, the sage transcends them, an act which may be called "following two courses at once."

The wisdom recorded on these plaques in the hilltop Daoist Memorial Hall above the Long River is universal. Parallel phrases are found halfway around the world in temples atop cliffs overlooking Ephesus. The inscriptions of the 5th-century B.C. Greek philosophers proclaimed, "the way upward and the way downward are one."

Chuang Tze, like the French philosopher Henri Bergson (1859-1942), stressed the value of intuition over reason and taught that duration is the heart of existence. The universe's Dao, or life force, is similar to Bergson's view of the *élan vital*. That force, like the rushing river, struggles with obstructive, static matter. Creation is everywhere and always in motion. Every being and the whole of life is engaged in a process Bergson called "creative evolution."

But motion, according to Chuang Tze, confronts an ultimate–it has a bottom line. Anticipating the Zen Buddhists' position, the Chinese sage wrote:

> *The common and ordinary things serve certain functions and therefore retain the wholeness of nature. From this wholeness one comprehends, and from comprehension one comes near to the Dao. There one stops.*

Thompson, the major and I were ready to stop. For this day, enough was enough. But more was in store for us.

The full moon cast silver bands on the houses and alleys. Shadows were thrown on the shopkeepers as they began securing their windows and doors for the night. We were more than ready to return to our junk, but our host and Wang Shi insisted we take in another experience–the *Fo Miao* (the Buddhist Temple).

On the far side of the hilltop, facing the western arch of the pavilion, we came to the Buddhist monastery. Facing the entrance, looking out at us from the courtyard, we confronted a large, gilded, iridescent figure. The serene one was Amitabha, the Enlightened One, who rules an Eden sought by self-negat-

ing persons of faith and good works. May's full moon bathed the tiered rows of bodhisattvas arrayed on either side. A barefoot priest, garbed in tattered maroon robe lit a red candle. At his side was a novitiate sounding the deeply-grooved fishhead drum. Large bronze tripods held smoking incense sticks. Their little red burning rings glowed in the darkness.

On the ceiling-high panel behind the Buddha, inscriptions of the Four Sacred Truths were emblazoned. The first concerned sorrow: "Birth is sorrow, age is sorrow, death is sorrow, all in the world is sorrow and suffering." The second Noble Truth holds

*Buddhist Sanctuary*

hat all suffering stems from craving the pleasures of life. Third, the end to suffering can come only by ending craving. And, finally, the way to end craving lies in an Eightfold Path whose steps are Right Views, Right Resolve, Right Speech, Right Conduct, Right Livelihood, Right Effort, Right Mindfulness and Right Concentration.

At the entrance of an ante room we heard the monks at prayer inside. "We must go in," urged our host: The way was across the courtyard, past two large prayer wheels lit by oil lamps. The colonnade leading to the inner sanctum was lit by burning wicks set in cups of peanut oil. In dim corridors we moved along walkways of worn stone slabs. Entering the sanctum we became aware that others were present in the blue, incense-filled haze. As eyes became accustomed to the dimness, we could see monks in yellow robes draped with maroon shawls sitting cross-legged on the floor. Heads bowed, they were chanting prayers.

Though they sensed that guests had joined them, the monks did not raise their eyes. They accepted us into their circle. We were motioned to take places on benches beside the worshipers and participate in the worship. We felt emanations, like the red rings on the incense sticks, sending off occasional sparks.

A mysterious power emerged out of the worship. Thoughts settled, fit more into place and came together. The quality of wholeness replaced the discord of the mind. Pieces of ourselves and the day's events were pulled together. The muddy waters of our lives became tranquil and clear, a mirror reflecting the depths and heights of our thoughts.

Celestial-toned cymbals sounded and prayers rose in unison. The assurances articulated were of the power and healing of love. As we allowed ourselves to be drawn into the atmosphere, we appreciated how the aspirations of each votary stirred the energies of the others. In the mounting chorus, individuals' thoughts blended and contributed to the unity of a growing fellowship.

The way inward had opened ways outward. There seemed to be artesian wells of wholeness in this now-luminous sanctum. It was as if inner doors had been opened and we became familiar with many things that had been strange before. The previously distant became near. New levels of knowing appeared as we sat in the sanctum, breathing in the monks' body odors, the rancid smell of burning oil and the heavy clouds of stale incense.

Our host was intrigued with our entranced response, but his attention span was short. He nudged Wang Shi and Wang Shi nudged me. And so we slipped out into the courtyard, bathed in moonglow. I was ready to confess my shortcomings to settled members of the brotherhood and go outside to have my head shaven and anointed with oil.

"We've had too much," the major said, stretching, taking a deep breath and walking away from the temple and the outer pavilion.

On that high knoll our minds had been expanded and our spirits touched.

Our enthusiastic co-traveler Wang Shi had introduced us to the great sage Chuang Tze and our hospitable proprietor had ushered us into the sanctuary of the monks.

No crickets chirped and no dogs howled at the moon. Half-asleep already, we made our way back through the picturesque town. Reaching the mooring cove, we picked our way through the jungle of stakes and other vessels to find our junk and fall exhausted on our sleeping mats over the stern hold hatch.

The major, quickly fast asleep, had been right: we had had too much. The over-full day had been demanding and fearful. Toward the close on the hill, however, the day had become thought-provoking and soul-stirring.

But the tranquility we yearned for in our need for rest seemed denied: We were tied to other junks, three rows out from the bank, and so were shackled to the movements and sounds of the turbulent river. Our *wu ban* pitched and rolled, lunged and jerked with all the others. The great wooden rudder creaked and banged. We jolted our so-very-close neighboring sleepers, and they jolted us. Upstream, the roar of the cataracts thundered. In some vague distant place, periodic drum beats resounded and, close by our boat, a baby wailed. The river splashed over our gunwales, spraying us through the edges of the matting which covered our sleeping stall and dampening our bedrolls. Attacked in body by relentless bed bugs, we were hounded in mind by the images of rocks and whirlpools. In our fitful attempts to sleep, it was easy to slip into the depressed mood Chuang Tze cautioned his readers against: "Finally, worn out and imprisoned, the mind is clogged up like an old drain, and in the failing one shall not see light again."

Instead of slipping off to sleep, it seemed as I peered into a mirror at my image-drenched soul, I saw reflections of my life and of the unseeable. Then, in the manner of half-dreams, the crew–including even the tough *lao ban*–became like the maroon robed faithfuls. I tried to find the aspirations and meditations that carried the loyal monks into their inner world of peace and quiet. I struggled to return to the sanctum's empowering atmosphere. Eventually the semblance of sleep deepened, moving toward the real thing. One after another, fears and certainties, confusions and clarity coalesced, and the daunting day was lost in the night.

# Mi Dan Chasm And Tea With Bandits

*Junks Sail Toward Mi Dan Chasm*

Before daylight, the cook was bustling about in his cramped galley, six feet from our still-weary heads. Behind us, *Lao Ma*, the skipper's wife, shuffled about on the stern deck above her quarters. Midship oarsmen began to stir. At the bow two sweepmen sat up, turned around to see golden dawn-lit peaks to the southeast and stretched.

The crew's ablutions were quick and simple–no teeth brushing, shaving, showers or change of clothes; only a splash of river water and a brisk face rub with a dirty rag.

The crew prepared themselves and the junk for the day's struggles, without the petulance of the previous morning. Later, while they squatted on the deck, downing their bowls of rice gruel, the lead oarsman and lead bowman gave pep talks.

The first officer, like a first violinist readying an orchestra, tuned the junk's instruments–oars, sail, sweeps, bamboo towhawser and iron-tipped poles. He then readied the crew and, stretching out his arms toward the Mi Dan Chasm, said, *"Sheng"*–the *I Ching* hexagram meaning "move upward." He voiced an ancient saying:

> *"Pushing upward with the time in confidence has*
> *Supreme success and brings great good fortune."*

Giving assurance, he continued, "The next stretch of river will be easy going compared with the troubles we had yesterday in the Xintan."

The Mi Dan Chasm's name included the ideograph for "rice" *(mi)*. Differing explanations of its origin were associated with Tang dynasty generals who had stock piled the grain for their troops in the cliffs' caves.

Calm waters and pastoral scenes marked the Mi Dan's entrance. On the south bank was an exquisite glen. Nearby was the historic Pure Jade Cave used centuries ago for storage, but now a tourist attraction with its grotesque stalactites. The tributary streams pouring through the glen were navigated by long, slender boats with high sterns manned by a single rower, reminiscent of Venetian gondolas.

As we moved upstream with sail and oars we found the Mi Dan's unique shorescapes were marred by recent rock and sand avalanches. Peaceful vistas soon gave way to bold, vertical cliffs rising 1,000 feet. Behind them towered serried peaks of higher mountains.

The rock faces were fissured with deep splits. Bisected promontories appeared ready to fall, as some already had, breaking into huge piles of angular boulders, which presented additional obstacles for the goat-footed trackers. Streaks of soft red sandstone in the strata added color and mystery. Always changing, the formations rising from the copper-colored river stirred images of battlements and cathedral spires. Torrents flowing over the lateral clefts made impressive bridal falls. Around the edges we saw cultivated fields, green with spring wheat. Here and there were brown-roofed villages, nestled among blossoming fruit trees.

As in the other chasms, the current ran faster where the channel narrowed. Instead of creating rapids, the fuller water ran quieter. This was hard to believe, considering the prevalence of reefs and jagged rocks we encountered close to shore. The unusual depth of this portion of the river–as much as 400 feet–was the explanation we were given.

The major, our engineer-geologist, told us these cliffs were granite batholith columns–formed by water, ice and earthquakes during the Mesozoic and Jurassic eras, 70 to 250 million years ago. This 400-foot-ditch was but a fraction of the abysmal trenches of the ocean. The Izu Trench in the Pacific Ocean southeast of Japan and the Mariana Trench south of that both run 31,700 feet below the surface–100 times the depth of waters we were plying.

The river's nadir suggested a metaphor to Wang Shi: "Much of life's journey involves negotiating close-to-the-surface troubles–whirlpools, shoals and hidden rocks. The journey is easily impeded by these surface dangers, but an underlying current provides a steadier and more reliable flow. A quality life must be more than merely floating on the surface. Survival on the river is between the quick and the dead. Staying alive amounts to battling surface obstructions, as well as finding life's powerful currents."

"Depth," Thompson started, "refers to qualities and forces underlying the surface events. Your Chinese word *shen* (deep) suggests 'unfathomable' and 'profound.' Significantly, the radical for the ideograph shen is water and water implies a natural force flowing toward the ocean's depth. *Shen yi*, 'profound significance,' is how Chinese describe the 400 feet of water below the surface of the *Mi Dan* Chasm."

"Psychologists use the term 'depth,'" I pointed out, "to describe the unconscious, that part of personality that is the source of habits, motives and thought patterns. These experiences come from underneath the shell of personality. They come from the heart, not face only. This is the realm of psychic drives and goals, and the arena where conflict occurs between them. We get in touch with these deeper characteristics by exploring dreams, fantasies, defenses and slips of the tongue."

"The type of person we become," the major offered, "depends to a great extent on how we acknowledge and harness these deep parts of ourselves. When the conflicting parts of personality are reconciled, the individual moves toward self-fulfillment. Entering these deeper currents of experience brings joys, also risks, similar to those of persons who face and overcome the Long River's hazards."

"When we talk of a person having depth," I suggested, "we mean the individual has qualities beyond the ordinary. Chinese *jun zi*, or complete human being, pictures such a person."

"Those meanings of 'depth' I understand," Wang Shi countered, "but you include religious meanings."

"Religious experiences," Thompson replied, "take people beyond what is normally seen and touched. They reach toward the full human experiences. In the 139th Psalm, for example, 'depth' has to do with the Almighty's inescapableness. The words say, 'If I ascend to Heaven, you are there! If I make my bed in hell, you are there.' The prophet Isaiah (7:11) wrote, 'The signs of God are deep as Hell and high as Heaven.'"

"That verse describes our experience now–under the open heavens and sailing over the gorges' deepest sections," I responded.

"Religious experiences have to do with feelings of being in touch with divine influences, sometimes with sadness and sometimes with exaltation. Strong, steady qualities like *Yi* (righteousness), *reng* (justice), or *shi* and *jen* (truth) are powerful ethical continuums. Paul Tillich, a respected Western philosopher and theologian, for example, says finding 'depth' means experiencing the ground of all being–i.e., God the Creator and Center of life."

Suddenly, caught simultaneously in a surge of faster current and a slackening of our supporting wind, the *wu ban* shuddered. Our attention was shaken from theology back to the realities of journeying on the river.

To make headway, the trackers on board were put to reinforcing our oarsmen. The bowmen worked around rock outcroppings, using their long hooking poles" to grab crevices or steel rings driven into the cliffs. Once they secured the poles, two men pulled on them and walked down the gunwale as far as they could, then disengaged the hook and walked up to the bow to start again. This repeated maneuver of the bowmen tugging hand over hand at their poles to keep us moving upstream had a hypnotic effect on us spectators. The patient bowmen repeated the same motions, again and again, to keep the junk moving against the current. Aft of these pullers, our rowers were straining, with three men on each of the four pairs of oars.

Reassured by our steady progress, we were optimistic as we started making what we thought would be an easy crossing of the outer part of a sheltered cove.

Caught unawares, we hardly noticed a smaller boat that darted around the point. In minutes it was clear it was rushing toward the *wu ban*. The boat was rowed by three pairs of fast-pulling rowers, carrying 15 fierce-looking, armed uffians, who shouted at us to head for the shore.

As the skipper steered the junk toward the glen, we saw on the beach an nsavory band of 50 to 60 gesticulating, gun-wielding characters. The skipper vas both seething and unnerved, and his wife cursed Heaven and everyone lse. The cook chattered nervously, the first officer was apprehensive, and Vang Shi mumbled, "Looks like trouble."

Rumblings from the crew increased. The initial phrases they used–*fei ren* bad men) and *jiao fei* (members of a secret sect)–were not alarming. But as hey rowed, their nervousness increased and they talked about *jien fei* (villain- us rebels). The closer we got to the motley gang ashore, the more the crew's nxiety escalated. Now the phrases they mouthed became ominous. They went rom describing them as *du fei* (local bandits) to *bang biao fei*, or (the worst of rigands, ones who carry away captives for ransom).

Warnings of bandits given by our Yichang hosts flashed through our houghts. My own memories were triggered. As a boy, I had heard stories, fre- uently from the servants, of the atrocities committed by the dreaded *du fei*, andit predators. There was the kidnaping of two missionary women, with a loody finger of one of them enclosed with the ransom note. On a lighter ote, a Westerner in the interior had suffered the indignity of having his pants tolen so that he had to make the trek home in the buff.

Several days ago, Thompson had talked off-handedly about how social nrest and abject poverty provide the conditions in which banditry grows. The najor and I asked about the seriousness of banditry in these upriver areas. Thompson's explanations helped minimize the threat by contending that ban- itry had its roots in poverty, injustice and the nature of isolated pockets of the isgruntled underemployed, and discharged soldiers of defeated warlords. Hordes of soldiers roamed the country, with fickle allegiance to the govern- nent, or greedy warlords, or local bandit chiefs or no one. They were undisci- lined and frequently merciless, following the ancient custom of looting and iving off the spoils of their misdeeds. Any act of resistance brought retaliation vhich, in turn, forced the peasants into the mountains, where the transforma- ion from citizen to bandit came easily.

But what we now faced was fast becoming more serious. The major, alert o use of arms, saw sharpshooters aiming at us and covering the flanks of the and. Thompson, usually calm, became nervous. With his fears building, he nade off-the-cuff, irrelevant comments, such as barking at the cook to heat up ome tea.

Within earshot of the men on the beach, the skipper gave loud shouts ffirming our having no contraband, no possessions of any worth. Standing to is full height, the first officer gave a strong back-up call, "We have only ordi- ary foreigners on their way to Wanxian. They have no rank and no wealth. We are only a cargo *wu ban*, a houseboat, so our cargo is limited to our supplies.'

Even before we touched shore, two pairs of the ruffians waded out and clambered aboard. A fierce-looking adjutant and other armed men followed when we beached. While his men searched the junk from bow to stern, the adjutant was taken aback when he found that Thompson and I spoke Chinese. For a moment he moderated his initial demands. He let it be known that the leader of the band was directing the operation from the farmhouse on a nearby knoll but was on his way to the *wu ban*.

The first officer spoke for our skipper and the adjutant for his chief. Demands for valuables and hard cash were repeated. "Worthless" paper money was unacceptable.

Our first officer remained cool and courteous. He took the initiative to ask the adjutant to allow the skipper and us passengers to go ashore to meet his impressive leader. We were prepared to pay deference to the intimidating giant of a man who approached. Firmly, but with tact, the *tai gong* assured the adjutant that we would cooperate as much as possible. The adjutant stepped up his show of hardness as he saw his superior and body guards approaching.

"Surely," the first officer said, seizing the moment to state our case, "ours is a humble voyage and we would like to be on our way with the westerly wind that's blowing. We simply ask that you let us get along toward Zi Gui, which we are trying to reach before dark." The skipper smiled pleadingly and we passengers did likewise.

Thompson, acquainted with the roving bands of this region, attempted a ploy: "Are you associated with the Song band (a Robin Hood-like group reputed to rob the rich to feed the poor)?" From the way the leader exploded and shook his saber in our faces, it was evident this was the wrong question. "Never! Heavens would have to fall before we'd associate with the Song. We're the Bai group, infinitely superior," he shouted.

"Our foreign friend, Mr. Tan (for Thompson), meant no harm, sir," the first officer said. "And, *gan ni di mian zi* (considering your superiority, or importance of your face), you will excuse him. Since he works in a county on the other side of the river, he is not well informed about the groups in your area south of the river. He is a special teacher of teachers and is known for his many good works and helps to children."

Thompson and I quickly apologized and began to admire his collection of firearms and his men's fascination with foreigners talking their tongue. Picking up on the chief's hypersensitivity regarding his band's identity, I took an alternate tack, suggesting his group must be of a special kind, a *hui fei*, or "a special secret organization"–a designation less pejorative than either *du fei*, the garden-variety brigand, or the feared *bang biao fei*, who bind up, take away and hold for ransom.

Trying to find some way to give them the respect they obviously considered their due, I spoke of the ancient Chinese tradition of banditry, embodied in the classic novel *The Water Margin*. In a fantastic mountain lair called Liang Shan Po, the outlaw heroes established a "liberated" zone, a renegades, republic. In this twilight world of magic and genius, good deeds were done along with suitable knavery. Stories of these noble thieves and rebels were known to everyone in China through the constant retelling and local dramatizations.

"One of your old proverbs," I ventured, remembering one a Chinese instructor had taught in language school, "wisely says, *Gao shan qi shan, gao sui qi xui.*" (If a person lives in the mountains, he must get his living there; if near the water, from the ocean or river. In short, a person must depend on his environment for his livelihood.)

This double entendre struck Chief Bai's fancy. He was a mountain man, and he was entitled to earn his living from the mountains. We were, in a sense, ocean and river people, entitled to protection and a livelihood from the river. The proverb had other subtle, humorous innuendoes, which tickled him, but most important it enabled both him and the skipper to save face.

Thompson, remembering the tea he had asked the cook to ready, invited the chief and his adjutant to go aboard the *wu ban* for a round of drinks. The lead bodyguard nodded, assuring security if his chief accepted the invitation. With great pomp he paraded aboard, more out of curiosity than reassured there would be no trickery.

Seated around the coil of bamboo cable, topped with a board to serve as a makeshift table, our exchanges became less tense. In addition to the tea, the enterprising cook added all the deserts and peanuts he could assemble. The major offered the chief two silver-plated Air Force medallions to adorn his blue jacket, and a handful of ballpoint pens and color postcards. The only valuables I could locate were Chinese-language pocket New Testaments–perhaps not the most appropriate gifts for unlettered recipients, but they were accepted.

I told the Bai chief the apocryphal story of the Fujian province mountain man (actually a notorious bandit chief) whose life was saved by a missionary surgeon. The Fujian outlaw had been severely wounded in a shootout with government gendarmes and was brought to a mission hospital for treatment. Following his recovery, the mountain man returned to ask the surgeon if some recompense could be made. The missionary asked but one favor–that the outlaw not attack and rob Christians. The Fujian leader agreed, but asked how he could distinguish Christians from non-Christians and was told that, since Christians knew the Lord's Prayer, he could ask them to recite that petition (*Women zai tian shang di fu. . .*) before deciding whether to take their money. A problem arose when the populace spread the word that claiming to be Christian might grant them immunity from bandit assaults. From then on, wealthy merchants about to be relieved of their wealth were asked not only if they were Christians, but were told that, if they could not recite the Lord's Prayer, they would be dispatched to the land of their ancestors.

The adjutant appreciated the story, whereas Chief Bai was not so enthusiastic. He nevertheless demanded that we recite the Lord's Prayer!

Cautiously, I asked whether, as a resident of Nanjing, it would help if I were to explore avenues in the capital to plead for improvement in services for the people of the chief's county. This prompted two of the bodyguards to speak up and initiate more amiable negotiations.

"I'll settle with you if you'll take four bundles to a man in Wanxian," their leader offered. "Ask no questions and get them there in three days."

Our skipper agreed and had two oarsmen transfer the sacks to the luggage hold. We speculated on what the sacks might contain: too large to be opium or precious stones, too tidy to be dried fruit or some other specialty of the area, so we concluded that they probably contained salt surrounding some hidden contraband.

In the ritual of leave-taking we offered words of gratitude for the Bai band's consideration in allowing our modest voyage to continue with minimal delay.

"You foreigners are fortunate," exclaimed the skipper as the band took to the shore and we poled out of the cove. "It's very unusual that these desperadoes didn't grab your wrist watches, gold rings and all your cash. Such loss is the minimum passengers usually suffer." The oarsmen remained pale and silent, thinking of the fates that could have befallen them. Lao Liu, the tough lead oarsman, halted his stroking long enough to tell us, "Lucky we had you foreigners. The Bai gang is *hen li hai* (very dangerous). They draw blood for pittances."

Reaching deeper waters and out from the lee of the chasm's rock wall, we were struck with a strong gust of counter winds which necessitated Lao Liu and helpers to trim our giant patched sail. Having to concentrate on pulling harder against stronger wind and current helped the crew calm their frayed nerves.

The calming effect, however, was short-lived. From upstream came a frantic uproar of shouts and drumming that became more strident by the second. Another large out-of-control cargo junk was bearing down toward us. Caught in the swift current and stiff wind it was rushing straight at us. In a split second it broadsided our bow, swung around, snapping in two one of our 30-foot *yulows*, smashing two oars, locked on our fenders and started dragging us downstream. Both crews seized iron-spiked bamboo poles and, with withering vituperations, began a free-for-all that threatened bloodshed.

Surprising all, with booming voices and frightening grimaces, Thompson and I boldly entered the fracas. Maximizing the available cramped space, I executed several maneuvers caricaturing the classical Chinese sword dance, punctuated with fierce grimaces and the most blood-curdling yells I could muster. Fending off the blows as best we could, we shouted out the proposal to negotiate.

Captivated by our pluck and posturing, both crews broke out in boisterous laughter and accepted our suggestion. We urged laying down the spiked poles and proposed untangling the snarled lines and crossed oars. Our boatmen muttered their dissatisfaction and urged the skipper to "go to the law" over the accident. The skipper's wife demanded we follow the offending junk so that we could be recompensed and avenged at the Zi Gui mooring.

We negotiators interceded and persuaded the other skipper to provide us with one of its giant sweeps and two oars. With faces of all saved, both crews set to work untangling ropes, oars, bumpers and tempers. The junks were separated. As we drew away, our men vented their residual spleen by pulling harder on oars and sweeps.

The first officer sounded the challenge to make ZiGui by nightfall, saying, "*Shen!*" (Make progress upward!)

Just before dark, on the north bank, we sighted billows of smoke from Zi Gui's lime-processing plants. Within half an hour, as the sun was setting, we moored at the river's edge below the city.

After having seen a series of small towns, we were impressed to find such a sizable city, but surprised at its small wharf. Lumber yards, junk-building sheds and warehouses crowded the lower part of the river bank. Along the slopes, on wellpaved streets parallel to the river, we saw rows of modern four- and six-storied buildings. These shut from view the city's older alley-ways of the era of Liu Bai, who had built a stone city in the Three Kingdom period.

The town appeared reasonably wealthy. Its several markets were large. We walked by peddlers hawking all sorts of wares. At their request we took photos of a pots-and-pans entrepreneur and a chestnuts cooker. A group of seniors playing Chinese checkers insisted we join their game. We started to put money in a blind man's begging basket, but hesitated when we found he was surrounded by paying customers waiting to have him tell their fortunes.

Zi Gui is renowned as the hometown of the poet and statesman Qu Yuan, in whose memory colorful dragon boats are raced once a year. He lived during the fratricidal 'Warring States' period (c. 5th to 3rd century B.C.). Rising to power during the fourth century B.C. The state of Chu was prosperous and the envy of its rapacious neighbors, known for developing the technology for making bronze ceremonial vessels and especially the two-tone ritual bells that had a quality found nowhere else in the world at that time. Corruption and intrigue spread and the peasants were burdened by heavier taxes and conscripted into warlords' armies. Social disorders and disintegration escalated. Many were the wars and the exploits of these troubled years. Many a story has been handed down of loyalty and prowess, of trickery and intrigue, and of generals and statesmen successful today and disgraced and banished or executed tomorrow

Qu Yuan, a renaissance man, while vice-premier of the Kingdom of Chu helped his monarch combine the northern culture of the Yellow River with the expanding newer Yangtze Valley culture. His vision at the court was critical marking a turning point in the amalgamation of Chinese culture. Deeply concerned for the common people, he advocated drastic reforms to make his state prosperous, strong and just, as well as a diplomatic alliance with the state of Q against the ambitious state of Qin.

Pro-Qin officials in Chu, bribed by an emissary (Zhang Yi) from Qin framed Qu Yuan and induced the Chu ruler to go to Qin, where he was betrayed and held prisoner until he died. The prince who succeeded the throne was more muddle-headed than his father and banished the much-loved Qu Yuan to a remote area south of the Long River. In his banishment the statesman-poet poured his bitterness and depression into powerful poetry. A line in QuYuan's autobiographical Li Sao (Encountering Sorrow) expressed his sadness

> *But the Fragrant One (King Chu) would not look into my heart;*
> *Instead, heeding slander, he turned on me in rage. . . .*

In 273 B.C. Qin captured the capital of Chu. Qu Yuan, who had been in exile for 20 years, was then 62 years old. He was overcome with sorrow at the defeat of his country and the suffering of his countrymen. In despair, he threw himself into the Mi Luo River and drowned. The tragedy took place on the fifth day of the fifth month, according to the Chinese lunar calendar. For more than 2,000 years, people have cherished the memory of Qu Yuan and woven moving tales about him.

One story recorded in an ancient text has to do with the naming of the city It recounts that on hearing that Qu Yuan had been dismissed from his post and had returned to his hometown, his kind and virtuous sister went to console her brother. She pleaded with him to keep up his spirits. The village folk hoped that Qu Yuan would heed his sister's advice. They gave the place the name Z Gui, which means "Sister Returning Home." When Qu Yuan died, the story goes, his body was swallowed by a large fish which brought it back home and threw it upon the bank at Zi-Gui. The villagers buried him, began to idolize him and built a temple in his memory. The style and themes of his verse influenced poets for generations.

On the anniversary of Qu Yuan's death, people go out on the river in dragon boats, a custom symbolizing their desire to rescue him. Families make *zong zi*, a dumpling of glutinous rice wrapped in broad bamboo leaves. These are for the river dragon to eat, so that he will not harm Qu Yuan.

A group of eager high school students surrounded us to practice their English. Surprised that we had not yet visited the Qu Yuan Temple, they insisted on escorting us up the hill overlooking the Long River's bend where the large fish is said to have deposited Qu Yuan.

Near the temple, at a tea house, pungent with the aroma of jasmine and orange blossoms from the bushes close by, we were treated to another distinctive evening. Sitting in the moonlight, we were served locally grown tea and fresh *zong zi*, (sweet dumplings) in this historic place.

The five students who had escorted us to the spot were intrigued when we told of some of our experiences in the Xiling. Curious about us, they all seemed to pose their questions at once: What brings you to this place so far away from Nanjing and your native country? What did we think of China? And the gorges? We fought a losing battle trying to get them to tell us about their families, their friends, their school.

Our telling the new friends about the day's adventures in the *Xintan* and the *Midan* didn't surprise them in the least. The events were not unlike happenings in the great myths, legends and art forms observable in ancient Chinese drama and verse. Somehow the happenings seemed rooted in prehistory beyond our separate individuals. Considering how we had navigated between some of the gorges' highest limestone walls and also over one of its deepest sections, the major noted: "Our day has been a 'high' and 'deep' one!"

"That image of the major catches me," Wang Shi broke in. "It calls to mind what you were talking about–the idea in Western psychology of archetypes. You said they are images shared by all people. I can imagine the poet Tu Fu, 1,300 years ago, sitting here drinking tea and sorting out the events at the end of one of his days saying: 'This has been a high and deep day.'"

Thompson replied, "Archetypes are the systematic arrangements of a person's thoughts, feelings and patterns of behavior. The *I Ching* and other Chinese classics provide archetypes. They offer prototypes for acceptable thoughts, feelings and patterns of behavior. These condition the individual's ways of perceiving the world. Archetypes are the nucleus of our being human. Accepted and wisely used, they release creativity and give our lives the quality of depth. Great art draws upon these images, as does psychosis. They can be beautiful, and they can also be hideous."

"Archetypes are often personified," I explained, "as in figures of the compassionate mother or the evil witch (like the skipper's wife), the good guys (like the first officer) and the bad guys (like the Bai bandit chief). They serve as patterns of looking at and coping with life's changes."

"That goes along with another angle you described last night," Wang Shi added. "If I heard you correctly, you were saying that the archtypes, represent the wisdom of the ages and point toward superior tendencies for individual.

Self-development consists in bringing persons into contact with their 'collective unconscious' where these archetypes are stored. This means that when
you're trying to become aware of archetypes, you're striving for a new center
and balance in life."

"Very good! You've got it!" I exclaimed. "If, for example, in dreams you
push associations beyond the immediate life of a person, you reach a deeper
level of experience. Thus a dream about father would finally come to a conception of all fatherhood, the father archetype. This awareness gives the person
energy not directly experienced in other ways."

Pausing to let these comments settle and Wang Shi to translate the gist to
the students, Thompson continued, "Yes, in light of this day's happenings we
can draw a parallel between nature's deeper currents and the person's collective unconscious. A person's freedom of choice, for example, needs to be
brought into line with the promptings of life's deeper currents. We chose to
make this journey to Wanxian knowing it would involve hardships and a strug
gle against the river.

"The river's current," Thompson continued, like the sweep of destiny
"flows with a strong directional force. After making such a choice, you must
exercise your freedom to triumph over the Long River. The potentials of peo
ple's finite freedom are limited by destiny. These boatmen, for days, have
applied their power, skill and perseverance to keep us moving toward Wanxian
Reaching that destination, accomplishing our goal, we will win a new degree
of freedom."

"Another example is found in individuals who decide not to rise above their
role as trackers, and to work to become bowmen and skippers. People are free
to triumph over the Great River when they understand and harness the deep
er levels of their circumstances."

"Individuals grow in freedom," the major observed, "when they venture
beyond the ordinary and create new worlds for themselves. The new worlds
may be technical, having to do with tools and products, or artistic expressions
in poetry or drama. And, paradoxically, people grow in freedom as they exercise the power of turning themselves around to discover and develop theirs and
others' essential or archetypal nature. They have used their freedom to search
for depth in their lives."

We had emptied five or six teapots and four plates of sweet dumplings. The
proprietor was closing shop and we had transformed from mellow to wearied

As we picked our moonlit way down the great stone steps, an appreciation
for having four such diverse personalities on a journey through the Long
River's gorges struck me. The opportunity to experience together the day's
astounding events is more than simple chance. The Great River's urgent neces
sities were the stuff of destiny. And perhaps the essence of God's limitless free

dom was translated into our arduous and amazing day.

As we made our way down toward the junk, Thompson concluded, "Depth understanding comes with recognizing that our freedom works within the frame of a universal destiny. In the cosmos, God, 'the ground of all being,' is His own destiny."

In minutes the four of us were stretched out in our bedrolls on the hard boards of our cramped space. The roar of waters pounding jagged rocks, the cracker's cries reverberating within chasms and all the other tumultuous sights and sounds which had bombarded us all day faded away into the night.

CHAPTER EIGHT

# Unsung Commoner Heros And Lessons Offered

*Trackers Bend Double Strain Hauling Junk*  *Courtesy Lyman Van Slyke*

At all times the Long River surrounded us, but it was the *wu ban's* crew that enveloped us. Elbow-to-elbow and shoulder-to-shoulder they circled us with their physical closeness and their inexhaustible curiosity over our strangeness. Each of them fulfilled his part in ensuring our survival with their dutifulness. We knew they were never to be taken for granted. Day by day our respect for their patience and skill grew. Uneducated and superstitious, raw and often explosive, we found them neither villains nor saints, but diamonds-in-the-rough. Always ready to share their humanness, they were loaded with surprises. Their lives of hard labor, unending struggle and hand-to-mouth existence stirred our deepest concern.

Though lackadaisical off duty, at their posts these crewmen stuck by their menial and backbreaking tasks. They knew their tasks and fulfilled them well. In emergencies, facing danger, they responded with split-second skill. Ordinary and lackluster in simple matters and by no means parlor dandies, their skillful handling of navigation crises and team work were amazing. Their meager fare and pay hardly rewarded their great exertions. They asked for no plaudits, but they well deserved special mention.

These boatmen also won our respect for their ancestry. They were the distant offspring of the heroes and villains of the romanticized Warring States period in the fifth to the third century B.C. We imagined our crewmen as descendants of benevolent rulers, wise ministers, daring generals and self-sacrificing commoners canonized for their courage and loyalty in classic lyrics and dramas associated with the gorges. Other ancestors may have been rapacious overlords, vile traitors and sadistic torturers who jabbed scissors in people's eyes and chopped off heads at will. National symbols, such as the warriors and villains of Chinese fables, stand for positive and negative cultural values. These evidences also served to exemplify universal myths about the perennial conflict between good and evil. Each of these rough boatmen demonstrated how a culture can reach all its members. Each of these rough boatmen seemed to possess a portion of China's uniqueness. Their Chineseness gave them an innate sensitivity which linked them to one another and made for easy sharing. Sharing with the crew's characters, some admirable and others dubious, helped us appreciate these commoners as unsung heroes.

Crew members were of the *lao bai xing*, "the people of the old one hundred names," the hoi poloi, "the run-of-the-mill" among the populace. Having very little close contact with foreigners, these rivermen reacted to us with both hesitancy and curiosity.

We in turn, found them intriguing and puzzling. Often their humor seemed obtuse and even derisive. Unfamiliar with their idioms and slurred dialects, we foreigners connected only fractionally in our communicating. Often their expressions that seemed illogical to us, were all together consistent for them. Their easy-going ways were

© Helen Howser

frustrating, particularly when it gave them a disregard for punctuality. Toward one another, they were alternately cooperative and companionable, then abusive and abrasive. Unbathed, garlic-breathed, bodies often lice-ridden and with infectious sores, they presented harsh contrasts of Westerners accustomed to white bathtubs, flush toilets and soap-scrubbed skin.

So paradoxical! They both loved and feared life. Some were wrinkled and gnarled, others young, supple–mere youths. Not a few were refugees, drifters and homeless. In performing assigned tasks, routine or tedious, they were reliable boatmen. Many were like the nephew of oarsman Lao Liu, whom the uncle described as "Having tough hands but a tender heart."

Though brutalized by their toil, a touch of joie de vivre broke through at unexpected times. Scratch the surface of their seeming stoicism, and they were good-natured, delighting in a joke, welcoming the chance to let go and forget their subsistence existence. Their faces easily broke open with ready smiles. Instead of anxious, knitted brows, they showed crows'-feet wrinkles from eyes to ears, formed from years of smiling and joking. At night, in their mat-shed hovel camps ashore, or in their cramped quarters in the wu ban's hold, they were often boisterous. Neither rascals nor paragons, they rose to heights of exertion when necessary. Un-tutored, yet one often would come up with some so yu (proverb, or saying), that triggered an immediate recognition from others.

Oarsmen, bowmen, trackers, pilots, skipper, cook and lifeboat sailors–all were regulated by their defined functions. Each had a part in helping the wu ban's passage. Each had his own station, his task to accomplish and his relationship with the others on which his own life depended. Though classified by their functions, they were known essentially for the way they talked, ate, snored, groaned, sang, dreamed, argued and propitiated the river gods. With all their anomalies, nevertheless, we came to appreciate these rough hewn boatmen as unsung heroes.

The lao ban, skipper, was the undisputed crew chief–the kingpin. The "lao" means "aged," also "experienced" and "honored." Though neither aged nor honored, our skipper was experienced–and that was what counted on this journey. Whether or not his hand was on the tiller, the wu ban's safety and course were his business. In dangerous places, like an experienced and vigilant coxswain, he threatened the crew with yells and gesticulations. Whether seeking greater exertion by the trackers, oarsmen or sweepsmen, or exhorting the cook to have the rice and vegetables ready, the captain's job was coordination, communication and motivation.

The lao ban's appearance was not commanding. A small, lean man with drawn features, he appeared old beyond his years. His yellow skin was like mildewed parchment stretched over his bones. His hawk-like face with sunken eyes and several missing teeth suggested craftiness and avarice. His was no sartorial splendor. He wore loose-fitting, blue cotton trousers and an oversized, attered, blue jacket that was forever blowing open, exposing his stooped shoulders and emaciated chest. This was his attire even in the chilliest weather.

His command manners were a mix of Capt. Bligh and Capt. Queg. At the start of the rapids, he dickered with trackers and their foremen to save the equivalent of a few pennies, though, on account of the delay, he had lost more than he'd saved. The skipper was not above grinding the boatmen down and feeding them inferior rice. He would not spend a few yuan on patching his ragged sail. His unexplained tardiness, like that at Yichang, irritated us Westerners who wanted to make efficient use of each minute. It seemed insane that an entrepreneur, setting out on a 200-mile voyage with what, for him, must have been a heavy investment and with responsibility for cargo and passengers, would not respond to the fact that upstream speed meant downriver profit.

The skipper's taller and more vociferous wife supplemented his force. Called *Lao Ma*, or Elderly Mother, she was a domineering wife, mother and grandmother. An overbearing nag and virago, her sharp tongue was rarely still. She coerced her husband into pecuniary and shifty ways. She was given to paroxysms of rage and was embarrassingly harsh with her offspring. Reputedly, she had beaten her eldest grandson to death a few months before. The remaining nine year-old boy lived in terror, lest he should share the same fate.

Lao Ma, the pregnant older daughter and *Xiao mei mei* (Little Sister, granddaughter) were the only females aboard. Consistently caustic, *Lao Ma* permitted the woman-starved crew no sexual innuendoes or advancements. The Chinese women portrayed by the great painters Ku Kai Chi and Ch'iu Chou suggest willows bending under a powerful wind (masculine) or beauteous gossamer clouds being chased across the sky (feminine). But these descriptions hardly applied to this female. Daily she dressed in the same loose-fitting, unprovocative men's clothing–a simple pair of trousers and a coat-shirt. The fluid blue fabric enveloped her movements. Only in the most hard-pressed fantasy could anyone describe her as feminine. Long ago, her womanliness had been abandoned, and along with it, any cooperativeness she might once have possessed. Whatever erotic dimensions may have been dormant in her, they now had been transformed into an unrelenting androgyny.

*Lao Ma's* magisterial manner commanded acquiescence; always she needed to be reckoned with. Her nettlesome determination for action made her impatient with sitting still, listening to others or rocking the cradle. Her rage erupted when things didn't turn out as she had planned. She showed little comprehension of the spiritual hell in which she trapped herself. There appeared to be no internal struggle waging within her soul. The inevitable result of this spiritual void, this tragic lack of introspection, was heavy-duty anger. There was no incoherence or ambiguity about her: she was what she was, period.

The second in command, the *tai gong*, was an A-1 first officer and a winsome person. He tripled as chief officer, as pilot and chief bowman. Tall, handsome and athletic, his demeanor was as open and direct as the *lao ban*'s were devious.On duty he was intense and untiring. He spent hours at the bow a look-out. His orders were clear and confident. His presence was masterful.

Off-duty, the *tai gong* was cheerful and engaging. Though a no-nonsens officer, as a person, he had a good sense of humor and sensitivity. His poise had not come from education, of which he had very little. His likeable qualitie seemed innate. People liked to have him around. A quick and accurate "people-reader," he was a born reconciler.

Toward us foreigners, he showed neither deference nor condescension. To him, we Westerners were more than *yang gui zi,* "barbarian devils," the lin gering nineteenth-century stereotypes applied to outsiders. We were represen tatives of a country where new things were happening and helpful machine were being made. At moorings, after our common meals or around the evening riverside campfires, he was full of questions about American rivers, ships, car goes, regulations and business ventures.

The cook well deserved his designation as second officer. A short, wiry man he was neither as gaunt as the skipper nor as well-built as the *tai gong.* Hi close-cropped hair set off his round face and square jaws. He possessed a blu cotton coat, like the skipper's, but he rarely wore it, preferring to work in hi sleeveless undershirt. From a *xian* (county) in Hubei province, he had worke with his father as a tenant farmer until eight years ago. Flood and famine struc the area and claimed the life of his parents and two brothers. Resorting to boat ing, he served three years as an oarsman. When the cook on another uprive voyage was killed in a fight, Lao Gou, or Old Dog, as he was called, volun teered to prepare the meals. For the last two years, he had served as cook o runs between Yichang and Wanxian.

Though a crucial crew member, he was the one most taken for granted. He was distinguished by his matter-of-fact and accommodating ways. In his cook ing he aimed to satisfy, but not necessarily to please. When squatting and chop ping vegetables, readying rice, fanning burners or stirring the woks, he was no to be interrupted. If anyone had the temerity to bother him at these crucia moments, he waved his cleaver and banged it against the supports of the hol where he was working. His menu lacked variety, but meals were served on tim and always maximized the limited supplies he had available. In a kitchen scarce ly 8' x 8', he was a genius at preparing meals for hungry people. Whether fo ten or 100 mouths, he made sure each dish was hot and ample. He accom plished these feats on two earthen charcoal burners.

The lead oarsman, Lao Liu, was stationed on the other side of the galle from the passenger hatch. Deeply wrinkled, bull-necked and sinewy, he was veritable rowing machine. With his left hand on the oar handle and his righ pushing on the shaft, every stroke he took bulged out his veins and muscles

When we passengers were in our section, he often talked to us in bursts through each rhythmic stroke. When Lao Liu was giving calls to the rowers, the cook would fill in bits of information about the man's hard life. We gauged him to be in his late fifties, but the cook assured us he was only 35, a fact Lao Liu confirmed.

The fifth son of a poor, indentured farmer, Lao Liu's choices of work when he reached age 13 were few. A typhus epidemic took the life of his father and three siblings, and Lao Liu's village offered him only seasonal work in the fields. He fell in with a band of rowers after a friend from his village told him about his trip through the gorges. Lao Liu considered himself lucky to have teamed up with an older brother to find work on the river.

For almost 20 years, he had served as bowman, sweepman, oarsman and tracker. His older brother had two sons who were also river boatmen. The youngest son was aboard our *wu ban* as one of the bowmen. Regarding our skipper, Lao Liu astutely observed, "The *Lao ban's* thoughts sometimes seem far away. The man has much on his mind." With no complaints, Liu said, nevertheless, he had found the man to be easily flustered and sometimes distracted in moments of crisis.

"This back-breaking work," leadman Liu said, "wears you out, gives pain and no future. Month by month your strength becomes less and less. The risk of injury and death goes up every month. . .My wife in Wanxian wants me to find other work and promises to coax my nephews away from becoming boatmen on the Long River."

Lao Liu voiced the same jaundiced views about the toil and travails of river life as his fellows. Their life stories, too, were just as fraught with back-breaking work. Like the majority of the others who were originally from the country, his expectations of finding less menial work had not been realized. Like the rest, Lao Liu still hoped to find less taxing work. In the mean time, like the others, he viewed boating as "temporary work" that he'd hang onto it until either their backs or their hearts or both broke.

Essential for the safety of the *wu ban*, but not a part of its immediate personnel, strong swimmers worked with red-and-white sailed "rescue boats." These men were powerful of body and indomitable in fortitude. They did what preventative work they could, alerting crews to changes in the channel and of special dangers. We were told they usually had experience as crew members on large upriver junks. Many had been shipwrecked and rescued by lifesavers themselves.

Rescue boats maneuvered on the turbulent waters above and below each of the worst rapids. Four to six strong oarsmen operated them, as they knew every rock and eddy in the most dreaded parts of the river. Buoyant as corks, they darted into the turmoil of scud and foam where confusion was at its worst, saving as many bodies from the raging waters as possible.

The trackers made up another group of boat people. The migrant workers of the gorges, they were considered the lowliest of the crew. Their function was simply to lend their energy and power to the massive bamboo tow lines which ran hundreds of feet from the wu ban's mid-mast to the shore.

During the navigation season, coolies migrated to the river, gathering in spots along the gorges where upstream junks were in the greatest need of pullers to supplement the few on board. Along the shore they lived in hovels–mats stretched over bamboo hoops. These settlements of itinerant trackers were both over-crowded and pathetic. Hucksters moved in and out of these refugee-like villages, peddling food, tobacco, samshu, opium, rice wine, matted sandals, shoulder harnesses and bandoliers.

Rough, dirty and noisy, the trackers were lean-jawed, odorous and explosive bunch. Invariably they were undernourished. As a group, they were short and wizened, yet wiry and muscular. They were scanty clothed in ill-fitting, heavily patched cotton pants. With wild, swinging fists and foul invectives, they fought with their foremen for the few coppers they received for their arduous day-long labor.

The tedium of the trackers' grinding work diminished their humanity. They seemed reduced to faithful cylinders in a diesel motor, up-down, up-down, up-down, providing the power necessary to haul us a little farther up the river. Some broke bones and were left in their tracks, without splints or treatment, to survive if they could. Severe strains and hernias were commonplace. Frequently, the thin, naked body of a fallen tracker was dragged, bumping over rocks, until he managed to extricate himself. Few men were free of cuts, bruises and sores. All suffered malnutrition. Those who fell over cliffs and drowned could cynically be said to have saved themselves from more years of hell.

The trackers' work was hard labor. Sometimes they pulled close to the water, edging over boulders with hardly a foothold for goats. At other times, they struggled along precipices on narrow tracks cut in the rock 200 feet above the river or on broken ledges where even a man free of any load would have trouble keeping his balance. Choosing their steps across angular spurs and scrambling along tow paths carved out of cliffs, they slid on their backs when rocks were smooth, barely holding on with their fingers and toes. Sometimes only their grass sandals saved them from slipping into the foaming race below.

Watching a column of trackers on a towline presented a disturbing and a hypnotic experience. Disturbing because, like observing a chain-gang at work, it stirred guilt-feelings. Hypnotic because the sight stirred amazement at this millennia-old application of man-power. Human teamwork was overcoming the river's drag. Here accommodation of physical and emotional human resources was being effectively applied. Wills were becoming involved with things they had not been concerned with since they were born. Yet tugging, leaning, plodding one-effortful-step-after-another, this pulling was a kind of anesthetic off duty, instead of bovine hauling bodies these men were much like school children at recess.

Behind the trackers came men whose duty it was to see that the tow line didn't get caught on the rocks or tangled with the cables of other junks. Should a line become fouled on an obstruction, swimmers were on hand to plunge into the racing waters to free it. These rear-guard boatmen also helped to fend off foolhardy crews of junks with lighter loads who tried to pass at inopportune times.

The astonishing trackers were engaging to watch. Agile, they scrambled from rock to rock on the river shore. Answering a demand beyond duty or promise of gain, they strained and persisted at their halters. With an unspoken loyalty to their fellows, they equitably shared their toil. Along level ground, they moved deliberately, step by chanted step. Along a ledge on the chasm's wall, they crept, leopard-footed, hauling the clumsy *wu bans* against the current. Large rollers of wood had been wedged into the rock so the cables could slide on them rather than be frayed through the toothed rock edges. Even then there were places where the rock was worn down in grooves several inches deep by centuries of abrasive, braided bamboo tow ropes.

Doing the work of draft animals, they were sustained by the ancient melodies which the lead tracker sang as he tugged at the head of the 1,000-foot towline. The cadence of his songs paced their labored steps, and their *"a yah, a yah"* served as a chorus. The head tracker's thread of mellow music was intended to suppress the groans or cries that accompanied each painful step, so that his crew gave him the title of *yin zhen di* (Noise Suppressor). River hymns of palaces, flights and beautiful maidens were given an *"a yah, a yah."*

Echoing from chasm walls, the rhythmic work cries were indescribably poignant. The chorus was of nature's harsh demands amidst beauty and grandeur. Melancholic, gutsy, joyous, tragic, exuberant, but always a united voice, it was a marvelous symphony of man's triumph over the river.

In the face of frequent demands for great physical exertion, these boatmen insisted on the need to take breaks. They called these pauses times for *xiu xi*. It was a simple method by which oarsmen, bowmen and trackers alike balanced work with repose. They seized chances to *xiu xi*, neither out of indolence nor indifference. A Chinese proverb counsels, "By breaking the fetters which fasten people to misery and the hum-drum, they achieve compassion."

Unexpected delays and slack times offered welcome bonus *xiu xi* time for sitting on the gunwales after meals or waiting without anxiety when the skipper was delayed.

This inclination to take breaks is derived from several characteristics of Chinese life. One contributing element is rooted in the fact that, from antiquity, China has continued as essentially a rural nation. Once agrarian boatmen brought with them to the river the custom of taking a rest at noon to escape the midday sun. We passengers welcomed the crew's *xiu xi* breaks that gave us the chance to talk with this or that tracker or oarsman. At first inspection, they had appeared untamed, animal-like, for enduring punishing drudgery, hour after hour and season after long, weary season. As we spoke and joked with them, we treasured their humanity.

Another factor is found in their eating habits. Chinese breakfasts are light, so people are ravenous at lunch and often devour large quantities of noodles and steamed bread, washed down with tea. Such a meal needs to be followed by *xiu xi*. Still another influence arises from the age-old teachings of moderation and patience. Chinese wonder at Westerners who drive themselves nonstop at the expense of their mental and physical health. Many generations of Chinese have found that regular times of rest are essential to a well-balanced life. Modern medicine and science have begun to give Westerners the same message.

"I'm sympathetic with rest breaks and the compassion it may achieve," the major put in, "but I worry about any system that wastes time. Time is one of life's great resources and must be conserved and maximized: first, because as mortals our time is limited; second, for the sake of efficiency; and third, because being on time is considerate of others. I'm not for robotizing people by making them slaves of time. But every hour we waste is lost forever."

Like his crew, the skipper's perception of life was realistic; his responses, like theirs, though guided by habit, more often than not, were strictly practical. Though essentially a very practical man, he had surprised us with flashes of sensitivity to the splendor of the gorges.

Wang Shi didn't share the major's and my assumption of the skipper's sensitivity. He was unwilling to concede that the *lao ban* went from feeling appreciation to a state of reverence. Wang Shi wasn't inclined to seek a superhuman purpose or deity through either artistic experience or scientific methods. He lso was skeptical about the suggestion that art mixed with cognition and faith ould be a way to experience divinity.

The first officer, also a pragmatist, said little about the beauty and terrors of he gorges. But the major and I sensed he had feelings about these matters that le had not expressed. His sensitivity for the grandeur of the gorges seemed nore inward than the skipper's. No more educated than the skipper or the ther boatmen, he nevertheless came forth with keen insights. On several occa- ions, with the sensitivity of a more cultured Han, he had responded to a spec- acular vista with an exclamation that showed feelings akin to awe. In our con- ersation the night before, for example, referring to his parents, he'd sponta- leously commented, "The tenderness that binds us to those we love is what we ake from our fathers and mothers to pass on to our children." This history ontains ideas, feelings and reaction patterns that are typical in all humanity. t's not out of line to suggest that the tai gong's thoughts and reactions were rchetypal. His outlook and behavior were representations from the 'collective unconscious.'

As to the unlettered rivermen, evidence of their self-education was striking, hough in contrast to the school-taught knowledge the major, Thompson, Vang Shi, and I treasured. Instead of passive absorption of other people's deas, the boatmen, blurted out their immediate reactions. Given the chance, hey talked outright about what they thought and felt. They told earthy stories bout their past and present, giving us an appreciation of what their life was like nd how they felt about it. As they talked to us we uncovered the full range of uman traits: the normal, the smart, the moral and the optimistic; also, the lullard, the immoral, the pessimistic and the depressed.

As we gained deeper appreciation of them we saw how easy it is to idealize hem for their efforts, tenacity and loyalty. Whether they were obstreperous or ompliant, scoundrels or fine characters, we viewed them for their sheer umanness. They weren't exactly heroes. Their continuing with age-old blind- rs, their imperfections and resignation to their treadmill lot kept them from leserving feckless admiration. Thompson called to our attention some of their diosyncracies, such as how at times commoners may suddenly break the stream of their drudgery to stare at others caught in a predicament or immersed in a umorous situation. He felt Chinese commoners show a wonderful universal uman capacity to take pleasure in an unusual happening that breaks the nonotony of their hard lot. Their resoluteness and ready sense of humor elicit- d our respect.

Several among the insights the commoners gave us included: the preemi- lent role of their *jia* (extended families), the dominance of their dependence n the vicissitudes of nature, the pervasiveness of a conservative and fatalistic trand and the ubiquitousness of appalling poverty.

Their *jia,* extended family, was a crucial part of these commoner-boatmens' uniqueness The skipper carrying his three generations aboard, the tai gong close feelings for his artist brother, the lead oarsman firm bond with his young nephew, were but a few of the networks of extended families aboard the wu ban. One after another a boatman showed that he saw himself in relation to particular ancestors, parents, siblings, children and relatives.

Before our eyes, here, in mid-20th century, was replayed the 3,000 year-old Chou Dynasty's social and political scenario. Commoners' obsession with Chineseness (The Han household) made them self-conscious in the face of the non-Chinese world and continued as a crucial force accounting for the civilization's durability. Emphasizing household relationships gives social cohesion primacy, but individual autonomy becomes secondary. A lack of individual autonomy has made the Chinese people conformist and vulnerable to collectivist passions. These two blind spots are linked: for a tribal pride of the Chinese as one huge family both obstructs the individual's search for truth and makes give-and-take with the non-Chinese world difficult.

Chinese society is an enlarged household or *jia*, Wang Shi told us. Having refined and preserved their society for millennia, Chinese understandably have been concerned to perpetuate it. Focusing attention and loyalty on one's own household is an essential way to maintain the social cohesion that keeps the culture intact.

Less effort and confidence goes into relationships beyond the immediate household. Within society, however, the function of the *jia* can be expanded to include the individual's or clan's work situation. The river people belong to the larger household of all boatmen. Theirs is a household of pain and want relief, happiness, security and full stomachs came only in dreams. By observing the protocol appropriate for their stations in life, however, the boatmen fulfil their cultural responsibility. They gained face by being reliable on their assigned job. Emphasizing household relationships gives social cohesion primacy and individual autonomy secondary status, which has made the Chinese vulnerable to collectivist passions.

Chinese commoners' loyalty and dependence on their 'households,' was a strong contrast to Western societies' individualism, which often entails a frenetic search for artificial experiences. In our hunger for new stimulations, we risk confusing originality with soliciting a reaction, as in show business, by cheap illusions. We are more interested in sensuality than the Chinese. We imagine glitzy circumstances to compensate for life's drabness. The appearance mirrors collective fantasy, not fundamental aims and beliefs. We fool ourselves by claiming we are purposeful individuals.

A veneration for nature's dominance was another characteristic of these commoner-boatmen. They showed strong respect for the earth, the heavens and "all that in them is." This reverence was powered by the crucial demands of harvests, the rivers' dual capacity to nourish fields and flood whole popula ions, and the sheer enormity and variety of China's geography. With their lives o dependent on natural conditions, their world view had to be naturalistic. Nature's dominance stamped boatmen and farmers alike with fatalism. City people may see this acceptance of the force of natural circumstances as timidi-y and naivete. Nevertheless, down the long corridor of time Chinese peasants' nd boatmen' wisdom has evolved a close dialogue with the natural order.

These boatmen lived according to the circumstances of the river. Its ways letermined their destiny. They lived their lives within the authority of skippers, unk owners, freight and passengers.

And what led us to consider the commoners' conservative and fatalistic trand? Chinese civilization could not have endured for five millennia without trong conservative forces. The down side, however, is that a society cannot epay to children of slaves the present cost of ancient bondage. The prospect or these commoner-boatmen was grim. The estimate of their fate was clear: When they died, some were given burial in the earth, others had their bodies lropped into the river. Fatalism was their realism. Fatalism is the opposite of ndividual initiative, and the attachment to place is an obstacle to cosmopoli-anism. Neither of these strong orientations reduce debilitating rigidities. These two persistent factors hold back modernization and relief for the com-noners from their grinding poverty. Change in 1946 required a breakthrough n China's millennia-old conservatism—a radical alteration of thought, techno-ogical instruments and socio-economic structures.

Heroes or villains, the core circumstance of their existence was that they are poor. These boatmen shared the condition of poverty with the majority of Chinese commoners. To talk of "source of income" or even "employment" was complete anomaly. Their being hired was chancey at best. When hired, for all heir exertion the rowers and trackers received but a few coppers pay and were lisposable always. Theirs was no ordinary labor; it was endless bitter toil. Theirs was a grim equation: row, man the sweep, hoist the sail, bend low giv-ng total strength to the bamboo hawser. In their poverty no ombudsman poke for them against the grotesqueness of their miseries and the hopelessness of their prospect.

Theirs was a culture of poverty: fatalism, belief in chance, present-time ori-ntation, impulsiveness, the inability to delay present gratification or to plan for he future; concrete rather than abstract thinking, feelings of inferiority, accep-ance of aggression and illegitimacy. Death was the only escape from the pains nd abuses of this world.

Was the sum of the boatmens' routines inconsequential, a lost drop in the Long River? Buddhist teachings, which to some degree influence all Chinese ommoners, would say "yes, self and the world are transitory, insubstantial." Was their lot the enactment of the Law of Karma? Retrospectively, karma—one's houghts and deeds have an ethical consequence fixing one's lot—is the cause of what was happening in these boatmen-commoners. Do these thoughts provide assurances that allow them to accept the misery of their marginal lives?–disposable and with no higher destiny?

With Wang Shi and the major, I was angered at the injustice, frustrated a the absence of programs to correct their exploitation and sad for their interminable toil and pain. We often asked: Were human beings created for such life as theirs?

Wang Shi in particular deplored the coolies' acceptance of their lot and the injustice of a social structure that perpetuated such a system. He was vocal with his recommendations for needed changes. Yes, he would say, a few, like the skipper, climb out of poverty and some become comparably well-off entrepreneurs. But the skipper's way out of poverty was at the expense of others. The new China cannot be only the search for relief for a few. Help will come as the pace of modernization is speeded. At best, however, the installation of the necessary technological applications will take years. The identification of the source and expressions of the culture of poverty are but a beginning. The need is to understand how environmental conditions produce psychological dispositions. Then must come an analysis of who are responsible to make the needed change. Changing long-enduring psycho-dynamic structures of individual may well become more difficult to accomplish than changing environmental conditions. But first, important changes must come in the values, faith and character of individuals.

Did we Westerners need to concern ourselves with the lot of these million of disinherited Chinese? In three weeks we would be back in our comfortable Nanjing compounds. Then, before long, we would return to the affluence of the United States. Conscientious Westerners, and particularly those who take their faith seriously, must ask themselves probing questions like:

What did the Bible verse "And the poor will be always among us" mean And what are the implications of humans being created in the image of the Creator?

Can we value human suffering, not as reflecting the will of an inscrutable God, but an active solidarity with all the world's weak and victimized persons Are we willing to face and change how our conception of what is human is so focused on ourselves that it is difficult to empathize with others, especially people who are different? Can we strive for a valid account of the reality of personal life and of the social exchanges of the disinherited? Can we Westerner make our goal less the pursuit of individual comfort and more a commitment to the humble trackers, oarsmen and bowsmen of the earth? Conceivably the race could continue perplexed, anxious and guilt-ridden about the human propensity to perpetuate poverty and abandon its disinherited. But that condition cannot be allowed to remain in a democratic society, much less in a committed Christian community.

It is easy to gloss over the tale of the suffering servant of Isaiah: "He hath no form nor comeliness; and when we shall see him, there is no beauty that we should desire him. He is despised and rejected of men; a man of sorrows, and acquainted with grief. He was despised and we esteemed him not."

Wang Shi's challenge was right. The existence of an oppressive and unequal system demeans the life of people in each society. Not only within China, but in Africa, India and South America–even in North America and Western Europe–poverty continues to be a cause of suffering, social cost and waste of human potential. The destructive influences affect us all. The seriousness of poverty as a critical world-wide problem demands that knowledge proceed to understanding, and that understanding engender change!

CHAPTER NINE

# New Life In The Witches Gorge

"By the gods," the agitated cook said, as he ladled rice gruel into our breakfast bowls, "today you'll see waters that toss *wu ban* on rocks like toys, waters stirring up quicksand that traps trackers on the shore." Serving the next in line, he added, "We'll need much good fortune today. Instead of only one, we should have sacrificed two roosters."

"The rapids we go through today," the first officer explained, "begin with the difficult Yedan. Then comes the Hengliangzi, or Cross Beam cataract, feared for their hidden rocks and treacherous sandbars. They also have the *fa shin*, or boiling caldrons, giant bubbles that explode without warning, then subside into a false calm, to erupt again. While we go through the the Witches Gorge's, however, we will be rewarded with some fine scenery."

Pulling the *wu ban* away from the shore, the skipper, in an uncharacteristic fashion, said, "You'd better ask one of your foreign gods to look well on today's journey."

For the first section we passengers chose again to follow the trackers' trail ashore. The way was difficult and got worse as we passed through another low ceiling tunnel. carved out of the cliff-side and had to bend over to keep from knocking our heads. Our progress, though, was easy compared with the harnessed and bent-over trackers who plodded at our heels.

A thousand feet behind us, the junk's drum beat out the message "steady forward." The men strained, hauling on the tow line even as they clambered barefoot over slippery boulders, between crevices, through treacherous sand nd up into the constricting carved-out tow tunnel. We empathized with them n their labored dragging and plaintive choral responses. We were pressed to hurry our pace to keep ahead of their column.

An unexpected and ominous jerk came in the tow line. The lead tracker shrieked a warning cry to his 100 pullers. The 1,000 foot towline had become tangled on a ledge jutting out over an inaccessible crevice and farther back it was caught on an underwater boulder. Our big *wu ban* slipped back, with the tow line serving as the only stay against the current.

In seconds strong swimmers dived in and freed the hawser. Simultaneously the trackers above slacked up on the cable and swung the line clear of the obstruction. This move was perilous because the last trackers in the column easily could have been jerked off the trail and whipped into the river. The lead tracker started his column of pullers again with a new chorale. And our precarious struggle through the Yedan continued.

On the edge of the hamlet Nanmuerh (South Cedar Garden), the skipper steered the junk into shore to take us and 24 of the trackers aboard.

The village was the last settlement in Hubei province. The thin line of its few houses straddled two glens. To the east of the village flowed the Dream Stream, a rivulet which formed a portion of the boundary between Hubei (north of the lake) and Sichuan (Four Streams) provinces. The dividing line was opposite a point called Cloth-Bag Mouth. Two narrow glens, dubbed the Portals of Awe, cradled the picturesque stream and were connected by a covered bridge. The late Guo Mo-ruo, a popular modern Chinese poet, described this little stream: "When the bow of my boat enters Sichuan province, the stern is still in Hubei."

More than 500 stone steps formed a terraced way leading to the quixotic place.

The gentle green slopes were marred by giant gashes. Above the pristine glen, the walls of the gorge again closed in.

Leaving the peaceful waters beside the village, our bow lurched and the entire junk trembled as we were caught in the downsweep of the current. Lao Ma, the skipper's wife, gave a series of yells from the stern that ricocheted off the canyon walls: *"Xiao Meimei xiang chuan wai! Diula, diula!* (Little sister fell overboard! We've lost her!)."

We saw the five-year-old thrashing and screaming in the calmer waters in the lee of the junk behind us. A tracker from that boat jumped into the water and swam jerkily toward the child. In a split second, the first officer and an oarsman jumped over the side of our *wu ban* into the dingy in tow and rowed to the rescue.

Lao Ma, the virago grandmother, exploded. She wept and crackled the air

116

with her curses and screams. Her paroxysms continued even after seeing that the tracker had reached Little Sister and that the first officer in the sampan was approaching the two. She choked on her outbursts as the first officer fished the little one out and wrapped her with his shirt.

When the shivering child was lifted up on our *wu ban*, the grandmother burst into tongue-lashing: "All this trip I've told you to stay away from the edges. . .You play around like you are on land."

The near tragedy unnerved all aboard. Grandfather, the skipper, was still shaking and at loose ends, not so much from the near loss of his granddaughter as from his wife's tantrum.

Oarsmen and bowmen maneuvered back into midstream and headed for the next rapids. The north shore was devoid of vegetation. Worn in places into colossal terraces and fluted with deep vertical potholes, it was caverned from the water line all the way up to its great heights. In contrast, the hills on the south shore sported woodlands and green fields.

Sweepmen worked with long poles to fend off rocks. The rowers, drummer and the lead tracker ashore, all were tense as we headed for the next two rapids. As we moved into the current, the water foamed and raged under the bow. By degrees we felt our way through rock strewn shoals.

The skipper was still distraught from Little Sister's mishap, when warning shouts came from the bowmen. The alarm was not soon enough for the helmsman to react. We heard a crunching and felt a jolt. We'd hit a submerged boulder, damaging one of the starboard holds.

Shouting out news of the leak, two oarsmen began bailing and the first officer jumped in to help. The chocolate-colored water, however, bubbled up faster than they could empty it. Lightning coordination swerved the *wu ban* toward the south bank to a sandy cove where it could be beached.

Conflicting estimates were exchanged about what needed doing and how the work was to be managed. The *lao ban* was indecisive about how to deal with this new emergency, but penurious as usual, he didn't want to summon carpenters from the nearby village. After much harranguing, the decision was made for the crew to do a patch-job. Cotton batting and clay were rammed into the hole and covered with a mixture of heavy tallow. Then, inner and outer boards covering the hole were bolted to the hull and coats of tar were applied to both surfaces.

While the repairs were in progress, passengers and unoccupied crew explored the small orchards along the south shore. This shore offered a sweeping view of the imposing north bank. Beishi (Black Rock), the first village in Sichuan was perched on an extended ledge of the precipitous hills. Not far away was Qu Yuan's whirlpool. The poet's house was in the nearby hills.

Beyond was the imposing Daba Mountain, with the small city of Badong nestled in its eastern foothills. A communications juncture and gateway to the mountainous regions of western Hubei province, the city had centuries-old roads fanning out into the neighboring counties. Here large cargo junks were loaded with downriver freight to be transhipped to the interior. The cargoes we could see were building supplies, tung oil, raw lacquer, hides and medicinal herbs.

After several hours we were called to the *wu ban* for lunch. Shortly afterward, repairs were completed and the crew was readied to return to the Witches Gorge. Bowmen poled out from the inlet back into the rock-strewn mainstream. The sweepmen and oarsmen skillfully maneuvered the *wu ban* through two short rapids in minutes.

A non-navigational emergency struck us as we approached the Hengliangzi, (Cross Beam) cataract. The *lao ban's* expectant daughter, who had been whimpering through the morning's accident and commotion that followed, now broke into sobs and went into labor.

Shifting fast into the role of midwife, Lao Ma, ordered all the hot water the cook could heat. She gathered towels and pillows and improvised a harness for her writhing daughter.

The first officer, nearby at the tiller, suggested that Lao Ma get the "foreign devils" to help. "Thompson," he said, "helps midwives at his clinic, and Mr. Cowles is a hell of a handyman." Lao Ma called us to the side of her daughter lying on a mat in the cramped captain's quarters below decks.

Thompson was ready for action with his emergency bag and had already taken out sterile instruments and gauze. I was by no means as ready. The optimistic first officer had oversold my experience and handiness. My experience in the life-and-death birthing procedures was mostly cerebral. In clinical training at a hospital in Boston, I witnessed a delivery and in 1940 during a Japanese air raid in wartime Chongqing , deep in a dugout under the Methodist Mission Hospital, I had held a flashlight for an obstetrician caring for an emergency delivery. And at the birth of my son in Alta Bates Hospital, Berkeley, California, hurrying nurses had relegated me to an outer waiting room. Those were my "handy" experiences.

In addition to my lack of experience, I was ambivalent about babies being born. In my masculine head, the amazing happening was both marvelous, and mysterious, enveloped in travail and unpredictabilities. I imagined births that were perfect, painless and joyous.

"Get the water kettle from the cook," Mother Lao Ma ordered me. Her tone made it clear that this was no time for a bumbling bystander.

While I went to get the water, I realized I needed to get my act together. The cook's nods helped. I returned to the mat with the kettle, still shaky, but determined to be reassuring, if not helpful.

The little mother-to-be clamped her fingers on my hand as the next spasm struck her. As her grip tightened and shook, I looked into her eyes. The fear I met reminded me of eyes of men facing shell fire. Giving birth must be the ultimate labor.

"Have Mr. Thompson's scissors ready," the commander directed me Suddenly, there was a spurt and a gush of fluid and the birthing exploded.

"There's the beginning of the head," barked the assured grandmother. "Mr Thompson, take your big, clean hands and pull!" After several attempts, the little mother pressed the baby out the birth canal and another Chinese was out into the world.

"Hurry," Lao Ma ordered me. "Take the gauze and tie the cord close and tight." I obeyed.

"Cut the cord with the scissors," she urged. I tried and I tried, but, it was slippery. The scissors wouldn't bite in.

"Mr. Thompson," she instructed, "stretch the cord and help him make the cut." That procedure was successful, but novice that I was, I had botched the previous step. I had not tied the gauze tight enough. The cord flopped around like a loose hose, squirting blood in every direction.

Mother Lao Ma applied the proper knot and cast a 'you're fired' glance in my direction.

Other crises came with the placenta and afterbirth bursting. Thompson, in helping Lao Ma with the remaining procedures, restored a semblance of the foreign-helper's "face."

The new mother's eyes now were dancing bright, deep and clear like some fir-shaded mountain pool. For a moment it was as if hers was the knowledge of all time and all worlds because she better understood life's sorrows and perplexities. She had gratitude and wonder from the inside out. The fresh arrival was healthy, but noisy. Thompson and I shook hands and offered silent prayers for the miracle of new life.

The skipper emerged haggard from his cabin and announced, "Our daughter has delivered a healthy baby! The young mother did well. She and the newborn are fine." With his dour mien he suggested that the only blot on the great event was the unfortunate fact that the baby was female.

The crew, busy fore and midship readying the *wu ban* for the next rapids, led by the drummer's fast beat, united in a welcoming hooray for the new life.

As we pulled out of this last cataract, the statuesque first officer, stepped back to congratulate the grandparents, then moved to his post at the bow ready for the next navigational ordeal.

Much impressed, Wang Shi quoted and translated lines from "Birth and

)eath" by a contemporary Chinese poet.

*Birth refines our view of man,*
*As dusk our view of stars.*
*Death refines our view of man,*
*As dawn our view of stars.*
*Dim at first? No, star and man alike*
*Reflect the amplitude of ageless light.*
*Gone, you say? No, shining still,*
*Each celebrates with us eternal day.*

This event, under such conditions in this faraway place, took the major into one of his frequent moods of awe and scientific analysis.

"Hmmm. Random egg. Random sperm. Random river. Random junk," He began. "And she won't have any more time than the rest of us, whether she's a queen or a coolie. But it goes to show you how intelligent God is. He does-n't fuss with our humans' small going's-on. He keeps His mind on the Big Plan! If she survives the dangers of her helpless infancy, she will begin to dis-cover that she is either queen of creation or only a mite on the surface of a minute planet. She, like all of us, will find her stay here brief and must face the fact of existence–time."

"I don't know what you are talking about," the cook inter-rupted. "But on the north bank we are passing the town of, Guandukou (Official Control Crossing). It's the beginning of the second string of gorges we call the Wuxia (Witches-Sorceress Gorge). Shorter than the first, only about 36 miles, the scenery is not as varied as that of the Xiling or as spectac-ular as the Wind Box Gorge. Its riverscape, however, is unique: Cliffs rise on both sides of the

*Courtesy Professor Van Slyke*

*Etching of Witches Gorge*

river. Forest-covered mountains stretch into the distance. Strange rock formations above and the river's fast waters below make very special sights."

The vistas in Iron Coffin Shoal, the first of Wuxia Gorge, leaped out. The magnificent palisades, arresting and mysterious with rich green ravines and forests, seemed to be the work of a landscape painter. In places narrowing to scarcely 300 yards, the river turned and twisted past immense mountains which dropped perpendicularly to the water. They seemed to block our passageway. Range after range of mountains that seemed never to reach the sky rose up and shut us in. As the mist cleared we saw the channel, which now in the sunlight looked like miles of enormous tunnels cut through sheer rock.

"Up ahead, on the other side, we are coming to Kong Ming Tablet," announced the cook. "The six large Chinese characters carved into the whitish rock carries the message: 'Cliff upon cliff, and peak upon peak, in the Wu Gorge.' Like a giant billboard the words describe the Peaks of the Immortals."

Legend has it that these ideographs were written by the great Shu Kingdom military strategist, Zhugeliang, during the Three Kingdoms period. Tradition has it that he carved a memorable poem here. The poem was so commanding that when the great Wu Kingdom general Lu Xun reached this spot with his armies, instead of attacking, he turned around and returned home with his troops.

Goddess Peak towered over mountain ranges on the northern bank. A single stone upthrust marked its spectacular pinnacle. From this distance, the peak had the appearance of a graceful woman, gazing down at the river. It is called Watcher of the Dawn and Sunset Glow, because, as the highest of the twelve peaks in this chain, it is the first to greet the dawn and the last to say goodbye to the setting sun.

Among the stories told about Goddess Peak is that of the goddess Yao Ji, the youngest daughter of the Mother of the Western Skies. Clever, intelligent and strong-minded, Yao Ji was given charge of Yao Pool by her mother, but she grew impatient with the monotonous life in Heaven and wanted to live on earth.

One day, she secretly asked her eleven sisters to go down to earth with her on a spree. Coming to Mt. Wu, she found the legendary hero Yu fighting a devastating flood stirred up by twelve dragons. She succeeded in killing them with the flood waters. Though the flood was tamed, the river's course remained hazardous and hidden rocks caused shipwrecks. So the heavenly maidens stayed behind to guide ships and help peasants with their harvests.

These heavenly maidens, along with the Peak of the Immortals above Kong Ming Tablet, touched the hearts of Chinese poets, who gave them the names they bear: Peak of the Holy Spring, Peak of Morning Glow, Pine Ridge Peak, Dragon Peak, Peak of the Cranes, Peak of the Emerald Screen, Peak of the

Flying Phoenix, Peak of the Pure Altar, Peak of the Rising Clouds and Soaring Peak.

Caves dotted the cliffs. Up the sides of many, in small patches of arable land, were small homes. These stone houses clung to the steep cliffs. The inhabitants lived by the fish they caught with small conical nets dipped into the current. The cliffs from low or high water levels are pockmarked by pot-holes bored like the holes of a cookstove upon the cliff face; these were formed by the stabs of boatmen's prongs and hooks as they had pushed and pulled their junks at the different water-levels during the last few thousand years. The eerie quietness was broken by the gurgle of a whirlpool or the whistle of the junkmen as they invoked the aid of the Wind God.

The inhabitants of these cliff-side houses must have spent a long time climbing from the water's edge. Clinging to promontories, some of these blue-gray hamlets with their high-arching bridges straddled streams. On the opposite shore, cultivated terraces ascended to the highest peaks.

Living at the sides and atop those precipitous mountains no doubt presented difficulties, but the superb vistas provided ample reward. Glimpsing into the depths of the gorges far below, these people must have seen the junks as toy boats. From these obscure little farms among the clouds must have come some of the sturdy trackers, their sure-footed and hardened bodies fit to endure the crushing work by which they lived and died.

A May cloudburst gave Sorceress Gorge an unusual cast, somber but grand. Under heavy rains, the soil had turned to a ruby red, the trees were a deep tropical blue-green, and the Long River kept its shade of copper, a gift from the sands of Tibet. The grotesque markings on the perpendicular walls, sculpted by the silt-filled waters, produced a weird and almost depressing scene, suggesting one of Salvador Dali's surreal paintings.

The immensity of the cliffs swallowed up the crashing waters. In such a vast landscape, we humans felt tiny and inconsequential. From the chasms upriver came a low throbbing, then the tell-tale falsetto refrain of feverish boatmen, *"A yah, A yah, A yah."*

From the mists ahead emerged the outlines of a junk headed downstream. The agitated rhythm of its drum beater and the anxious chant of its lead oarsman kept its extra bank of oarsmen and sweepmen stroking double-time. It was a furious sound, muffled in the fog, much as memories emerge from the lower mind.

Their desperate cries grew louder and louder in the otherwise silent afternoon. Suddenly we saw the form of a great junk, revealing the frenzied labors of the crew that matched the sounds we heard. Just as quickly, it disappeared. The Doppler effect of the noise decreased as we moved apart, adding to the mystery of the chasm. The noises faded until we heard only the drummer's frantic thumping, then absolute silence.

Powerful winds descended, blew off the rain and left fleecy clouds swirling about the higher summits. The freakish formations gave way to a bridal falls and a glen nestled in an evergreen grove. The delicate portions, set against the surrounding confusions of crags and gashes of this rugged part, transformed the picture. This seemed more like an artist's dream on a Japanese screen than anything in the real world.

Small wonder the poets of China visit the Three Chasms of the Wuxia Gorge if they can. Li Tai Po, one of the greatest of them, recorded his experience on the wall of an inn:

> *Last night below the Sorceress Mountain*
> *Wind blows, gone is the rain color.*
> *On the high hill from which four quarters can be seen,*
> *treasure thoughts of Song Yu,*
> *Thus visiting ancient sites,*
> *tears fall on my garments.*

The reference to Song Yu comes from an ancient tale. Prince Xiang of Qu (c. 300 B.C.) asked Song Yu about the mysterious beauty of the filmy clouds as they traveled this gorge. The poet told the prince the mists were those of a beautiful maiden named the Cloud of Dawn:

> *When it first rises, its vigor is like the pine,*
> *erect, lofty. A little later it comes nearer. It is*
> *brightly illuminated, like a beautiful woman*
> *who raises the sleeve of her robe to ward off the sun's*
> *rays,. . .Suddenly the form changes, and in an instant*
> *it is like a chariot with four horses; like a standard*
> *with fluttering banners; refreshing like wind and cool*
> *as rain. . .Looking down one sees the whirling waters*
> *of meeting; it is beautiful, unusual and grand. The*
> *viewer cannot praise it sufficiently.*

Immediately, so the story goes, the prince commissioned Song Yu to express these mysteries and beauties in verse.

The ravine above Wen Shan, or Mountain of Learning, sheltered the village where the lovely daughter of the Wang clan was born and reared. Her sad story is given in the Fir-Flower Tablets, taken from a book devoted to biographies of famous beauties. In 33 B.C., the emperor cemented an alliance with the Mongol khan of the feared *xiung-nu*, or northern barbarians. He bestowed Lady Wang Chiang to the khan in marriage. Though made queen and given he title of Ning Hu, she was not well treated and wrote pathetic letters to her emperor-father. After the death of her husband, custom decreed that the succeeding khan marry his father's widow. With this prospect, the beautiful Lady Wang Chiang took poison and died.

The doughty Captain Plant, the early 20th-century British sea captain become Chinese, who knew each pebble of this gorge's winding length, described it: "The river winds round the base of precipitous thousand-foot cliffs, their peaks barely showing above the fleecy clouds and the whole row running back to distant mountain ranges. . .The rocky wall-like sides are fluted along their faces by thousands of terraces and potholes making it resemble the great pipes of an organ."

Decades later, in 1925, another Caucasian, Elizabeth Crump Enders, traveled past these sculpted square coves, cut as though by skillful craftsmen, with their giant pudding stones washed along the shore. She reported seeing "stalactite formations and caves in long rows washed out of solid rock, pebble grooves, deep round holes like monster pieces of Swiss cheese, and gray sandy beaches the color of the rocks."

With all its spectacular scenery, the Witches Gorge's waters proved a constant and formidable opponent for the boatmen. The assorted cataracts necessitating poling by the bowmen to "feel out" the least risky channel.

Trackers were landed at the start of the cataract. Bowmen with their long sweeps pulled the boat's head out into the current to clear the rocky shore and then clawed with hooked poles the sheer palisades. The head tracker stepped up the tempo of his work refrain. Soon we were into the Cuo Gai, or Wrongly Opened Chasm. Ashore the foreman's lilting refrain stirred the trackers to scramble and pull harder. When an unexpected emergency arose, like the tow line becoming caught in a crevice, his chorus would instantly change to an order to lower a man over the precipice with a rope to free the line.

Our progress was rough and slow. The trackers seemed to hang, slip back and give way. Gongs and drums beat, bells rang, firearms sounded, hundreds of trackers on all fours yelled and bellowed. The foreman shouted like a madman, rushing along the gasping, struggling lines of bare-backed men. He howled, leaped and thrashed about the column. Often our boat quivered and seemed about to gyrate out of control. When the cliffs became inaccessible to the trackers, they came aboard and helped claw the junk along the deep water using long bamboo poles with iron-beaked tips hooked into the rocks. This maneuver was made easier in the gorge's Iron Coffin section, where helpful iron chains bolted into the cliffs had been installed 25 feet above the water.

The westerly end of the Witches Gorge brought us underneath the 1,500-foot high Witch's Mountain, where, reputedly, an evil spirit lived. Once we were past this point we entered a calm section that opened a clear passage to

Wushan City.

We wondered what drove junk owners up and down the Great River's gorges. Perhaps the incentives that propelled them were different from those of Westerners. Our experiences had taught us much of the Chinese suffering, and a bit about their sensitivity to loss of face. The motives that impelled them must have been more than mere mercantilism. Their motivation must have been both the profit and the adventure that have fired traders from time immemorial. A feeling for the image of the archetypal quest crept into our thinking.

Like the ventures of the Spanish and Portuguese galleons of the 15th and 16th centuries, these voyages were costly and risky. Often the great expense did not pay off; sometimes all was lost. Yet once accomplished, these perilous journeys became internalized into the psyche of the river people.

Another impetus, through the millennia, that sparked these laborious treks was the persistent pressure to connect China's east and west. Yet another motive inducing ordinary people to struggle through the gorges is found in the sheer challenge they offer. The revered Sichuan poet Du Fu, marveling at the stuff of which these boat people were made, wrote:

> *The men of the chasms regard death lightly.*
> *Avoiding whirlpools, carried on by the rushing*
> *water, no danger delays them.*
> *These men . . .are very able in surmounting these dangers.*

The Witches Gorge had been both harrowing and awe-inspiring. There was isolation where the river bent away from civilization; beauty where clouds, mountains and shore lines struck some memorable poses; peace when the river flattened for short stretches. Neither ancient poets nor sensitive moderns could escape the grandeur of its chasms.

The cataracts had been treacherous and nerve-racking, but the hole in our hull had been repaired. Two trackers, however, had been injured: one had fallen, another had been trampled.

There had been the excitement of the new arrival among us. The birth presented a scream of pain and a cry of joy. The little one now was launched on the great river of life, destined to meet all its turbulence.

In appreciating more fully the motivations that fired Chinese to travel this and the Xiling Gorges we gained additional insights about the secrets of the Long River and its people. The river gods and poems etched on the serrated rock walls and the pagodas built on the heights gave clues to anxieties and aspirations of Chinese. The Witches Sorceress Gorge opened windows into many paradoxes that concern Chinese: consistently inconsistent and practically impractical. In its chasms questions continue about the symbolic and mystical in nature's secrets and in humans' predicaments. In these reaches, to see their destiny more clearly, persons feel the need to come to terms with archetypes, the original models from which similar things are patterned, things that transcend any one culture.

As we approached the city where we were to moor for the night, thoughts about supernatural forces were left behind. Our stress and tumult receded. The calmer land-and-riverscape pacified hearts roiled by the harrowing hours in the river's turbulence. Gulls soared in and out of shadowy ravines, up into the amethyst clouds and back down around our wu ban. The steep hills were marked by occasional coal miners' caves. The slopes along the city's outskirts were dotted with clusters of shacks and little houses. The softening afternoon light from beyond the western hills rendered the distinction between sky, hills and water uncertain. The magical scene became opalescent accented by the straw-yellow rising moon.

The crew was invigorated in this river-shore-and-sky combination. No longer jerky, the oarsmen and yulowmen's strokings blended into a smooth and strong unity. The rhythm they struck wasn't clock time. It had the urgency of anticipating a night on the town. Their pulling harmonized with our breathing. Its pulse spoke of the confidence that comes with having conquered a formidable section of the Gorges.

Wu Mountain, which gave the city its name and provided an imposing backdrop, symbolized the antiquity the city was striving to leave behind. The buildings appeared as if they would, at any moment, jump free of Wu Mountain.

CHAPTER TEN

# Wushan City And Our Search For The Zhou Ancestral Hall

*Wushan Junk Mooring At dusk*

Wushan City we were nearing presented a chimera. Other towns and cities we had seen on our westward journey blended into the shores. Not so this city. When the sun's rays pierced the clouds, the towers of the fifteen-centuries-old wall and the green-and-yellow tiled roofs were set aglow. A quixotic luster enveloped the ramparts and the mysterious structures within. As if turned into a cosmic neon sign, Wushan seemed to advertise itself as distinct. When racing clouds blocked the afternoon sun, the city's profile on its mountain perch remained striking. Each impression augmented our feeling that here was a unique city.

Now within sight of the day's destination we saw the forest of masts rocking against the background of Wushan City steps rising to wooded promontories. We saw the white walls of suburban villas spreading out from the North Gate and up toward the base of Wu Mountain. Those ostentatious modern developments beyond the city wall suggested forces at work to defy the mountain's sacredness and the age-old practice of leaving things exactly as they always had been. Many interior river cities wanted to stay the way they had been for centuries, but not this city toward which our oarsmen and sweepmen were pulling us.

From midstream, the rowers pulled us toward a flotilla of large junks. The skipper steered us into a mooring slip near the base of the 300 broad granite steps leading to the South Gate.

Once off our junk, we had to wait at the end of the gangplank for the afternoon's "water carriers' parade," the interminably long line of coolies hauling king-size wooden buckets they had filled with river water. The upward procession rhythmically swung their weighty sloshing burdens from carrying poles. Keeping a hurried pace in their steady climb, the carriers chanted a heart-melting melody: *"A yah, A yah, A yah."*

Stalled for a time on the river's edge pontoon, we found ourselves adjacent to Wushan Shan's boat-building sheds. The major and Thompson were fascinated with the rows of slips with river boats in all stages of construction. The teams of busy carpenters, in turn, were intrigued with the curious foreigners.

*Water Carrier*

The manner of production was elemental by Western standards. The planks of these small and mid-sized boats were fastened together with wrought iron cleats and spikes. The spaces between them were filled with bamboo shavings, caulking and tar. There is a continuous tradition of both boat building and boat handling that reaches back to where history mingles with legend. Long experimentation has led the builders to combine the most suitable and available raw materials with the best size and cut of boat for the particular local conditions. The resulting river boats are both beautiful and functional in design. These Long River's generic wooden boats are one of the principal material expressions of the region's culture. People traveled on these river boats, worked on them and lived on them.

Finishing our tour of the boat-builders' sheds, we found the line of water-carriers had thinned out. With the stragglers of the coolie caravan ahead of us, we joined the stream of people making the trudge up to the South Gate. Pedestrians gave the coolies a wide berth, particularly when they switched their burdened poles from one tired shoulder to the other. Their cries of "Clear the way" and "Get to the side" rung with authority. Reaching the top of the steps and quickening their pace, they swung through the broad gate and emptied their splashing loads into the large tank for public use in the center of the square.

Outside the imposing Gate, we paused to note the signs of Wushan's growth and efforts to change. The small plaza at the top of the wide steps outside the gate provided a panoramic view of Wushan's burgeoning transport and trading enterprises. From this vantage we could see how the city was strategically located. At a bend in the river, it also was the hub of age-old, cobblestone roads reaching out to a series of bustling county seats. Intense activity along the waterfront provided impressive evidence of the city's successful efforts to capitalize on its location. Evident also was the way the city was expanding its commerce and managing to assimilate the influx of refugees–war-displaced persons from the west returning to the coast and people from the north fleeing famine-stricken areas.

In this time of reconstruction, Wushan, like the other up-river cities, was being blown by new winds from downriver. Pressures to update thought, technology and architecture were evident. New, more efficient and more profitable businesses were pushing aside antedated establishments entangled in century-old ways and family networks. Other signs–even the unconventional ways in which junks were assembled and moored–reinforced our estimate that some people of Wushan were risking change.

A different picture faced us as we turned to go through the massive 30-foot-high wall into the city. Unchanged in 1,500 years, the wall was amazingly well-preserved. Built at great expense of materials and toil, it remained impressive. With continuous crenelations and four visible gate towers, it followed the contour of the city limits. At both the East and West Gates were miniature pagodas, long past their former glory.

The remnant of the city wall symbolized both the perennial human drive for security and permanence and also the ineffectiveness of this way of achieving that goal. The wall proclaimed the futility of keeping out foreigners and change. This imposing structure was revered by the population as a monument to the ancient city's unique history.

Walking through the 20-foot-high open doors of the gate towers, we were inside an ancient Chinese city. Accustomed to China's westernized metropolitan coastal cities–with their wide boulevards, European-style buildings, traffic jams, polluted air, garish billboards and cacophonies of noise–we were surprised. Within the plaza we saw that Wushan was what some city planner in the remote past saw as the model for every Chinese city.

We faced two-storied 600-year-old government buildings with the jasper-colored tiled roofs we had sighted from the river. Back of these were 1000-year-old yamen headquarters where the gentry had held forth. Still farther back stood older yellow-roofed temples.

These dilapidated ancient structures dominating the plaza seemed to stand firm, resisting change. Here we saw little evidence of modernization. We sensed that many in Wushan continued to feel nostalgia amid a world of rapid change.

This city possessed a puzzling and bewitching air. Small wonder that the legend of the Good-and-Bad Monster, Wang Shi briefed us about, originated in this city! That mythological one-legged creature was notoriously ambivalent

and hopped unpredictably from helpful to hindering behavior. Perhaps the "something more" that we sensed about Wushan was its intriguing ambivalence–it embraced both the new and the old. Entering it meant entering a zone of altered possibilities

The first officer and Wang Shi had briefed us about the two millennia-old history associated with Wushan. The city played a significant role during the turbulent Three Kingdoms era (221-265 A.D.) which followed the collapse of the Later Han Dynasty. This age was immortalized in the famous cycle of stories, half history, half legend, known as *Sanguozhi yanyi* (History of the Three Kingdoms). Owing to the popularity of this book and the many plays it has inspired, the The Three Kingdom period became wrapped in mystique and adventure. Though, in reality, an age of bloodshed, turmoil, violence and treachery–has become idealized in the Chinese mind as the golden age of chivalry and romance. One illustrative event, for example, still honored by the city, was the historic meeting of two warrior-adventurers, Shu and Wu, who lived, fought and loved in Wushan City.

In the centuries since then, the city has served as the home of kings, strategists, politicians, warriors, dramatists and poets. Tu Fu (712-770 A.D.), the Tang dynasty poet, struggled and wrote some of his most moving and treasured poems in this tradition-laden city. Much of its romance had faded by the time of our visit, though, as county (xien) seat and administrative and trade center, Wushan still retained a kind of glory, albeit a glory of the material and not of the spiritual world.

Since the Zhou family, as Wang Shi had explained, were prominent among the city's founders more than 3,000 years ago, we decided to seek out the Zhou ancestral hall. Beginning our search with respect, we hoped to find history written in alleys, stairwells, tablets and hills. We found less history and more evidence of inland cities' urban problems–crowding, sanitation and inadequate infrastructures.

We came to a congested street the cook had recommended we take. He spoke of it as one of the main thoroughfares. We found it narrow, dingy and jammed with pedestrians. At its extreme width it was barely twenty feet, and even part of that was not available for pedestrian use, since shopkeepers on both sides had put out portable counters to display their wares. For potential customers and foreigners out for a stroll this left free only a few feet to squeeze through. In these labyrinthine alleys we were exposed to family after family living in packed quarters unchanged from the cramped way of their ancestors.

The side streets feeding into this thoroughfare were also narrow, dirty and dark. Many so-called streets were but slits between high walls or a narrow flight of stone steps cut out from rock.

Sickening sewer smells from unscreened latrines pushed out the appealing odors of roasted chestnuts and hot-dipped crullers. Rancid odors arose from piles of decaying refuse. The sewers under the center of the street, covered only by loose stone slabs, emitted their characteristic foul stenches.
Such conditions prompted Westerners' revulsion, but elicited no emotional discomfort in these street folk.

The moving panorama of good-natured and easy going people on the narrow streets and alleys, however, was fascinating. Fortunately, the Chinese did not cherish privacy as we Westerners did. They didn't appear to mind having their daily affairs seen by anyone who cared to look. Weaving, tailoring, brass working, blacksmithing, and scores of other occupations were carried on in public view. Food shops and itinerant 'tuck shops,' carried on shoulder poles tempted the hungry. It was as if each person had determined that forebearance must guide conduct in every human encounter. A laughter-loving people, they enjoyed jokes, funny stories, people's predicaments and everything that stirs a chuckle.

Our exploring eventually brought us out to a street bordering the north wall. We followed this wider street flanked by an array of once-magnificent buildings. We looked for Moon Tooth Way, where the Zhou ancestral hall was said to be located. Taking a nondescript alley leading up a hill we finally found the now neglected hall.

A decrepit gateman, with eyebrows like caterpillars and a faltering gait like a turtle, escorted us around the courtyard and into the meandering rooms and anterooms. His face lit up and his garbled dialect became clearer as he told of one after another Zhou ancestor. Their histories were lavishly inscribed on the memorial tablets and plaques covering the walls.

Many clans had ancestral halls. These had their prototypes in the religious practices of early historic times. Managed by elders elected from the clan's various branches, these establishments and the ceremonies in them were usually maintained by endowments, which also supported the aged, poor and widows of the clan.

In their heyday these halls were sumptuous. Set apart and usually surrounded by high walls, they included several large assembly rooms separated by courts. In the central room were memorial tablets to the deceased male members of the clan. These were arranged on steps, those of the same generation on the same step, the oldest being on the highest with the founder of the clan at its center. A poorer living member of the clan may be in attendance to keep incense continuously burning and light candles before the tablets twice a month. At winter solstice a major ceremony and sacrifice were held at the

ncestral temple. The custom pre-dates
Confucius. A similar sacrifice was conducted for a funeral.

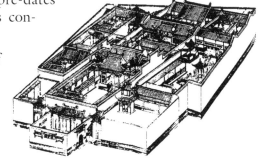

The clan took the occasion of
he ceremony to meet and trans-
ct business. A section in the hall
ften was used for a school, and
nother meeting place often
ecame a court of justice in which
he clan pronounced judgment on
ts members. Around New Year's
he spirits of the dead were welcomed into the homes of the clan members and
few days later, sent back to their customary residences. During Qingming,
he great spring festival, graves are cleaned and repaired, and offerings made of
ood and incense. At other times, like the birthday of the deceased, commem-
rations were also made. These practices were meant to strengthen the family
nd uphold habits of filial reverence and obedience.

For centuries the cult of ancestor worship has been sanctioned by each of
China's main religions. In addition to conserving much of the past, this wor-
hip has important social results. It has enabled the family to form the back-
one of China's social and economic life. It has been a means of moral and
ocial control, and it has acted as a check on individualism.

The Hall of Ten Worthies, which housed copies of Song dynasty paintings,
vas another place we wanted to locate. We hoped to find paintings of the
Three Kingdom "worthies" who could help us capture the adventure and
omance memorialized in the literature and drama of that turbulent period.
Disappointed that we were unsuccessful in finding anyone who could direct us
o the hall, we nevertheless did find, atop a hill, a monument marking the well
vhere Liu Pei's wife drowned herself. Generation after generation has retold
he story of her grief and suicide over the loss of her husband, one of the three
sworn brothers of the Three Kingdoms and one of China's great heroes.

High up in the town was a large stone tablet marking the spot reached by
he flood of 1870, which destroyed much of the city and took thousands of
ives. From this marker we took the worn stone path on the other side of the
ill and headed for the commanding towers of the North Gate.

As we made our way through the exit under the tower, an arresting vista of
Wushan's northern suburb spread out before us. In the distance, on Mount
Wu's 1,500-foot cone, we spotted the silhouette of the graceful Temple to the
God of Literature in a grove of evergreens. A slender pagoda below the peak
ose out of an orange grove. "Like bamboo," Wang Shi noted, "delicate, flex-
ble and strong." A display of lustrous azure emerged as the twilight illuminated lilac bushes dotting the hills.

The nearby scenes were less ethereal and romantic, but no less interesting, clusters of small shops with impatient merchants anxious for closing-time sales and crowds in a festive mood, gay and noisy, sporting bursts of firecrackers in celebration of a spring holiday.

A short way to the east, we came into a section with larger homes and villas whose white walls we had seen from the river. Broken blue and white porcelain mosaic, suggesting huge pieces of Delft pottery, decorated the façades of the homes of the more affluent. Not a few of these walled residences could be seen to have "pleasure grounds" (bistros), tea houses, gardens and orchards. The contrast to the miserable mat-shed hovels squeezed outside the South Gate did not go unnoticed by Wang Shi.

Back in the city not far from the North Gate, we found the courtyard, with its famed little pool in the center, where the beloved poet Tu Fu had lived 1,200 years ago. No signs or displays proclaimed "Tu Fu slept here."

The quiet and simplicity of the place exuded a poignancy, reflecting a bit of the sadness which had marked much of the great poet's life. Early in his life he had failed the imperial examinations and was given an irksome assignment as a minor official. Triumphing over this demeaning apprenticeship, he had won the attention of Emperor Ming Huang, the only benefactor Tu Fu ever had. But upon that emperor's death, Tu Fu suffered disgrace at the hands of his successor.

Here indeed was a great "worthy," perhaps not one of the ten painted by the Song artists, but one whose life had attested to a sensitive and innovative spirit. As a poet, it is said, he took great pains with his composition. He did not match the daring lyrical quality of his contemporary Li Po, or the colorful metaphors and penetrating insights of Chuang Tzi, but Tu Fu was loved as the poet of the people. Greatly admired, he has been often quoted by Chinese through the centuries. Even twelve centuries following his death, he is widely read, loved and respected. A faithful public servant, he is honored for the pain he bore and the empathy he had for the suffering of commoners.

Outside the courtyard gate we found a tiny stall, dusty and dingy. We bought a scroll on which was written, in beautiful calligraphy, Tu Fu's moving poem "Very Able," in which he eulogized the hard and all-too-brief lives of the boatmen and trackers of the gorges.

*The men of the chasms regard death lightly.*
*Few are within the gates of official residence, many are on the water.*
*The wealthy, possessed of money, embark on great vessels.*
*The poor and humble seize their livelihood in tiny boats.*
*Larger youths tie bundles, pack luggage and follow traveling merchants.*
*They attend the sails, the inclined rudder, as it enters the waves and billows;*
*Avoiding whirlpools, carried on by the rushing water, no danger delays them.*
*Just now what strikes the eye is surely a proof,*
*The terrifying embankment is boundless to the sky—the tiger's beard is raging.*
*The old men of Gui Zhou are very able in surmounting these dangers.*

Heading back through the center of the city toward the South Gate in the fast-fading daylight, Wang Shi recalled one of Chuang Tzi's insights we'd talked about the other evening and said, "The wise old philosopher, in his famous 'Autumn Floods,' speaks of the small which reflects the large, and the large which reflects the small."

This concept of the infinite contained within the infinitesimal, of the inextricable connection between the microcosm and the macrocosm, made sense to the major and me. We recalled that the French thinker Pascal had spoken of "nature's immensity in the womb of this abridged atom." The insight encapsulated our experience of Wushan City.

As the night settled upon us we returned to the still-crowded South Gate plaza. Again, as we faced Wushan's city wall, Wang Shi reminded us of the human costs of these walls.

"Let's not forget," he insisted, "these many walls of brick and stone are tributes to the bitter labors of the common people." To make his point, he recited an inscription we had found in Tu Fu's courtyard:

*The iron had entered deeply into his soul and*
*He was a stark realist, portraying the suffering*
*Of the common people in a very moving fashion.*

On our way down the long stone steps a water carrier called out, "Move over or I'll bump you." We obliged him.

When we reached our mooring, we were again fascinated by the river's magic and furor. In the twilight, we saw below us a stream of limpid blue-green water from a small side gorge. Almost before we could identify the stream from which it flowed, it entered and mingled its clear waters with the brown torrent of the great river. Back in our constricted quarters the realities of the seething currents continued to possess us. All our thoughts were again blended with the sounds of rushing water, of the hiss of the crisp surge against the wooden sides of our junk, of seeing the heart of a vicious whirlpool and a feeling again of human impotence and the irresistible power of the wild river. But as we often discovered, on the Long River, periods of contemplative calm alternated with moments of exhilaration or terror.

"The Long River," Wang Shi mused, "reminds Chinese of the flow of history. Like the river the flow of history is but one cycle subsumed under the larger cycle of heaven and earth, of seasons, of renewal and decay. Like the river, also, the stream of our people has been flowing for millennia. So that Chinese historians–unlike what I understand about their Japanese, Jewish or Christian counterparts–are reluctant to assign a temporal beginning or end to the history of the world or the nation. For the culture our 5,000-year history gives us a sense of destiny. For persons, however, the flow of time slaps the individual in the face with the facts of aging and death. These provide inescapable reminders of one's mortality."

Thinking less about the flow either of the river or of China's history, Thompson was more still focused on Wushan. He asked, "Did you find it the special city you anticipated when you saw it from downriver?"

"Yes and no," the major and I both answered. "No, it was no city of Oz," the major said. "Wushan was better. It was for real. A microcosm of China, it well reflects the people and their culture–so old at the core, yet struggling to become new."

The major's reactions started each of us to reflect on the collage we'd gained in this venerable place: ancestral halls, *pailou* arches to memorialize faithful widows, cobblestone streets, narrow alleys with noxious odors, red and yellow temples, gate towers, crowded sidewalk markets, little children playing in courtyards, rings of smoke from curbside braziers, pavement slabs etched by millions of footsteps over thousands of years, plaques and sites of ancient "worthies" and a frightfully costly 30-foot-high wall that was ineffective in keeping ıt invaders and looters.

We wondered how much meaning this sensory tapestry held for the young ıd old around us. We were reminded again of how much of China emerged ɔt from its cities, but from farms and villages surrounding cities like Wushan. ut for ourselves, we knew that what we had seen, smelled, heard, and touched ıat day in Wushan would be preserved in our memories for as long as we lived.

By now, flat on our backs, in our sleeping bags, we gazed up at a black sky nholed with stars. In the awesome darkness we could count all of the leiades, the Seven Sisters, and see the faint little star partway down the handle f the Big Dipper. The Milky Way was a glowing trail of platinum dust cutting ıe blackness in half. Before long, snug in our bedrolls, we were fast asleep.

CHAPTER ELEVEN

# Awe and Terror, Beauty and Death In The Embankment Chasm

*Trackers Strain In Qu Tang Gorge*

The Qu Tang, the most westerly of the Three Gorges, is also the shortest less than seven miles long, and perhaps the most spectacular. The wind and the waves constantly change direction around the headlands and make its current especially treacherous. The gorge forms a corridor so narrow that the river rushing through thunders like a stampede of wild horses. The Chinese ideographs for its name suggest "embankment," "corridor" and "to gaze at terror, and account for how it's variously called the Wind Box Bellows or Terrifying Embankment Gorge.

Legends tell that some 3,500 years ago Yu Wang, the Great God of the Waters, sat on Wu Mountain directing the course of the Long River. The subterranean powers of the rocks of this stretch, called the False Gorge, defied the Great Yu's determination to push the river through. Then Wu Zi, the mighty wizard and resident of the lower Wushan Gorge, in the form of an ape, came to Yu's aid. Breathing fire, he cleaved the hills farther westward by a fearful blast of wind from his nostrils to form the gorge and thereby allow the water to flow through.

The *I Ching* suggests the creation of the Qu Tang, also known as the Terrifying Embankment Chasm, stands as a witness to a basic natural and human process. According to this classic, it was the taming power and handiwork of Da Qu (the great Earth Spirit) that accomplished this:

> *Heaven within the mountain*
> *When innocence (faithfulness to virtue) is present,*
> *It is possible to tame.*
> *Thus the superior man acquaints himself with*
> *Many deeds of the past*
> *In order to strengthen his character.*

In other words, Heaven points to character and virtue. The mountain suggests strength. Decision and bold action are called for. The enlightened one manifests the genuine and the true. To go forward may be uncertain, but to hold back is dangerous.

These men, Wang Shi explained, believe that spirits of the past from the World of Shade revisit the scenes of their earthly sojourn. Given this, the spirits of the heroes of the Terrifying Embankment Chasm must also return for visits.

The portals of the Terrifying Embankment, or Wind Box Gorge, are guarded by Cat Rock, which lies at the end of the race created by Long Snake Reef. The current sent tremors through the *wu ban*. Terraced shelves of black rock and giant spurs, ominous enough at low water, produced dangerous passages at high level.

Two millennia ago, when China's strongest kingdoms were in this section, the Long River provided strategic access to eastern peoples. Since it serves as a portal from eastern Sichuan to western Hubei province, it is often referred to as the *Qu Tang Xia* (Gateway Gorge), as the Chinese say, "the valve which controls the waters of the Long River." Contemporary hydraulic engineers have proposed building dams here to harness the river's force.

The cliffs rose more than a thousand feet. Some background peaks soared a mile high, their tips flirting among wisps of clouds during bright sunshine and bathed in gloom during rainy weather.

On the south bank opposite Heroes Coffin Cliff were rock formations that had stirred the fantasies of the ancients. One was called Cattle Horn Looking at the Moon, and strangely was associated with the paradox, "Become rich if you have the money." Another had been dubbed *Kongqueyin Quan*, Peacock's Drinking Fountain). Still another was titled *Daodiaohe Shang*, Upside-down Hanging Monk), a derisive epitaph to an unfaithful monk who betrayed his ruler.

Behind the south-bank cliffs was a row of lofty peaks, the highest of which was White Salt Mountain. On the north bank was Ji Jia Mountain, soaring

2,000 feet above the river. Shaped like a ripe peach, it was known as Peach Mountain among the local people. Under the bright sun it glowed, and so it was also called Huoyen Shan, or Flaming Mountain.

Seen from a junk struggling in the current far below, these cliffs appeared to slant inward, narrowing the sky to a ribbon. The waters of the Terrifying Embankment Chasm stirred feelings of careening through a crack in the earth. The Water Barrier Corridor, with rock walls standing sheer on both banks, was magnificent and ominous .

On a flat rock on a cliff midway through the gorge, Emperor Tao Kuan had long ago placed an iron pillar. As ruler of the *Shu*, he had ordered chains to be stretched across the river to prevent junks from carrying salt to Hubei, the province to the east, which was also the seat of the kingdom with which he was at war.

The sobering vistas, perilous passages and tactical importance inspired 8th-century poets Li Bai (Li Po), Tu Fu and Lu You to write romantic verses dear to Chinese hearts. Scores of the country's well-loved novelists and dramatists also felt the throb of this region and penned imaginative stories and plays about Qu Tang Gorge's splendors and dangers.

Quiet and melancholy during low water, the gorge became a torrent when melting snows in Tibet poured down. At low water the red sandstone narrowed the river to scarcely two hundred yards. At its flood stage, the waters often rose a hundred feet transforming the river into a demon. Silty yellow waters dashed from wall to wall, boiling around half-submerged rocks and breaking into whirlpools. Junks bound upstream could spend days navigating this gorge. When especially dangerous calloused Chinese junkmen would not enter it.

On the south bank, opposite the eastern gateway town of Daixizhen, was a small tributary with the fanciful name of Da Qu, or Great Stream. The skipper steered our junk to a landing where we put ashore the remaining reserve trackers.

The skipper ordered the huge lug sail hoisted and all oarsmen and yulows-men to begin pulling. We needed maximum power to move our *wu ban* through the raging current in the Kitten Race and the Get-Down-From-Horse Cataracts ahead.

Between the two cataracts the bowmen of an eastbound junk yelled to our skipper that the river had risen 20 feet in three days. The feared black Goose Tail Rock at the western mouth of the gorge now submerged, was more hazardous than usual. We would encounter fast water in the 300-yard channel ahead. Trackers and oarsmen would have to use their strength sparingly, saving it for the heavier current and more treacherous eddies of the Fengxiang, (Wind Box or Bellows) section of the gorge.

As we made our way through the Kitten Race, the drum signals were for ready pulling by oarsmen and trackers. Although we grazed one after another rock, we emerged safe. Following a short breather, we began plowing through the Get-Down-From-Horse Cataracts. All through this rocky chasm, trackers ashore and rowers aboard strained, tugging the junk against the convulsions.

The river jerked the junk as if it were a toy. This jerking made it difficult for the trackers to keep a steady pull on the bamboo hawser. With recent rains having washed out portions of their path, the trackers' footing was in constant jeopardy, and the rhythm of their steps was often disrupted. The sudden breaks in their pulling chorus gave foreboding signals about the troubles they were encountering.

"Look ahead on the north bank," broke in the cook. "See the rows of caves there. They're long and thin. That is the Chinese Wind Box." We saw deep-gouged crevices on the limestone that gave the impression of a bellows. Entering the funnel made by the lofty walls on either side, we were struck with strong gusts of wind.

"Take another look," the cook continued, "and you'll see the famous rock coffins–formations that resemble the ends of coffins sticking out from the cliff."

These cliff tombs were all the rage in Sichuan during Han times. They predated Buddhist cave temples and burial sites. Murals show primitive men bearing torches, cutting holes in the sheer rock faces to erect temporary scaffolding. The entrance shafts were dug into the rock and gravel of the hillside and lined with stone blocks. The tomb chambers were hewn from solid rock.

Wang Shi added that legend has it that these were the coffins of heroes placed in their lofty sepulcher by the wizard Wu Zi as a tribute to their valiant deeds. He explained that recent research had shown that these caves were a burial site during the time of the Warring States (403-221 B.C.). Nine different coffins, with various funerary objects, had been excavated.

Farther upriver, on the face of a cliff, we saw a zigzag line of square holes. These were where the Song dynasty (A.D. 963-1127) General Meng Liang from Hubei province cut an escape ladder for his beleaguered army. Known as Meng the Good for his bravery and loyalty to his brother-in-arms Qiao Zan, Meng became commander-in-chief when his superior, Yang the Extended Brilliant, was killed in battle. While advancing upriver to attack the city of Kuifu, Meng Liang was trapped in the gorge by enemy forces who had secured both ends of the chasm. Genius that he was, he ordered holes 14 inches square and two feet deep cut in the rock and then had wooden beams inserted. His men were thus able to scale the cliff, reach the plateau, catch Meng's foes unawares and defeat them..

On a promontory opposite Meng Liang's ladder we saw the remnants of the White Emperor's city, built by the great Shu Kingdom ruler, Kungsun. In 25 A.D. Kungsun succeeded in establishing the independence of his kingdom from Emperor Juangwu of the Han dynasty. During construction of the city, a white dragon supposedly appeared to him from out of a well, so he chose white as his color and gave his city this name. Long ago it was a citadel, protected by water on three sides and by the Wushan Mountains behind. Formerly a walled town, it guarded the break in the mountains called Kuimen Gate.

The place was roughly half-way along the Long River's 450 mile stretch between Chongqing and Yichang. From the waters' edge emerged the proverbial "ten thousand steps." An ancient temple at the top, the cook told us housed the beginnings of a museum displaying some of the region's recent archeological findings. The artifacts included calligraphy carved in stone tablets and dioramas with life-sized statues of historical and mythological figures. The buildings in the background were the villa of the contemporary Guomindang poet-general Wu Peifu.

Long before Europeans had known Charlemagne and William the Conqueror, the precarious path in the rock 60 feet above the high-water mark of the river had been hand-hewn by workmen whose only tools were mallets and chisels. The deep gash in the rock wall was illumined by the particular angle of the sun. The brilliant rays highlighted details of the trackers' life-and-death toil. We saw the trail, like a tunnel with one side open. Surely, often enough they must have gashed their arms and legs on the jagged rock walls. All the while, death waited for any tracker hapless enough to stray but a few inches from the trail.

In the channel below, the sweepmen maneuvered around a rock outcropping and the skipper steered farther into midstream. The towline tightened and the trackers above hugged the inner wall to keep from being pulled off the trail. Suddenly the already tight hawser jerked. The effect on the pullers was horrifying. The last two trackers were wrenched from the tunnel and swung screaming out over the river, suspended only by their bandoliers. The lead tracker ordered his men to keep moving forward, lest the junk get dragged back and pull more trackers over the cliff.

The unflappable first officer worked to draw the junk closer to the shore to ease the gathering tension on the towline in hopes of swinging the two unfortunates back onto the trail. The trackers in front of the fallen ones squeezed against the inner wall of the tunnel, bearing the weight of the ones over the edge. By keeping the hawser taut, they maintained their share of the junk's drag. As the vessel drew closer to shore, the two dangling trackers were whipped against the cliff.

Every second the imperiled men's screams became more desperate. Since they had been the last two of the column, the effort to haul them up over the edge and back on the trail depended on the next in line, who were the youngest, weakest and least experienced. Nevertheless, their fellows tried frantically to lift the two back up onto the trail. By this time, the lead tracker was ffering what limited help the tight space and his strength allowed.

The skipper on the *wu ban* below had to decide. At stake were cargo, junk, assengers, crew and other trackers.

"Cut them off!" he shouted, "Quickly, quickly!"

The lead tracker above drew a blade and hacked at the taut slings holding ne men.

"Faster, faster!" the skipper shouted, "the junk is slipping back!" The second tracker's sustaining band was severed first, then the one in front of him.

Both plummeted, then thrashed in the convulsed brown current. Blue coat-ails emerged and then two heads and pairs of arms battling the torrent. They ere dragged under, then bobbed up again. Help was not available from the sual guard-swimmers, because, with too little space for walking at the base of ne cliff, they had been put on the tracking line above.

"A yah! A yah! A yah!" shrieked trackers and crewmen alike. The oblivion ney'd constantly feared now possessed them. A ghastly silence, broken only by ne river's battering of the rocks, swallowed us.

The first officer bounded to the stern and jumped into the sampan we had a tow. He swung oars into place, and the tiny skiff heaved. Whirling away, he nouted over the tumult words of hope to the two struggling trackers whom e would save if he could.

The trembling skipper ordered the drummer to signal a faster pace. The eavier beat became a funereal rhythm reverberating between the cliffs. The ad tracker, back at the head of his pullers, broke out in a refrain we hadn't eard before. The usual lilt was absent, and the tune he voiced was sober and eliberate. The measured antiphonal response of the trackers became deeper nd more unified. Like the tough bamboo towline, there were many strands: ar of personal death, anger at the dehumanizing conditions of the boatman's fe and helplessness in the face of the life-taking river that rendered individu-s expendable. The lead tracker again sounded his melancholic melody, and ne trackers' response displayed a renewed resolve to survive the river.

River demons were claiming two of our number. The crew knew they were aught up in powers greater than themselves. Mesmerized, we passengers oticed little else around us. An eternity crowded into this moment.

Navigating the final miles of the gorge called for the crew's extreme exertion nd coordination. The heavier than usual drag on the towline strained hearts as ell as muscles. The current so rolled and yawed the junk that our oarsmen found hard, as one of them said, "for the oar to get a bite of the river." Foot by tor-rous foot, the junk moved along the Terrible Embankment Chasm.

Rounding a bend, on the south shore, we approached the magnificent Gui Ien, a 1,500-foot rock wall rising sheer from the river. It reminded me of rock faces I'd seen in the Alps and the High Sierra. The name comes from th ancient Kingdom of Gui, said to have existed at the beginning of the Sprin and Autumn Period (770-476 B.C.) The *gui*, a mythical dragon-like creatur with a single hind leg, is thought to have been the totem of a local tribe. Fc those traveling west, Gui Men provides the western exit to the Qu Tang Gorg

It was only minutes, though it seemed like days, before the westerly mout of the gorge was in sight. Approaching the exit, we neared the enormous ser tinel *Yen Yu Dui* (Goose Tail Rock) that pierced the angry waters and divide the channel. At low water, this polished, black, spiraling mass towered abov the surface. The subject of many poems, the Chinese also called it Whirlin Water Rock. When it was submerged and thus an unpredictable dange authorities at the city five miles upstream did not allow junks to go downstrea until it reappeared.

The major called to our attention the river's force as it tumbled abou Goose Tail. "A hell of a job for the boatmen to pull us against such force!" h commented.

With the unyielding efforts of the oarsmen and trackers, in time, the *wu ba* was pulled into calmer waters west of the gorge. We passengers, numbed froi the awful happening, had said nothing.

"A tracker's life," Thompson broke our silence, "is hitched to the towlin For a short while he's attached, then suddenly he's cut off and dies." The con ment shook the major and me out of our shock.

Wang Shi tried to distract us with the history of these parts. Like WuSha Qu Tang had been the site of much political, military and literary activity.

Liu Bei the Prepared and his prime minister, Zhuge Liang, were two loc: heroes. Liu was a benevolent ruler who listened to the counsel of his ministe whose name became a synonym for devotion and loyalty. So completely did Li Bei the Prepared and Zhuge Liang act in unison that shrines to the officer ar always placed beside those erected to his master. As the story goes, the youn ruler was depressed and in ill health following a humiliating defeat. He sent fc his minister to inform him of his abdication of the throne. But the faithfu Zhuge Liang, his voice choked with tears, declared that he could only serv descendants of the Han dynasty. He then uttered words for which he has bee famous ever since: "My body shall toil; I will suffer and exert myself to the la: extremity. Only after death has come shall my service have an end."

Another venerated spirit was the much-loved poet Du Fu, who spent tw years on the shores of Terrifying Embankment Chasm and left a record of hi impressions in five volumes of poetry. Some he wrote when, exiled to the edg of the empire, he was ill and despondent, separated from his loved ones, dis contented and isolated. He compensated by writing of the grandeur and awe someness of the scenery about him. "The endowments of nature, howeve

and triumphant!"

*The kingfisher color is deep—it opens the sheer-cut wall.*
*The far-off red is knotted with the flying pavilion.*
*The sun comes up as I gaze at the bright river.*
*The soft warmth dispels the stranger's grief.*
*The shadow of the chasm enters deep into the river.*

Other poetry about salt wells, fish, women gathering firewood and fathers careless in arranging marriages further displayed his sensitivity. Regarding inequities, corruption and oppression he also spoke the truth. "The manners and customs of the land are bad."

Out of the Qu Tang Xia or Wind Box Gorge, with its legends and references, we entered a less spectacular but nevertheless engaging section of the river. We passed temples on craggy spurs above picturesque villages. Cliffs gave way to valleys with manicured miniature farms. Distant forest-covered mountains, which would become snow-splashed in winter, provided a majestic backdrop.

The cook identified a tributary we passed as Stinking Salt Stream. It was the natural salt springs said to have been discovered by a beggar during the reign of Emperor Xian Feng. Flowing from a bed of shingle, the salt water is evaporated in large iron pans. The salt is then recovered by men from the nearby village only when the water is not too high to cover the flats.

Toward twilight, on the far horizon above the right bank, peculiar tornado twists of darkness connected earth and sky. We made out curls of eerie gray smoke rising against the sunset. The cook, never missing a chance to serve as instructor, told us that was steam from the brine boilers for which Feng Jie city was known. We were lucky, he said, to see this because the season's work would soon be cut off with the river rising and so curtailing travel. He whetted our curiosity by telling us about the city of Feng Jie, known as the Venice of the Long River. Once the seat of kings, it was still romantic with sing-song girls in sampans and gondola-like boats that plyed the side streams.

A hour later, we pulled into a flotilla of junks on the north bank, just east of the salt-producing city. The cook had been especially busy in this last stretch of calmer water, preparing an extra kettle of rice and a large wok of vegetables for the crew who had not been able to eat all day. He started the first shift as soon as we made fast to the mooring stakes. Acting as priest, the cook portioned out three servings that would have gone to the two lost trackers and the first officer. The squatting trackers attacked their servings, working their chopsticks double time. Bolting their first offerings, they returned for seconds.

Finished, the boatmen rose from their haunches, rolled out their mats on the midship deck and laid down in a row like a series of ten pins. They were too exhausted for their usual rehash of the day's happenings. The exception was Lao Liu, the lead oarsman, who had lost his father and two brothers to the river and today had lost his favorite nephew. On the poop deck, the skipper puffed on his pipe, staring vacantly.

We passengers were physically knotted and emotionally spent. We talked of the lot of these snoring boatmen sprawled next to us from the galley to the bow. From the way they jerked and broke wind in their sleep, we were aware that however idealized we viewed them during the day, in their twitching sleep they lost their aura.

Perhaps it was "natural" that these men became boatmen, but we asked "Was it natural that they should sweat and toil, live and die the way they did? What did they have to hold onto beyond mere survival?" Whatever the attitude that sustained them, it was not one that included much hope of liberation.

# Fengjie, City Of Brine, Coal And Ghosts

*Fengie's Poet's Gate*   *Photo enhanced by Helen Houser*

Courtesy Caroline Walker

The pall of yesterday's tragedy darkened the new day's colorful sunrise. A haunting silence pervaded all on board. Lao Ma, the skipper's usually articulate wife, held her tongue and glowered at the river's churning. Oarsmen, trackers and bowmen stared blankly at one another. Wang Shi alternated his attention between the river and the immobile crew as if pondering the tragic character of life.

The major, Thompson and I continued shaken by having two of the trackers we'd talked and joked with washed away. All we could do now was to calculate their chances of survival. And, of course, we wondered about the fate of the esteemed first officer. Feelings over the strong likelihood of loss drew crew and passengers closer together. We shared a sense of helplessness. Each of us was numbed by the immediacy of death–we had to reckon with our own mortality, making it difficult to focus on simple tasks. The prospect of exploring Guifu, now called Fengjie, where we were moored, gave little lift to our spirits. Dulled, we found few positive feelings to prepare for later in the day, negotiating two minor rapids and making a stop at Yunyang, the next city west.

Bowls of rice gruel in hand, Lao Liu, the cook, the skipper and Wang Shi. squeezed around us. For once they didn't gulp down their food. Instead, they shared their feelings. Listening, we heard their differing grief voices. As with the actors in a Greek tragedy, time, place and action were welded. Each showed how with the loss of crew members something of their own selves were lost.

Lao Liu, the untutored oarsman, suffered the greatest personal loss: his nephew, as close to him as a son, was the one person who could help him climb out of poverty. The deprivations that had been his lot from birth would continue. Lao Liu shook his head and, staring into the distance toward the rising sun, sadly said, "In a flash, the inevitable strikes down even the strongest. *Mei you ban fa* (there's no way to beat it)."

The cook expressed his sadness by making a rite out of food-serving. By word and manner he gave the day's first meal symbolic meaning. Ladling out the morning's gruel, he added words of personal assurance to each crewman. Though a lapsing Buddhist, and by no means a Christian, he nevertheless conveyed the impression of a clergyperson presiding at a Communion table. It was as if, with each serving of rice, he was saying, "Take, eat. . .in remembrance of____." This hallowing of their simple fare seemed to help the crew cope with their fears.

The skipper tightened his belt, fastened his tattered jacket and stood taller than usual. The loss seemed to have sent a steel rod down his spine. Loosening his usually tight lips, he commented, "Such sorrow must be lived away, not into. Though very lamentable, such accidents must be accepted. Only a thin line divides life from death. It is especially so traveling the San Xia (Three Gorges).

"*Wo bu zhi dao* (I don't know)," was his answer to my anxious question about the possibility that the three had been saved. Shaking his head, he admitted that the first officer's prospects of rescuing the two fallen trackers were slim. "But if anything could be done," he said, "the first officer was the man to do it." He added, "That officer is *shi fen hao di* (ten parts genuinely great)." I hope we will find him waiting at one of our moorings on the downriver trip."

Wang Shi, unnerved from the time he had disentangled himself from his bedroll, had been quiet up 'til now. His hand showed a slight tremor as he held his bowl of gruel.

"Our crew," he observed pensively, "being mostly superstitious villagers, no doubt are guarded, lest in thinking the worst, they bring more death about. What thoughts about death they allow themselves are wrapped in fatalism. They most likely anticipate the conventional responses of rural communities: sobbing women, expensive coffins, funeral processions and necromancer's recommendations for grave sites."

Finishing his rice, he voiced some of his other feelings: "In China death is always near. We see it often and, as most humans, are unnerved by it. Depressed moods, loss of treasured possessions and harvest failures disturb us greatly, but death is the most disturbing of all—especially the sudden death of young, active friends. The skipper is right: for Chinese the line between life and death is thin. Death stalks life and leaves no family unscathed. While I was growing up, one brother and one sister of mine died as infants, while disease and accidents took two uncles and three cousins. The life expectancy of a Chinese is now only 40 years. No Chinese is untouched by a fear of death: infant mortality, fatal accidents, natural disasters, recurrent wars devastating entire regions, bringing death often and close."

"For the more thoughtful Chinese," said Wang Shi, setting down his rice bowl with chopsticks laid across the rim and moving over to sit on the gunwale. "A recurrent question is the one Li Zhi, a revolutionary 17th-century intellectual, asked: 'As man is born for some good reason, how can he die but for some good cause?' In his famous essay, 'Five Ways to Die,' he gave his answer: Death for a worthy cause was the finest, followed by death in battle, death as a martyr, death as a loyal minister unfairly calumniated and premature death after finishing some good piece of work. According to Li Zhi, then, we should rather ask whether our two trackers died for 'some good cause.'"

"For Westerners in China," Thompson quickly added, "It's the millions upon millions who die without 'some good cause' that's China's appalling tragedy."

The unsophisticated responses of Lao Liu, the cook and the skipper to the challenge to their mortality impressed Thompson and moved him to cite the biblical verse: "For the worldly are more astute than the other-worldly in dealing with sudden catastrophe (Luke 16.8)." Then reflecting on China's chronic political upheavals he had lived through in the last 20 years, he added: "Hundreds of thousands died from the convulsive struggles that finally brought down the moribund Manchu empire in 1911. Conditions never settled after the 1911 revolution."

"An incalculable number died in the political upheavals of the 19th century," I put in. "Many killings resulted from resistance to the Western powers' interventions in the 1840 and 1860 Opium Wars and the 1900 Tientsin-Peking Expeditions. But most costly was the Tai P'ing Rebellion, occurring about the same time as our Civil War, which took an estimated 20,000,000 lives."

"Throughout the 20th century the Chinese have experienced a series of death-dealing upheavals. After the 1911 Revolution came one violent regime after another spreading death. In the late '20s, came the killings connected with Chiang Kai-shek's Northern Expeditional War of Unification and the beginnings of his campaigns to 'exterminate' the Communists. In the '30s, the Japanese began their invasion, which cost the lives of at least 10,000,000 Chinese."

"Yes," interrupted Wang Shi, "I experienced part of that slaughter firsthand. I was only a boy ten years ago when the Japanese entered and raped Nanjing. One estimate has it that at least 300,000 Chinese were slaughtered in the five-day rampage. I shall never forget seeing torn bodies everywhere."

"The killing of our people goes on," he continued. With the Guomindang's stepped-up witch hunts and the fast spreading civil war, blood

is again running in the streets. Today political executions, open conflicts and man-made famines (caused by blockades) bring death to more millions. Protesters are slaughtered as they rise against governments that have been cruel, corrupt and unjust. Our Chinese revolutions, like the Great Wall, are built on corpses. So many innocents, usually enlisted under duress, are the first casualties. They are our martyrs and heroes. There is not a village or a part of a town which did not lose dozens of its youth commandeered by either the Guomindang or Gungchandang (Chinese Communists)."

"You'd better go ashore to see some of the city," the cook insisted as he finished cleaning the galley. "Eager hucksters and would-be-escorts into the old city are waiting for you on the pontoon out there. Feng Jie is revered as the City of Ghosts and is said to beckon souls after death. People's lives are judged after they cross the city's suspension bridge and either enter nirvana or plunge into hell. Despite its otherworldly connections it's worth your visit. It's a center for coal mining and a brine processing. You can see parts of the 2000 year-old City Wall and one of the still standing Gates."

Without further words he was off to market fresh supplies.

The skipper pulled himself out of his gloom and started ashore to talk with neighboring skippers about replacing the lost lifeboat. He said he would go along the embankment to a shipwright with whom he could bargain for another small sampan. As he crossed the floppy gangplank, he muttered, "I wish I could dicker to find another *ten-parts-good* first officer."

As the crew finished their routine jobs, we passengers rolled up our bedrolls and packed our knapsacks. With prospective guides pressing around the *wu ban*, it was time to enter this bustling city of Fengjie on the bank above us.

Fengjie had the longest set of steps we'd

*Column Of Salt Carriers*

149

et seen. When we reached the top we faced the South Gate and the remnants of what had been the extensive city wall. The entrance was about 18 feet high and 20 feet wide. Above were inscribed three ideographs, including the pictographic character men (or gate). When it was rebuilt during the Qing Dynasty, it was named Poet's Gate.

On either side of the Gate the once-20-foot wall simply disappeared into the surrounding buildings. Like so many things in China, the once-mighty walls, with their strategic and social importance were gone. At various times in history, the tamped earth ramparts may have been faced with brick or stone, but both those materials are eminently reusable and much in demand. We passed through Poet's Gate, appreciating it as a serendipitous remnant of the old city and its entire valley.

The major, Wang Shi and I accepted Thompson's suggestion that we visit one of the local industries.

On our way to a salt-processing plant, Wang Shi briefed us on the historic significance of salt and its production and distribution in China. Important for its dietary, medicinal and preservative uses, salt also possessed symbolic and religious significance. From antiquity, the importance of salt had expanded far beyond its basic culinary usages. Chinese artisans used salt in leather-working, enamel-making and chemical-processing. As salt's importance in Chinese life expanded, it also became susceptible to unauthorized production, widespread corruption, smuggling, theft and embargoes.

*Steaming Vats Of Brine*

The combination of trade volume, aggregate worth and the development of means to control it made extraction of revenue from salt production and distribution a compelling issue for Chinese rulers. Its primacy in the life of the people and the comparative ease of gaining a monopoly made salt an ideal commodity to control and tax. Early in Chinese history, salt became a major source of government revenue.

In China salt is derived from three sources: brine from wells, sea water and crystals mined from dry salt lakes. It is processed by solar evaporation or boiling. The largest share of the country's salt comes from the coast, particularly the Lianghuai solar and boiling evaporation yards north and south of the Huai River. That obtained from mining salt beds has had chiefly local significance.

Sichuan has produced its own salt in numerous local industries that date back at least 2,500 years. Large underground solid salt or brine deposits were accompanied by beds of coal and pockets of natural gas. These additional resources made it possible for the brine to be boiled with gas conveyed by bamboo pipes. With much patience and labor, wells were drilled that reached depths of 3,000 feet. High-concentration brine was drawn up by long buckets attached to a windlass, then taken by shoulder pole or bamboo pipe to the evaporators. This supply of salt was licensed to provide Sichuan and the neighboring provinces of Guizhou and Yunnan, but it was often smuggled downriver through the gorges to compete illegally with sea salt from the Lianghua works along the coast. Except for distant mountainous areas, almost all bulk salt was transported by junk on the intricate river systems above and below the Three Gorges.

The major, Wang Shi and I walked eastward toward the cluster of nearby salt-processing units. On a cleared section of the riverbank, we found enormous, half-buried, steaming cauldrons, emitting a caustic spray. Underneath bricked-in natural gas burners, fired day and night, kept the brine boiling. Above the giant pots, illuminated by the slanting rays of the morning sun, the steam resembled vapors escaping around active volcanoes. Teams of coolies streaked with perspiration and encrusted with gray-black ash, tended the fires.

On raised platforms, the cauldron stirrers, their noses covered with tied rags, strained with long-handled paddles. Stripped to the waist, they wore no protective aprons or gloves. On the side away from the cauldrons were pits which stored chunks of raw rock salt mixed with brine solutions for the seething cast-iron pots.

Up and down from the huge conical wells, on slippery paths, hundreds of near-naked men–some mere youths–toiled with their heavy, brine-laden buckets. Another stream of sweating carriers wound downward for refills. These brine carriers were not tied to a towline. Instead, their two swinging wooden buckets dangled from bamboo poles that seemed to be fastened to their shoulders. Instead of rock ledges and unforgiving currents, these workers faced the filth, burns and fumes. They functioned as a human conveyor belt.

From dawn until sundown one shift labored, and from sundown to dawn another. This was no dream, no Dantean fantasy. This was slave labor on a massive scale. We circled from the brink of one huge conical pit to another, and in each place we saw the same pattern of human exploitation. These worker's bovine acceptance of servitude was pathetic. Their submission stirred us with pain and anger.

"Another awful injustice!" Wang Shi broke out. "The system that allows such degradation is terribly wrong. It's the brine plant owners and the wealthy city salt merchants who need changing, not the laborers. Radical changes are long overdue!"

The major, engineer that he was, suggested that modern equipment could easily free millions of coolies from such demeaning labor. A large submersible pump with salt-resistant pipes, he explained, could be installed to bring the brine up from the pits. Such machines could be purchased at reasonable prices and easily maintained.

"But, Major," countered Wang Shi, "we have little foreign exchange to pay for such equipment. We have so many mouths to feed. Menial as their jobs are, the pittance pay they get provides them with money to buy rice and rags. Coolies are considered expendable. Without capital to purchase pumps and pipes, coolies will have to go on scooping up the briny mud with their buckets."

A tracker arrived to call us back to the boat. Both the skipper and the cook had returned, and our junk was ready to sail to the nearby city of Yunyang. Shortly after we boarded, the sweepmen cast off.

Pulling away from our mooring the cook pointed to the mine shafts which seem to have been dug straight into the rocky banks. Fengjie, he explained, is a major coal center. We saw how the miners simply dumped the laden ore carts down the slope and dock workers shoveled it into baskets and carried it onto barges.

We saw a dreamy hill on the left, once the site of the ancient stronghold of the White Emperor's City, which flourished in the days of the Three Kingdoms (3rd century A.D.). Instead of the antique temples and stone tablets that had stood there for centuries, the area was spread with the gaudy, pseudo-foreign palace of Wu Pei Fu, a warlord in the 1920's.

A brisk wind at our stern helped the junk move upriver at a steady pace. Blue and silver fissured limestone cliffs hemmed us in. The cleavages in the walls, looking like rouged lips, were pierced by sprays of cascading streams.

Before long we entered a double channel with the inner one narrowing with reddish-gray sandstone walls.

Before noon, the trackers were put ashore to help pull us through the next series of minor rapids. The first, called Lao Ma, or Old Horse, was long and rough, but minor compared with the others we had struggled through. The second, Miao Jizi, or Temple Stairs, had a swift channel in its center. Once clear, we saw the outlines of Yunyang, City of the Clouded Sun. Like Fengjie its brine-processing plants poured clouds of saline steam into the skies.

Within two hours we approached Yunyang, a small city in a glen scooped out from the surrounding mountains. The skipper steered the *wu ban* into the fast-flowing tributary the city straddled. Again, for our convenience, he chose a central mooring a short distance from Yunyang's central stairs.

# Cloud City's Temple, Mission And Inquirers

Ascending Yunyang's daunting set of steps to the city's main entrance, instead of columns of water carriers, we had to make way for haulers of twelve-foot stone building slabs. Inside the central plaza the early afternoon's lull had thinned the number of vendors. Morning produce stalls were closed, but clothing and dry-goods were open with salesmen tending a sprinkling of customers. On the side streets tin smiths, carpenters, weavers and other artisans were busy in their side-walk workshops. In front of the few tiny houses squeezed between the shops grannies doted over toddlers playing in their wicker roller-carts.

Walking up a knoll, we came to the Palace of the Patron Saint of Literature. Looking more like a museum than a residence, its 300 year-old buildings were distinct for their green-and yellow-tiled roofs. Beyond the central section we found the Temple of Longevity, with curved roofs and large red columns. Inside, its walls were decorated in high relief and adorned with bronze tablets. We came upon residences distinguished by black beams and white gables. On the outskirts of town, bungalows surrounded by blooming orange trees dotted the slopes.

Citizens were proud of the jeweled memorial temple nestled on the opposite bank. Frequented by boatmen seeking a blessing for their voyage, the more worldly shoot off firecrackers to frighten away evil spirits.

The flimsy, leaky and overloaded ferry we took to cross the river was anything but reassuring. The major and Thompson found spots on cross-boards. Wang Shi and I sat on our haunches, squeezed by the additional passengers the ferrymen kept accepting. As we got underway, Wang Shi pointed to the *Longji Shi* (Dragon Spine Stone) midstream, an ominous rock pile over which the copper waters were crashing. An old custom, he said, was for young couples to row out to the rock in the third lunar month to sacrifice a chicken to ensure a good year. Local boatmen sang a song that claims the rock grows or shrinks to help or hinder passage. With overloaded sampan nearly capsizing, I had little interest in the Dragon Spine Rocks.

By the Almighty's grace and the phenomenal skill of the four determined oarsmen, we made the crossing without incident. From the rickety make-shift landing covering the slippery shoreline rocks we turned right and climbed the 150 steep steps to the temple.

On the face of the vertical cliff we climbed to the temple were four enormous ideographs that read: *Ethereal, Bell, Thousand, Ages.* Near the top, amid the graffiti and markings of countless pilgrims, was the inscription: "Let us unite as one, against great gusts of wind."

This temple was erected to honor the Three Kingdoms warrior-ruler Zhang Fei and his colleagues Liu Bei the Prepared and Guan Yü the Just Counselor. The three became sworn brothers, having made a famous oath in a peach orchard. According to accounts in China's much-loved historical novel *Romance of the Three Kingdoms,* they performed heroic deeds.

The short-lived League they forged was fraught with tragedy. Guan Yü was assassinated and Zhang Fei was captured and executed. Though a memorable warrior, Zhang Fei proved an impetuous and arbitrary administrator. He incurred his people's wrath when, in his grief over the deaths of his two brothers-in-arms, he ordered unreasonable mourning observances. Ten thousand white grief garments had to be cut, tailored and ready in three days to clothe each of his soldiers. Finding this and other such orders intolerably harsh, his officers murdered the hero.

Zhang Fei was so feared by his enemies that his head was buried in the temple and his body in Shensi province, 700 miles to the north. Posthumous glory and reverence accumulated around his character and led to his being extolled in Chinese drama and verse.

The temple bell was believed to ring of its own accord in case of fire in the district. The temple had three courts, one three-storied pavilion, another two-storied one and a central Friendship Tower. Porches with ornate balustrades surrounded the Great Hall. Curled roofs were decorated with blazing green. Corridors made of elaborate wood filigree carved in a peony motif, connected the courts. Pilgrims from afar lit firecrackers to foil demons. Petitioners knelt, prayed and made offerings. The incense they burned sent smoke curling up into the dusty eaves. The walls were lined with fine old things, and wizen monks peddled scrolls and paintings.

Beside the temple was a deep, narrow glen with a well-kept garden and woods. In the background was a bridal falls. Over it, an arched stone bridge started upward from the temple's south gate. Nature and the work of the designers and builders of centuries long gone had combined to make the tem-

ple an architectural gem. The *feng xui* (location of water and the temple's position on the hill) were correct.

To return we risked another precarious crossing in the same dilapidated
ferry. We did not want to keep our skipper waiting.

Back at our mooring, however, the skipper told us our departure would b
delayed for several hours. The cook suggested we visit the Catholic missior
located near the Drum Tower and not far from the West Gate.

When we reached the mission the gnarled gateman turned our calling card
over and over and took his time limping off toward the compound's centra
building to summon his superior.

Nearby was the grammar school where students chanted their lessons
Chinese education was in progress! Each class, with its particular repetition o
set phrases, seemed trying to outdo the others.

Soon we saw a slender, graying priest emerge from one of the classrooms
surrounded by children breaking for recess. Surprised by the rare appearanc
of three Westerners, he introduced himself as Father Albert in French-accent
ed English. He was elated to have visitors especially those interested in his cen
ter.

With his enthusiasm rising, the Father had much to show us. After walking
through the dispensary, Father Albert took us to the moderate-sized sanctuar
at the far end of the courtyard. Close to the entrance, in an adjoining chapel
three elderly women with rosaries knelt in prayer, reminding me of worshiper
in Paris' Notre Dame or New York's St. Patrick's Cathedral.

At the chancel steps, one of the black-gowned Chinese padres was leading
a funeral rosary for an extended family. While Father Albert lingered in the
narthex with Thompson, the major, Wang Shi and I joined the worshiper
around a white casket.

The deceased, a 73-year-old father of six, was from an outlying village
Months ago his eldest son had brought him in to the mission's dispensary or
the back of a bicycle. The diagnosis had been inoperable colon cancer. The
family did not tell the old man, but he knew his end was not far away when hi
son began giving him better food than usual.

Years before, the gentleman had come to town and bought his own buria
suit, a black gown with a formal jacket and black cloth shoes to match. Only
"semi-believer," the man had secured from a Buddhist friend a "soul passport,"
a certificate into the life beyond, which his wife had sewn into the burial gown
The two older sons had become Christians during their attendance at a missior
school. Though they had gone along with the village's burial practices, they
had also brought the body to the church for a Christian memorial service.

Father Albert then took us past the gatehouse to the rectory and the priests sidences. The flower beds lining the path showed more care than the disrepaired entrance walkway with its broken tile slabs.

Over tea the priest put aside his initial shyness and warmed to the opportunity of having an audience of Westerners. With each question we raised, he became more animated. Upon his arrival in China at the age of 26, fresh from seminary in Louvain, Belgium, he had begun his service in Shanghai. Completing his language study at the Zikawei Catholic Training Center, he had traveled the 800 miles to Yichang by steamship and then upriver to Yunyang by junk.

By this time we were joined by Father Liu En, the distinguished looking Chinese senior priest whom we had seen officiating at the funeral. Together they told us of the severe trials churches, schools and dispensaries had experienced since the mission's beginnings in 1870.

The two pointed to the framed portraits of the pioneer priests who had guided the mission's work through the early decades. Centered in the row of portraits was a slender, almost gaunt priest, the brilliant Father Marcel. Below was the inscription, "Buildings should be places from which we go to work rather than at which we work." During the 1900 Boxer Rebellion, he and three Chinese priests were dragged out the East Gate and beheaded for their faith.

Before World War I, Catholic missionaries stressed direct evangelism rather than new schools or hospitals. In retrospect, this course of action cost the defection of Chinese intellectuals who sought training for their offspring.

"Those who broke away from Catholicism," Father Albert commented wryly, "became *de facto* materialistic rationalists."

By the end of World War I, Catholicism seemed to have reached an impasse. It was not only losing ground to Protestants, but was not challenging young Chinese intellectuals or second and third-generation Chinese Catholics who were the most promising source for an indigenous leadership.

"Do you offer help to the poor, the unemployed and refugees?" asked Wang Shi.

"We've a history for pioneering humanitarian work," Father Albert responded, "but during the war years we have had to struggle with our own limited resources to keep from being refugees ourselves. Having only a small flock, reduced staff and no funds coming from the diocese, we've been hard-pressed to keep the church alive. For the most part, converts at this time are poor and illiterate. Most are from peasant families. We have neither the skills nor the experience to help them with rural reform programs. But when floods, war and famine struck, we provided what emergency relief we could. This does not prevent us, however, from teaching and preaching against the root causes of the social injustice."

With the rising tide of nationalism after 1925, Father Albert told us, both foreign and Chinese clergy tried to remain neutral, while continuing medical educational and worship programs.

In the mid-'30s, when he had started his work here, the consensus seemed to be that Chiang Kai-shek was an alternative to chaos in China. The Generalisimo, after all, had brought about some governmental reforms and raised the army from a rabble to a disciplined corps. But renewed Chinese-Japanese hostilities in 1937 and the growing Chinese Communist influence torpedoed this generally optimistic picture.

By 1940 there were fourteen American Catholic missions in China staffed by Maryknollers, Vincentians, Dominicans, Jesuits, Passionists, Marianists, Columbans, Benedictines and Franciscans. These North Americans reinforced the depleted number of European priests and sisters. Priests from these orders and sisterhoods carried out the work of catechizing, ministering to the sick and orphans, and educaating their parishoner's children.

The domination of the French clergy in China, Father Albert continued frustrated American missionaries who came later. To complicate matters, the French fathers often were prejudiced against their Americans counterparts.

With the outbreak of the Sino-Japanese War, like many other upriver missions, Yunyang became flooded with refugees. Much mission property was damaged by air raids, funds were drained, personnel were taxed to their limit and replacements of catechists was slowed by delays with their entrance visas. Foreign clergy who remained suffered severe financial hardships because poor exchange rates seriously devalued their dwindling incomes. Crippling reductions in the mission's personnel, supplies and funds worsened as the war dragged on. Despite frequent air raids, recurrent natural disasters and diminishing resources, the mission continued its relief work. Regardless of a persons political persuasions, wounded and destitute families were cared for. This humanitarian work of the mission served to break down prejudices and win the respect of Chinese authorities.

In the postwar months, the hoped for return to normalcy and easier times had not yet materialized. Reconstruction was more difficult than providing emergency relief. Families and entire villages faced widespread uneasiness about political instability and worsening currency inflation. Refugee groups and church leaders who started the long trek back to their east coast homes needed traveling aid. Refugees who chose to remain, required continuing help to get their basic needs met. (Repeat of the same frustrating condition throughout the country!)

Hardly a church, dispensary or school had not been looted by either the Japanese or local bandits. In the 11 stations outlying Yunyang, buildings had been, for the most part, reduced to empty shells. In some cases, the flooring and beams had been stripped away, and in one area a chapel had sustained a hit from Japanese bombs.

Meanwhile, bargeloads of United Nations relief food and medicines accumulated. Mission workers, trusted as being honest and fair, were pressed into serving as distribution agents. These and other humanitarian projects, however, drained the energy of scarce personnel, and limited their evangelistic and educational work.

Instead of only 'catch up work,' the priests said, they would like to be working on plans for meeting the wide range of opportunities to renovate chapels, hospitals, dispensaries, schools and to launch new programs. The opening of schools, particularly on the middle level, was given the highest priority, the priests said. It was hoped these schools would provide the proper training for the future leaders of China, offset the long-established Protestant hegemony in education and fulfill the desires of young Chinese for Western education, especially in English.

The Church in post-war China, they said, faced both old and new troubles. Internal problems of congregations surfaced when abruptly the surrender of Japan came. Short of staff and funds, with diminished membership, the missionaries and their Chinese colleagues were unprepared for t he new economic instability, political intrigue and social upheavals that followed. The rise and fall of Guomindang factions and the inroads of Communists, bandits and guerilla groups made current church work difficult.

"We've begun now," the father said, "to better understand what we mean when we speak of the self-revealing God, of the Word that both confronts and addresses us. It's more than some deathless intuition of a Presence that inhabits Eternity. The Word that has come to our fellowship is special. It comes to us in the mutuality of forgiving and serving love, battering down the walls of our loneliness, shaking the fear of our isolation. The Word has a power of its own. And it comes to create what it says."

Father Liu En's talk about the power of the Christian message raised questions with Wang Shi, but his broad-mindedness and frankness won approval. Our colleague was glad to hear the priest say he considered the Guomindang corrupt and ineffective in meeting the country's economic and political problems.

Political instability, Wang Shi noted, seemed to increase in direct proportion to the area's distance from the capital at Nanjing. He also sensed that neither clergy was aware of the scope of Nanjing's political confusion, and even less aware of the Guomindang's in-fighting or its duplicity in dialoguing with the Gungchandang (Chinese Communist Party). The mission's humanitarian good works were commendable, but their hope for the country reaching some stability in the near future was unrealistic. In this context the Church, for a long time, would have to work in conditions that were at best an "equilibrium of chaos."

In view of all they had said regarding their flock's plight, the priest explained, defections from the faith were understandable. But most trouble some of all was the realization of their own lack of vision. With their 20-2( hindsight they saw how inadequate had been their assessment of the problem of their congregations and communities around them. In other words, the not only were discouraged, they were depressed! And, sadly, it was time for u to leave.

Their generous farewells, with sincere good wishes, assured us we ha( gained new friends.

Passing through the West Gate we returned to our mooring. Before w boarded the junk, the skipper called out to tell us we would not be sailing fo another hour. The delay suited the curious followers we had gathered. A num ber of those who elbowed their way to the inside ring were street urchins. Soo these wiggling, ragtag, runny-nosed front-row youngsters were pushed asid by uniformed upper middle-schoolers. Well-dressed adults, including sever; elders, pressed at the edges of the growing circle. The assemblage, like th river, swelled and swirled.

With his height, full head of salt-and-pepper hair and charisma, Thompso1 was a powerful attraction. When they heard him and me speaking Chinese albeit with a downriver accent, the circle around us squeezed tighter. A barrag of questions jumped out like popcorn from a hot pan.

"*Wei shenma ni lai? Zung shenma di fang?* (Why have you come? And from where?)" asked one bright-eyed fellow at our elbows. His companion added "Very few foreigners come this far upriver. What brings you here?"

"We are on our way to Wanxian," responded Thompson.

"And what will you do in Wanxian?" pressed another.

"Mr. Tan (Thompson)," Wang Shi broke in on our behalf, "is on his wa to teach and preach in a county center 70 *li* north of Wanxian. These other tw( and myself are journeying through our renowned San Xia. True, it is many ، from Shanghai and Nanjing, but we have heard much about your celebrate( San Xia and the people in these parts."

"*Yang jiao dai biao*, (representatives of foreign religion)," rumbled a stu dent in a loud whisper. "*Tamen shi jiao shih gen mu shi*, (they're teacher-pastors).

"Yes," Thompson responded, "we teach, preach and *tsaw li bai*, (conduc worship)."

"Our Chinese worship," commented one young adult, "is chiefly in time of famine, drought or other trouble. We propitiate the spirits by burnin; incense, putting out food for them and getting Buddhist monks to say prayer Is that the way with your *zung jiao* (religion)?"

This stirred another student at our side to press the question, "How is your worship any different from that of our Buddhist monks?" The companion beside him added, "And how is your teaching any different from the superstitions of Taoist beggars?"

Thompson was in his element. He had heard such questions many times and he was ready with answers. "Christian worship," he began, "brings believers and inquirers together for teaching and encouragement. Then it sends them back to serve people where they live."

Before he could finish his sentence, a tall fellow on our left explained, "You gather converts into halls on Sundays to sing foreign melodies. And sometimes your people are given pieces of bread and grape juice that they take together."

"People standing outside Christian meeting places hear and see our worship the way you say," Thompson said. "But, what is done is more than ritual. Christians worship to help one another see God at work in the world and what is his will or path for us. . ."

"You talk as if your God is at the center of our lives and active in everyday affairs," interrupted the questioner. "How do you know?"

Thompson affirmed that God was at the center, as creator, governor and loving heavenly father. "What's more," he said, "God not only acts but speaks."

"We would like to have the name and address of anybody who has heard your God speak," the eager man said. He pressed his point, saying, "People are victims of forces beyond their control, so they have to do the best they can, assuming that they can master them singlehanded and shape their own destiny. If you can give people something they can use right now, where they are, to their own advantage, well and good. But, please, no more talk about things which are not, and yet bring to nought things that are."

"We believe," Thompson said with confidence, "one of God's greatest acts was sending his son into the world precisely to show people what he is like—it was the eternal Word coming to earth in a historical event. The close-at-hand Son of Heaven, Jesus, walked, taught and healed on earth showing people how God acts."

"Son of Heaven?" one of the students interrupted. "Is your Jesus an emperor?. . .You have two gods, one you call Shang Di and another Jesus?"

"No, not two gods, but one God," Thompson replied, keeping his composure. "Our belief is that this one God showed His nature and purpose by sending His son, Jesus, to live on earth. God also continues as a guiding spirit."

"Oh, like the Buddha and his disciples?" an older student asked.

"Similar in some ways, but also different," Thompson explained.

"Christians believe God has showed Himself through thousands of years as more loving and self-giving than Buddha or other deities."

"Jesus was more than a disciple and closer to God than Buddha. Buddha as a wealthy prince, spent his life in looking for ways he and his followers could escape the world's pain, aging, death and other miseries. In contrast, Jesus, a *laobaixing*, (commoner) and a carpenter, came into the world to guide people toward Heaven. Always Jesus' words and deeds pointed to God (Heaven) as wise, just and loving. And the way Jesus lived, taught and died demonstrates for people that this God is personal, caring and loving, like a wise and good father."

"You say 'personal, caring and loving'? How can 'Heaven,' which is so far away and so often angry, be personal and loving?" blurted out an incredulous fellow.

One of his friends elbowed him, explaining, "The foreign teacher must be talking of our *Dian Lao Yeh*–the heavenly old uncle, the giver of food, peace and comfort!"

Thompson let that question and the friend's comment pass and continued "Jesus the son was sent to demonstrate how God is personal and loving. Jesus gives you and me new life. We talk about Jesus showing us the goodness and loving kindness of God as 'the good news.'"

"Teacher, the goodness and better living you talk about sounds like the wisdom of our Chinese classics," broke in an elderly man who had squeezed toward the center of the crowd. "Our great books say much about benevolence, righteousness and other virtues."

"Yes, our ancestors poured high-sounding counsel upon us," an older student broke in. "Parents, teachers and administrators trying to control young people surround us with old and new platitudes. The government plasters city walls with giant words like '*li*,' propriety, good manners, respect; '*ren*,' benevolence, selflessness; and '*chung*,' loyalty, faithfulness, patriotism. We are told to live out such virtues to improve and strengthen China!"

The restless student beside him asked, "What did your Jesus say about evil invaders that kill and rape? And a government that lets the cost of rice climb higher and higher? And rapacious landlords who make poor farmers poorer?"

"Jesus had much to say about feeding the hungry, freeing the oppressed and imprisoned. Once he 'cleansed' a temple where priests had became corrupt," Thompson explained. "But more than talk and teaching, Jesus went about healing and helping those broken in body and spirit."

Many see and hear about Jesus' teachings and works, but few of us live our lives by those teachings. A verse from one of the Christian classics says:

*The bad that we would not, we often do; and the*
*good that we say we would like to do, we do not do.*

We pretend to be better than we are. Like a Peking opera, we wear masks ) make good Impressions. We need reminders to stop falling short, doing rong and hurting others.

"But why do you talk about 'falling short' and 'doing wrong'?" asked the lder, who now was in the front row under our noses. "Are not people at their earts good? And why do we need forgiveness from an unseen you've not njured?"

"Wrong-doing and evil must be talked about," Thompson explained. "The nderside of the good is evil. Your Chinese principle of opposites teaches us to )ok at both sides of behavior, the wrong and the right, the dark and the light, ne unjust and the just. People in their hearts may be good, but also they 'miss ne mark,' harm others and make them lose face. We all fall short of our best. Vhen we injure others and ourselves, we injure God."

"Injure God?" exclaimed another skeptic in the restless throng. "How can nat ever be?"

"We injure God in many ways," Thompson held his ground. "We disrespect iod, or worse, we disregard God, deny God and cut ourselves off from the Ieavenly Father."

"How can people cut themselves off from Heaven?" asked another.

"When we are honest with ourselves," Thompson continued, "we admit nat we need God's forgiveness. Being human, as well as divine, Jesus knew ow people got themselves into misdeeds and failures. Then Jesus assured peo-le that God is ready to forgive them. We believe this assurance because Jesus, n his life as the Son of Heaven, showed that the Heavenly Father is loving and )rgiving. In our remorse over our failure to live up to the good in us, our ten-ency to hurt others and turn our backs on God, we need the encouragement nd cleansing of God's love."

Thompson continued undaunted, but not I. I was uncomfortable with giv-ng a free-for-all 'witness' from Yunyang's waterfront stairs. I didn't disagree ith Thompson's witness, though I was more hesitant. The quality of heart-)-heart encounters have a way of being diminished when they are made into narket transactions. Though my convictions were strong, I still felt that one's uth is also personal. Also, I was ill at ease presuming that these people want-d to hear about our faith; I wanted to avoid spiritual imperialism. This tena-ious audience asked questions different from those I was used to hearing from lanjing University history and philosophy majors. These earthy questions )uched life-and-death matters. These questions showed how new and foreign the Christian faith was to these hearers. For these people Christianity, mos assuredly, was *yang jiao* (a foreign religion).

In our talking with these people Thompson and I were connecting only par tially. We were only beginning to bridge the chasm between their belief system and ours. Simultaneously, we were forced to search our own convictions.

I felt we'd pressed our welcome about as far as we should. More crew mem bers were weaving through the crowd, returning to the *wu ban*. It seemed clos ing time. I moved away from Thompson to encourage him to wind down th exchanges that were heating up, but his arm drew me back and his eyes gav me the message that it was my turn to field some of these curious people' questions.

"Sir," I said, turning toward the elder facing me, "you make an importan point when you say we do not see or hear God. We may not see God in th same way the sun above strikes our eyes with its brightness."

"But have you seen the *Tian* (Heaven) or the *Shang Di* (Highest of gods that you believe in?" I asked, reaching for practical Chinese words to expres my conviction. "You see the sky, the clouds, the sun and stars, but you do no in the same way see the infinitely grander *Tian*. I believe that if historical event have significance at all they have to be seen as the underside of that huge tapes try which on God's side is his dealing with human life to redeem it. We 'see God through our 'inner eye.' The Jesus we are talking about answered th same question you asked. He said, 'You say aright that we have not seen God not as you and I see one another, but you do see me and I reflect the fathe God.

"You, elders and students, raise worthy questions," I continued. "We als ask such questions. We too are seekers. We don't have all the answers. We ar like the man, 2,000 years ago, who went up to Jesus and said, 'Master, believe; help Thou my unbelief.' We come to listen to your wisdom. We hav come as friends to learn your wisdom about life. After all, we are only *da biz* ('the big-nosed ones,' an expression used humorously and sometimes derisive ly to describe Westerners).

This berating personal reference electrified the crowd, which exploded i laughter and won approval.

Pointing to my nose, I said, "You may see it as big compared with Chines noses, but at least I have a nose to smell with, just like you." And taking th little pocket knife from my pocket I made a tiny incision in my thumb and hel it up as a drop of blood formed. "And, what is this and what color is it?"

"*Xue, xue* (blood, blood), and *hong, hong* (red, red)," called out the front row urchins.

"Is it not the same as yours?" I asked. "You and I have noses to smel mouths to feed, ears to hear and red blood to give us life. Look up into the sky. Is there a Chinese sun? An American sun? Isn't the sun for all people? Is it not true, as your great novel says: 'In the four seas, all men are brothers?' An important conviction we hold is that *Ji Du* (Jesus) was both Son of Man and Son of Heaven. With this double nature he unites all people. He invites both Christian and non-Christians to follow him."

"You don't want me to lose face, do you?" I asked. "Is it wise to discard the Jesus faith because it is *jang jiao* (a foreign religion)? After all, didn't some of our Daoist beliefs come from treasured truths of the Ba and Shu people who were 'outsiders.' And, didn't your *fo chiao* (Buddhism) come from India? And, *ui chiao* (Islam) come from Arabia? Do we not help one another by sharing the unique faiths each of us has discovered? We come to share the good news of another great master, *Ji Du*. By his own suffering and death Ji Du gave meaning to life's hardest troubles and pointed to finding a 'new life.' And with Shang Di (the greatest Spirit) our lives are made new and given direction."

"Chinese place much trust in *Tian* (Heaven) and *Shang Di* (the great spirit). These great truths strengthen each of us. This great river and your beautiful temple on the south bank stir our respect and awe of *Tian* and *Shang Di*. The beauty and magnificence we have seen have opened our hearts to good feelings for ourselves and for others."

"This gratitude and awe make us bow our heads with respect," I explained. "Our worship calls for the same reverence the Buddhists feel. We direct our reverence not to Buddha and the bodhisattvas but to *Ji Du* and *Shang Di*. We hold that Jesus entered history. He came into the world to lift people–individuals, families, towns and whole countries. The great Gautama for years traveled the earth searching for personal escape from pain and death. We are drawn to Jesus, who, as a human being, is our friend, counselor and guide to God in Heaven."

"Belief and worship of *Ji Du*, however," I explained, "cannot be only talk or show. Belief must bear fruit in behavior. You honor virtues such as *de* (righteousness) and *jen* (benevolence) and you honor illustrious men in your temples and preserve the bones of the warrior Zhang Fei and the loyal counselor Chu Ko-liang."

"*Lai, lai, lai,* (come, come, come!)" bellowed our skipper from the stern of the waiting junk. "Get yourselves aboard. We're leaving!"

The elderly gentlemen and several students asked for our cards. This opened the floodgates for all the others to ask for the same tokens.

We felt, as we had in taking leave of Father François the week before and Father Albert an hour before, there was much more to be heard, said and shared. Many among the persistent inquirers clasped their hands together in front of their chests and said, "*I lu ping an*, (may every road of your journey bring you peace)." Also, how little we truly knew of the feelings, thoughts an faith of those in the crowd we were taking our leave of!

We had participated in the universal search for basic answers to life's crucia questions. We had seen the convergence of people, not only of differing race and cultures, but of different faiths. The crime of racism and imperialistic cul ture is to deny the humanity of people with skin of a different color. Toleranc arises from a recognition of oneself in others, from seeing in a separate bein all one's own possibilities, weaknesses, appetites, loves, lapses, brutalities an decencies.

The effect of yesterday's losses lingered. We had expected these crewmen t live for many more years. When our expectations were shattered in this way, s were our security and confidence. Now we saw plainly that we are mortal. W had to live on intimate terms with that fact. We felt what Ray Bradbury woul later call "the briefness of life and the sadness of eternity." We were haunted b the need to do with our lives the good that we had been intending to do bu had put off.

# Talking About Truth We Nearly Missed Beauty

*Bridal Falls And Shrine*

Courtesy Ah Bing, Nanjing

A gentle crosswind puffed out and gave a push to our giant lug sail as the bowmen poled away from the Yunyang mooring. Trackers, still on board, helped rowers give more pull to the oars. The sweepmen, cutting the waters with deep, curving swaths, further powered us to gain on the current and move westward. Aft, the *lao ban* gripped the tiller and stared ahead, while his glowering wife castigated him for not getting the *wu ban* underway earlier. Midships we four packed-in and, unobtrusive passengers were absorbed in our grief feelings and search for hope.

"Look up," said the cook, pointing to the massive rock columns along the shore. "They're the Eight Canyon Cliffs. At flood level the river covers these walls. Now with the river level low, you see the rock formations." They looked like organ pipes decorated with wildflowers.

Farther along we saw the deep crevices comprising Three Water Guardians. The ledges and recesses were accented with crimson, blue and gold foliage, giving the appearance of a solemn row of divinities in full canonicals.

These spectacular rock monuments west of the Qu T'ang's couldn't erase the terrible image of the trackers being jerked off the towpath and into river's whirlpools. Feelings of distress and disbelief hemmed us in more than the sandstone cliffs. The men's plunge continued to drag us down too. Still, a part of ourselves was lost and feelings of our own finitude and fragility were overwhelming.

"Losses like these shake us from head and heart to toe," the major said quietly. "It's death's irretrievable loss, that always hits me the hardest. With time some breakthrough comes, but the sudden evaporation of life is a lightening-bolt reminder no one of us can escape the finality of death."

From just back of us, at the tiller, the skipper surprised us with broodings addressed to Wang Shi.

A seasoned observer of death, the skipper had escaped its clutches more than once and knew his time would come eventually. Since he carried no life insurance for his crew, he viewed any loss of crewmen's lives in terms of supply-and-demand forces. He accepted the loss of the trackers as payment for his junk's safe passage upriver. His primary concern was not that of loss of life and threats to the crew's safety, but of protecting his own and the other junk owners' proprietary interests. As skipper, he didn't have to sign death certificates, or even report the deaths. These two were expendable, like a frayed section of a tow cable or a split oar. Repair it or rescue it if you can; otherwise, cast it off as part of the cost of the enterprise.

Just in front of us was the down-to-earth lead rower, Lao Liu, silently, single-mindedly stroking, like the other crewmen, numbed by the catastrophe. Already Lao Liu and his fellow boatmen had entered several grief stages. Struck with death's inexorable reality, they were inwardly disorganized and despairing. They needed to be able to bury their dead with ritual and argue in anger that some deity, if he be loving, should not have done this. Since they didn't have these options, they lapsed into fatalism. The monotony of physical exertion allowed them to slip into the safety of their routines.

The cook, a self-appointed ritual master, encouraged crew members to "talk away from their fear" of death and the river. He sensed diversionary expressions were important for putting a cap on grief, so he sparked conversations with Lao Liu and, through him, stirred chatter among the oarsmen. It was as if, in unison, they were to psych themselves into saying, "Fie on the tragic character of existence. We need no extra rites of mourning beyond our immediate work, which makes us feel powerful and invulnerable, at least in this moment."

Spirits that had drooped were lifted up by the companionship of being, physically and emotionally, in the same boat, all with the goal of getting the *wu ban* to Wanxian.

These men, Wang Shi explained, were falling back on Chinese folk religion. Unlettered peasants that they were, the responses open to them were limited. Unacquainted with the sophisticated strands of Chinese thought about death,

aving to sort out relevant Buddhist, Daoist and Confucian teachings about
he subject was far from their concern.

The boatmen were from villages where people held that the world is alive
ith spirits and gods. Families had gods of the kitchen, earth, cities and rivers.
hese deities wielded magical powers over nature and people. Feared lest they
ecome angry and vindictive, they were placated. When the gods failed to
eliver on some earnest request, the idols representing them were often cursed
r slapped.

"Death is always a problem and a great mystery," the cook broke out as he
nished cleaning up the galley. As usual, a person who could be relied upon to
ave an opinion and to be ready to express it, he continued, "Those who trav-
l into that unknown land of perpetual shadows and gloomy torture chambers
or the unrepentant don't send messages back telling what it's like. When my
ather died, my mother in her grief consulted the village *wu po* (sorcerer, witch)
nd was told: 'The Land is a gloomy one, and there is no sun to be seen.
hadows lie everywhere, and an air of depression rests upon the hills and on
he plains that stretch before me. Men and women pass up and down the roads,
ut they all look like specters, for there is no laughter on their faces, and no
igns of joy about them. They seem to be oppressed with a sense of their des-
late condition.'"

Though a secret that none may fathom, Chinese built up a mythical and at
he same time a very human conception of what the "Shadowy World" is like.
hey have imagined that Hades is an exact counterpart of China and that it had
s emperor and great and small mandarins, and provinces and counties with
he same names that these have in the actual and visible lands of the Celestial
mpire. Regarding the afterlife, all three belief systems held that the realms of
arthly life and the hereafter were continuous and related. The world of spirits
s like the world of humans: As in this life, it is impossible to live without eat-
ng or to obtain comforts without money; so in the life to come. Later, under
Buddhist influence, the view prevailed that where it had not been visited upon
 person in this life, retribution would be meted out in full measure by the
hadow Land's King.

In grieving, the problem was to estimate what the gods or spirits had
ntended in taking the life of a fellow. Commoners turned to divination, astrol-
ogy, palm reading, geomancy, witchcraft, phrenology, dream interpretation,
ortunetelling and charms. The boatmen's response to death was forged from
his mixture of custom and superstition. Fate demanded acceptance, an unex-
mined determination to keep rowing as long as the body held out.

Such fatalism, Wang Shi contended, posed problems as China seeks to
ecome a modern society free from irrationality and subservience.

Thompson was prompted by Wang Shi's comments to speak about the differing attitudes toward death he'd noticed from his participation in both tra ditional Chinese and the usual Western funerals. Chinese, he said, see deat more as a personal, rather than a social or metaphysical, catastrophe. They loo at it more as an inevitable event.

"That sounds about right as a starter," Wang Shi responded. "We Chines are pragmatic about death, as we are about other things. A natural necessity, a unavoidable fact of life, death, for the Chinese, is not necessarily a tragedy. is not conquered by avoiding the finite, but rather by accepting life's finitud while you are living it."

"Is it true," I asked Wang Shi, "that Chinese believe that upon death th two aspects that comprise the individual are separated?"

"Yes, that view is part of the mix," he explained. "The idea of a split come down from the magico-religious view dating back to the Chou dynasty (12t to 3rd century B.C.). It was believed that the *bo* (*p'o*, = soul) part of the per son, or essence created at conception, continues to reside in the tomb with th corpse. It draws nourishment from the offerings which are made by the livin at the tomb. The afterlife of individual's *bo* is limited. When the body ha decayed it gradually loses its vitality and takes on a shadowy existence in th underworld.

"At death the higher part of the soul, or *hun*, ascends to the palace of *Shan Di*. There *hun* leads a life similar to that of a nobleman at his prince's cour The journey is not without perils. There are evil forces to be outwitted–th earth spirit who devours the soul and the Heavenly Wolf, who guards th Shang Di's palace. To escape these dangers, the sacrifices and prayers of the liv ing members of the deceased's clan are necessary."

"Chinese find great social significance in death," I added. "Death is nc merely an event in an individual's existence, but it involves one's family in long lasting and elaborate bonds. Common folk, for instance, are sustained by confidence in the eventual triumph of the race."

"For families and communities the significance of death goes farther, Thompson said. "The dead are seen as dependent upon the living. Ceremonie in honor of ancestors solidify family and clan ties. No other phase of Chines religious life has been more prominent than ceremonies for the departed. Thei maintenance, therefore, has depended upon a mixture of motives–tradition an social convention, respect and affection for the departed, the desire for th prosperity of the living and, last but not least, fear."

"To this day ancestor worship remains the one creed to which all Chines pay homage. It remains unquestioned by all classes and requires no state-main tained temples or priests."

"Father Liu En at the mission," said Wang Shi, surprising us, "opened ne windows into viewing death. At the funeral he conducted, he presented a point not mentioned by the geomancers who preside over Chinese funerals. The spirit of the father's prayers were positive–quite different from the resignation in Chinese eulogies. The father stood above the usual helplessness. He spoke from a deep conviction that death is an entrance into a greater life."

"The passage he read from your sacred writings (Psalms 16) was powerful for me:"

> *My heart and soul rejoice, my body rests secure;*
> *For never wilt you let me sink to death,*
> *nor leave your loyal one to the grave;*

"'Rejoice in soul,' 'rest secure' and 'reveal the path to life'," Thompson added, "are not elements heard in Chinese mourning ceremonies. Like children's fear of the dark, death for many Chinese stirs terror."

"True!" Wang Shi observed. "I've never heard words of praise and petitions like Father Liu En gave in his prayer. He praised the Eternal One for creating life. Then he said when death comes we will be taken by the hand as we go to realms we know not of. No longer an enemy, death is the gateway to life eternal."

Our discussion was interrupted as the *wu ban* entered a short stretch of rapids. More effort and attention was demanded of the crew. The cook provided a brief history of the temple on the left bank.

Our conversation resumed when Wang Shi asked Thompson, "What did you mean when you told Mr. Gao (Cowles) he'd given a sermon to the Yunyang crowd? I thought sermons were lectures ministers give inside a church during worship. *Zhuan dao*, Chinese for 'sermon,' means both to explain doctrines and to win people to a faith."

"What I meant," Thompson replied, "was that in a few minutes and in understandable language he told about trying to lead a Christian life. That's a sermon. Many people nowaddays don't want to hear sermons with a string of 'shoulds' and 'should nots.' Sermons, actually, are not intended to be lectures. They're what you noted–a declaration of faith, an example of faith and a challenge to do something about your faith. In this sense, Confucius 'preached' to his followers."

"Sermons don't have to be inside churches or part of a worship service. Jesus gave sermons under a tree, walking along a country road, in homes, in marketplaces and on the shore of a lake. The location doesn't matter. All that are required are eager listeners and a faithful telling of truth about the Good News."

"Whatever you call it," Wang Shi responded, "Mr. Gao's down-to-earth words made sense to the students and elders. You didn't talk down to them as if they were ignorant children. And I liked your comparison of the river's deep currents to the ageless force running through life. The image suggests that strong convictions, like the Long River, come from some higher place and go out to the greatness of the ocean."

"Yes," Thompson replied, "Our faith is that *Shang Di*, as supreme and cosmic, flows through all creation: nature, individuals, communities and nations. The Chinese *Shang Di* suggests *zhaoran* (that which is ultimately superior) and *xiang wai* (that which is transcendental) Shang Di also is a source or force—a creative and life-giving energy that gives purpose and direction in all of it expressions and finally empties into the immense ocean of being. But the river is still only an analogy of God's greatness."

"Your conviction that *Shang Di* is a timeless spirit," Wang Shi pressed, "isn't easy for me to understand".

"Because *Shang Di* as the source existed before creation," Thompson explained, "we use the description 'timeless,' or before and beyond time. Also we consider God gives us time as a resource, as a period to fulfill life. We are 'stewards' of this special resource; we have the responsibility to 'redeem the time,' i.e. to maximize what we do in our minutes, hours and days."

"Yes, what Mr. Tan says about the transcendent," I added, "is true. Yet there really is no way to prove the existence of such a divine creator who oversees the world. If you see it, you see it. If you don't see it, no one can convince you its there. It's a venture of faith that you do or don't place on things. This faith is a pilgrimage we move in and out of through life. Doubting is part of the religious experience–even the so-called 'religious', like Jesus' disciple Thomas, doubted. The pilgrimage of faith includes the continuing effort to look at one's whole life and perceive some sort of pattern. Then comes death. You have either despair or hope. And the hope is not supported by very much evidence if you're going to approach it through the scientific method."

"Death of a friend or fellow worker, such as we have possibly seen, is one of life's important moments. It's then that we hope to be allied with those who came before us. We want to be rooted in tradition, also to see the prospect of something better."

"You talk about 'religion' and 'religious' in several ways," Wang Shi followed. "What do you mean by 'religious?'"

"You and I experience certain times, places, ideas, attitudes as other than the ordinary," Thompson said. "Those different experiences are 'religious' moments in the sense that they are better aligned than ordinary life to 'transhuman' powers, planes of living and centers of meaning. The 'other' involved may be no more than a realization of one's finite nature or ancestral spirits, or it may be the ultimate, unconditional Reality of the Buddhist Nirvana or the Christian God. Vital and genuine religious experience makes a difference in a person's life. That's when the sense of right-and-wrong, justice and righteousness is lived out. The person vibrates with a sense of purpose, which is lived, not merely contemplated. Reading a manual about marriage and children is not the same as marrying and having children. Those who have traveled the Long River's Three Gorges gain a much richer experience than someone who has only read of them .

"We begin with the practical and immediate that we can see and touch, but we're challenged to keep reaching for truth, beauty, love and a *Shang Di* we can't see or touch. Life-transforming conviction comes from finding meaning and destiny in the events and people in everyday life."

"What an assignment!" I burst out. "Applied to us right now, we are to appreciate all we've encountered on our journey today—the cliffs, glens, grief and wonder, smells, words, glances, every drop of water in this great river."

The major nodded and said, "Engineers like me are trained to test and order facts. Not so the artists, dramatists or poets who create myths. In religious experience sometimes we do both. We are challenged to go beyond the ordinary, seeking ways to redeem and fulfill individuals and societies."

"Religious experience, then," Wang Shi ventured, "is more than common sense, or even wisdom. It's getting hold of the power and sense of urgency that comes with an experience of 'the other' you're talking about and letting that outlook and spirit guide you."

"I still am skeptical, however, of talk about *Shang Di* as personal," he continued. "How can qualities such as caring, empathy and responsibility be associated with *Shang Di*? Why assign *Shang Di* a personal side? Can't *Shang Di* give life its ethical dimension without having human characteristics?"

"Good point," I ventured. "*Shang Di*, rather than staying detached and merely contemplating otherworldly thoughts, is rooted in the stuff of creation, in humans and their communities, in the world and its history. We feel *Shang Di*, since He created persons, must have a personal side: Also he continues to work through history and people: wholly inward and also a cultural and social reality. Likewise individuals' and communities' ideas, stories and practices are doors between them and the transcendent."

"Since we are created 'in His image,'" the major added, "both *Shang Di* and we humans are inextricably involved. Instead of talking about poverty, war and corruption, we must act to right these injustices—and ask God to help and guide us to make a better world according to His plan."

"You talk, Wang Shi," I added, "about the most difficult decisions in life which are moral. And the most difficult acts in life are those that demand moral courage. Many of your penetrating questions are those asked by people of religious faith. Your persistent searching reaches for the answers that can only come from solid convictions. Religious convictions grow in conditions where individuals in different cultural and historical situations share deep concerns such as yours. Today too few ask the questions you ask, and today's antireligious sentiment is not a favor to humankind. For virtually everything we do is on faith: our actions, thoughts and feelings can not be proved. In a world in which one does not hear much about religious faith, concerned persons need to unite to share their deepest convictions and, with give-and-take, develop action plans."

"You talking people," interrupted the cook, "are missing some of the best sights of this important section of the Long River. You ought to look around! We've been going through the western section of the gorges. If you'd been noticing, you would have been struck by its grandeur and beauty."

We had survived and exited the Three Gorges. Instead of a sense of accomplishment, we experienced a letdown. Spectacular scenes and sobering events had pushed our sensitivities to their limits. Our serious give-and-take about our convictions had initiated the healing of our shared grief. We needed this peering at our convictions to restore a feeling of individual worth and a sense of our common humanity. We were ready for a quiet evening break and an easier day tomorrow on the last leg of our way west.

# Unique Scenes And Sharing Crowd Last Day West

*Riverscape West Of Qu Tang Gorge*

The next morning, our cook/tour guide allowed us no rest. The landscape, though not as grandiose or perilous as the Qu Tang, was nevertheless worth missing a few winks to see.

For the moment the cook insisted that we appreciate the broader and more placid reaches of the river which revealed but a hint of itself in the uncertain morning light.

"We have passed through," he said, "the river's most lethal part, that for centuries terrified boatmen, destroyed junks and flooded the country-side. Here, before it crashes into the gorges and nearly 1,300 miles from its mouth, the Long River is still a noble river, nobler yet when the summer rise covers the grand confusions of its rocky bed."

This stretch, he told us, is where the river dragon loiters. From the Tibetan highlands lofty birth the river has crossed the lush province of Sichuan like a changeful dragon, racing here, sweeping there, toward the gorges and thence to the sea. On this journey the river feeds on the scale befitting a dragon, swallowing people and tons of earth as it moves across the land.

This estimate annoyed the no-nonsense *lao ban* at the tiller behind us, and led him to assert: "The river is for the ordinary life of the people, not for poetry."

*Conicle Peaks Shrouded With Mist*

The undaunted commentator resumed his imaginative view, and before th
fog lifted briefed us about the unique features this section of the river presen
ed. For days on the river in the gorges, it was perpendicular walls that confine
us. the rock banks loomed above us, dwarfing our *wu ban* in walls that rose t
a narrow thread of sky, clear blue and inconsequntial in the distance. Now th
banks we were about to see were red earth from which the mountains wer
pushed back. Here, as an old legend puts it, 'The monstrous waters embrac
the mountains and overtop the hills.'

The fog melted as the day advanced, revealing austere green mountains tha
climbed down into the plains back of the river bank and then out of it agai
into the distant clouds. Our commentator accommodated to the expande
panorama and started telling us of the nuances unique to this section. The in
tial landscape was mountainous and confusing, changing from hills to peak
from peaks to palisades, from palisades to ridges. Distinct from the gorge
chasms and rapids, this part of the river's course featured mountains and plain

Blue-clad mountains continued to hem us in. About their peaks, cloud
hovered, then cleared, then circled again. Slopes were draped in undulatin
scarfs of fog. Behind the hills were taller companion mountains, range upo
range. These background peaks occasionally pierced the dense sunlit cloud
Interspersed were low hills that seemed pushing up to join the surroundin
ranges. Low palisades abruptly halted the cloud-enshrouded valleys. Erodin
they spilled broken rock into the river. Jagged ridges descending from th
clouds seem to tug the mountains down to the river. Pyramidal hills sproute
lollipop-like trees. Chocolate-colored waterfalls poured from gashes in th
mountains , some spraying delicate bridal veils, others gushing over enormou

*Sunrise Qutang Gorge • S. Macon Cowles, Jr.*

*Baidicheng City • Dr. Lita Singer*

*)utang Gorge – Gui Men • S. Macon Cowles, Jr.*

*Qutang Gorge – Fast Water, Deep Chasms*

*Cuokai – The Gods Made A Mistake* • *Dr. Lita Singer*

*Junk Mooring East of Qutang*

*Wu Gorge – A Wider Section* • *R. Hayman*

*Gaundukou – Wu Gorge, with Escarpment • Dr. Lita Singer*

*Gui, Western Edge of Xiling Gorge • Dr. Lita Singer*

*Wu Gorges, Daning Tributary • R. Hayman*

*XiLing Gorge – Another Dead End?*

*Broken Mountain Spilling Into River • Dr. Lita Singer*

*XiLing Gorge, Ox Liver Rock • Dr. Lita Singer*

*Shennongxi, Near Badong* • *R. Hayman*

*ier Upon Tier of Fields, XiLing Gorge*

*Eastern Entrance, XiLing Gorge • Dr. Lita Singer*

ɔck slabs. Run-off from recent rains washed away gray-brown silt lines that ᴍarked changes in the river's level.

On abutments in river bends, a few clustered houses suggested a village. ᴊlong slender roads camouflaged by clumps of trees, an occasional pedestrian ᵣ cyclist could be seen. Lonely dwellings protruded from a few promontories. ᴌow mud-plastered houses surrounded by tight clumps of trees sat in isolation. ᴄelvety plateaus emerged from hillsides marked by gray-roofed whitewashed ᴀrmhouses. Small junks ferried passengers across the river. On shore, gesticu-ᴀtion and babble suggested haggling for prize passengers and cargo. Some ᴏats were taking on passengers who boarded over precarious gangplanks. Still ᴛhers were moored offshore, like taxis at an airport, cuing up for customers.

The channel narrowed, then broadened again. The shoreline was alternate-ᴊ marked by silt and rock piles. In coves the river became placid, while in mid-ᴛream the current presented a formidable down drag for our crew. Passing ᴛhrough a low canyon, we emerged into a narrow lake with calmer waters. ᴊradually the heights we had grown accustomed to began to soften. The hills ᴀded into distant slopes. We recalled the intrepid Victorian traveler, Isabelle ᴊird Bishop's description of this section 50 years ago (1897), "The country ᴏpens out and the verdure and fertility are most charming."

The westerly wind gave us a full sail, allowing trackers to come aboard and ᴄeinforce the oarsmen and sweepmen. Our non-stop guide pointed out tem-ᴘles that peeked from behind bamboo groves and blossoming cherry trees. ᴊalling our attention to hill after hill peaked by white towers with painted red ᴜns, he explained, "In the past, those towers issued smoke signals, alerting ᴜpriver towns to impending dangers. Now they double as distance markers."

On level ground beyond the river banks were small farms with brown-red ᴏil, the same that colored the river. So close were we to the shore, I felt as if ᴊ were walking through the lush fields we passed. In addition to the usual rice, ᴛhere were plantings of sugar cane, rape (out of which comes a staple cooking ᴏil) and row upon row of sesame with bright yellow tops. Nervous dogs dart-d back and forth around stoic water buffalo led by barefoot boys.

The ever-observant cook sensed my romanticized perceptions of the pas-ᴏral scene. "You may well smile at these country scenes, Mr. Gao," he said, ᵀbut the people here are neither fine nor beautiful." Betraying his downriver ᴘrejudice against this province, he began to explain how Sichuan was a far cry ᴄrom Nirvana.

Fire came into his eyes as he told stories of the peasants' uncouthness and ᴀpacity. "They skin dogs alive," he contended, "and let them run loose with ᴛheir skins hanging between their legs. Sodomy and incest are common in these ᴘeaceful-looking farmhouses."

Then, coming closer and cupping his hand beside his mouth, he told stories about our crew: "Some of the haulers are homosexuals, others go in search of opium or strong white wine or both. Indeed, the young have a hard life. There is no law to protect the young, who are made to work as soon as they can stand."

He was perplexing: first he spread tales, then he made excuses for the malfeasance.

Wang Shi confirmed that such wild behavior is reported in these "less civilized" parts of the interior, but asked us to remember that the cook was a prejudiced Hubei native. He also hurried to insist that "corrections of such conditions as the cook described are coming about fast."

"Let me come back," Wang Shi said, "to questions I didn't ask yesterday when we were leaving Yunyang. As I heard you, Mr. Tan, saying the Christian religion has to do with people reaching to connect with the cosmic order ruled by your *Shang Di* and living their lives accordingly. Trying to understand your view, I am wondering if it compares with our Chinese idea of *shu dao* (reciprocity)."

"The essential 'connecting'–drawing people together–part of religious experience," Thompson said, "certainly involves the idea of reciprocity, but the experience is more than people-to-people connectedness. Reciprocity comes in the person's honest and persistent openness, then ordering one's life and relations to others accordingly."

"There's a personal acknowledgment," hecontinued, "of human limitation and recognition of a kingdom not of this world only. Your Chinese idea for seeking *zui zhong* (the ultimate) touches on this. Your Chinese term includes 'exceeding' or 'absolutely superlative' and 'the entire,' suggesting qualities and forces beyond earthly powers. You also have the meaningful phrase *cheng shi yu*, ('the business of becoming more perfect and universal in your motives). Lao Tze's emphasis on ordering life according to the 'Ultimate Way,' or the Tao, conveys much of the same meaning."

"How to reconcile your Western view with the traditional Chinese *Shang Di* puzzles me," Wang Shi said. "For Chinese *Shang Di* includes many gods believed in from primordial times. One was regarded as supreme and was variously called *Tian* (usually translated as Heaven) and *Shang Di* (probably best translated as the Supreme Ruler). Originally *Tian* and *Shang Di* were probably distinct, *Tian* perhaps meaning the heavenly abode, or city of the dead, and *Shang Di* having more of a personal theistic significance. Eventually *Tian* and *Shang Di* practically coalesced. *Tian* or *Shang Di* was sovereign over gods and men. As such it was the source of the mandate by which the head of state ruled. It seems what you call the 'cosmic order' is similar to the Chinese 'totally ultimate.'"

"The 'cosmic order' we are talking about is revealed and lived in day-to-day experience," Thompson said. "Routine living deals with surface happenings.

more purposeful life seeks to find deeper forces and destiny. The discoveries may come from nature, from society or from one's inner voice, the 'God within.' Religion has much to do with listening for these ultimate forces and thereby refining and broadening our motives. The more we're aligned with this cosmic order, the more our lives are intensified and enlarged in all dimensions and given direction and meaning."

"Religion is subject to cultural and historical influences," I suggested. "Its traditions develop relative to particular times and places. Religious impulses spring from their surroundings. Likewise religion influences its surroundings. Various branches of faith develop and organize in societies. These differing world beliefs and traditions intersect with and nourish the cultures around them."

"I see indications," the major commented, "that within Chinese society spirits are everywhere, every meaningful act is in one sense religious or sacred and nothing is seen as nonreligious or profane. Often it appears that in China the various streams of religious tradition have become blended."

"Yes, you find quite a mix," Wang Shi began. "Referring to their religion, Chinese speak of the *San Jiao* (the three religions)–Taoism, Buddhism and Confucianism."

"With commoners the ancient folk religions continue to have strong influence," Wang Shi cautioned. "Commoners for whom life was frustrating and bitter sought relief from suffering and ways to ward off evil spirits. Over five millennia ago Chinese devised and embraced beliefs in unearthly powers (primitive religion, if you will) to meet these spiritual needs. The boatmen's superstitions, for example, showed elemental, but still prevalent folk beliefs and practices."

"This strong cultural sensitivity began to be organized more than 3,000 years ago, eventually resulting in China's three great religions. Taoism and Confucianism emerged in the 6th century B.C. and Buddhism entered from India in the 2nd century A.D. Centuries later, Islam and Christianity were introduced. Over the years there's been much blending and combining."

"Confucianism has been the central tradition molding China's culture," Wang Shi said. "At one level, it has been a moral code for the ruling class. Confucius (551-479 B.C.) rooted his ethical system in the cult of Heaven, which had grown up in North China during the Chou dynasty (1122-221 B.C.). Heaven was not conceived of as the dwelling place of empyrean gods, as with the Greeks, or the abode of a personal god, as in the Judeo-Christian-Islamic tradition, but rather as a cosmic order. Just as nature moved in accord with this ultimate law, so should people. If they followed the ways of Heaven, their lot would be good; if they did not, disease, drought, famine, earthquakes, poverty and other calamities would befall them."

"Heaven and earth were brought into harmony as the emperor regularly performed prescribed rites. If the emperor didn't perform these rites properly, or if he did not rule with concern for his people, he could lose the mandate of Heaven."

The Confucian philosopher Mencius wrote:

*'Heaven sees as my people see; Heaven hears as my people hear.' The emperor's right to rule, then, ultimately rested on the people's view of him.*

"Confucian thought and practice is really humanistic rather than religious. Moral law is not revealed to mankind, as it was to the Hebrew prophets. According to Confucius, moral society requires that people live in harmony with Heaven's way and the place to start one's moral life is in the family. Chinese thinkers felt that people could be moral without being religious. The notion of sin was absent. Human nature was basically good. The evils of society were due to immoral leaders and the failure to order society according to known moral wisdom. Over the centuries, Confucian honoring of ancestors developed complicated rituals that made the reverence of families a near religion."

"Five Principal Relationships," Wang Shi explained, "were spelled out by Confucians, patterned after the family and extended to society as a whole. These were the relation of father to eldest son, husband to wife, elder brother to younger brother, friend to friend, and emperor to subject. Thus the family pattern helped tie the state together in a harmonious whole. If these relationships were followed, all would be harmonious throughout the family, village, nation and world."

"Taoism," I interjected, "has both philosophical and applied sides. It stems from the legendary Lao Tze, who, like Confucius, lived in the 6th century B.C. A later follower, Chuang Tze, memorialized in the Qing Fan temple visited last week, deepened Lao Tze's thought. How, precisely, one is to harmonize one's life with the Tao is difficult to articulate. As the Chinese saying goes,"

*Those who say, do not know.*
*Those who know, do not say.*

"The Tao is experienced when we retire from society and cultivate a condition of 'creative quietude,'" Wang Shi continued. "This state, called *wu wei*, is developed through the contemplation of nature. We allow our deepest human qualities to surface from beneath the artificial expectations society imposes."

"Taoism that gathered religious overtones," I suggested, "espoused an extensive and often colorful pantheon of otherworldly creatures–spirits, gods.

ghosts, pixies and fairies who affected human fate in countless ways and had to be propitiated to prevent natural disasters and assure personal well-being."

"Scarcely a basis for government—as Confucianism succeeded in becoming—Taoism was nevertheless of great influence, particularly in times of social instability. It challenged conventional views of the good and the acceptable, exposed the hypocrisy of Confucian morals that chiefly benefitted the rich and powerful, and questioned the Buddhists' pursuit of a nebulous Nirvana. Religious Taoism provided spiritual comfort in the face of death and the unknown, but it also retained superstition that has condemned it in the eyes of many modern Chinese."

"Buddhism, like Islam and Christianity, came from outside China," Thompson explained. "It originated in India through the teachings of Siddhartha Gautama (580-460 B.C.). It spread across the trade routes of Central Asia and took root in China during the turbulent period accompanying the breakup of the Han dynasty (220 A.D.). It was established primarily by monks and others who came by sea to Tonkin (modern Vietnam). Strongly resisted at first as a foreign religion, Buddhism began to take hold during the 4th century A.D. Some Taoists asserted that Lao Tzu, after his sojourn in China, had traveled to India and become the Buddha. In this way, Chinese ethnocentrism allowed for a Chinese basis for a popular new religion. Buddhism and Taoism grew together in those early centuries, with the Buddha and Huang Lo, the major Taoist deity, placed on the same altar."

"Buddhist thought and practice," Wang Shi explained, "underwent many adaptations to make it fit Chinese culture. It gave an answer to people's hunger for the assurance of life after death. The humanistic Chinese were not comfortable with the Indian view of life as simply one incarnation among many. The Pure Land sect of Chinese Buddhism held that salvation in this life could be achieved through devotion to the Buddha, the performance of meritorious deeds and unswerving faith. The reward was entry into a Western-style paradise in which the individual maintained his or her identity, instead of merging into a larger spiritual unity, as held by Indian Buddhism."

"The heart of Buddhist life in China was the monastery," Wang Shi continued. "In these communities men and women retreated from the problems of secular life and engaged in spiritual disciplines. Frequently located on picturesque mountains or other out-of-the-way settings, nature provided inspiration for the monks' spirit. Rather than begging as Indian monks did, most Chinese monks depended upon income from lands donated by rich converts. Monasteries and temples were supported by the rents of tenant farmers. In recent years, this arrangement made them part of the hated landlord class."

"Monasteries were open to travelers, and hospitality was freely offered," Thompson said, continuing his explanation. "They served as one of the few social service agencies in a society where people without families were generally doomed to death. Many widows, widowers, orphans and other resourceless persons found homes in monasteries. Buddhism strongly linked religion to morality. Acts of charity became the basis for salvation, and kindness and compassion were supreme virtues contributing to saintliness."

Thompson paused in his discourse, as Wang Shi affirmed what was said about monasteries at their compassionate best. The major asked about subsequent developments.

"An amalgam of philosophies and influences," I explained, "that were held by a minority of elite scholars, contributed another stream of Chinese religious thought. Though intellectual, its adherents managed to avoid losing themselves in intricate abstractions. Aiming at synthesis, this small but prestigious group of intellectuals was more directed toward solving the practical ethical problems of everyday life—social relationships and difficulties of governmental systems. Philosophy was viewed as the finest product of human faculties, while religion was associated with superstition, to which scholars felt superior. Religion was left to commoners.

"Throughout its long history," I added, "China's rulers have sought to control religion rather than be controlled by it. China has no tradition of any one religion being superior to the state—no Chinese emperor stood barefoot in the snow before a Buddhist or Taoist temple begging forgiveness. Nevertheless, very few Chinese, educated or not, found difficulty in satisfying the comparatively loose requirements of the various religious traditions. Each was regarded simply as a different road to the same destination. An ancient saying expresses it well:

*The great majority of Chinese wear a Confucian crown, a Taoist robe and a pair of Buddhist sandals.*

"The Yunyang elders who questioned you," Wang Shih observed, "were respected for how they followed the honored admonition to 'learn from Confucius his attitude of inquiring into everything.'"

"Christians," Thompson explained, "coming overland from Central Asia, made a presence in Xian (Chang An), the capital of the Tang dynasty (618-907 A.D.). Their presence is evidenced in an inscription preserved on a nine-foot stone tablet now in the Provincial Museum at Xian. In the 16th and 17th centuries Jesuit missionaries came to China by sea. The large Protestant missionary influx began in the early part of the 19th century. The person of Christ—his life, teachings, works and death—were stressed. The conviction is that the presence of Christ's spirit, called the Holy Spirit, continues and guides the fellowship of believers. Christianity invokes a Father God, who is seen as the ultimate orce in the trinity. Charity becomes Christian charity when performed with a God-centered consciousness. Optimism is Christian optimism when grounded in God's purpose."

"Ritual is not as central in Protestant worship as it is in Catholicism," I said. "Protestants, however, accept the divine authority that underlies ritual. Communion and baptism are shared to remember how Jesus used them to sanctify and unite his followers. These sacraments channel God's grace and challenge believers to renew their commitment."

The redoubtable cook, who had held his tongue for almost two hours, broke in "I don't know what you four were talking about, but you certainly let a great deal of beauty slip by."

The cook brought us back in sync with Taoist teachings! Though true that it was appropriate to talk about how in our journey through the gorges, we had seen China's religious expressions played out before us. The elder who had questioned us represented Confucianism, while Taoism had appeared at Qing Tan in the form of the ancient philosopher Chuang Tze. Buddhism had been apparent in graceful temples and reverent monks. But the cook was correct: We needed to stop living in our heads, quiet our tongues and merge with the aesthetic harmony of the river.

"Thompson, Wang Shi and Ben, you've been long-winded, but your review has clarified much." the major exclaimed. "I'm more convinced of the existence of something in the nature of things which is higher and stronger than the mind of man."

"From childhood, I was taught to believe in God", he contiuned. "But I have trouble understanding, let alone accepting, the meanings ascribed to God by different faiths. For Christians, God is good; for Jews, God is righteous and just; to the Buddhists, God is the wondrous beauty of emptiness. . .For tonight, can we leave it at that?"

The skipper at the tiller barked over our conversation, "We're in sight of Wanxian, the city we've been heading for all these days."

On the north shore, perched atop of a small hill, surrounded by cypress trees, stood the Wanxian Sentinel Pagoda. For centuries it had guarded the city against the malign influences of the "demons of the South," who may well have been others like our bigoted Hubei cook. Referring to this pagoda, he gave details of when it was built, who had it erected and how the city fathers through the centuries had given it more fame than it deserved. He declined to mention how its purpose was to ward off violent creatures who spread monstrous tales about a neighboring province that shipped so much high-quality rice downriver to feed them.

At the far end of this broad section of water, the river swung to the southwest. At the bend, on the north shore, on a promontory split down the middle by a tributary stream, was the city. The late afternoon sun highlighted the city wall and made golden lines on the stone stairway that led to the South Gate.

Wanxian gave many indications that it was more than another picturesque ancient-walled river city. Known as the *Myriad City*, it promised surprises and adventures.

Backed by shrub-covered hills with misty peaks, the city rose high above stone stairways flanked by arched and towered gates. The city wall, which started well above the yellow-red water line, seemed to float along the contoured palisades.

A two-mile-long cluster of junks crowded its shore. Below the wall along the water could be seen the yards of junk builders and repairers–little wonder our skipper had opted to wait until reaching Wanxian to have the *wu ban*' leaks fixed. Wanxian was a boatman's paradise, offering cypress from nearby hills for the construction of hulls and plenty of pretty girls for amorous adventures.

Docks along the river's edge were piled high with freight. Stevedores, bent over and scantily clad, rushed about, loading and unloading rice, malt, cooking oil, cotton and coal. Large warehouses vied for space along the shore. Above were bamboo huts in which coolies purchased their meager meals. As a visible sign of Chinese resourcefulness, these huts could be moved upward as the water rose.

The main part of the city was built above the highest flood marker. Buddhist temples with belled towers and moon-arch bridges broke the monotony of roofs green with moss. White and gray shops and dwellings and yellow-green red pavilions and public buildings rose in tiers up the gray sandstone walls. Outside the eastern and western walls, additional sections spoke of expansion and prosperity. The cliffs were dotted with the makeshift villages of refugees. The river disappeared into higher western mountains that dissolved into fleecy blue clouds. In the misty twilight the multitude of flickering lights, the gurgle of water swirling around the junk and the musical tones of Chinese voice enchanted us.

In mooring we joined fleets of *wu bans* that looked like bees clustered around their queen. Traffic from the western interior and from the east was heavy. The chants, shouts and haggling of hundreds of coolies created a great chorus.

In these past nine days, we had come to respect the crew's skill and fortitude. True, they had at times been fractious, but they had gotten their cargo and passengers to Wanxian safely and in good time.

Such boatmen they were! Garlic-ridden, sweaty and lice-infested, they were a tested, testy and motley lot. How the oarsmen, trackers and men on the giant ow sweeps had labored! And the skipper–unscheduled and shylock though he ⁄as–had been a creditable *lao ban*. The lead tracker, a veritable choirmaster, ⁄ith his enduring strength and dogged persistence, was never to be forgotten. ʰe cook, even with his Hubei prejudices, had fed us consistently and suffi-ᵢently, if not well. From him, too, we had learned much about the gorges. *Lao* ᵢᵤ, the hard-muscled, soft-hearted lead oarsman, *Lao Ma*, the skipper's wife, ᵉr intimidated son, her daughter with her three-day-old baby and her grand-ₐughter *Mei-mei*, who had come so close to drowning, have remained strong ₁ my memory over the decades.

Towering over them all was the statuesque model first officer *tai gong*. The ⁄ords he quoted from the *I Ching* haunted me:

*Pushing upward with confidence in time*
*Has success and brings good fortune.*

Wang Shi insisted that the next phrase from the classic also applied:

*One sees the greatness of humanity in a great man,. . .*
*The reason for lasting success is not an earthly*
*quality alone, but a transcendental one.*

We three Westerners realized how closely, through perils and magnificence, ⱱe had lived with these indomitable persons. We felt privileged to have entered ₙto this microcosm of China's *laobaixing*. No ordinary adieu would suffice. ⱱe waved and saluted. Thompson and I said a private benediction, then turned ₒ mount the wide stone steps leading to the massive towers of the city's South ʒate. With our gear we debarked and joined the files of water carriers sloshing ₚlashes upon the slippery stone steps.

We had scarcely taken two steps, however, when we found the cook, now ᶠunctioning as the boat's steward, at our elbows: "*Jiuqian bugou!* (Wine money ᵢ.e., tip) is not enough!"

These few words dashed our sentiments. This was no time or place to be ₛquabbling over what had already been an ample tip. We offered him a supple-ₘent sufficient to let him and his *lao ban* save face with the skipper's wife who ₛhook her fist at us.

Our feet took us up toward the South Gate, but our hearts remained below ₒn the junk the bowmen were poling away. A tall, poised, younger lead bow-ₘan returned our final wave. Our eyes followed the junk to one of the repair ₛhips we had just passed. As it became lost in the forest of other masts, we pon-ₗered the fact that the journey we had just ended had been taking place for some 3,000 years.

What was most real to me in those parting moments were the 500-foot long bamboo rafts, the 95-foot-long cargo *wu ban*, the hard-bitten but heroic river people, the oarsmen and sweepmen stroking against the current, the vicious whirlpools and treacherous rapids, the way my heart had leaped into my throat when suddenly we had seen below us a bloated body float past and above us the golden rays of the setting sun illuminate a hilltop pagoda.

All these events, places and people were reminders once again that the world, beyond all telling, is both a beautiful and an ugly place.

We held our breath, aware that having been baptized in a few of the Long River's fearsome mysteries, we would never be the same because of this journey.

CHAPTER SIXTEEN

# A Promising Welcome

*Van Xian's Tang Dynasty Bridge by Helen Houser*

The energy and confidence of this bustling upriver port was contagious. No time to grieve leaving the *wu ban* and its resolute crew. Making our way from the river's edge, we had to increase our pace or risk being trampled by those intent upon their business. Fast-climbing carriers and hucksters pressed us to the edge of the steps.

What a bonus we gained at the steps edge! A full view of the stunning 1,200 year-old (Tang Dynasty) Heavenly Bridge that bursts out of the rock on either side of the city's central tributary.

This spectacular bridge nearest the river bore the inscription *"Dian shen iao"* (Bridge Created by Heaven). A delicate pavilion surmounted the center f the bridge's single arch. Slender, well-proportioned pagodas and a three-sto-

ried, ornate *ding tzi* (tea house), guarded the approaches. The airy span of th
bridge connected the walled city with its sprawling western suburb. In times c
low water, the tributary stream, which the bridge spanned, offered loc
women their favorite laundering spot.

It's elegant arch uniting the banks presented a classic picture. We had t
pause!

From the stairs summit, we funneled through the immense, iron-studde
city gates and into a spacious plaza.

Even at this twilight hour, the plaza was alive with shoppers darting in an
out of stores festooned for the Spring Festival. Noises echoed between th
massive towers and the walls of the surrounding ancient buildings. From th
far end came the rat-a-tat-tat of stone masons' chisels cutting limestone block
From other angles came a tinsmith's hammering, the hawking of vendors, th
laughter of children, the kitten cries of infants, the banter of flirting couple
the chants of magicians, the moans of beggars, the music of flutes and fiddle
Small groups gathered to gossip, bicker or listen to storytellers.

We made our way past terraces and up steep connecting streets through th
city's old section. Above the crowded lanes rose the aromas of deep-fried pas
tries, roasted chestnuts, barbecued chicken and flotsam in open sewers. Withi
the recesses of squalid alleyways we could see ragged, sore-encrusted beggars

On higher ground, we came upon broader streets with substantial housc
and well-kept guild lodges. This upper tier afforded a panoramic view of th
Myriad City. Below us we could see the river, its docks and the great ston
stairs that conveyed streams of burdened people to the enormous South Gatc

To the east, a half-moon was rising. On the western horizon, the distar
mountains were red and gold against the sinking sun. Below them were dark
er ranges of flat-topped hills, which stood in a mysterious, low-lying purpl
mist like cardboard cut-outs, one in front of the other. Nearer still were ter
raced slopes luxuriant with tung-oil trees, early wheat, barley, rape seeds, bear
and blooming poppies. The near hills, delicately split by tributary streams, sur
rounded the city in a protective embrace.

Wanxian's *feng shui* (good-omened location), so desired by Chinesc
approached perfection. The city blended with the water, earth, wind and star:
The organic fusion of nature's elements with human structures has pleasc
even the most exacting necromancers.

Centuries ago, the city had begun spreading out along the north riverbank
These developments expanded the boundaries miles on either side of the eas
and west walls. A rivulet from the northern hills swelled to a sizable stream an
split the city into two sections. What nature had divided, however, the inhabi
tants long ago had connected with a series of bridges.

Thompson had served in Wanxian his first missionary term, so he guided us to the China Inland Mission. Reaching the high-walled compound, we announced our arrival in the usual way of pounding on the large gate. Inside, the gatekeeper labored to slide clear the bolts, then swung one of the great doors open. Using his sleeve to wipe remnants of a supper we had interrupted, he grilled us concerning our identities. Finally, he let us in and sent his son scampering to call the head of the house.

Beyond the servants' quarters were the goat stables. A walkway bounded by well tended flower beds and blossoming plum trees led to an inner court. In a red sandstone mound was a cave which had been used as a bomb shelter during the war. From the cave's musty interior two mongrels bounded. After quieting them, the gatekeeper ordered them to escort us through a moon gate into another large courtyard. Offices and receiving rooms surrounded a small amphitheater. Next door were the primary school's classrooms. Through another moon gate to our right was a barn-like church.

Dormitories and guest houses lay in back of the central courtyard. Each unit was set apart by latticed screens. Windows were decorated with bamboo paper. Curved tiled roofs pointed skyward with their ends supported by protruding eaves, carved beams.

At the second moon gate we were met by three hosts, Horace Harlow and two young Chinese, Pastor Wang and Ms. Chen, a high school teacher. They apologized for not meeting us at the entrance, explaining they had just finished vespers.

Tall and almost gaunt, Harlow appeared stern and reserved. His friendly greeting and firm handshake, however, conveyed a generous hospitality. He cut the introductory amenities to a minimum, sensing our eagerness for hot baths. Pastor Wang promised to have the gardener, who doubled as a handyman, carry in buckets of hot water. Ms. Chen led us to our rooms on the second floor.

We took turns using the large iron tub that years ago had been shipped here as cargo on a junk like our *wu ban*. Thompson, who considered himself the most in need of cleansing, went first. He exuded words of ecstasy as he soaked and lathered in the hot water. In time the others of us enjoyed the same bliss.

The guest quarters, though simple, were attractively furnished. Walls, roofs and pillars of fine-grained wood displayed exacting craftsmanship. Our windows opened to the courtyard and provided a superb view of the city and the eastern stretch of the river. Through a door on the north, steps ascended a wooden tower with a pagoda-like roof. From that vantage, we saw the encircling city wall and the roofs of neighboring houses, temples and shrines. On distant peaks and ridges behind the city, the last rays of sun outlined the villas of high officials and wealthy merchants.

Around the supper table we became acquainted with our host, whom

*C.I.M. Guest House, 1898 Photo by Bird Bishop enhanced by Helen Houser*

Thompson had already described. From Minnesota, Harlow's mother, an emi gre from Sweden, had met her Yankee husband in the Midwest. Born an raised in Minnesota and reared on a farm, Harlow had been late entering th university, where he had initially planned to become a mechanical engineer.

"In those days," Harlow explained, "I was an enlightened modern wh took Genesis as a myth. Thoughts about Heaven and Hell were not my cor cern. I saw Christ as an historical character. Engineering and success were m aims. Over weekends, my roommate and I were quite the rounders."

Pausing to finish dessert, he continued, "I was bent on science's realist approach to life, but on account of a blonde I was pursuing, I began attendin a study group at the campus Student Christian Association."

"It's been a long haul from those days 30 years ago," he mused, sipping h tea. "The longer I went to those study groups, the more I had to consider th possibility of a God who might have an other-than-engineering plan for me My imagination was caught by the graphic accounts missionaries gave abou the missions in China being 'white unto the harvest.' And deeper still was th contagion of these men and women's clear sense of vocation. They felt they' been 'called' to go to China. Those impassioned interpreters challenged wit the question: why not you?"

Harlow explained that the young lady he'd been courting and then marrie was ahead of him in answering "yes" to overseas service. At 25 he too answere "yes" and entered seminary. Upon graduation he was sent across the Pacifi After a year of language study, he was assigned to Wanxian.

"What about your family?" asked the major.

Harlow explained that their two sons and one daughter were born in Chin

Now, almost grown, they would remain in the States to complete their college. His wife planned to return to China in a few months.

Impressed with Harlow's straightforward manner, the major explained that he, too, had studied engineering. He further explained, "When the draft was about to catch me, I joined the Air Force and I'm glad I was eventually assigned to duty in China."

"Before coming to China I had always been leery of missionaries, holding the usual misconceptions of would-be Western sophisticates. I considered missionaries misguided, but harmless. They were to be tolerated as long as their 'fulfilling their calling' made them feel better. I didn't buy their imposition of Western beliefs on a people who seemed already to have a rich religious background of their own. I saw missionaries as religious imperialists. It seemed presumptuous for Caucasians from distant lands to urge Christianity over established Buddhism, Daoism and Confucianism. I was embarrassed to hear of Bible-thumping, hell-fire-and-damnation types. I also doubted their motives, thinking they hadn't made the grade in their own country, so they counted on becoming better off in China. What an eye-opener to see what you missionaries do!"

"So good to hear you've seen the light!" Harlow responded with a twinkle. "Stateside people have little comprehension of what the China missionaries do or how they live. I often wish I could transport the officers of my sponsoring churches to Wanxian for a couple days."

"Big changes, however, are coming fast. Beginning my fourth seven-year term and close to retirement, I have not reneged on John R. Mott's great vision of 'evangelizing the world in one generation'. But it's going to take more than one generation."

"China today is much different from what it was before the war. For centuries the majority of Chinese officials and intelligentsia resented and resisted Christianity as 'foreign.' It was seen as part of the West's carving up of China. Now more than ever, messengers of the Gospel must dissociate themselves from any vestiges of imperialism."

"In this post-war period, missionaries must be responsive to the many radical changes sweeping China. One big change is that foreign missionary influence must wane. Our job has become strengthening the Chinese church to be self-supporting, self-governing and self-propagating."

"Recently a deacon and I visited an ailing elder. In his small room was also his Western-educated younger brother. In the past, the younger brother has been antagonistic toward the elder's 'foolish preoccupation with Christianity.' For a change, the critic was friendly. Several times when I turned from conversations with the elder, I found the younger man's eyes searching mine. In time he asked questions concerning Christianity. Over the months a bond grew

between us. His parting comment to me today was telling: 'I'm glad you ar
you and that you came here today. May I come to see you some time this weel
to talk over changes in my life?'..."

"We are finding increasing numbers of officials and commoners who ar
reaching for hope, faith, and a vital connection to a new type of community.

Though Harlow's words were hopeful, he felt the weight of responsibilit
in meeting these challenges. Thompson had told us of Harlow's 'whole-soulec
response' to living in the crossfire of a changing China. We were glad to kno·
from Thompson that Harlow knew the importance of periodically findin
times of Zen-like stillness and renewal.

From outside came bursts of laughter and the clapping of servants and thei
friends gathered in the dim courtyard. Without movies and dances as diver
sions, and being for the most part illiterate, commoners found professional sto
rytellers, such as the one who was weaving his tales below us, a welcome trea
As their favorite raconteur, Old Zhu sometimes enhanced his stories with son
or made use of his weather-beaten stereopticon. We were intrigued with th
rousing melodies with which he embellished his heroic tales. With skill an
gusto, he dramatized the fears and absurdities, majesty and tragedy of th
Three Kingdoms period some 17 centuries ago.

Overpowering Old Zhu for a moment was a cry accompanied by a tinn
wistful peal. Coming from beyond the compound wall, it was the plaintiv
gong of the district timekeeper, signaling to all that the hour had grown late

Whereas Thompson wished to journey via bus to his former station in th
morning, Harlow insisted that we other three downriver guests, who migl
never again have the chance to visit the Myriad City, extend our stay at lea
three days. Saturday, he said, we could visit two rural "preaching points." O
Sunday we could participate in the two worship services. In the meantim
there was much to see.

While grateful for his offer, this concerned dollars, not hospitality. Th
major, Wang Shi and I remained firm about our need to leave the day afto
tomorrow. In reply, Harlow and his two Chinese co-workers shook their heac
at our slighting of the Myriad City. "Why are you so determined to start bac
so soon?" they asked. To which we explained that we must keep the rer
dezvous with the pilot in Yichang, else we would miss our flight back t
Nanjing.

"Let's talk it over in the morning," Harlow suggested as he accompanied ι
to our quarters. "You have had a long and strenuous day."

# Wanxian, The Myriad City

The peals of the church bell at daybreak the next morning failed to awaken us. Soon afterward, however, Thompson's knocking did. With enthusiasm he invited us to join him at Harlow's house in a half hour for the staff's morning prayers. The major and I agreed: the major out of consideration for our hosts, and I out of guilt for my long neglect of a recommended practice of my respected Southern grandmother.

Still not fully awake, we reached the living room where young Pastor Wang welcomed us with the same cordiality he'd shown before. His black robe and dignified manner alerted us to be ready for a somber thirty minutes. "In our ten-minute matin the ten of us have at least ten things to be grateful for," he said, then prayed:

> *The Father seeks such to worship him—in spirit and*
> *in truth. God is a spirit, and those who worship him*
> *must worship in spirit and truth. (John 4:23)*

In an eager tone, he continued with invitational words from Psalms:

> *Arise and tell the commandments to their children, so*
> *that they should not be like their fathers, stubborn,*
> *rebellious and ignorant. (78: 6-8)*

He then deferred to his mentor, Pastor Ban Dian, who said he was thankful for the way his faith had been quickened by the zeal of two new communicants. He used "mission-speak words" like "spirituality" and "salvation." Then, face brightening, short and to the point, he declared, "Though we see Him not, our Heavenly Father is with us even in this moment. Let us open to his Spirit. Let us listen to what it tells us about how to live this day."

All now on our knees, each in turn offered simple, direct words of thanks and praise. One woman voiced the prayer, "O great Father, you have big ears and much wisdom; listen to us and guide us through another day." Another in the circle spoke from the heart, "Great Sustainer, we often stumble and fall on our faces. Forgive our weaknesses, pick us up and put us on the right path." A pastor intern invoked blessings for the "visitors from downriver," adding, "Bless the major, who, with his brave fellow airmen, helped our people defeat the enemy."

After a pause, each in the circle stood up, clasped hands and sang a verse of "What a Friend We Have in Jesus." Two Chinese pastors invited us to attend the mid-week services that night.

Following breakfast, the major, Wang Shi and I sought out the business manager, the "travel specialist," to book passage for our return. He agreed to contact *lao ban* at the riverbank for us.

Leaving the office, we stepped into a group of colorfully dressed, well scrubbed kindergartners lining up for class. They could not keep their eyes off us foreigners and resisted marching into their room. Grinning and chuckling, they were intrigued by the major's 6'2" height and auburn hair. Across the courtyard, adults found it difficult to go about their business as usual. Many lingered to gawk and to catch a word with us.

Harlow's cook returning from market, pulled his bicycle through the outer moon gate. He had a phenomenal load: bundles of white cabbage, spinach, turnips, a large river trout, a straw bag full of eggs, a bottle of rape-seed oil and, on top of the crowded carrier, a squirming hen with wings and legs tied.

Noticing our curiosity, Miss Johnson, one of the younger missionaries, explained, "Chinese cooks are wonderful! We could not get along without ours. They perform culinary miracles! Mrs. Harlow is from the South, so our chef cooks the best grits, gravy and hot biscuits you've ever tasted."

Miss Johnson assured us that missionary cooks did much more than plan and prepare meals. They were adroit at haggling amidst the confusion of the Chinese markets. In their purchases, it was understood that they deserved a "modest percentage," provided they managed to save their employer money wherever possible. They were adept at designing menus with in-season produce and stockpiling surplus. The year's supply of sugar, for example, was delivered 30 pounds at a time in large bamboo baskets. Coming from the open boiling vats used during the harvest, the sugar was coarse and dirty. The cook had to refine it, adding water, boiling, straining and recooking it.

"Our cook," she said, "doubles as waiter. After preparing the food, he dons his white serving coat. What's more, he is foreman of the other servants, supervising their work, pay, quarters and complaints. He has even cajoled his wife into being our laundress. Likewise, he is one of our chief sources of information, which he picks up gossiping with other cooks while he does the shopping."

Harlow appeared with bicycles for our tour of the Myriad City. He proposed an itinerary including the hillside missionary cemetery, the North Gate, the Drum and Bell Towers, the old town, the City Temple and a famous antique shop near the Bridge From Heaven.

In an aside to me, Wang Shi expressed apprehension about visiting a burial place. By explaining that perhaps our host wanted to "pay respect to the ancesors," I allayed his reluctance. I encouraged him to go with us, insisting that we needed him to check the *feng xui* (location appropriateness) of the cemetery.

The cobblestone road led us through a valley surrounded by rolling green hills. Along the way we passed clusters of mud-walled, bamboo-thatched farmhouses. Every square inch was put to use with crops planted right up to walls of the huts and the edges of the road. Up the hillsides were terraces with a few walled in compounds.

The harder we pedaled uphill, the more lucid were Harlow's introspections. "There's more than nostalgia or a sense of duty to visiting 'the sacred hill,'" he commented. "I'll never forget how, on my very first day in Wanxian, Reverend Warren Abernathy, who started here at the end of the 19th century and was completing his third term, took me to the cemetery. 'You need to walk up here regularly,' he told me, 'for meditative remembrance of the high price so many of our colleagues paid for serving the Lord in Wanxian.'"

"Visits to the hill remind me of my limitations. The psalmist's words come back: 'The days of our years. . .are soon cut off, and we fly away.'

I think often of Abraham Willoby's powerful comments about death. After his wife, the mother of five, died in a dreadful typhus epidemic, he told me, 'Her death brought me face-to-face with myself as finite. Usually we look at death from the outside, in relation to the world. But we must consider death also from the inside, in relation to the self. In her prime, Gertrude, my wife, was enthusiastic and full of energy. Embracing her family, she seemed to embrace eternity. Beyond her family, many were touched by her affection, loyalty and courage. I realize now that, even before her illness, she saw life as a preparation for death.'"

Of the 'sacred hill' Wang Shi noted, "Practical location on the hillside keeps buildings off prime farmland. It's best to have highland behind and lower reaches on the sides and in front. The place is well chosen, intertwined in the rhythm of surrounding land."

The cemetery was circled by an eight-foot wall much in need of repair. The arch over the entrance gate was inscribed with three characters: *An Lo Yuan* (Paradise). The supporting columns were circled by a *lung* (dragon), imparting a mystical dimension. The tarnished brass plaque read "Sacred Mount–Final earthly resting place for faithful and beloved servants of the Lord. In their resurrection they rest in peace."

The tombstones' disarray and the grounds' neglect accentuated the haunting solemnity. The Chinese elms, azaleas and stately Lombardy poplars conveyed a sense of peace and order suggestive of Wordsworth's "Lines Composed Above Tintern Abbey:"

*. . .Hearing oftentimes*
*The still, sad music of humanity,*
*Nor harsh, nor grating, though of ample power*
*To chasten and subdue. And I have felt*
*A presence that disturbs me with the joy*
*Of elevated thoughts; a sense sublime,*
*Of something far more deeply interfused,*

Wang Shi had been reluctant to visit "the foreigners' burial place," but now was intrigued by the headstones.

"Chinese tombstones are usually rather dull," he said. "On top is the name of the dynasty or place where the person was born, then, on a perpendicular line in the center, is the sex and family name of the deceased. To the left, in smaller characters, is the name of the deceased's sons. Nothing else–no loving record of their virtues, no hope expressed about reuniting with the deceased."

Despite the garden's unkemptness, he said, this place has a more positive atmosphere than that of the "Shadowy World of Death" associated with Chinese burial places. The Chinese enshroud their grave sites, imagining them to be a spirit land that is the counterpart of their threatening present-day world. Like many Chinese, Wang Shi was not religious in the way Jews, Christians and Muslims understand the term, but he certainly was spiritual in appreciating nature and humanity's place in it.

"These stones," Harlow pointed out, "also tell of stark realities, particularly of the awful death toll on young missionaries in the 19th century."

|  |  |
|---|---|
| Mary Anne McDonald | Jonathan David Bowron, M.D. |
| b. March 1871 d. July 1898 | b. January 1864 d. June 1895 |
| Beloved wife of Robert | Irreplaceable Mission Physician |
| Mother of Kenneth and Anne | Beloved husband and father |

"Both died during their first term: Mary in childbirth when she was only 27 and Dr.Bowron in the cholera plague, after saving countless others, when he was only 31. Instead of the biblical 'three score and ten,' theirs was but one score and ten."We found the markers of even younger persons all the more sobering:"

|  |  |
|---|---|
| Susan Roberts | David Lloyd Smithfield |
| Called to the Lord | b. Emporia '11 d. Wan Hsien '16 |
| In her third year | An Everlasting Joy |
| Beloved by John and Ruth | Remembered forever by Fred and Naomi |

Children and young women were especially vulnerable to the onslaught of oriental viruses. In the first three generations of the mission, in the days before vaccines and other preventive medicines, diphtheria, dysentery, small pox and typhoid fever frequently decimated entire missionary families.

On a mound near the back wall, we found the tombs of Abraham and Gertrude Willoby. Two tall and elegant basalt markers bore them tribute:

|  |  |
|---|---|
| Abraham Douglas Willoby | Gertrude Alexander Willoby |
| b. Cleveland 1875 d. Wan Hsien l940 | b. Toledo 1879 d. Wan Hsien 1935 |
| Make me to know mine end, | God is our Refuge and Strength |
| And the measure of my days | A very present Help in trouble |
| Dedicated Missionary Leader | "I vowed I'd serve my husband, |
| Deeply Respected Lover of Chinese | And with him live and die." |

Harlow explained that the second quote on Gertrude's stone was from a verse titled "Till Death Do Us Part," written by the Tang dynasty poet Zhang Ji. Abraham Willoby had died of a heart attack, five years after Gertrude's death. After the memorial service in the packed sanctuary, twelve deacons had carried the elaborate catafalque donated by the city fathers up the hill. Though it was raining, a huge procession, many of whom were not professing Christians, followed. In the throng were officials, generals, teachers, smugglers, fishermen, hilltop villagers and both reformed and unrepentant pirates and bandits.

Bolting the gate and turning the key in the latch were the only sounds as we exited.

Wang Shi broke the silence with, "I don't know about 'Protestant Paradise,' but the quiet of this place is more powerful than the stillness we found in the Buddhist monastery. I'm beginning to understand why Mr. Harlow brought us here. Our visit is much superior to the Spring Rite of dusting off the graves of ancestors."

"This has stirred so many turbulent feelings!" was the major's reaction as we bumped downhill over the cobblestones. "What tremendous courage these early missionaries demonstrated! Half the world away from their loved ones, their loneliness at times must have been excruciating. A few months ago, in France, I visited the American cemetery of World War I heroes lost at the Marne. In this Sacred Mount lie heroes as well!"

We dropped into a canyon, crowded with wall-to-wall shacks and shops, then labored up another steep and narrow cobblestone street. Wanxian's streets, like those of other Three Gorges' cities and towns, didn't follow the regular grid pattern of Chinese plain cities, but instead clung to hillsides and precipices. They didn't occupy land so much as they defied gravity. As a consequence, the streets were not parallel but followed natural contours and ledges. Coexisting with the roads was a network of stairs and ramps that carried pedestrian traffic. A large portion of the goods were still carried on human backs.

We came to a cliff-side niche that housed a gilded statue of *Li Dai Bo*, famed 4th-century poet who had studied here in his youth. Like those in other Three Gorges settlements, the people of Wanxian labored to keep the memory of *Li Dai Bo* fresh in their minds and hearts–"very green," as the Chinese say. The spot where he had read, wrote and played checkers was the promontory that crowned this cliff. The effigy in the niche showed the poet smiling down at the copper-colored river, appreciating what is called "the most beautiful view in the prefecture."

The three-storied *Chung Gu Lo* (Bell and Drum Tower) overlooked the river on one side and a jewel of a canyon on the other. In the 19th century its large stage had been the setting for Confucian, Buddhist and Taoist dramas. Two miles back, atop a rocky peak, was the imposing Temple of the Three Religions, reached by climbing 1,570 stone steps.

That day happened to be the birthday of *Matzu*, the androgynous god/goddess of ocean and river. A huge parade was making its way to the temple, and along the wider streets, we saw colorful floats depicting scenes from Chinese history and literature–tableaus of pretty women in traditional costumes and athletic men twirling ancient weapons.

As we overtook the slow-moving procession, we had to dodge the zigzagging 'god carriages' and the firecrackers exploding around them. On each palanquin was the image of a god, who was honored by the boisterous antics and shouts of the carrier. As the deity passed, he or she 'blessed' each doorway. The air was so thick with smoke and gunpowder that a man with a small bellows ran alongside the palanquins to give the bearers fresher air.

Reaching the colorful pavilion, we found hundreds of people milling about the courtyard, restless in anticipation of the coming excitement.

Near the entrance a woman in a trance wrote messages she received from the spirit world in a tray of sand. Other mediums, given the more magical name of sorcerers, also fell into trances after engaging in elaborate dances accompanied by music and drumming. A divinity or ancestral spirit entered the woman's body and used her voice as a channel for its message. Wang Shi took a dim view of sorcerers' practices, decrying them as 'archaic habits from feudal days.'

At another spot sat a man whose back had been pierced with long brass skewers resembling knitting needles. Objects fastened to the skewers pulled against his skin. In a trance as well, he appeared immune to pain. The devout knelt and bowed, lighting incense sticks and placing them before shrines and ancestral plaques. Around the central altar attendants dressed in street clothes and priests in yellow robes chanted verses from Buddhist scriptures.

A group of 40 or 50 people entered the temple and, with much aplomb, handed a small bundle decorated with pennants and flowers to an attendant, who passed it to a second attendant at another altar, who passed it over the smoke of incense sticks, and so on until the bundle reached the main altar, where it was placed in front of the *Matzu* image. After a few minutes of bowing and chanting, the attendants handed the bundle back cross the altars until it was received by the waiting group with a tumultuous shout of joy. Holding it high, they danced out of the temple as another group came in and the ceremony was repeated.

These groups brought *Matzu* images from their respective village temples to be "recharged" with power from the central *Matzu* shrine. In this way, the god/goddess's power would be more effective in their lives during the year ahead. Skippers, too, often returned recharged bundles to their junks to serve as protective talismans. After leaving the temple, the renewed images were carried through the streets via palanquins like those we had dodged earlier.

In the Chinese mind, "God power" can deteriorate but can also be revived. Select people are able to contact the spirit world; others, while in a trance, can be physically "hurt" but feel no pain. A Buddhist priest may participate in the worship of a non-Buddhist god, and a bodhisattva's likeness may be associated with tablets honoring the ancestors.

Later we passed through stone-columned "widow's arches," for which Sichuan was renowned. Called *pai lo* in north China, these splendid structures were known as *pai fangs* in this province. Widows who adhered to grieving protocols and thereafter remained faithful to their deceased husbands were honored by these arches, but *pai fangs* had also been raised to honor women who had suffered wrongs, dealt heroically with the trials of life and faced death to uphold their chastity. Such women might even become goddesses to the local villagers, prayed to by men and women alike.

The Sichuan *pai fangs* sometimes rose to 75 feet, towering above two-storied shops and houses. Often hand-carved in intractable granite with inscriptions, dragons, lions and other symbolic decorations, they stood as striking tributes, not only to the celebrated women and goddesses, but to the rich who had commissioned them and the artists and laborers who had built them.

Neither Confucius nor his disciples sought to deify women. Rather, they had canonized lesser male literary and military figures. In contrast, these *pai fangs* honored women who served their parents-in-law and did good works. These tributes were to women who had helped hold society together, which was certainly at the apex of the Chinese hierarchy of virtues. While Chinese society was patriarchal, these arches served as powerful acknowledgments of what the psychiatrist Carl Jung called the *anima*–the feminine component inherent in both individuals and societies.

Sadly, these unique sculptural masterpieces were being dismantled to make way for wider avenues. In the days of automobiles, buses and trucks, the magnificent creations proved little more than inconveniences and traffic hazards.

In his book *Cosmos and History*, Mircea Eliade speaks of modern man's effort to come to terms with the "terror of history," in short, the struggle to make tolerable powerful pressures. In their bones, I knew the Chinese felt and respected their history, yet they were anxious and insecure in facing the radical changes which gripped their land during post-war reconstruction. Nonetheless, I found the systematic leveling of these arches disheartening.

The remaining *pai fangs* manifested a distressing irony. Camped at their bases were often miserable poor and diseased beggar-widows. The alleys over which the arches rose had stone slabs which barely covered the wretched sewers below and, by no means, covered the stench. On either side of the arches, against the abutments of the intricately carved pillars, were rows of lean-to hovels, the abject abodes of starving squatters.

On the way back to the mission compound, Harlow took us by one of his favorite antique shops. At such places, the oriental aficionado might find porcelain and bronze from the Ming dynasty, or even a Song dynasty (10th century A.D.) piece. A browser with particular good fortune might even take home a Tang bronze or terra-cotta horse. This was no hole-in-the-wall shop. In its aged building and collections of period treasures, it had the makings of a provincial museum.

For those who must travel light, little signature "chops"– stones carved with the purchaser's name in ideographs of many different styles–were of particular interest. Atop the two-or three-inch-high, ¾ inch square pieces was carved the person's animal of choice: dragons, lions, tigers, rabbits and elephants. But for

e connoisseur and the novice alike, pieces of jade never failed to prove attrac-
ve. For the benefit of foreigners, the owner of this shop had framed above his
splay of jade objects the English translation by the scholar Legge of a famous
ssage from Li Ji:

> *In ancient times. . .men found the likeness of all excellent qualities
> in jade. Soft, smooth and glossy, it appeared to them like benevolence;
> fine, compact and strong like intelligence; angular, but not sharp
> and cutting like righteousness; hanging down (in beads), as if it would
> fall to the ground like (the humility of) propriety; when struck, yielding
> a note clear and prolonged, yet terminating abruptly like music; its
> flaws not concealing its beauty, nor its beauty concealing its flaws
> like loyalty; with an internal radiance issuing from it on every side
> like good faith; bright as a brilliant rainbow like heaven; exquisite
> and mysterious, appearing in the hills and streams like the earth;
> standing out conspicuously in the symbols of rank like virtue;
> esteemed by all under the sky like the path of truth and duty.*

We saw ancient relics, both genuine and imitations. The workmanship of
ese early craftsmen was good, and the ancient people's work worthy of imi-
tion, though it was sad, we thought, that maintaining tradition was more
ghly valued than self-expression.

We were glad to find folk art, a celebration of the ordinary. As the Three
orges abound in bamboo, bamboo baskets, vases, plates, figurines, whistles,
d painted strips were commonplace. Handcrafted furniture, weaving, bead-
ork, jewelry, rug making and leather work were also regional traditions. Large
rnate fans were a local specialty, though not as delicate as those made in
angzhou and Suzhou. We were particularly taken with Three Gorges' peb-
les. Nature's weathering of stones is an art form in itself. Some pieces were
tractive for their shapes, smallness and mixed surfaces. Others were fascinat-
g for the artists' adornments.

A culture is kept vital by the harmony of its members, expressed here in
esigns of good luck, happiness, kindness, longevity, bountiful harvest, love of
eauty, joy and, most of all, hope in the future. In keeping with his persistent
ragmatism, Wang Shi simply commented, "All these crafts have strong poten-
al for development."

As we pushed our bicycles back up the long hill leading to the mission com-
ound, in the background loomed the revered Tian Shan, or Heavenly
lountain. Its south face, now emblazoned by the noonday sun, revealed a set-
ement near the hard-to-reach summit. This was a resort built and maintained
y the wealthy who, over the centuries, had sought protection from bandits
d invading soldiers. Tian Shan was impregnable and so required a minimal

number of guards.

Back at the mission, the administrator told us he had succeeded in bookin our downriver passage to Yichang. He had haggled long and hard to arrive a fare that was "reasonable."

We were interrupted by wailing from the room next door. A hysteric mother seated on the front bench was rocking back and forth on her heel moaning a frightened and anguished "*A yah, A yah, A yah!* I don't know wh took my little four-year-old. What can I do?"

She was so distraught that all our words of comfort were in vain. "I sha die! I shall die!" she repeated. Two women lay workers tried to quiet her, o embracing her and the other mopping her brow and giving her a cup of tea.

Not long afterwards, the gatekeeper came running, announcing, "*Xiao h tze lai la,* The child has come." Following him was a woman holding a sm girl by the hand.

"Coming here on the *da ma lu* (the big thoroughfare)," the woman sai "Little Sister was pushed down on the stone slabs by rushing carriers. She w screaming. But she's not seriously hurt, only frightened. You'll have to take h to the clinic where her bleeding head and arm can be treated."

After a touching reunion, the mother and her precious child walked han in-hand toward the clinic in the corner of the courtyard–a moving end to th first half of a day that had been both pensive and riotous.

# CHAPTER EIGHTEEN

# Feminine Enthusiasm And Power

Mrs. Chen Yu overflowed with enthusiasm for the challenging work in which she was engaged. We downriver guests simply had to come to her afternoon Women's Bible Class.

Having finished lunch, the major, Wang Shi and I were ready for a break: At sunrise we'd participated in the mission's matins, at the hillside cemetery we were sobered by reminders of fallen heroes, then we had circled the city on our bicycles, joined a parade, paused with refugees beside *pai fang* (memorial arches) and had been intrigued by a sorceress in a temple courtyard. We were ready to digest these experiences and relax.

Mrs. Chen graciously, but firmly, brushed aside our excuses. As one of our hosts, she had just begun with us. Despite our hesitance we succumbed to her insistence.

Already assembled in the chapel, the women were buzzing in clusters of conversation. The city and country types were apparent by their different attire. All wore trousers, those from country or lower class being wrapped round the ankles and tied, those from upper class being wide and decorated. The city women's clothes were more recently ironed and their shoes were of cloth, while the country women's coat-blouses were rumpled and their sandals made of straw. But as they chattered busily, what a person was wearing or where she was from did not seem to matter. Instead of hindering conversation, differences in education and status enhanced the vivacity of the 35 ladies.

Marguerite Johnson, a single missionary recently returned to China from her furlough in Nebraska, told us how surprisingly easy it was to start and expand these classes. Many women were eager to learn and hungry for social contacts. The temptation was to let these study-service clusters multiply, but tending them, took much time and effort. The members of these weekly afternoon groups, Miss Johnson explained, devoured the Bible for nuggets of wisdom and inspiration.

They also spoke of their efforts to transform good words into good deeds. For example, they had banded together to help widows and other needy friends and neighbors.

Some of their concerns were, of necessity, self-motivated. They shared strategies about extending the purchasing power of their already scarce money and sought advice about handling family misunderstandings and jealousies, and village or neighborhood feuds. Surrounded with uncertainties, they were reassured by hearing how other Christians handled daily difficulties. They asked, for instance: "Is it better to tell a neighbor off for a wrong she'd done to you? Or should you try to reason with her? Or visit the neighbor with a friend and negotiate the trouble?"

Sister Ji Ling-xi, a recent graduate from the mission high school, was the instructor. The daughter of a third-generation Christian family, her parents had taught her to read the Bible. Her favorite scripture was Psalm 19, she told us. When she was only 14 years old, she heard about becoming "a certified and card-carrying Christian" and had said, "Me too! That's what I want." She sought confirmation and joined the church.

Living with this decision had often been difficult. Her schoolmates argued with her about the existence of God, calling her *zhi jiao* (religion-eater). In senior middle school her convictions were so consistently challenged she said she often wondered why she had chosen this foreign faith.

The war years had brought unspeakable hardships: fleeing from advancing enemy soldiers, loss of loved ones and possessions, times of near-starvation. Eventually she worked through these struggles to a stronger, more vibrant faith.

Ji Ling-xi called for order twice without getting the group's attention. By raising her voice and giving a third call, all talking stopped. In a conversational manner, she focused on some of the life problems the women had been so intensely chattering about. In time she read the assigned scripture, pointed out its wisdom and asked for reactions. When she found the women receptive, she engaged them in a discussion about the meaning and implications of commitment, renewal, and service. A lively interaction began which evidenced wide divergence in biblical knowledge and religious experience.

"I see what you are saying about God's nature," said Mrs. Li Hua, who with two peasant friends, had walked from her village seven *li* (about five miles) away to attend class. "It's simple: the old gods we had in the country are made out of clay, but that of the Christians is made of wood."

"No, not wood only," interrupted Mrs. Eng, a two-year class veteran. "God not a thing but a special spirit, like a trusted friend."

"True," added Mrs. Chou from a neighboring village. "The God we honor nd serve is not made of either mud or wood, but is a caring and loving [eavenly Parent. The source of all wisdom, justice and love, this great God vites our respect and obedience."

"Jesus, the son of the Heavenly Father," suggested Mr. Tang, a young stu- :nt instructor who had slipped in and was sitting in the back row, "by his xample, his teachings and his sacrificial death, shows us what God is like. It's xplained well in the verse we are studying today:"

*If any one is in Christ, he is a new creation, the old has passed away, behold the new has come. (II Cor.5: 17)*

Making reference to the postwar deprivations and frustrations they were xperiencing, Mr. Tang added, "When anyone is united to Christ, old ways are ushed aside and new ways come to people."

Puzzled, Mrs. Li Hua persisted, "With my heart I feel you are telling me ɔmething true, but I've not experienced what you are talking about. My head an't picture what's not mud, wood or rice."

"It's easy to get locked into only what's right in front of our noses," Mrs. ;en Gai, a small, plainly dressed woman, offered. Though she gave the out- /ard appearance of simplicity, when she spoke, she showed herself to be refined nd perceptive. "We all have difficulty taking hold of what's 'not mud, wood r rice.' But since we think easily of the rich spiritual idea of the Tao, should it e hard to grasp the notion of a non-material god?"

"Something you can see and hold onto must be at the heart of being a Christian. We find God in 'the witness of deeds'—the caring way Christians are alled to behave day by day."

"Yes, yes," Mrs. Tang added. "Our Chinese phrase for 'witness' combines wo characters meaning 'to see with one's own eyes' and 'to provide proof or ive testimony.' To witness is to 'run in the blood of,' to get involved in, per- on-to-person relations. It's expressing care and support to family, friends, eighbors and people we work with."

"Let me tell you what I mean," Mrs. Ren Gai returned: "*Yue-han Xiao-jiei* Miss Johnson) knows my story. When I was in middle school here years ago, he found me rebellious, argumentative and difficult to teach. Nevertheless, he remained patient and loving. I was the oldest daughter of a wealthy offi- ial. Well-dressed and popular, I was impressed chiefly with myself. Before the apanese captured Yichang my father was transferred there and was unable to escape before the occupation. The Japanese confiscated my parents' home and treasures. Shortly afterward, both Father and Mother died within the space of a week–probably suicide. Then my blind grandmother was held in jail, awaiting investigation for their deaths. When Grandmother died only a few days after her release from prison, I was left as the head of the family and the sole support for four younger brothers and sisters."

"Frantic and back in Wanxian, I looked up my former teacher and poured out my desperation to her. Instead of lecturing me, she listened and encouraged me to put the pieces of my life and those of my brothers and sisters into new patterns. The love she showed me was tied to the confidence she had in power greater than all of us. Miss Yue-han steadied me, opened doors I had not seen and gave me strength to keep my family together, resisting offers of 'good' marriage into officials' families that would have compromised what had come to believe and how I want to live."

Ren Gai paused, eyeing Mrs. Wang and other new members who might not understand. "The 'new creation,'" she explained, "is an inner change. I was remade. I became different from what I was at my former best. The change is radical. It goes to the roots–to the head, heart and deeds. The difference is not just a blanking out of suffering, as some of our Buddhist friends recommend. The old self-centered, insecure person is no more. You become a new person and see the world more positively."

"Mrs. Ren Gai's confidence and enthusiasm came from much spiritual struggle," Miss Ji said empathetically. "Her moving experience didn't come from formal teaching or custom, but from personal study, prayer and service. She demonstrates what Pastor Ban says about people of genuine spiritual experience: 'As soon as one opens one's mouth to pray, you know immediately whether he or she is a true Christian.' Mrs. Ren Gai's journey of faith led her to put Christ at the center of her life. Since Christ means everything to her, she cannot but tell others of him."

Miss Ji encouraged Mrs. Li Hua and her villager friends to talk further during the week with Miss Ren Gai. "We grow," she assured them, "as we listen to others who have found the Christian way."

When the time came for adjournment, the women extended a special welcome to those visiting for the first time. Quickly, we Western visitors were surrounded by questioning women: Did churches in America have Bible study groups? Did country and city folk mix? Did our youth accept the Christian faith?

We visitors drew Miss Ji Ling-si aside to ask her about these lively grassroots groups. She told us the questions they raised indicated how the women stumbled over words like "amen" and "Alleluia." Then came questions regarding Bible history and teachings about which they had no background.

Coastal refugees shared their treasured dog-eared Bibles with people they met in the interior. In the exchange, it was customary to explain that owning Bible is great, but greater is studying and meditating on it, and greatest is living according to its message. The expanding number of Bible readers studied in light of the sufferings and deprivations of the war years. Though Bibles were still hard to come by, direct use of the Bible was growing, due in part to increasing literacy. With this greater accessibility to the Bible came a strengthening of bonds between Protestant denominations. Believers with differing backgrounds—mainline Protestants to conservative evangelicals—were held together by the relevance of the Bible's message in the people's struggle to survive and rebuild their bombed buildings and disrupted lives.

Before the war, most churches had been concentrated in cities and had made little contact with country people, who made up the vast majority of China's population. Today, Miss Ji observed, church leaders and sometimes whole congregations reached out into rural areas to win grassroots Christians among the country folk. Efforts to present the person of Christ's oriental qualities help to lesson the stigma of Christianity being a foreign religion. It is in presenting Christ's universal characteristics, however, that the faith is most convincing.

Two young adults edged through the circle of questioners and gave their English a try. After introducing themselves as an engineer and a government economist, they enthusiastically told of having recently received baptism.

Harlow observed, "The new converts' exuberant faith and the way they make it the center of their lives pale Westerners' casual convictions. Thoughtful young Chinese professionals who come to accept Christ, more often than not, have a long, hard struggle to reach that decision. While Chinese find it comparatively easy to identify with the oriental aspects of Christ, joining a Christian community often is more difficult. Accepting Christianity often brings serious social problems. Many new converts face being cut off from family members and friends."

"Making shifts in cultural gears is never easy," Harlow continued. "And so it is no small wonder that thoughtful and patriotic Chinese find it difficult to free themselves from the amorphous amalgam of Taoism, Confucianism, Buddhism and the powerful attraction of the secular faiths of communism, nihilism and scientism. Two of our best-trained high school teachers went through such inner tussles. One told me, 'I came to the point that I simply had to throw myself upon the mercy of Christ.'"

# A New Mandarin And Wanxian Mission's "Holy Trinity"

From out of th crowd, Huang Fu, magisterial elder approached us. Harlo introduced us, com menting that M Huang served now one of the church elders. Called away an assistant, Harlo left us alone with th distinguished-lookin gentleman.

"May we sit on th stone bench and talk He began. With arn folded and his wisp goatee bouncing u and down as he spok he seemed to be th classic Chinese vener ble, but his tri Western style trouser shirt and jacket mad him appear more mo ern. He did not fr over to what etiquett he was to confor himself; he wanted t talk to foreign guest

The wrinkles that appeared as he smiled suggested he was in his late '70s, bu his erect posture and energetic speech suggested a younger man. We conclud ed he was a new style Chinese elderly who presented himself with the grace an felicity of a timeless Confucian.

He engaged us immediately, posing the usual personal questions: age, num ber of children, residence, purpose of our trip, occupation, state of our healt developments in Nanjing, conditions in American hometowns and, of cours how we liked Wanxian. He had all day, and he assumed that we did too.

At our insistence, Mr. Huang told of himself. He had come from a county
at 35 li away to attend this mission middle school. For a father from the gen-
ry class to send an eldest son and heir to Wanxian to a foreign mission school
vas a most untraditional thing to do. It was also a radical departure for the
*uai jia zi di* (scion of an official family).

"The action was unusual for a well-connected, gentry or mandarin family,"
vas Wang Shi's translation.

"What is meant by mandarin?" the major asked Wang Shi to inquire.

"Describing my grandfather," our new friend began, "is perhaps the best
vay to tell you about a mandarin."

"Grandfather came from the gentry class, a family of landowners and offi-
ials. He shared the intense longing that every young Chinese, who had any
mbition for the future, had to some day become a mandarin. Hardly a son
vorn in the Empire about whom the father did not at once begin to have his
lreams of the son succeeding in the civil service exams and becoming a man-
larin. Like many of his forebears, he had a yearning and admiration for schol-
rly knowledge. The ideal was the man who was willing to fit into the norm of
he Tao, the cultured individual who was not exceptionally endowed by nature,
vut gives perfect expression to this norm according to tradition.

Since government service was the only prestige bestowing, face-giving occu-
vation open to him, Grandfather's main duty was to succeed in his examina-
ions, to cram as much theoretical knowledge as possible into his mind in as
hort a time as possible. After many years of studious mastering of classical
exts, of memorizing poetry, of becoming intellectually learned and emotion-
lly steeped in Confucianist orthodoxy and classical culture, and after satisfying
arsh judges, he sat for the stiff state examinations and passed.

"Having succeeded in going through the mill, he was given a government
vost—a reward for his intellectual accomplishments and his achievement of a
ertain mental conformism. His efficiency and performance of duties were of
econdary importance. He was admitted to the *guan jia* (officialdom house-
old). He no longer needed to remember all he'd learned; he had become a
*mandarin.*"

"Grandfather, though hardly an innovative civil servant, was a creditable
mandarin, something of a private scholar, poet or philosopher, versed in
Confucianism and in the refinements of Chinese life. As such he always com-
nanded the respect of his tenant farmers. He was, then, all of one piece, a har-
nonious representative of a great civilization, the essential although standard-
zed cog in the huge mechanism which keeps the cosmic play of Yin and Yang
vithin the bonds of heavenly harmony."

"His son, my father," Mr. Huang Fu said, "was a new mandarin, one in the
vest and truest sense. In 1905 the two-millennia-old civil-service and exami-

nation systems were abolished, so Father was saved from having to strugg|
through the old route. It was fortuitous, because Father was a renegade to tra
dition. An original and exceptional personality like my father could never hav
expressed himself adequately and fitted into the immense machinery of state
He was caught, nevertheless, in a social upheaval of volcanic proportions in th
decades that followed the 1911 revolution. Groping toward a substitute for th
verities and structures that had been swept aside, Father joined several loca
intellectuals who had ventured to Peking and come in touch with the "New
Tide" movement. The determined band of young turks and their avant-gard
professors, emphasized the value of science and the scientific approach in socia
studies, psychology and education.

"Fortunately for me, my father inherited and passed on the legacy of th
Confucianist "gentleman" who pursues wisdom and morality. For Father, tru
wisdom was not a mere matter of knowing with the mind but one of alterin
the whole human being and the society."

"Culture cannot be enclosed within the covers of abstract books or mori
bund tradition," he said thoughtfully. "It needs to be won by the long an
hard work of each generation. Father espoused a fundamental socialism that i
one of the remarkable characteristics of China's political and social instincts
He believed in state ownership of all natural resources in order to protect th
lower classes against the greed of the wealthy. He considered the justificatio
of a land-owning gentry living off the labor of tenant farmers lies in its bein
the warden of a precious cultural heritage which is at the disposal of all wh
care to master it."

The system provided many of the artists, poets and philosophers who stud
ied, preserved and annotated the great classics. The order brought the teach
ing of the classics up to date; preserved the ethical values of the traditiona
philosophies, and served the state. All this was the responsibility of the ill-pai
*mandarins*. This sort of *mandarin* or Chinese gentry who were responsibl
public servants, *mandarins* in the best sense, had a moral right to its existenc
as a contributing social class. The vision of the culture they espoused must b
"lived," failing which it would disappear from the surface of the earth. The rad
ical changes that came over China in the early part of the twentieth century
and the consequent loss of moral standards and sense of responsibility by th
landowning gentry, prepared the ground for a cyclonic uprising of the agrari
an masses.

True *mandarins* were scions of gentry and others whose personal integrit
was beyond question and who, in fact, were living China's highest visions o
culture.

"Father had no first-hand contact with Westerners," Mr. Huang Fu contin
ued, "but he was open to Western thought and was determined that his son
would be introduced to different learning and new thought. Forty years ag

ny brother and I were sent here to attend the middle school. I took to the new learning, including music and especially the piano. I was active as a pianist in he mission's musical programs, even though as a single adult going to church was not one of my most important concerns."

"After graduation, like my father  decades before," Mr. Huang Fu said, "I also was a renegade to tradition. I too was caught in a series of giant social upheavals. I felt myself an abandoned and betrayed victim as traditional forms collapsed during the war, and chaos separated me from my father, for whom I was to long all my life."

His account reviewed the devastations and violence that characterized the warlord years, the Guomindang's campaigns in the early '30s to 'exterminate' the Red bandits, and the recent decade of Japanese occupation.

"In 1941, while downriver on business in Yichang," he explained, "I was trapped by the Japanese advance and for four years was unable to get back upriver. The recollections of hardships and sufferings given by other war survivors had usually been imprecise, warped by the personal indignity, loss or pain they had been subjected to. Not so with me. These experiences were seared into m heart."

Mr. Huang's memoir was mesmerizing. With a calm that suggested stoicism, even more than patience, he gave graphic descriptions of his family's struggles, telling their intimate and immediate pain and horror that were often cloaked in silence.

He described how, under the Japanese, influential citizens were restricted in travel. Later Pastor Wang An gave an account of the persecution Huang Fu had suffered because of his influence in the business community and among Christians. The beatings he sustained had so badly damaged his right hand that he could no longer play the piano.

"In those dark days we saw no end to the occupation and began to fear that we might suffer the enemy's presence the rest of our lives," Mr. Huang explained. "The saying that 'the Han people eventually will conquer their conquerors' gave us little consolation. In the midst of our suffering, often all we had to hold on to was our integrity. But even that was wiped out when the virtue of patience seemed so much spineless resignation."

His way of thinking resided in its synthetic and concrete, almost feminine apprehension of reality. He shunned generalizations and analytical reasoning. The Chinese type of thinking or reasoning often springs from the master recipe, the "special" key formula which, once it is meditated upon and understood in all its implications, will unveil secrets and mysteries of the universe and of the human heart. He gave the famous example from the classic, Great Learning:

> *We are informed that the "men of old who wished to shine with*
> *the illustrious power of personality throughout the Great Society*
> *first had to govern their own fiefs efficiently. Wishing to do this,*
> *they first had to make an ordered harmony in their families.*
> *Wishing to do this, they first had to cultivate their individual*
> *selves (hsiu sheng). Wishing to do this, they first had to*
> *put their minds right. Wishing to do this, they first had*
> *to make their purpose genuine. Wishing to do this,*
> *they first had to extend their knowledge to the utmost.*

"You see," Mr. Huang said triumphantly, ". . . this is how to reach the ke formula: 'Such extension of knowledge consists in appreciating the nature c things.' Purposes then become genuine, mind becomes right, individual sel comes into flower, family becomes an ordered harmony, the state is governe efficiently, bringing peace to the Great Society.

This explanation helped us see how after a long string of difficulties, h found solace and meaning in being a Protestant convert; and following that even in his sunset years he was apparently poised for some new internal (an perhaps external) move. We were convinced that Mr. Huang himself wa indeed a new mandarin. He asked Wang Shi to translate a tribute to the majo He wanted to convey thanks to the American servicemen who helped defea the Japanese.

As three friends of his walked by, Mr. Huang stopped and introduced them Dr. Chen, a physician; Mr. Liu, a teacher in the middle school; and Mr. Zhang a flood-control engineer. "All three are graduates of this mission's middl school and are serving as deacons," Mr. Huang explained with pride.

We anticipated learning of Wanxian's medical network, educational systen and hydraulic problems, but a call to supper intervened.

Mr. Huang was reluctant to let us go, and added, "These three friends ar new and true *mandarins*."

Now the term had powerful meaning for us. Mr. Huang, these thre younger friends, and others like them are working to lay the foundations for structure of Chinese thought and society which would equal or excel the old

After a lengthy leavetaking, we walked to Harlow's house, where we wer greeted with a generous spread.

During supper, Harlow continued the conversation interrupted earlier "New converts," he said, "continue to experience the suspicions and ostracisn of non-Christian friends and relatives. Hardships, however, are matched witl new joys and new strengths. When they decide to become Christian, nev power accompanies their change into 'those who have found and been foun

y Christ.' Then, even though resistance to them may continue, the new con-
erts begin to find a new sense of identity."

"Just a moment," interjected the major. "How does accepting a foreign
aith help the Chinese? How do they cope with resistance from relatives and
riends?"

"Gaining a new faith introduces a burst of new ideas and new patterns of
ving," Harlow explained. "Just yesterday, for example, Mrs. Zhang, a newly
aptized middle-aged teacher, reported her new faith had strengthened her in
oticeable ways. She told that when she learned how Jesus met life's difficul-
ies with wisdom and love, she felt encouraged and renewed. When she
emembers how he overcame temptations and opposition, she's better able to
bsorb ridicule and resistance."

"These new Christians," Harlow continued, "elderly or young, commoner
r gentry, reach out and find supportive friends. The young reinforce older
hurch members and attract other young people. It is reassuring how their
ewfound lives validate the mission enterprise, but more important is the way
heir transformation wins positive response. It is chastening to see their devo-
ion to the church, their patience in suffering and their growth in hope and
ove. It is a joy to share meals, simple recreation and times of prayer with ded-
cated people like these. They strengthen the faith of the rest of us."

Over after-dinner tea, Harlow leaned back in his chair and became more
ntrospective, saying, "As as a backwoods teacher in the Dakotas, I started off
eeing life narrowly and legally through the first five chapters of the Bible. Over
he years, however, my message has become less dogmatic and more open, less
loctrinaire and more realistic. Also, since I'm a farmboy at heart, I've enjoyed
working with ordinary folk, the *laobaixing*. The longer I've stayed in China,
10wever, the more I've come to see the importance of working as well with the
ducated and official classes, such as Huang Fu and his friends whom you met.
30metimes we missionaries feel that, against the ancient social and philosophi-
al system of China, our creeds and sects wage war in vain. The Chinese are
ssentially a practical people, and any ethical system must appeal to their rea-
on. It must also be made to harmonize with fundamental principles of life
ransmitted through countless generations. The conversion of this great peo-
le must be both from the bottom up and from the top down."

We saw from our window mid-week worshipers assembling more than an
10ur early for the evening service. There were men of all ages and a few young
eople, but the majority were women. As we joined the early-comers in the
ourtyard, we heard one lady say, "This is better than going to the market."
And so it was.

When the bell rang to signal worship, the crowd flowed into the sanctuary.
After all the pews were full, other people entered with stools, hoping to find

space in the aisles. The latest arrivals were relegated to standing outside around open windows.

*Wanxian Mid-week Worship Service*

Two clergymen, a woman Bible teacher and several elders were seated in the chancel. In the pews many, with oversized Wanxian fans, were fanning themselves for relief from the heat rising from so many bodies. The pre-service singing was marked more for its gusto than its harmony. Hymns were Chinese translations of 18th- and 19th- century Western favorites: "Rock of Ages," "What a Friend we Have in Jesus," "He Leadeth Me" and "Love Divine, All Loves Excelling." Chatter and bustle accompanied the praise. A parade of dogs sniffed in and out of the crowded aisles.

With the *Yamen* at the end of one hymn, the diminutive Bible teacher rose and in an assured voice announced the evening's selection:

> *Behold, this is the day the Lord has made,*
> *Let us rejoice and be glad in it;*
> *O give thanks to the Lord, for he is good;*
> *His steadfast love endures forever. (Ps. 118: 1-3)*

She paused to command fuller attention, then with an eager smile, began to orchestrate the assembly for worship: "*Wo men di zhu ai di fu* (Our very loving heavenly Father) created this day. Let us make full use of each moment to praise the Lord. Let us bring our troubles and sufferings for His correction, always remembering God labors and feels with us. His patience and love never end."

"Idle phrases, empty promises and mumbled prayers are not enough," this mite of a lady affirmed. "Let us pray not with self-centered requests, but with earts full of thanks for God's gifts. Let us prepare for inner change, allowing ₁e Holy Spirit, our friend and counselor, to enter our hearts and help us reflect od's truth and love."

"So small a lady, such a fast mind and such a big heart," whispered the oman beside us. "Like the best jade, Miss Chen's genuineness glows through er presence. To see and hear her is to believe her."

After another hymn, Pastor Ban Dian, sartorial in his gray silk gown, rose. he hanging gaslight threw a halo on his thick salt-and-pepper hair. At 65, he lled his responsibilities as senior pastor with dignity.

With a strong, mellow voice he read from the New Testament:

> *You shall love the Lord your God with all your heart, and*
> *with all your soul, and with all your mind. This is the*
> *great and first commandment. And the second is like it:*
> *You shall love your neighbor as yourself. (Mt. 22: 37)*

His were not ordinary Sunday-go-to-meeting words. Spending little time ith incident and anecdote, he spoke powerfully of how the Word of God lays old on the stuff of human existence and reshapes it. It first appropriates. But does more than appropriate: it transforms. It takes the things that are, and ith them brings to birth the things that are not. It adopts some known pat-ern, and by standing over against it fashions the new. He challenged his con-regation to apply all their resources to finding and keeping a three-part rela-onship between God, neighbor and self: "All our capacities must be harnessed ₁ this venture of following Christ, just as the trackers pull with all their trength on their towline.

"Love is from the beginning; it is built into the world God created. Being t the heart of creation, it is as if the universe itself calls us to love one anoth-r. We must not take the invitation lightly. You and I are responsible to love the ₁uman temple God created in each of us. The call is to take good care of the est persons we can become. Each one of us is to embody this quality the liv-ng God shows us."

A hush consumed the restless, sweltering assemblage. By their nodding ₁eads they affirmed. One worshiper whispered, "Behold, the servant of the ₋ord has spoken!"

Just as male characters in Chinese opera use a large black folding fan to sig-₁ify magisterial authority, Pastor Ban wielded his with grace and drama. With . deft snap of his wrist, he collapsed the black fan with a resounding crack and imed it at the parishioners to drive home his first point: "Love isn't merely a ₁ne thought or some teaching handed down from our ancestors. It has meaning every time persons meet face-to-face."

Catching his breath, he moved a few paces to the left and repeated the dra
matic fan gesture to emphasize his second point: "Christians are to love, no
only while sitting in church, but in all occasions and relationships." Moving
farther left and now using his fan symbolically to touch hearts, he declared
"It's the unbounded love of Jesus that gives us our surest guideline."

Citing the story about the blind man Jesus healed, Wang An noted how or
regaining his sight the first thing the once-blind man saw was a fellow humar
being, not money or rice. Next he saw the Pharisees, those who considerec
themselves righteous. Finally he saw Jesus.

Men and women should never forget the gift of their special creation–being
made in the image of God, the fervent preacher declared. Christians have the
responsibility to fulfill the inestimable value of human beings, God's preciou
children. At the same time they must face and hold in check their fallible anc
rebellious tendencies.

Another hymn was sung and a series of intercessory prayers were given by
Elder Huang Fu. Suddenly, young pastor Wang An sprung out of his chair and

## 165    My Heart Looks in Faith

China

The Yangtze Boatman
Chinese Chantey

*Moderately slow, In unison*

My   heart   looks in . faith   To   the   Lamb di - vine·

His   pre-cious blood He shed   For   this   life of mine.   A - men.

1. My heart looks in faith
   To the Lamb divine;
   His precious blood He shed
   For this life of mine.

2. My heart waits in hope
   The great God to see;
   Sure are His promises,
   They encompass me.

3. My heart dwells in love
   By the Spirit blest;
   He heals my sicknesses,
   Sets my soul at rest.

4. All faith, hope and love
   Are by Jesus given,
   On earth to give us strength,
   And His peace in heaven.

ounded to the pulpit. Shorter and more fiery than his senior colleague, he xploded with, "Our revered Brother Ban is *shi fen dui* (100% right)! From our eginnings as Christians, we find that love is both a measuring rod and a source f power."

The closing hymn, "My Heart Looks in Faith," reached our hearts. The ine the pianist played in her introduction was a melody adapted from the angzi boatmen. The sanctuary vibrated with song, and stirred my memories f the trackers' melodious processional as they had hauled us through the orges. The worshipers' voices reached a glorious crescendo in the fourth and nal verse:

*All faith, hope and love*
*Are by Jesus given,*
*On earth to give us strength,*
*And His peace in heaven.*

"Those three share fire from their bellies," Wang Shi commented as we exit-d the sanctuary. "They gave us much to think about. They know people's urts, sorrows and betrayals. They know why the *laobaixing* are unsure and ngry over taxes, rising food prices, corrupt magistrates, cruelties of oppres-ors, and sufferings from famines and floods. They sense how even after indi-iduals and communities pledge to change, corrections never are made. They vork hard to help people see beyond what is habitual and self-centered. I was stening to hear what they would say about the specifics as to how faith in Jesus . going to accomplish all this. They gave a lot more."

"They were talking about a radical transaction–not just of mind but of per-ons," Wang Shi continued. "They were getting down to the bottom of things. hey weren't talking about peace, plenty or happiness. The Almighty they rought us face to face with was not so much a source of rest, but the cause of nrest. Not the provider of life's goods, instead, He is the one who often vades our lives by smashing life's goods.

For these three there can be no toning down of the lively Word of a living od, no softening of its power and severity. Like all truth the message they ave was rigorous and demanding. The purposes they talked about neither elent nor excuse: They require and exact. The God they referred to never says Please.' Life never says it. There is very little of the 'ought,' Or the 'should,' r 'It would be a good thing if you would.' There's only the indicative of what he world is as God made it, followed by the imperative that under penalty of leath commands us away from what we have done with it to what he has done bout it. . .They were impressive."

"These three preachers," Harlow concluded, "are endearingly called 'the trinity.' Pastor Ban Dian, strong in his faith, is considered the Father. Young Pastor Wang An, exuberant, busy in good works, is the Son. And Miss Chen the ever-ready counselor and comforter, is the Holy Spirit."

The major, who didn't speak Chinese, regretted he had missed the content. He commented, however, that he had not missed the drama of the preacher and the responsiveness of the congregation. He noted, "Great worship service but exhausting. This 'day the Lord hath made' has filled me to the brim; I can not absorb more!"

The door opened suddenly and Wang Shi ushered in Pastor Wang An and an instructor from the normal college.

"There's more for the evening!" Pastor Wang An declared. "It's only 8:30. Come with us to a faculty *hui-hua* (discussion-and-action meeting)."

Harlow urged us to go, promising the meeting would present us with a representative cross-section of teachers from these parts. Though I had wanted to go to bed long ago, I convinced myself to attend with the argument that always worn out on this journey: If I don't go now, will I ever be here to have this experience again?

# Teacher's Visions Of A New China

The major's, Wang shi's and my footsteps echoed through the dismal hall-way as, with some reluctance being already saturated with the day's experiences, we approached the faculty lounge. When we joined the overflow of teachers standing outside the doorway they courteously cleared a path for us and insisted we go in. Once in we tried to blend in unnoticed with those standing along the back wall.

In a flash we realized that this was no routine gathering! Each chair held two and the sofas four and five persons. Some sat on stools, others were cross-legged on the red rug in the center of the room. Rows of those standing lined the walls and still others were perched on window sills. The vigourous discussion in progress was not about plans for the next faculty outing or complaints about the school board, but about troubling political developments in Wanxian city and the province. The pulsing meeting was vigorous as any dormitory bull-session and fervent as a session of Pilgrims in a Plymouth meetinghouse. Those talking were enthusiastic as pep-rally cheer leaders. The vibrations were such that we would not have been surprised if a string of fire-crackers had exploded to celebrate the teacher's chance to share opinions and concerns.

Our intention to remain unnoticed was summarily foiled. With our entrance the lively interchanges stopped cold. Surprised and quiet for a moment, the teachers' eager faces showed they were steamed up to say much more. The chair-lady urged us to take places on a centrally placed sofa just vacated by the four occupants who slipped down to sit on the floor.

"*Huanying mei guo di dai biao gan xia nin lai!*" (Welcome, American delegates. Thank you very much for coming), said Tang Mei, the science teacher at the small head table. A bright-eyed, no-nonsense thirtyish woman, she introduced us with graciousness, as important travelers from the capital, Nanjing. She noted that the major and I were among the few foreign visitors who had ever attended their forum.

"We teachers," Tang Mei explained, "are from different provinces, but most are graduates of this mission school. Since we live and work in humble circumstances, these Third Day evening meetings highlight our week."

Yü Ying-shi, the co-chairperson beside her, interrupted her and bantered. "Another name we have for Tan Mei is *Zu chi jia* (the Organizer)–a biology teacher, she classifies us into phylum and species." To which Tan Mei quipped back, "And Yü, our co-chair, is a political science teacher whom we call *Fa xue jia* (the Legalist) since he tries to keeps us in line."

Wang Shi thanked the faculty for allowing us to share their *hui hua* (forum literally "return commenting" or "give-and-take talk-fest") and said we were eager to listen and learn from them.

## HOW CAN THE CANCER OF CORRUPTION BE CONTROLLED?

"Tonight," Tang Mei began, sparking the discussion again. "We started talking about teachers' *tze ren* (responsibility) during reconstructions days. We are disturbed over another instance of goverment corruption described in the morning newspaper's feature article. The report gave sordid details, also quotations about this worsening problem from writings of the esteemed Chinese revolutionary Lu Hsun. . .As we continue, we hope you visitors will share your ideas."

Immediately the fast flowing interchanges resumed and we were caught up in the whirlpool of the teachers' engaging *hui-hua*.

"Corruption goes back to Shang dynasty times (over 3000 years ago)," Wu Chen-liang, a history instructor, said, "And it builds up in times of social and political breakdown."

He reviewed the age-old conditions which engender corruption. Officials have *guanxi* (influence), but receive meager salaries. Officials have many hangers-on, especially relatives, to support, so their small stipends in no way cover their expenses. Looking for means to supplement their incomes, they readily find ways to conduct under-the-table transactions with individuals and groups that are willing to pay for their influence.

"An official told me recently," Wu reported, "I am like a water spigot. verybody comes to me to turn on special favors for them. They are sucking y blood. So, as these demands increased, despite wanting to remain an hon-st official, I take their gratuities and rationalize, 'Everybody else is doing it, so hy not me?'

"Look at the case of that 56-year-old county coal company cashier woman the Northeast," broke in Chin An-bing, a female math teacher known as *uan xue jia* (The Calculator). "She developed a syndicate of nearly a hundred fficials who embezzled tens of thousands of dollars–all under the nose of the unty's bloated police apparatus. The police's omnipresent armies of regular d secret gendarmes enforce their authority. They are self-serving, not public-rving."

"Above all," Wu said, "corruption hurts the poor who are the least capable f paying the extra costs caused by the evil. Corruption is a cancer in the body olitic that we must fight."

## O DEMOCRATIC WAY FOR THE POPULACE TO AFFECT PEACEFUL CHANGE

"But how are we going to fight this cancer?" challenged Yu Ying-shi, the o-Chairperson, poltical science teacher called Legalist. "Voicing our opinions, s we do in this forum, may be a start toward democracy, but, voicing com-laints about officials, or even giving positive suggestions, could easily land us jail."

"China doesn't have the democratic mechanisms," noted Chiu (The tatesman), "for changing a government that no longer serves the people. The resent Guomindang came to power without a traditional legitimating mech-nism. Since initially (1927) forging the semblance of unity and stability, and aking some constructive changes, it was accepted. Then, before it could con-olidate a new political system, the Japanese started their invasion. People are illing to make allowances for the terrible drain those nine war years put upon e Guomindang. But now, during these months of peace, people have waited vain for evidences of renewal."

"Here it is, ten months after the defeat of the Japanese," Yu commented ith disdain, "and we are still only cleaning up debris and doing piecemeal building. It appears the Nationalists' strength continues drained. Their effec-veness and concern has become weaker and weaker the greater distance from e capital. Here, 1200 miles west of Nanjing, we see neglect and loss of deter-ination in the government's agents. We see no plans, funds or personnel to build our city, curb runaway inflation, reduce usery, right injustices, correct efficiencies in industries and agriculture, and improve health care. And, as Yu ays, we citizens have no democratic way to push the government to tend to ese urgent problems."

"Again, this lack of a peaceful way to change regimes is an old problem fo China," Wu Qing, the young history instructor observed. "For millennia th only recourse the populace have when venality of officials becomes unbearabl is for them to rise up in a bloody rebellion and bring down the corrupt regim Such revolts brought down many of China's great dynasties. In earlier cer turies the revolts were spearheaded by exasperated peasants who were squeeze by officials for higher taxes and by landlords for exorbitant rents and interes In the 19th and 20th centuries it's been studesnts and teachers who hav fought for reform. The student-teacher uprisings of 1910-1911, 1919 an 1926-1927, for instance, were triggered by the yearning for democracy as we as by outrage over corrupt officials and oppressive landlords."

"True! As Wu explained, the political system spawns corruption and th weakened social system feeds it," cut in Tu Eng, a social science teacher in h mid-'30s, who wielded influence as the forthright editor of the school's poli ical news sheet. Short of stature, full of 'dynamite and pepper' like many in h native Hunan province, he was respected for having survived student uprisin skirmishes and more than his share of personal tragedies. He was admired fo his fearless editorials that targeted China's problems of unresponsive goverr ment, the plight of education, soaring inflation, nepotism, neglect of youtl poverty and oppression of peasants. His colleagues also appreciated his acerbi writings about Chinese addiction to 'saving face' and their propensity for cu tivating sly circumlocutions to neglect priorities.

## HARDSHIPS ACCOMPANYING ACCELERATING INFLATION

Zh'en Jo-shui, a home-economics teacher, known as *Nei wu jia* (On Devoted to Household Affairs), voiced her feeling that one serious effect c corruption was how it added to the rising cost of food and other necessities.

"Inflation wasn't bad six months ago," she said, "but now each month gets worse. The cost of living for us ordinary people keeps going up and up Corruption eats away at the efforts of people to improve their living standard It undermines the country's economic and social stability."

"Feeding mouths gets more difficult each week," Gao Eng, an economi teacher in his mid-'30s echoed. "We have to use the 'back door' more ofter When your neighborhood market ups the price and no longer displays bea curd, you send your sister to shop. She has former schoolmates who work i the market and can pull out reserves hidden under the counter."

This prompted Yu (the Legalist) to note, "You see why we call Gao Eng *Ju lueh chia* (the Strategist)!. . .'back door' shenanigans won't cure inflation, bu it's a common strategy people feel forced to use."

# CHINA'S EDUCATIONAL SYSTEM NEEDS MUCH MORE SUPPORT

"Education, our vocation, will take more than the 'back door' strategy to x," countered Zhiang Mei-li, a pretty language teacher, wiggling forward om her tight fit on a sofas to emphasize her point. "All levels of education in ur country cry for improvement. We all know the obstacles are many. Iardships endured during the war years continue–third-rate food, jamming six :udents into two-person dormitory rooms, limiting access to libraries to only few hours per week. To graduate requires more discipline and concentration ıan many students can muster."

"Yes," I said, by way of reinforcement. "Six years ago, in 1940, when I trav-led to Kunming, Chongqing and Chengdu, I stayed in refugee university ormitories and saw first-hand these hard conditions. The teachers' and stu-ents' unified and determined spirit was heroic. You who struggled through ıose punishing years, understandably, question why can't the same spirit of nity and determination be rallied now to improve China's basic institutions–and articulary education?"

"Chinese value education," asserted Kung Yi-an, a tall refugee from ıandung province, now a history instructor. "Teachers esteem the privilege of :aching. Only a few in our country have the chance to finish upper middle :hool and fewer still manage to finish university. We feel a special responsibli- / for teaching and for the role people give us to speak out against injusticies, orruption and poverty."

"So true!" affirmed Wu Chen-liang, the history teacher. "In critical times, :udents and teachers marched at the forefront of movements demanding ıange. Our grandfathers, who were teachers and students rallied peasants and orkers. Teachers and students fought against the Qing dynasty in the 1910-1 Revolution and marched in the vanguard of the first Tian An Men (May th, 1919) demonstrators protesting against the Versailles Treaty's unfair pro-isions. Later, our fathers, as students stood against rapacious warlords and ppressive landlords. With the same spirit we took part in the resistance to the ıpanese invaders. Today teachers and students seek ways to help broken peo-le and blighted neighborhoods."

# NEGLECT AND SUPPRESSION OF YOUTH

"Neglect and misuse of young people is another kind of corruption," Liu )a Wei was quick to assert. "In a fractured and confused society, where older dults themselves are harried and worn, our young people seem to have a hard-r than usual time entering the mainstream. The difficulties our middle school raduates have finding positions for which they are qualified is a case in point. acked with knowledge and sharp with training, they feel superfluous."

"True! China has had a history of slighting its youth," Liu the Reformer

commented. "The elderly are respected and given deference; youth are su
pected and considered expendable. Now, in the mid-twentieth century, mi
lions of urban youth are neglected and hundreds of millions country youth a
oppressed. Neither of these enormous groups are acknowledged as treasure
resources, let alone provided with needed education and helped with their pa
ticular complex problems."

"I am reminded of the Shenxi province peasant youth I taught in the 194
1943 years," added Tu Eng. "Mostly 16 to 25 year-olds, their marginal exi
tence under the thumb of landlords left the majority malnourished and exploi
ed. For many, acts of mental and physical cruelty were the formative exper
ences  of their childhood and early adolescence. Having been beaten and otl
erwise mistreated for years, the peasant youth developed an inbred fatalisi
toward their lives of degradation and exploitation and etched vivid memori
of countless incidents of humiliation by the landlords. These conditions playe
into the hands of the landlords, enabling them to perpetuate their oppressiv
system. It's little wonder that the explosions of youth's repressed resentmei
and hopelessness contribute the chief dynamic in radical agrarian movements

Continuing, Tu Eng told about the intensive youth training program
Formal education was not possible with these young people who had had n
previous schooling and whose remote communities had no text books, schoo
or curriculum. The teachers carried on 'cadre' training and *cheng feng* (rectif
cation campaign indoctrination). Linking theory and practice the instructo
tried to forge a working consensus on ultimate values and develop strategies fc
immediate action. Improved communication was sought within the cadres an
between cadres and the people. The *cheng feng* cadres acted forcefully c
shared values and a vision of China's revolutionary future.

Liu, whom they referred to as *Ke ming chia* (The Reformer), elaborate
"Our country not only slights the young, but accuses them and engages i
wanton killing of tens upon tens of thousands of revolutionary youths wh
might one day replace the rotten officials. Many city youth and many mo
country youth are accused of contributing to society's troubles because they'
rebellious and disregard traditional values. Thousands upon thousands hav
been imprisoned and many horribly tortured."

"It's frustrating to be considered unimportant in the country's reconstru
tion," Chiu Bing-an (The Statesman), said. "It's disillusioning to see how tl
government fears young people will undermine the status quo. It's worse st
to find that if we speak out against the wrongs we are jailed. In Nanjin
Beijing, Wuhan and Shanghai, students who questioned authorities we
arrested by the secret police and 'disappear.' Something serious is amiss with
society that blames its young for its woes and treats them like enemies."

Applause cut Chiu's comments short, and the audience reverberated wi
affirmations.

The teachers' use of their local dialects, accompanied by their outpouring of rong feelings, often garbled what they were saying and made many of their omments difficult to understand. We had to rely on reading their facial expres- ons and body movements. Wang Shi and I whispered summary translations ) the major, who sat between us. At one point, the major whispered back bout how amazed he was at the teachers' intensity and their forthrightness. le was surprised at how they spoke their minds without hesitation, even nough a government informer could have been among them. (Harlow had old us that student and faculty forums frequently were attended by "thought :aders," government agents who sniffed for subversive comments. To be crit- al was dangerous.)

## S THE RISING GUNGCHANDANG (CHINESE COMMUNIST) TRUSTWORTHY ALTERNATIVE?

"The fast growing Gungchandang (Chinese Communist Party) offers an ppealing alternative," Tu Eng asserted. "But, to even suggest this is risky. levertheless, facts are facts. The Gungchandang has detailed and comprehen- ve plans of action for improving the country's economy and social structure. 'heir alternative looks attractive, if for no other reason than the Guomindang as put forth no such plans."

"The Gungchandang welcomes and puts to work teachers and students, and oth country and city young people," Wu Chen-liang added. "Small wonder nat a growing number of students and professors lean toward Marxism. The ociferous opposing officials in power, of course, say the Communists are using neir class-war thesis to exploiting the rifts between young and old, peasants nd city folk, workers and entrepreneurs."

"The Gungchandang's plans for China's betterment have been tested in the Jorthwest," Tu Eng reported.

Tu Eng also told how the Communists responded to the peasantry's basic :eeds for military security, reduced tenanat rents and interest rates and an equi- ible tax scale. New political institutions enabled many peasants to speak for 1e first time with pride of 'our government,' rather than with fear of a remote nd threatening state. At the same time, elite participation was secured through ppeals to anti-Japanese nationalism and economic and political accommoda- on. By winning the active support of peasants, the Communists have suc- ceded in breaking the political monopoly of the landlord class in several key punties.

"Dispite their appeal," cautioned Liu Da-wei, "Communist theories and ractices arouse questions. The Communists' appeal is less that their alterna- ve is so good and more that the status quo's option is so bad. The ommunist gloss over the ways their regime tramples on personal freedom. heir system's cure might be as painful as the present ills."

"Yes," agreed the major, after we interpreted what Liu Da-wei had said "Some American teachers and students in the '20s and early '30s toyed wit Marxism as an alternative to the market crash and inequities of capitalism. Bu teachers and students in the United States were not the powerful force fo change as are their Chinese brothers and sisters. The intensity of tonight' debate shows the potential power of Chinese intellectuals. Activists among yo hold the initiative of possible leadership over China's 85% illiterate populace.

"Let's remember that giving allegiance to either the Nationalists or th Communists bring problems," Chiu, The Statesman, spoke up. "Loyalty to th Guomindang allies us with the stallers of progress and puts us at risk of goin to jail if we object. Loyalty to the Gungchandang aligns us with an untried an equally dictatorial regime that promises even harsher punitive measures fo nonconformity."

## MOST OF US ARE CITY PEOPLE, BUT 90% OF CHINESE ARE COUNTRY PEOPLE

"Our country," Liu the Reformer said, beginning to describe another larg need, "with more than 90 percent of its population living in rural areas, als has great need for agrarian reform."

"How true!" exclaimed Tu Eng as he told more about the Northwest peas ant youth. Describing the millennia old tapestry of China's rural life in the are he explained its continuing crisis. And uneasy balance of terror over the peas ant population was maintained by landlord-sponsored local militia and mobil armed rebels-bandits who swept down from the hills in swift raids. Natural dis asters, perpetual warlord-bandit strife, famine, war, chronic debt, overcrowde villages, heavy taxation and destruction of the soil compounded the peasant poverty, oppression and inability to meet minimum needs of survival. Famin in these areas have always been a periodic natural phenomenon, but recently i has been a product, too, of half a centruy of political collapse and incessan warfare, which so drained resources that even minor natural disturbances no result in immense suffering and loss of life.

Everywhere, he said, were evidences of the peasants' sufferings and hop lessness. Ruthless landlords, supplemented by the few farmers who becom rich and turn miserly and conservative, tightened their life and death grip o peasants throats. Forging a new order is a peoples struggle, so in this time c reconstuction country people as well as city people must be rallied to build society based on egalitarian values.

Where peasants have been freed from the bondage of the landlord system he reported, surprising improvements were achieved. Given the chance, back water tillers began to make their farms more productive. Others were enable to join ranks of workers in expanding industries.

# CHINA'S ABORTED DEMOCRACY REDEEMABLE?

"Whether or not China's aborted democracy can be redeemed is a big question," observed Wu Chen-liang, the history instructor.

He pointed out that after the 1911 Revolution, intellectuals urged China to adopt the political structure which had become widespread in many Western countries. The new regime that deposed the moribund Qing dynasty chose democracy and called itself a 'republic.' Ironically, the Chinese adopted portions of representative democracy even while fighting to overcome imperialists who proclaimed the idea. Western experts on democratic systems journeyed to China to help in the new Chinese republic. After World War I the English philosopher Bertrand Russell and the American John Dewey exerted great influence as they lectured throughout China.

Chinese presidents from 1911 until Sun Yat Sen's death in 1924, Wu continued to explain, went through the motions of developing a representative system. Due to inexperience and ignorance, also venality and arrogance, they sabotaged the fledgling system. From the 1911 Revolution onward China was a republic in name only and its few existing elected organizations were powerless. Professors and students have complained correctly that, apart from rhetoric-laden articles and speeches, there is no people's rule.

Asked to say a word about democracy in Western countries, I pointed out that Western democracy has been a long time developing and that representative government is a set of inventions come late upon the human scene.

"The mind does not take naturally to the subject," I said. "People tend to live by myths that favor hierarchies and tight command without the delays and hindrances representational government involves. Democracy springs out of philosophic and religious soil. It requires deep roots. Its structure and practices grow out of much experimentation."

I went on to describe how the beginnings of democracy in European countries reach back 2500 years. Greek city states experimented with representative rule and Judeo-Christian traditions, held kings responsible for providing justice. Over a millennia later the practice of representation sprang to life in France, England and the Low Lands as a means of choosing knights and townspeople to bargain with the king over public services and taxes. Bloody times followed. Then came the Anglo Saxons in Britain confronting King John with the Magna Carta to guarantee the people's basic rights. The French philosopher Rousseau and the English thinker John Locke propounded theories to explain and reinforce national democratic administrations. Thus, the foundations for American democratic governance were being laid centuries before the colonists defied King George's taxes with the Boston Tea Party in 1775. There followed four draining Revolutionary War years, and twenty-year struggle to forge a representative government and another two years to outline the political structure in a consititution that the quarrelsome thirteen colonies woul‹ accept.

"Establishing a democracy," I observed, "requires developing means c controlling authority by popular vote and ways of making peaceable changes a the repubic grows. Over the centuries, Western democracies have had to strug gle to keep their political system working. New laws had to be written t‹ replace outworn statues and present political action needs to be examined i‹ light of the Consititution's intentions. Mistakes, omissions and inconsistencie‹ must be corrected. The right to vote, petition, assemble and displute is alway‹ in need of protection and regulation. In America too few citizens take advan tage of the representation they do have–many don't vote. More serious is ou‹ failure to apply the egaliatrian theories on which democracy is based, notabl‹ our continued failure to match economic and racial equality with politic‹ equality."

"I can verify how the Nationalists' brand of democracy is off the mark," th‹ major broke in. "As an American Army advisor in Nanjing, I see firsthand th‹ Guomindang's weaknesses and abuses. More than even this, however, i‹ Nanjing we see a lot that is 'off-center.' For China, whose name is *Zhong gu‹* or 'middle' or 'central' such as condition is especially serious. A motor, w‹ know, whose fly-wheel is 'off-center' soon flies itself apart. Your country'‹ chaos is similar to that of Western nations after World War I, about which th‹ Irish poet Yeats wrote, 'The center no longer holds.' You tonight seem to hav‹ been saying: Of course, China continues to be *Zhong guo* (The Middl‹ Kingdom), but where and how is the center holding? I know many thoughtfu‹ concerned Chinese in Nanjing are aware of these deficiencies and are lookin‹ for alternatives."

"Quite right!" affirmed Wang Shi. Exploring the roots of democracy an‹ ways of getting China's so-called democracy on track are concerns that kee‹ history and political science instructors busy at our univeristy in Nanjing. On‹ task force currently is searching Chinese history for evidences of theories an‹ practices of Chinese experiments in representative government. Ancient writ ings suggest that the idea of the people's participation in and responsibility fo‹ ruling themselves long has been a Chinese concern. Confucius taught that ‹ govermnent exists for the welfare of the people. Chinese tradition reminds us ‹ 'Heaven sees as the people see,' and 'All must work within history to improv‹ the bit of society were he lives.'

Wang Shi explained how, throughout Chinese history, in practice officia‹ have resisted representative rule. The Emperor, cloaked in the Mandate o‹ Heaven, was at the pinnacle. Orders going out from his office descended th‹ bureaucratic ladder to the elders of the village and then to the male head of th‹ family. The essence of China's three millennia-old political system has bee‹ government by administration. It's a socio-political system Chinese cultur‹

ractically invented and then kept perfecting. It was the ancient imperial idea f top-to-bottom dictation. Politics was *deciding* a policy; administration was *xecuting* it. Nevertheless, contemporary Chinese speak and write of democra- y as *min zhu* (people's rule). The associated phrase, *minqüan-zhuyi* implies ghts or authority of the people. Another phrase, *minxia zhuyi*, means to be  harmony with the people, or the people's responsibility in the social order.

"Democracy requires convictions and participation," Tang Mei at the lead- rs' table declared, "As we know from its absence in our country. This is high- ghted by what we understand of American democracy which we teachers tend  idealize."

"As to some of the fundamentals of American democracy," the major said, I agree with Mr. Gao (Cowles) in his emphasis that religious roots are essen- al. Religious convictions provide authority, priorities and ethical guidelines at are bacic for democracy.

"I would add," he said, "To function democracy needs both balances and ontrols. It must find ways to hold together divergent strands of its history and ulture, develop political mechanisms for uniting change with the wisdom of ultural values and protect individual freedoms. It also needs an efficient ureaucracy to monitor and support the full range of democracy's workings in omplex modern societies. And, of course, democracy needs an alert electorate. itizens who, along with dedication and conviction, are well informed are ssential to making government more effcient and responsible."

## SURPRISING COMPARISON: LU XUN AND T. S. ELIOT

From an unassuming 29-year-old language teacher, Li Zi-ren, came an nexpected comparisons between the Chinese writer Lu Xun and the merican-English poet T.S. Eliot. He suggested that "the hollowness of our ge," "the waste land" and "the emptiness of existence" described current con- itions in China."

The group gave positive response to his surprising comparison. The insight elped Wang Shi and me to appreciate Li Zi-ren's nickname *Wen Hsueh Chia* The Literati)!

"Yes, we have such feelings," responded Liu Da-wei, and eager, boyish- ooking, 30-year-old math teacher. "Paradoxically, the 'emptiness' and 'hol- ownness' seems sometimes to come from being over full–being flooded by so any big social and political problems. Feelings of emptiness and hollowness row when teachers and students are ignored and denied a role in reconstruc- on. But we feel more than emptiness when we see and hear corrupt bureau- rats who stall, make excuses and offer no assurance of a better future.

"As frustration deepens," Gao Eng, the Strategist, asserted, "students' and teachers' patience wears thin and defiance grows. The times demands bold ne\* ideas and renewed institutions.

"Teachers feel betrayed," editor Tu Eng declared as he jumped to the floc from his perch in a north window. "Conditions in our country are not s much an empty existence as a time bomb about to explode! Face-lifting ol buildings helps, but key institutions cry for bacic corrections and expansion. T correct our present problems we've identified not only the government but th whole social order needs reconstruction! The Guomindang began as a revolu tionary movement, but it has betrayed its founders. Those now in power tal of relieving the people's sufferings, but what we see is the selfish struggling c the militarists for power and nothing to alleviate the people's misery. Chir needs so many fundamental changes! And needs them now!

Pausing a moment, he added in his native peppery Hunanese dialect. "Ou eagerness as teachers to bring about change is great and noble, but without being a part of a strong organization with an overall plan, we only blow hot ai Intensive work must be done to extend democracy to the family, school an work place. We're in a race against time. We cannot wait for foreign gov ermnents to become benevolent and pull us into the 20th century. So we' better hurry up!"

"We mustn't allow our country to become a sleeping society," Gao En insisted. "With eyes and ears open, we must identify the forces and agencie that cause people's suffering. We must oppose instances of oppression, injustic or abuse by lords, corrupt officials or imperialist. Our Mr. Editor (Tu Eng) right. More than patch-and-repair is called for. We must find, or create if ne essary, organizations that will bring about the necessary radical changes. "It time," Tu Eng broke in, "to rip open taboos that have plagued Chinese cu ture for millennia. New ways of thinking and acting must be developed! Yo Westerners do not stand at the edge of a revolutionary precipice as we do."

Looking at the major and me, he smiled and commented, "Do Liu and sound like your Patrick Henry? Can you American friends tell us the democra tic way to get rid of inequities and corruption? Will democratic ways do? Or blood-letting in order?"

### THE PRECIOUS JADE ONE: A WOMAN TESTED BY FIRE AND STRONG OF FAIT.

Pausing a moment after Tu Eng's climatic appeal, Chairperson Tang Me the Organizer, invited comments from a most respected teacher who ha remained quiet all evening.

Turning to Wu Yi next to her she said, "This distinguished woman teach social studies and religion. We think of her as *Bao yü chia* (The Precious Jac One–and not without reason). Two Chinese phrases apply well to her: *Yü* b *ch'iu bu ji* (If jade is not cut and polished, it cannot be of use and beauty) an

*Chun tze bu ji* (A person of complete virtue is not a utensil having but one use). In Wu Yi we have a gem. A versatile person, she applies her abilities in many good works. Her unfailing religious faith makes her an enviable example of a devoted Christian."

"*Wo bu gan dang* (I don't dare accept such glowing compliments)," 35-year-old Wu Yi responded. "Amazing this forum! Together we have spelled out many of the day's urgent issues."

"The question of 'Where and what is China's true center?'." Wu Yi started, accentuating her observations with gracious gestures, "raised by our visitor the major needs to concerns all of us greatly. In many ways the Irish poet's estimate 'The center no longer holds' applies to China. Where is our real center? Our people are cleaved down the middle in many ways. We have many serious splits, people of influence vs. those with none, the young vs. the old, businessmen vs. educators, traditionalists vs. advocates of change, 95% Han vs. 5% minorities, the obscenely rich vs. the desperately poor.

"Deprivations and inflation are bad, imprisonment and loss of liberty are worse, but a rotting at the core of individuals and society is the worst. Lu Hsun warned that corruption, poverty and ignorance are 'malignant tumors on the body of society. If we let these spread unchecked, our society will be ruined.' The struggle against corruption poverty and ignorance is a battle for China's very life. So, as the major said, we need to ask, what about China's real center?

"In addition to healing these great 'splits'," Wu Yi continued, "we're challenged to find and cultivate our spiritual centers. At the heart of peoples' and societies' problems are spiritual concerns. This reinforces what Mr. Gao (Cowles) emphasized: that religious convictions and vision must undergird democracy. Without a core of sound spiritual base we lack grounds for judgment. Lacking a far-sighted and balanced look, we become prejudiced and self-absorbed like the persons now in power whom we criticize. China needs the solid convictions that deep-rooted religious concern can provide."

"What 'deep-rooted riligious concern' are you talikg about?" challenged Liu Da-wei.

"More than an attachment to an orgainization, a temple or even a set of rules." explained Wu Yi. "It includes what we call *kuanxin* (to give total attention to), or *kuan she* (to be concerned or connected with)–but it's more. The intense zeal for the common good, shown here tonight, is an example of religious experience's 'ultimate concern'. What we teachers consider most derserving of the full and immediate investment of our lives is our religion."

When Wu Yi spoke, her colleagues listened. She was respected as a survior. When her parents were murdered in the 1935 rape of Nanjing, relatives sent her to Wanxian to be raised by an educated, widowed aunt. Though her adolescence was clouded with the deprivations and the chaos of the war years, her aunt saw to it that Wu Yi complete two years at West China Union Christian College in Chengdu, the provincial capital.

Through her trials and difficulties, her aunt guided Wu Yi in untraditional ways. Instead of accepting male domination, Wu Yi was encouraged to become a person in her own right. Free of pretension, she retained her femininity. Instead of hardening her, life's blows made her determined to fight against injustice. From her suffering, a contagious joy of life had emerged.

"This day of reconstruction," Wu Yi started again, "as many of you have said, cries out for radical changes. The other day a merchant we all know told me, 'All government officials are bandits. They used to have only two hands each. Now they have 30 or 40, all of them busy grabbing for money, our country is becoming not so much an autocracy as a kleptocracy.'"

"Consider the religious meaning of the Chinese phrases *hu hui* (mutuality +graciousnes=reciprocity) and *shu dao* (merciful-forgiving+way-truth=reciprocity). In China, truth is often determined less by empirical facts and more by deep cultural considerations. These beliefs are about concern, reconciliation and reciprocity rooted in the religious dimensions of the culture they develop and share. One of the central functions of the worldwide Christian church is to serve as a force of reconciliation. Concerned Christians hold that it is precisely the revolution of the oppressed in our day that is one great sign of God's activity in history."

"One hard message about battling corruption, poverty and ignorance is that each individual bears responsibility for working to correct these evils. I have learned from my Christian faith to face the fact that I, too, am venal. I look around for *guanxi*, a beneficial connection and influence that can help me get what I want. I too ask for favors. I allow my faith to fade in the face of trouble, my enthusiasm to fizzle out, and I do not pursue the hope I parade. Turning around our venality calls for deep personal change that in turn calls for the help of a 'higher power.' Help in correcting our moral weaknesses can come from our relating to the loving and all-powerful Heaveny Father."

Wu Yi then described how strongly she was impressed by Sun Yat Sen telling in his autobiography about finding the teachings of the Hebrew prophets (in the Old Testament) and later the Sermon on the Mount (in the New Testament). These powerful insights, he said, provided sound eithical guidelines for himself and his vision for China. He told of the impact on him when he read Micah 6:5-8–'But what does the Lord require of you? But to do justly, love mercy and walk humbly with the Lord your God.'. . .She concluded: "How wonderful!"

"Lasting reconstruction requires facing both the evil and the good. We need to look at the predicament of human failings–so obvious with the corrupt persons in our government, not so obvious when we search ourselves. Tonight e've challenged one another to reach beyond ourselves to universals –to the *n gu* (forever, or eternal)," Wu Yi affirmed. We must face the specific :mands of this larger vision. Genuine religion holds that to believe is to care, id to care is to do. To believe that human beings are created in the likeness f God gives each individual the challenge to mirror the Creator. Religion ivolves both redeeming the person and creating social structures consistent ith those convictions. I believe we as a nation will find the right path when e accept our human weakness and call on assistance from the Creator. If we ace our trust in the positive force of God's work in history, forgiveness and ·conciliation become possible."

A hush of awareness came over the room. In expressing confusions and frus- ations, anxieties had been relieved and matters of ultimate concern had been Jentified and wrested with.

Tang Mei, in bringing the *hui hua* (give-and-take talk-fest) to a close, said, It was our good fortune for you downriver and overseas guests to include our Jrum in your journey."

"You teachers have filled our minds and hearts to overflowing," I :sponded. "We guests were privileged and inspired to be with you. You have 1ade us wiser. Life is a long journey–much like traveling through the San ia. You have greatly enriched this part of our journey. May you keep your /es open to see the opportunites before you and may you have the courage ) make the most of them. Power to each one of you! And again, thank you :ry much."

As the meeting ended, we wondered how the sardine-packed teachers could :come unpacked, squeezed into every square foot of the lounge. But they did 1anage, and quickly.

As they exited, the teachers clustered around one or the other of us three Jests. If any of the teachers harbored antipathies for us foreigners, they cov- ·ed such feelings well. Aware that we would probably never meet again, they ssured us that they would remember us always. They offered the heart-warm- 1g desire for continued friendship across all distances and time. We recipro- ited and assured them of how much we appreciated their vim and vigor and dmired their boldness. Considering their impatience with chaotic conditions f their country, we wished them success in finding and joining organizations 1at would implement and help them realize their strong social concerns. lthough we were not able to thank each one for her or his particular insight ·e did express our gratitude to Tang Mei the Organizer for orchestrating the *ui hua* so masterly and to Wu Yi for sharing her strong faith and her undaunt- d search for "better ways" that her vision outlined.

The teachers' enthusiasm was contagious. The difficult lives they confront- d was not enviable. Their education, patriotism and for some their faith had given them intimations of a better society. But their visions were frustratin for they lacked experience and training in political matters and had not four an organization in which they could work to realize their hopes. Realisticall they were hemmed in by marginal pay, nutritional deficiencies, slim chances fe professional enrichment or advancement, restricted mobility and political pow erlessness. Many were open to new and deeper religious experiences, but wor dered where and how to start such a journey. Constricted by these limitatior they easily could succumb to the age-old way of isolating themselves to a lin ited reality, while defending themselves against the intrusion of a greater rea ty. But they said no to such a course. They wanted to broaden their horizor and join life's wider and deeper flow. Such hope they demonstated!

Their eagerness and determination to right wrongs and serve as agents change was commendable but sobering. Neither they nor we had the pr science to see that in less than three years their lives would be turned upsic down: the Guomindang would have fled to Taiwan and they would be livir in the sharply different People's Republic of China which would impose rac cal personal and social changes.

Now midnight, we downriver visitors were both inundated and exhilarate The vibrant expectaions with which the day began were far exceeded by its en

# CHAPTER TWENTY-ONE

# Downriver Through Qutang Gorge

*Kui Men Promontory, Qutang Gorge By Helen Houser*

At breakfast the next morning, Harlow again expressed disappointment over our determination to leave after we had just arrived. When, however, Mr. Chiu, the business manager, appeared at the door to escort Wang Shi, the major and me to our junk, he agreed to accompany us to the river.

Making our way through the northern suburb, we found roads coexisting with a network of stairs and ramps that carried only pedestrian traffic. Here were many examples of the old-style roads, interconnected with complexes of stairways, some grand and wide and some little more than alleys with narrow steps. All along, the way was enlivened by shiny orange foliage and dark formal cypress.

Coming to the north gate, we met with carts and burdened donkeys pouring into the city's old section. Reaching the heart of the city, we noticed how the few remaining *yamens* (offices of officials) and other key public buildings had been handsomely restored. The rising sun sent scarlet and golden shafts into the chasms of the narrow streets. At the graceful spires and pavilions guarding its approaches, we again were captivated by the 1,200 year-old Heavenly Bridge. It seemed to spring out of the rock without any visible abutments and its lofty single stone arch, with its fascinating tea house over th middle of the span, linked the banks of the tributary. Wanxian's elegant *fen xue* became apparent again, and we felt the folly of our overly-tight itinerar that cut so short our stay in this myriad city to which we'd already becom attached.

Roads and alleys leading to the South Gate plaza were gridlocked Merchants contributed to the congestion as they opened their store fronts and left their protective boards sticking out from the sidewalks.

Reaching the riverbank, we found that while the enchanting old town ha been just waking up, the riverport had been busy since before dawn. The col umn of junks, docked in tiers, extended for miles around the edges o Wanxian's famed horseshoe bend. Armies of coolies crowded the pontoo wharves, loading Sichuan tung oil, lumber, ox hides, pig gut, bristles, tobacco gall nuts, quicksilver and opium onto junks bound for Yichang and Hankou Downriver craft were being unloaded of salt, yarn, cotton, matches, kerosene medicines, wheat flour, sugar and light consumer goods.

The moored *wu bans,* stretching row upon row along the north shore, n longer looked alike. Now we were sophisticated enough in junk lore to recog nize from where they hailed. We could spot the *mayang zi* (king of junks) which were brightly colored and sometimes gold-painted. Behemoths among the junks, their bows were square and aft they had raised poops and stern hous es for *lao bans* and their families.

Among these monarchs of the river, Mr. Chiu found the one that was t take us downriver. Introducing us to the skipper, he said, "His name, *Chun Shi* (Strong Rock), is well deserved."

Thompson offered additional assurance, "Chung Shi, friendly and outgoing as a person, also is a boatman with unmatched skill and reliability. He'll get you to Yichang safely if anyone can and you'll enjoy his company."

Strong Rock's youth surprised the major and me. We shared raised eye brows and shrugged shoulders, realizing the die was cast. We were in no posi tion to reject our friends' recommendations. We were reassured by the fact tha this *lao ban's* proprietary welcome was backed by his being both skipper an half-owner. Young though he looked, he came across as strong, business-lik and experienced, so we were satisfied to entrust ourselves to this master.

Compared with our upriver vessel, this junk was ten feet longer and carrie fewer trackers, but twelve more oarsmen. Since it was larger than our previou junk, this *wu ban* provided more deck space.

"It's no grand guestroom," our new host said, pointing to our assigne 12" x 12" section, "but it's a section to which you are most welcome."

No longer having Thompson with us, the three of us would now not be a ramped as we had been going upriver.

While we were settling our gear, the skipper said, "Carrying aboard a Chinese scholar and two Americans makes for a good omen. Americans make good friends. As a boy in upper Sichuan, I attended an American missionary primary school. During the war, I met *mei guo chun* (American soldiers). Always they were easy to get along with."

Whatever his skills at navigation, he was adept at public relations.

Relishing interaction with us, he supplied detailed nautical information about the downriver trip. In his systematic description of what was to come, we almost expected him to bring out maps and channel charts. He explained that our departure time was planned to put us through the *Qu Tang* (Wind Box Gorge) in the afternoon so as to reach a mooring on the other side by sundown. That one gorge had consumed three days in our upriver journey; it was hard to believe we could make the 80 miles downriver in nine hours.

When the final cargo was loaded and the hatches battened down, the crew polled away from the crowded mooring. The new *tai gong* (first officer) was matter-of-fact and precise. Like many Sichuanese, he was short and stocky, but unlike most, curt and close mouthed. He simply said, "We're leaving. Let's go." He ordered the stake ropes loosened, the bow trackers to pole out, the oarsmen and sweepmen to haul away, and the trackers midship to hoist sail. We were off. We missed the stylish departure rituals of our westbound first officer.

Each *yulow*, three on either side, was sculled by four hardy bowmen. These wide, long, finlike blades tucked alongside were operated from the walkways in the bow gunwales. Deftly rolled and swished astern, they provided strong additional propellants. Two, and sometimes three, men pushed on each oar. Under the triple power—the crew's muscle, the current's force and a southerly breeze swelling the sails—we swept by the shoreline.

With the outlines of its skyline fast receding, the appreciation for the vitality and generosity of the Myriad City's people welled up within us. So many rich experiences its enthusiastic people had shared with us! The genuine friendliness, vigor and vision which we encountered in Wanxian was remarkable.

"In last night's forum I again saw evidences of missionaries' contributions," the major reflected. "The majority of those teachers got their start in missionary schools. The missionaries' work, though relatively small compared with China's great size, plays an often unrecognized part in the development of this country's emerging educational, medical and scientific work. Also again I realized how little knowledge about and appreciation of the foreign missionary enterprise I and the majority of Americans have."

Christian work needs to transcend being thought of as a "foreign" religion, I thought. From the seventh century, when the Nestorians introduced their faith to China, Christianity's acceptance and growth have been handicapped by its being *wai chiao* (foreign religion). In recent decades, and particularly during the war with Japan, significant gains have been made in Chinese seeing Christianity as a universal faith. In this period of reconstruction missionaries needed to disassociate themselves as much as possible from gun boats and other arms of foreign imperialism. This includes helping the Chinese church to become self-supporting financially.

Missionaries need to be learners and partners in the enterprise. Sherwood Eddy, often called a 'missionary to the world,' proclaimed this view in the 1920's, holding that the missionary purpose should not include cramming Western dogma down the throats of unwilling people. Instead, the work must be guided by an empathetic approach to non-Christians. Eddy, in telling of his motivation and work, explained:

> *We held no ideas of a narrow orthodoxy of 'perishing millions,' who were eternally lost. . .We went not to destroy but to fulfill, and sought to include value from the past in the new order.*

"Christian missionaries," I said, thinking out loud, "early found it self defeating either to embrace indigenous religious, expressions into an overly simple synthesis, or to attack them with dogmatic opposition. The idea that all religions are created equal is unrealistic. On the other hand, to stand in judgment of deep-rooted faiths is an un-Christian affront that invites antagonism."

"An important development has been the diminishing role of foreign missionaries and the increasing role of Chinese clergy in the formation of a truly Chinese church. For the Chinese, differences between the Protestant denominations are confusing, whereas unity in Christ has deep meaning. Foreign missionaries with authoritarian and separatist approaches are being pushed aside. The enormity and complexity of the task facing Christian educators, medical workers and evangelists force them to find common ground."

"Upheavals in Asia, and particularly in China," I concluded, "are pressing missionaries to face and try to understand revolutionary thoughts. The demand is for new ways of thinking and working together, in the cities and countryside, with the educated elite also with the *laobaixing*."

Before we realized it, we approached and quickly passed the eastern guardian of Wanxian, the Sentinel Pagoda. We were struck by how the morning sun lit the delicate traceries in each of its seven stories and outlined its graceful symmetry. How could we, on our westward trip, have passed this architectural treasure with so little notice? We wished we hadn't sped by—too fast to savor its beauty.

Recalling the upriver cook mentioning that the monument was built to ard off demons, the major asked, "With its fragility, how, through thirteen nturies, has it accomplished its mission of staving off demons from the southeast?"

"Pagodas are supposed to ward off demons," Wang Shi spoke out, "but a umber of other reasons account for the importance of pagodas in China. As gathered meaning across the centuries, the pagoda as a popular emblem or mbol shed light on the literature, fine arts, industry, and daily life of hinese."

"In few other countries has the art of tower-building become such a fine art in China. Whether a slender spire of carved marble or a multi-colored tower ' finest porcelain or a great structure of wood or stone, the pagoda, or idol wer, has long stood as a symbol of the Middle Kingdom. When one climbs e steep spiral stairway and takes in the view, one gains a unique perspective ' the land and its people."

Pagodas originated in India, where like a stupa, or dhagoba, meaning "relic eserver," they marked the spot where sacred relics were interred. First erect-l in China during the third century, pagodas usually are circular or octagonal uildings of seven or nine storeys. In most cases the walls are double, and tween the inner and outer walls a staircase winds, leading to the summit, om which, by means of doorways, access is gained to the rooms on each level.

Pagodas always stand for at least two things–protection and luck. They have so been erected in commemora-n of unusual acts of devotion, as ood omens or as observation tow-s. Pagodas sometimes were built secure geomantic influences for e good of the surrounding dis-ict. Small stone pagodas, in the rm of Chinese brush-pens, fre-iently were erected to improve the *ng xue* of the locality.

Happy is the person whose home ' burial site is shadowed by a pago-'s presence. This Wanxian sentinel as almost an exact replica of Jade ill Pagoda in Beijing's western lls Imperial Hunting Park. Of that autiful spire it was said that jade aters bubbled up from the rock low giving the pagoda an aura of e eternal. Above the spring is the mous Marble Pagoda, to the west the beautiful Porcelain Pagoda, while on the crest of the hill towered the loft *Yu Feng Ta* (Jade Hill Pagoda).

These beautiful Buddhist towers with their bedecked sides were considere important regulators of *feng xue* (good influence) and symbols of peace an security. Often encased with green and gold tiles, these sentinels were th guardians of imperial hunting grounds, the entrance of some fine old templ or sentinels standing watch on a hill overlooking a city. Now only the tiny, tin kling bells, drooping like pomegranates from green and gold eaves, remain t tell of past glories of an Imperial Park, a sanctuary or a particular locality.

Wang Shi noted changes in the eastern Sichuan plains. The new vistas le him to quote the old proverb, "The favorableness of conditions comes fror the invisible world."

"That old saying," he commented, "tells us to be aware of our surround ings and to make the most of opportunities through work and vigilanc Departure toward the south and east, as we now are doing, is propitious bu requires work. The south is the region of the heavens between Sun and Moor between the gentle and penetrating and the receptive and devoted."

In this, calmer section of the river, the first officer took the tiller, allowin, the skipper to join us passengers. A laid-back and engaging person, he did no live under the shadow of an ill-tempered spouse, nor did he arouse suspicion that he was involved in arcane schemes, as had our first *lao ban*. Fitting readi ly into our circle, he eagerly questioned: Did we have a good trip fror Yichang, his home city? What did we think of Wanxian? And, since we wer from Nanjing, what did we think of Chiang Kai-shek's government? Woul Chiang carry out much-needed reconstruction programs?

Skipper Chung was concerned over the unfulfilled promises and uncertain ties of the post-war months. "Very troublesome," he said. "There are risin, costs—rice, vegetables, meat and *wu ban* parts and repairs. Also, with more an more country people moving into the city, overcrowding and unemploymen are worsening. And there's not much we can do about these troubles. Sinc there's more than enough pessimism being spread, it's better to try to be hopeful.

No longer absorbed in the crew's constant struggle against the current, a we were when going west, we passengers were more relaxed and enjoyed th easier passage. We noticed more about our surroundings. Our present oarsme stroked a steady pace and the sweepmen maintained a measured rhythm wit their sculling to keep the junk in mid-channel and ahead of the current. W could see the skipper's strategy to steer a midstream course.

Before we realized it, on the banks of the eastern Sichuan, flat fertile field gave way to hills and rose up toward the palisades in the distance. The majo noted that the crops along the sloping banks were planted vertically, instead c paralleling, to the river. He assumed that on such slopes that was the onl ay the farmers could make their furrows.

A short distance further, we swept past the carved figures of the Three 'ater Guardians peering from their stone alcoves. We missed the point-by-int narrative of our upriver cook-guide.

With the guardian palisades on the banks and the Dragon Spine Rocks lternately called *yanyudui* or Goosetail Rock) midstream fast approaching, ir young *lao ban* was prompted to speak about the dragons associated with e river.

"It's the name Dragon Spine that's important," he said in a matter-of-fact ay. "The name stands as a warning about this potential danger in the chan-el. Giving the rocks a dragon name recognizes some of the dragon qualities f the Long River. These danger spots are not so much to be feared as to be nderstood and steered around.

"We Chinese," the *lao ban* said to Wang Shi with a broad grin, "heap upon ragons too many meanings–power and force, the old and the new, our tradi-ons and our expectations."

This triggered an animated conversation about the river's dragons. The old-me naturalists, they said, counted the dragon and the tortoise as leaders of the caly" and "shelly" tribes–the other three tribes being the "feathered", airy" (e.g. unicorn), and "naked" (humans). Chinese proverb-makers long ave described all manner of human life and conduct in terms of the habits and stincts of the animated beings around them.

One legend, Wang Shi told us, holds that the rock stood above the Dragon astle. One day, long ago, *Long Wang*, the Dragon King, decided to leave his alace under the rock and tour his underwater domain. This he did against the lvice of his ministers. He transformed himself into a fish and was so distract-l by the wonderful things he was seeing that he became careless and was ught in a fisherman's net. Soon he was being sold in the market. Before he lew it the woman who had bought him had him split and frying in her wok. 'hen he disengaged himself, he went directly to the palace of Ya Hwang, the ief ruler of the gods, and complained about the way he had been treated. Ya wang told the Dragon King that since he had left his proper place and turned mself into a fish he had only himself to blame for his misfortune. The story, 'ang Shi noted, may have its underlying Confucian ethic about staying in our signed stations in life.

Hardly a gruesome monster, they agreed, the river dragon is a force to be spected. It is the spirit of change, therefore, of life itself. It wields the power f transformation and the gift of rendering itself visible or invisible. In the pring it ascends to the skies, and in the autumn it buries itself in the watery epths. It covers itself with mud in the autumnal equinox, and awakening in e spring it sparks the return of nature's energies. Thus, the dragon Is a metaphor for the river's power and the human quest for strength and goodness.

Their conversation enlightened us long after we had safely circumvented the Dragon Spine Rocks. Wang Shi summarized their conversation: "There are three chief species of dragons: the *long* (the most powerful, who inhabits the sky); the *li* (hornless, which lives in the ocean); and the *chiao* (scaly and resides in marshes and dens). But, significantly, the primitive form of dragon known as *gui* (or k'uei) is a beneficent creature, said to exert a restraining influence against the sin of greed. Significantly, this *gui* is the Chinese character that gives the magnificent Gui Men promontory in the Qutang Gorge its name."

We sighted the picturesque palisade where the memorial temple to the choleric Zhang Fei stood. Coming from the west and flowing east gave us a different perspective. Our large *wu ban* was more stable by far than the leaky sam pan ferry by which we had previously approached the honored place. In the fast, wide-angle exposure, our eyes' captured the chief items of identification the four enormous ideographs–Ethereal, Bell, Thousand, Ages–on the face of the vertical cliff, the traditional styled central hall with its curled-up roof-end the pavilion for prayers and the orange and loquat trees enveloping the grounds. We gained, in the new clearer and wider-range view, the uniqueness of the temple's location. Instead of perched atop a nondescript bluff, we now saw the complex as symmetrically situated in a beautiful glen opening into valley flanked by steep slopes that climbed to a lofty pinnacle in the distance.

While the *feng xue* was superb and the atmosphere brilliant, it was not so with the meaning of the enigmatic inscription emblazoned near the fabled place: "Let us unite as one against great gusts of wind." Wang Shi hoped the "wind" people were summoned to unite against was corruption.

On the north bank was Yun Yang, the City of the Clouded Sun. Today instead of its usual misty wrapping, on this clear afternoon the sun outlined against an azure sky. The city's riverfront stone stairway, where students and elders had engaged us the week before, stood out in bold relief. The angle of the sun was such that the entrances to the riverside coal mines were accentuated. The skipper called our attention to the coolies hauling fuel and elaborate on the importance of coal in the local economy. He explained how everything from industry to home heating and cooking relies on coal. He pointed out places on the banks where people were molding coal-dust briquettes for household cooking.

Our attention was called to the majestic heights in the distance. The spectacular highest peak, now illuminated by the western brilliance, was *Chija Shan* (Peach Mountain). It's more flamboyant name was *Huoyen Shan* (Flame Mountain). Opposite it stood *Bai Di Shan* (White Salt Mountain). The two presented sharp, exotic color-contrast.

Far below, also on the north bank, were the remnants of *Bazhentu* (Eight

Mounds Locale), whose origins were much disputed–ruins of General Zhuge Liang's fortifications against the armies of the Wu Kingdom? Or stone piles from the Later Stone and Bronze Ages?

Within minutes we approached *Fengjie* (Kuei-fu), the gray-walled county seat with the venerable Poets Gate atop its riverside entrance stairs. We looked in vain for signs of the Iron Posts that were said to have once held "toll control" chains across the river. The skipper, not having scheduled a stop, took it upon himself to review how the historic town stands as a fragment of the area's heritage. He told how what little was left of the old wall and inner divisions into *fangs* (districts) showed that the city was a beacon of order. But the town had changed more in the last decades than it had in centuries before, evolving into a center for coal mining and transfer point for growing river traffic.

Before either he or we could say more about Fengjie, we had passed it and reached *Baidicheng* (White King City), where we would make a short stop to ready the *wu ban* for negotiating the Qutang Gorge. The sail was to be lowered and the mast swung back from its central-well pivot, lowered by ropes, unpinned from its base, dragged forward fifteen feet and lashed to the side. The skipper insisted we at least set foot ashore at Baidicheng, immortalized in one of Li Po's epic poems. The *lao ban* sent us off with Yang, the new lead oarsman, with instructions: take them to the citadel and the temple, and get them back in two hours.

Yang took us first to the city's ancient fortress, now serving as a sort of municipal museum. Displayed were brush-and-ink works, by which painters create another world with trees, stones, currents, streams, rivers and gardens. Examples of plastic and modeling arts were also expressed, with lifesize statues of historical personages such as Liu Bei and Zhu Geliang. At the temple galleries we found Chinese poems. Our attention was drawn to the painting of the twelve Wushan mountains that we were to see the next day. On a plaque with the question, "Which mountain did the poets most praise?" was the answer "Fairy Mount." Liu Yuxi's poem expresses well why so many poets chose to praise that one peak: "Whatever its height, so long as celestials and immortals exist, Fairy Mount will be famous."

By the time oarsman Yang corralled and got us down Baidicheng's precipitous cliffs, the preparations for the *wu ban* were complete. The skipper steered the vessel into the river's narrower and faster channel headed toward Qutang Gorge's entrance. Called the Chasm of the Terrifying Embankment or Wind Box Gorge, it is the first gorge approaching from the west. Though only five miles in length, it offered both spectacular vistas and great perils. Afternoon rays set ablaze the gorge's dramatic opening, but also highlighted the ominous Yen Yu Rock protruding from the turbulent rush of waters. Over the centuries boatmen had sung a cautionary doggerel about the fateful rock pile:

> *When Yen-yu's an elephant, upstream you shan't*
> *When Yen-yu's a horse, don't downstream course.*

Coming to the rocks and to the first of the gorge's rapids, we passenger chattered nervously. The anticipation was like the prelude of a symphony, complete with the blare of the winds, the delicate cues of the strings and the heav rumble of the percussions. "These minor rapids are no cause for worry," th skipper reassured us, "They're tame compared with the fierce *Yeh Dan* an *Qing Dan*."

According to the skipper, on this particular day, the rock pile was a comparatively "low horse," thereby diminishing its risk. Nevertheless, to us passengers, Whirling Water Rock loomed high and menacing with spray shootin from the eddies surrounding it. Our junk appeared to be dashing straigh toward it. A faulty pressure from any hand, or an eddy caught wrong at eithe bow or stern, could have sent the junk broadside into the current, out of con trol, capsizing and in ruins. Would the helmsman and sweepmen react fas enough to swerve away? Our hearts seemed to stop and only ever so slowl start pounding again.

The *lao ban's* timing was precise and his hands deft on the tiller. The oars men at midship exerted extra strength. Up in the bow, full power of arms shoulders and legs were applied to the sweeps. In the prow, the new-to-us an matter-of-fact *tai gong* carried out his job with equal skill. Catastrophe wa avoided.

The racing current sucked us into the gorge. The choppy surface was fille with swirls and eddies whipped by the heavier wind into froth and spray Perpendicular cliffs framed the gate and constricted the channel to a mere 37 feet in width. The river water forced in between roared like stampeding wil horses. When flood conditions prevailed, the current sometimes attained four teen knots, but it normally moved at about half that speed. The inward-slant ing cliffs seemed about to swallow the river. The mountain at the horizo ahead gave the illusion that the river was coming to an abrupt end.

The crew remained alert as we negotiated other minor rapids. Their con centration and steadiness took us through Eight Cliffs Canyon, and around bend we found the sky.

Suddenly, here in the heart of the *Qutang*, the usual gloom was transforme by the afternoon sun. Cliffs and glens on the north bank came alive with deli cate, exotic contours. The crisscrossing of light shafts and lengthening shadow created scenes like those in Song paintings.

Simultaneously, Gui Men Promontory loomed dead ahead. The afternoo sun had cleared the peaks that framed the Gate it formed. The pink stone wa the north face burned with light. The sheer south side, still in shadows, was back. The rays glinted off the *wu ban's* bow and illuminated the eddies and whirlpools that showed the river's violent current. Each swerve in the boat's passage revealed another view of vertical rock rising up straight as a ramrod and majestic. The grandness of the vista struck chords in our hearts and stirred our admiration.

The major spoke out from his long silence: "That promontory is one of the most beautiful scenes I have ever seen in my life." Pausing, as if to test some of his new learning, he added, "Such an example of a *yin-yang* contrast! We see *yin* the dark overcast clouds and *yang* in the sun's brilliance. The mountains on the north side are dark, or *yin*, and on the south side bright, or *yang*. The river's south bank with its shadows shows *yin*, while the north bank as it receives the sun shows us *yang*. Water is *yin*-natured, yet its turbulence is *yang*."

"This view of Gui Men from the west," Wang Shi responded, "has long been a popular subject for Chinese landscape poetry. Seeing how they try to present nature in its pure and original forms, the reader is brought into closer contact with nature itself."

Before reaching the *Qutang* we were astounded by the way our fast down-river pace telescoped our experiences. We swept past one after another village, historic spot or special scene long before we were finished with it. As we shot along on the racing current, it was sobering to realize that here the whole mighty flow of the Long River, collected from the melting ice of the Himalayas, the rivers that drain the vast Sichuan plain and hundreds of named and unnamed tributaries, was channeled into a rock-walled passage hardly wide enough for two large ships to pass.

East of Gui Men pass the *Qutang* was not as frightening today as when we had labored through it on the way west. Then, preoccupied with the stressful passage, we took but a few glances at the Wind Box Cliffs, cleaved open by the river god *Yu*, the picturesque temples perched on the rim and Flame Mountain looming majestic in the background.

Along the cliffs on the northern bank, the recessed tow path for the teams of trackers who had hauled our 95-foot *wu ban* the week before was visible. We passed so swiftly the south cliffs that bore markers of Meng Liang's Ladder and the Wind Box, or Bellows, that we almost missed identifying them. Given the absence of footholds in the stone wall beyond halfway up, we began to question the Meng Liang legend. We also saw the crevices high above the river into which large cypress coffins were once vertically positioned, giving the appearance of bellows from below. This gave meaning to Meng Qiao's 8th-century lines:

*Trees lock their roots in rotted coffins*
*And the twisted skeletons hang tilted upright.*

The superb views tranquilized us. Before we realized it, however, we were into the tumult of another set of races. It was the *allegro vivace* of this gorge. Our downward speed accelerated, but instead of slacking their rhythm, the boatmen quickened their strokes.

Following a short lull, we were into the second section. Our junk lurched now this way, then that. The drummer increased his rhythm, and the extra aboard jumped to assist the sweep operators in their labored sculling. With extraordinary exertion, they responded to the slightest order-by-gesture of the tai gong as he stood on the bow, eyes riveted ahead. Oarsmen pushing with broad strokes did double time over the *yulow* operators narrowed their sweeping swaths to speed their pace. Their chants lifted from one crescendo to another.

Once through the *Qutang*, the massive palisades that had surrounded us gradually receded into the horizon. On the southern bank, however two dark peaks soared. According to legend, twelve fierce dragons were chasing each other playing hide-and-seek around Wushan Mountain. Baring their fangs and brandishing their claws, they darkened the sky and whipped up a hurricane which demolished houses and left in its wake thousands of dead. Goddess Yao Ji, the youngest daughter of the Mother of the Western Skies happened to pass by, riding on a colorful floating cloud. Pointing her finger at the dragons, she conjured up a deafening thunderbolt. The dragons were struck down and turned into huge rocks that blocked parts of the Long River channel.

But *Yu* the Great rushed in and with the help of the Goddess corrected the wrongly blocked passage. This short stretch was given the name "*Cuoka* Chasm," (Wrongly-Opened Gorge).

Our oarsmen had an easier time stroking and soon pulled the *wu ban* into a clearer, wider portion of the river. The crew and we passengers welcomed the sight of the quiet cove on the south bank where we were to moor for the night.

Wushan city, so intriguing for us on our westward journey, dominated the high ground on the north bank across the Long River. It was quite different in its appearance from the places we had passed further west. Instead of rising directly out of the river as does Wanxian, Yunyang and Fengjie, this town is set back from the main channel of the river. Between the town and the riverbank are sloping red clay flats that were exposed at this time of year. In the twilight the city stood silhouetted against its backdrop of sawtooth peaks which loomed iridescent. In between, the uppermost houses and temples were turning golden in the fast-setting sunlight. The city's riverport, at the base of the cliffs and on the west shore of the Daning River, swarmed with craft snuggled up to pontoons like suckling piglets. In between the rows of docks we spotted the junk builders' slips we had visited the week before.

Flowing in from its scenic northern reaches, the Daning tributary was pouring its green stream into the Long River's copper waters. The shores at the Daning's confluence were lined with smaller craft that navigated "the miniaıre three gorges." The mouth of this important tributary was dotted with ondola-like sampans loaded with large burlap bags of salt from the up-coun-ıy brine wells.

Pulling into a protected inlet, we joined a flotilla of junks tied thwart-to-ıwart. With wide sterns, these boats resembled river fowl clustered against the ıind. Our docking was near the foot of a cone-shaped hill capped by a pago-ıa dedicated to the God of Literature.

The glen where we were moored provided welcome sanctuary from the ıeafening convulsions of the *Qutang* cataracts. Cool shadows on the sheer ıliffs and the cove's alcoves formed a mystical partnership, soothing and ıestorative.

The bossy downriver cook bellowed out, "Night meal not for an hour." The ırew accepted the announcement without grumbling and as soon as their ıssignments were finished, lapsed into *xiu xi* time.

Wang Shi, the major and I walked along the inlet to a nearby fishing settle-ıent. In this tranquil cove a tributary stream lapped the hulls of slim wooden ıoats nosed up to the riverbank. A woman emerged from one sampan's low ıicker canopy and began kindling a fire in a brazier on the stern. Her son and ıaughter tumbled and giggled on a purple blanket of safflower blossoms. Off ıhore fishermen dragged in their haul of *hui yu* (black carp) and other com-ıercial fish, which, on the morrow, they would take to market.

The broad steps behind us were inviting, so we strode uphill toward the ıod of Literature Pagoda, luminous and solitary, rising from the promontory ıbove our mooring.

Climbing the seven-storied pagoda, we joined an elderly man carrying a ıable lute. On the platform at the top we engaged Mr. Wang, as he introduced ıimself, in talk about the river below and the magnificent vista beyond. He ıas full of questions about us. As soon as we could, we turned to question him ıbout the instrument he treated as a special companion.

His *qin* (lute, lyre or zither) was a large, seven-stringed piece, in contrast to ıhe smaller twenty-five stringed version. These instruments, he told us, were ınvented by the first legendary emperor, Fu Xi, 2953 B.C., and are among the ınost ancient and honorable of Chinese stringed instruments. Originally they ıere made of tung wood, afterwards of stones, by which its sounds resembled ıhose of the drum under the influence of the wind. Wang Shi explained, the ıin carries many associations. By its particular length, the instrument repre-ıents 360 days; by its breath, the six points of the universe; by its thickness, the ıour seasons; by its five strings, the original elements, to which two other ıtrings were added to express the harmony subsisting between princes and min-ısters; the thirteen resemblances or changes are equivalent to the twelve notes ıf music; one for each month, and then one more for the intercalary month.

The *qin*, closely related to the *pi pa* (lyre, or zither), Wang Shi continued is often taken as a kind of generic musical instrument. Thus, knowledge of and ability to perform on the lute was considered by ancients as one of the four signs of a scholar, the other three being chess, literature and painting. This elegant and distinguished foursome is often employed for decorative purposes on bronzes and porcelains.  In other periods of Chinese history the four were increased to include training in rites, archery, chariot-driving, writing and reckoning.

Wang Shi cited Confucius' answer to a disciple who had difficulty picturing the practical aspects of aesthetics his Master was expounding. The disciple claimed, for example, that grace, as described in the *I Ching* (Number 22) suggested pure beauty and points to a full aesthetic dimension of life. Confucius told his follower, "The thing or person that is beautiful must be expressed. That is why I, for instance, must play the lute."

Mr. Wang was on his way to join other lute players who often gathered in the garden at the far side of the pagoda which offered a suitable setting for the lute. The surroundings provided the appropriate *shan xui* (scenery and ambience). He invited us to accompany him and took us to a rock grotto with a stone table and seats. Drawing his lute from its green-and-gold brocade pouch he placed it on the table and began playing plaintive folk songs.

Mr. Wang's music was well balanced, although his more northern tune tended to be sentimental and somewhat vaguely despondent. With Wang Shi's help we explored what the sages meant when they proclaimed that people should hear and be taught music in order to dissipate the melancholy of their souls. For all their subtle differences, Taoists and Confucianists agreed on music having both a functional meaning in people's lives and cosmic implications. The twin arts of rites and music, for instance, symbolized this eternal interplay of the two fundamental principles of union and dissociation–rite, symbolizing the necessary distinctions between people, music the harmonic association binding people.

Individuals' rhythms and society's collective rhythms, should correspond to each other and harmonize with the universe's rhythms. Mr. Wang then plucked two tunes which he introduced as pieces often played at wedding feasts. He explained that the harmony produced by the musical strains of the *qin* is emblematic of matrimonial happiness. To say of a family that 'their lutes are in tune' is to say that husband and wife are in harmony. The friendship of either sex is also symbolized by the sweet sounds these instruments make. The sounds similarly convey the experience of purity and moderation expected of officials. The name *qin*, Mr. Wang said, was derived from the word "prohibit," because its sounds restrain evil passions. Music used with the observance of rites or other sacred occasions is accompanied by burning incense and reciting venerable odes to remind people of their rich heritage.

These pieces and Mr. Wang's suggestions gave us a haunting echo of the old onfucian insistence that music affects behavior.

Patriot that he was, Wang Shi had a request, Tian Han's immortalized *"Qi i! Qi lai!* (Stand up! Stand up!). Lutist Mr. Wang obliged and our colleague oke into song,

> *Stand up, all you who refuse to be slaves!*
> *With our blood and flesh a great wall will be built.*
> *The Chinese nation now faces its greatest danger.*
> *From each comes forth his loudest call: "Stand up! Stand up!"*

Called the "March of the Volunteers," during China's war against Japan it as practically a national anthem. Wang Shi's day was made, but our new friend e lutist apologized, I regret the qin is neither loud or strident enough to do stice to our *"Qi lai! Qi lai!"*

The major and I had a series of questions for Mr. Wang. From his replies we thered that:

The essence of Chinese music, like all Asiatic, non-Western music, is the redominance of melody. Its striking feature is its pentatonic scale, which elim- ated all but five whole tones—roughly equivalent to our A, C, D, F and G— hich the Chinese entitled Emperor, Chancellor, Subject People, State Affairs d Picture of the Universe. This simple music, whether it is pure melody from e north or more rhythmic in the south, is essentially optimistic and sooth- g—neither sublime nor soaring, like Western music, nor subtle and vague, like do-Persian tunes.

After playing two tunes he had composed, Mr. Wang gestured toward the scription carved in the grotto wall. The central character, *en* (grace), referred a saying from the classics: "Grace has success. Grace, both solid and lucid, eates beauty." Once again we were dependent on Wang Shi to help us deci- her the meaning. "The saying," he explained, "encourages risking something w. Grace paves the way for success. Grace, however, must be accompanied y *ken*, 'keeping still and firm as the mountain.'"

"Sounds like your Western Socrates, remembered for his reasonableness and aching," Wang Shi noted. "The venerable Greek started playing the lute after s demon counseled him to make more music. However that may be, the onfucian point was that harmonious music accompanies great truths, and in rn, profound principles need to be expressed with charm and grace. Gracious ving, like graceful art, emerges when aesthetic appreciation is strong and abid- g as the mountains."

Genial Mr. Wang was perplexed as our dialogue in English dragged on but his tolerance he followed our gestures and facial expressions, and maintained his friendly mood. He carefully wrapped his lute, excused himself and walked off to keep his engagement with a friend in the village. We felt privileged to have met this amazing gentleman. We realized that with his lute he had expressed grace and beauty in a way that we could only imply with our words and our philosophy.

Back at our mooring we found boatmen clustered around a wizened fortuneteller seated at a rickety bamboo table. With an authoritative pose, one hand on his dog-eared copy of the *I Ching* and the other hand holding a brush and tablet, he was ready for his customers. Some threw coins, while others had the soothsayer count through his handful of 64 yarrow sticks. This wisp of man then flicked through pages of the ancient book to draw clues about their prospects.

This demonstration of the coolies' addictive gaming and reliance on the whirligig of chance exasperated the major. Uncomfortable with their trust in a random toss and broken reeds, he asked Wang Shi: "How can a throw of the dice or a chance selection of yarrow sticks, give any comfort for these boat men's hard and short lives?"

Also troubled, Wang Shi said, "True. I too don't believe in chance and soothsayers. But what's insignificant for the educated still has meaning for these uneducated laborers. Who else but soothsayers can the commoners talk with about their fear of the future?

"You, good major, are a specialist in mathematical calculation of *time*. But do you have answers for questions Chinese ask about *time*, such as: Why does each little segment of time possess the quality peculiar to that moment? Can you calculate why one particular moment follows another?"

Our stoical downriver *tai gong* stepped up to the shriveled soothsayer and put down coins for a choice of sticks. Getting a response, he walked off without sharing the wisdom he had drawn.

The encounter emboldened the soothsayer to ask the major to make a draw and commented, "Risking a draw with me is much less hazardous than going through the *Qutang* Chasm."

The major surprised us–and himself–by putting down coins for a yarrow stick count. Out of the 64, the number 13 was drawn. We Americans shook our heads. Noticing our consternation, Wang Shi explained, "This is an excellent draw: *dung ren* (fellowship with people)."

Reinforcement came from the skipper, who announced that the major's lucky draw bestowed honor on him and his crew, as well as on his "guests."

"Friendships that last," Wang Shi mused, "need to be open and trusting and often take time to mellow. Only then are unique possibilities gained. On this journey, we've been more than a mere random mixing of individuals. Our versity has been enriched by its being pointed toward a purpose. Friendships row among people who care for one another. Open-mindedness and common urpose stimulate needed cooperation and respect. I like the verse from one of ne Chinese classics which outlines these qualities:"

> *The will of persons under heaven must show li, enlightened will. Creative, it is from heaven, and has the power to draw good persons together in a positive bond. . .Open fellowship with persons leads to love. . .Success! Fellowship is furthered by the leadership of persevering superior persons. . .It enables one to pass through the most perilous chasms.*

"Fellowship must include love. When this love is expressed, the most difficult of adventures can be accomplished."

Through our openness to chance encounters at dusk, we had gained much. The lute player and the grotto's etched oracle and now this random gathering f boatmen around the Chinese gypsy enriched us.

Our evening meal around the glowing charcoal brassier left us mellow. Long fter we had cleaned our last bowl of rice, we lingered over jasmine tea. Century after century, the tea ritual had been a way in which Chinese culture ad wedded leisure, contemplation, gossip and refreshment.

"Culture is a product of leisure," once wrote Lin Yu-tang, "and the Chinese ave had the immense leisure of 4,000 years to develop it." In these millennia hey have had plenty of time to look at life over their tea cups. They have elighted in taking time to discuss their forefathers, to ponder their failures and chievements, to review changes in art and life, and to see their own ways in ght of the long-ago past.

The friendly *lao ban* joined our circle, but instead of his ancestors, he talked f his native province, Sichuan. "Where we are, opposite the town of Wushan, acing the Daning, is one of Sichuan's frontiers. Tomorrow we move out of my rovince and into Hubei. You must come back some day to see more of this reat province."

Like a Texan bragging about the Lone Star State, the skipper felt a need to ell us of his homeland. Expansive and wild, Sichuan bore many similarities to exas. Sichuan was renowned for its low fertile plains, mountains on the ibetan border that tower 20,000 feet and agricultural products that sustained eighboring provinces. Mineral-rich, the province produced salt, coal, iron, atural gas, lead and copper. Population-rich, it supported three times as many eople as California.

Through the centuries, Sichuan has often stood on its own, self-sufficien and rebellious against the central government. In 25 A.D. the great warrio and wise leader Jung Sun-shu broke away from Han dynasty Emperor Kuan Wu and established himself as the White Emperor. Only a few miles away, nea Meng's Ladder, was the site of Jung Sun-shu's capital city.

"In my father's day," the skipper recalled, "this province was one of the firs to join the revolution against the Qing Empire. Many leaders of the new republic came from this region."

Unbeknownst to any of us in 1946, Deng Xiao-ping, the man destined thir ty years later to become the nation's premier, hailed from a small village not fa from where we were docked that night.

*"Gao hsien sheng.* (Mr. Gao Cowles) *Gao hsien sheng!"* Came an excite summons from behind us which interruped these partisan descriptions of Sichuan

Turning to respond, I saw the unbelievable! There, in the flesh, standing i front of us was none other than our feared-for-lost upriver *tai gong* and besid him the gangly young nephew of oarsman Lao Liu. The major, Wang Shi an I couldn't believe our eyes. What very good fortune! Indeed, this was our lucky da

We embraced, as befitting the brothers we had become on our westwar journey, then asked, "Where is Chiu, the other tracker who fell?"

The *tai gong's* face saddened and he shook his head, saying, "We couldn' save him. He was sucked under and didn't come up."

"I too was sucked under," Xiao Liu (Little Liu) spoke out, "but I came up Plunging into the river I was dumped into a whirlpool to die. It pulled me t the bottom, but I did not know how to think of death. I fought the river an finally got to the side of the whirlpool and it just lifted me out and by the god the *tai gong* rowed over in his little boat."

The westbound skipper's most optimistic scenario had unfolded. There wa a chance, though slim, he had said, that the *tai gong* would be waiting at som *wu ban* mooring east of the Qutang Gorge.

A loud cry broke into our unbelievable reunion. Two boatmen ran up insisting *"Wai guo ren, kuai lai gan!* (Foreigners, come quickly to look!)"

At the riverbank, now darkened with shadows, a procession of many-col ored miniature lanterns on blocks of wood floated downriver. Minute circle were reflected in the dark waters, first sparkling, then iridescent. On and on th river bore the gossamer thread of lights. For a few luminous moments thought I saw the dorsal fins of the River Dragon gamboling downstream.

The skipper, also awed, said he had heard of such displays but had neve seen such an elaborate funeral observance for a member of a well-to-do fami ly. "It's hard to believe," he said, "that any of these tiny floats can survive th urrent. It's as if the great river is showing respect for this one's passing."

Several six-by-six bamboo rafts with torches blazing held fireworks which, with their delayed fuses, went off at varying intervals. Clustered lights cast eerie rays against the cliffs. From time to time, fish sprang at the lights to take them under. These tiny floats launched by unknown upriver hands swished by and were soon lost beyond the bend.

Back on the junk, Wang Shi commented, "You can see the strength of 'natural religion' that is so ingrained in Chinese thought and feeling."

"Yes," I agreed, "the Taoist emphasis on nature's power, serenity and beauty contributes an important strand to the tapestry of Chinese thought. Animism is still the basic religion of rural people—certainly most of the boatmen. It's easy to idealize awesome mountains, streams, rocks and chasms. We have seen shrines devoted to the river god, to snakes, fish, lions and tigers. The vistas, flora and fauna suggest super powers and creatures outside people's control. These natural objects and forces command respect, if not awe. And, of course, from a Westerner's view, a pantheistic stress on nature's beauty can lead persons to focus devotion on nature itself, rather than looking through nature to God."

"Another possible twist in natural religion," Wang Shi observed, "happens when people use the natural glories of their country to proclaim their own supremacy. The Chinese proclaim to be the people of *Zhung Guo* (the middle kingdom = China), while Japanese Shintoism captures the loyalty of the people through reverence for its unique natural beauty, such as Mt Fuji. Recognition of special bounty in the environment may lead, not to higher reverence for the God of all persons, but to arrogant nationalism."

"Tonight's delicate parade of lights," I said, "like the created order that has enveloped us on the Long River, brings us face to face with matters eternal. John Dunne said that three natural strangers invade our lives: the world, morality and sexuality. Buddhists and older adults would add a fourth: aging. These are the forces that track each of us. These realities are symbolized by the Long River's dragon, ready not so much to consume us as to offer power as we navigate life's river. It's awesome at moments of peril to realize that we depend upon natural powers we cannot control, against which we have no resistance."

Back from watching the funeral parade of lights at the river bank, we three welcomed our 12' x 12' section of the *wu ban*, nodded, slipped into our bedrolls and were quickly off to sleep.

# Wuxia And Xiling Gorges' Rapids And Legends

*Junk Readied For Downriver Passage – Mast Lowered, Crew Alerted*

As the sun began to light the rim of the palisades above our mooring, I wa
yet lost in dreams of the river's convulsions and wonders. My dream self wa
lifted into the shadows of the Pagoda of Learning and caught in the lute play
er's melodies.

The charcoal fumes from the galley and the pungent smell of breakfast cab
bage drifted into my consciousness. The major and I pulled deeper into ou
bedrolls, but Wang Shi's summons shook us awake. My night visions gave wa
to the reality of loud arguments from neighboring junks readying for the day
struggle with the river.

The sweepmen poled us away from the mooring into the Daning's gree
waters. Wushan city on the north shore receded as we passed eastward. Th
current and our rowers swept us into the *Wuxia* (Witches Gorge). Starting a
the Daning River in Sichuan province, this gorge ends at Guandu Ferry i
Badong Country, Hubei province. The gorge runs about twenty-five mile
Again, as we navigated the chasm's constricted channel, the mountains sud
denly seemed to block the passage only to fade back and allow us into an ope
passage once more. Austere rock towers served as sentinels for the chasm
entrance. The surrounding mountain peaks blocked the rising sun, permittin
only rays reflected off the sheer cliffs to stab their way into the canyon's depth

One after another we encountered *chipa* (races)–usually caused by a pro-
cting point or spur of rock below which there was an eddy. The rowers cleared
e first series of hazards in only minutes, compared with the hours it required
n our upward journey.

Gossamer mists blanketed the river within the Wuxia. Far above on the
orth shore, rolls of white clouds smothered the precipices surrounding *Fu
'an* (Fu Mountain). On the south side, the morning sun bathed tree-covered
lls. The scenery unfolded much like the veteran English captain Plant had
escribed it in 1902:

> *The river winds round the base of precipitous cliffs, which rise
> perpendicular in places to a thousand feet and are backed by
> lofty peaks shaped in fantastic formations. The solid rock walls,
> gashed by great faults, are streaked with strata that look like
> crumpled paper set at strange angles. Where the strata run
> vertically and are fluted with thousands of potholes, the towering
> rock walls resemble the pipes of an enormous organ.*

The spectacular jagged peaks of this gorge differed from the massive round-
d crests in the Qutang and the talus piles that were to follow in the Xiling. Its
eep walls and spire-like peaks blocked the sun during much of the day in tes-
ment to its reputation as the most foreboding and somber of the Three
orges.

"There they are!" exclaimed Wang Shi. "The famous twelve immortals,
eautiful peaks that touch travelers' hearts."

They were of various shapes, ribboned with drifting clouds. Six of the peaks
ood in a row on the north side and the other six lined the south bank.

The first three peaks bore the exotic names of Pure Altar, Wise Man Springs
nd Ascending Dragon. *Shennu Feng* (Pure Altar or Goddess Peak), the best
nown, took its name from a smallish rock formation at its peak. Viewed from
e river a thousand feet below, it appeared as if a robed woman were bent in
orrowful meditation. Austere and ominous, this supernatural woman and her
leven sisters hovered over voyagers as if ready to pounce at any moment.

On the north bank, near the Hengshi tributary, the sheer cliffs rose on both
des of the stream's valley. Thin layers of greyish-white limestone in curved folds
ced the cliffs, looking like the armor ancient warriors wore. The surface of the
ounded mountaintop has been tinted a yellowish-brown by underground water
ontaining ferric oxide. It resembled the golden helmet on a warrior's head. The
vine was known as *The Valley of the Golden Helmet and Silver Armor.*

Our bowmen were hard-pressed to pull the *wu ban* through a series of sharp
ends. On both left and right banks were many fabled sites–the trackers' road,

Phoenix Spring, rock formations, a plank road, temples, caves. Fishermen wei
sheltering in coves made by the rock cliffs. The skipper talked about *Ching s.
dung* (Green Rock Cave), twelve miles inland to the south. He mentioned tha
it was one of the gorges' most important archaeological sites. Wushan Coun
authorities spoke of it as *Longgupo* (Dragon Bone Hill).

Wang Shi kept his eyes on the eastern foothills of the Peaks of the Immorta
searching for the renowned Kong Ming Tablet. Spotting it on a high knoll, h
explained that it was a superb carved stone monument that bore the famou
inscription, "The Wuxia Gorge has peaks rising higher and higher." It wa
reputed to have been written by the esteemed Three Kingdoms prime ministe
Zhuge Liang. Also inscribed on the tablet were passages describing Zhug
Liang's political wisdom upholding an alliance between the States of *Shu* an
*Wu* against the State of *Wei*. Weather-beaten and time-worn, these passage
had become almost illegible. Legend has it that during a battle between th
states of *Wu* and *Shu* at Yiling, General Lu Xun of the State of *Wu*, upon reac
ing Zhuge Liang's wise counsel, was deeply moved, gave up the chase an
withdrew his troops.

Sweeping downriver we approached *Bei Shi* (Engraved Rock), a small tow
on the southern bank. Before Wang Shi was able to tell us about either th
unusual name of the rock or the town's, our *wu ban* was propeled into wha
the skipper called the *Hei Shi Dan* (Black Rock Rapids or Fan Water Course
Still absorbed in our sightseeing, we had to change modes fast. The confusin
name no longer mattered. Erupting crests of rampaging waters struck our w
ban. The swirling current sent vibrations from the keel to the floor boards. Ou
large junk quivered as it swerved to port and then starboard. Next we bur
into tumultuous sections running past the twin precipices that signal th
Portals of Awe. The crew pulled desperately to maneuver the junk nearer th
south shore to avoid the midstream danger of the Qu Yuan Whirlpool.

Relief came at the little north bank town of *Guan Du Kou* (Official Fer
Portal), which marks the eastern limit of the Wuxia Gorge. We came out int
a wider, slower stretch of water. To the south was Badong, a communicatio
juncture and the gateway to the mountains of western Hubei province
Highways fan out to neighboring counties that supply tung oil, raw lacque
medicinal herbs and hides. It was here on its short beach where our uprive
junk was run ashore for repairs and where our first *lao ban's* grandbaby was bor

We were given no time for reminiscing. The of crashing waters announce
our approach to the fierce *Xie Dan* (Yeh Dan) cluster of rapids. The towerin
rock phalanxes closed in and narrowed the channel, speeding up the curren
Our junk accelerated as it neared the first whitewater, called the Three-Tw
and-One Cataracts. Even though there was hardly time for suspense, the majo
commented, "I'm glad for the additional size and weight of skipper Chung
*wu ban.*"

Suddenly, *presto agitato*, the waters around us churned convulsive waves, ddies and whirlpools. The surging current exploded over submerged boulders nd dashed against the banks. The river's furor proved breath-stopping. Even fter emerging from the mad rush of the first cataract the channel continued to e roiled for miles downstream. We soon were in sight of *Xie Dan's* second run f rapids, the Cross Beam Cataracts. Our stress continued as the *wu ban* ashed into this middle section of the *Xie Dan*. Another turbulent race fol-wed shortly. Although not as ferocious as the first series, these last two rapids ere stomach-churning.

As fast as they had closed in on us, the rock walls opened wide. The chasms ave way to easier slopes and the river slowed to an amble, flowing down oward a series of wide bends. On the north bank, the city of Zigui reflected e noonday sun.

Since we had visited Zigui going upriver, for our mid-day stop Skipper hung planned instead to go a mile east of Zigui to Quyuantuo, a small village id to have been the birthplace of the esteemed Three Kingdoms statesman u Yuan. Having made it through the *Xie Dan's* gauntlets, crew and passen-ers needed a respite. The cook, particular about serving meals on time, was dgety. Our skipper, eager to avoid irritating that indispensable crewman, eered the *wu ban* toward shore. Oarsmen and sweepmen pulled us into an viting glen downriver from Zigui.

We had hardly moored before the cook gave the call for lunch. A chuanese, he had prepared generous portions of the province's spicy special-es. The skipper had sent one of the oarsmen ashore to buy *zongzi* (sweet umplings made by wrapping glutinous rice in broad bamboo leaves) for which e village was noted.

While we were enjoying the skipper's treat, he and Wang Shi told us about e tributary *Xian Qi* (Fragrant Stream), nine miles further east.

Fragrant Stream flows by the birthplace of Wang Zhaojun, who was an nperial concubine of Emperor Yuandi of the Han dynasty. Legend has it that nce when Zhaojun was washing in the stream, a pearl from one of her orna-ents fell into the water. Since then, the stream has carried the scent of per-me, hence the name, Fragrant Stream. The stream was clear since it flowed rough a limestone area which served as a filter. Another story tells that after siting her parents, the esteemed beauty set off on her journey beyond the reat Wall to be married to the chieftan of a northern tribe. As she sailed along ragrant Stream, she plucked the *pipa*, a stringed Chinese musical instrument imilar to the *qi* we had heard the evening before), and sang of her deep love r her kinsfolk and native land. The lyrical music moved everyone who heard . Even the peach blossoms on both banks shed their petals.

Before returning to the river's fury, the skipper described features of the

Xiling Gorge we were to enter. Beginning at Fragrant Stream and runnin
forty-five miles eastward, Xiling Gorge is the longest of the three gorges. I
turbulent rapids and zigzag channel run through four smaller gorges: th
Gorge of the Sword and Book on the Art of War, the Gorge of the Ox's Live
and Horse's Lung, the Kongling Gorge and the Gorge of the Shadow Pla
The major and I, still unclear from our upriver struggle with these section
yearned for a map that would specify the identity, location and sequence c
these chasms within Xiling Gorge. The skipper helped by sketching on a shee
of the major's notebook the Long River's channel in the Xiling and locatin
the chasms he had referred to.

"We would need many more sheets of paper," Wang Shi added, "to list th
legends, poetry and dramas associated with each of these sections. After all, th
'Three Gorges' are a human construct. The separate stories and historic
events connected with these separate chasms outnumber the population
Archaeologists have identified three main cultural layers in this region: *Da*
(4500-3500 B.C.), *Qujialing* (3500-2500 B.C.) and *Erlitou* (2500-100
B.C.)."

Travelers, the skipper said, were interested in the unique *shan xue* (mour
tains and waters, i.e., scenery) of each of these Xiling's parts. Boatmen, how
ever, have to navigate its perilous shoals and rapids. He explained its many hic
den rocks and dangerous shoals were formed as the river cut through shale an
unstable layers of the Huang-ling anticline. For junkmen the Xiling Gorge
known and feared for the *Xin Dan* (New Shoal, formerly known as the Blu
Shoal), the Discharge Shoal, the *Kongling Shoal* and the *Yaochahe Shoal*.

Xiling Gorge starts with high mountains, the valley opens wide, then hig
mountains close in once again. The first chasm of interest is the Gorge c
Sword and Book on the Art of War. Among the several legends associated wit
the section, one claims that it was so named because this was where Zhug
Liang stored his grain and a book on the art of war. On the sheer cliff on th
north bank, a rock shaped like a book stood high in a crevice. On one side c
it a long rock resembled a sword. This account says that Zhuge Liang wrote
book on how he commanded his troops. When he was seriously ill, he coul
not find a worthy follower who would appreciate the book, so he had it pu
away on the sheer cliff, hoping that some day a talented person would read i
Another legend holds that the sword and book belonged to Zhang Liang, wis
and resourceful military adviser to Liu Bang, who established the Han dynast
After Zhang Liang died, his sword and military book were stored here.

For a short stretch, the shore was marked by low, rolling hills and terrace
fields of corn and mulberry trees. Making a bend around a promontory, w
were brought to the portals of another series of precipices. The early afternoo
sun highlighted the towering stone bastions. Distant abutments rose across th
channel to the east, bringing us, it appeared, to another dead end. In minute

owever, the entrance to the Xiling opened.

The first officer announced the chasm as the *Mi Dan* (Military Code and recious Blade Gorge), the name we remembered as perplexing when we had rst heard it on our trip upriver. Again we turned to Wang Shi for clarification.

"Military," he began, "is expressed by the literary word, *shi*, referring to maral arts. The ideograph is one of the 64 hexagrams of the *I-Ching*, which says:"

> *The army requires perseverance*
> *And a strong man.*
> *Perseverance means discipline.*
> *The man who can effect discipline through*
> *Power and wealth may attain mastery of the world.*
> *The superior man increases his masses*
> *By generosity toward the people.*

"That's an appropriate but not very clear quotation," Wang Shi noted. "As eceptive ground receives and stores water, so military strength is stored up in ne people–invisible in times of peace, but ready for use when rallied to war. igid discipline is needed to reduce the double dangers of sedition from with1 and sabotage from outside. Like poison, war is always dangerous. If justice nd perseverance govern actions, the poisons and perils can be minimized."

Though grateful for Wang Shi's explanation, we still felt the various ccounts were more fanciful than plausible. We found the connection, howevr, if not with "military," at least with "blade." The 1,000-foot wedge that ormed the chasm looked like it had been sliced down the middle of the cliffs n the south bank, seemingly by some cosmic swordsman. The wall that emmed us in and constricted the channel seemed destined to hold the river 1 its present course forever. Then, in the distance we could see an opening, nat suggested the glen where the Pure Jade Cave was found.

Passing the glen, laced with reflections and shadows, Skipper Chung preared us for the *Xin Dan* (Qing Dan or Blue Shoals as formerly called), one of ne roughest rapids. He said it was formed by the collapse of sheer cliffs into ne river. During low water season (we were in mid-water season), the current owed at the rate of nine feet per second. At one place, the water dropped bruptly three feet. Numerous submerged rocks cluttered the channel. Their onstant shifting made the course unpredictable. These obstructions agitated ne river with whirlpools and tossing waves. The slightest carelessness could ause a junkwreck. Instead of one continuous shoal, there were three succesive cataracts–Head Rapids, First Rapids and Second Rapids. They together ran mile and a half, and boatmen spoke of them as *Yi, Er* and *San* (First, Second nd Third). Head Rapids was the most hazardous. All boatman knew the folkong, "May the gods protect us as we sail through the *Xin Dan*. If the Dragon

King gets angry, then both men and boat are finished."

Captains who failed to chose the optimum channel risked serious damage to their junks and possible death to their crews. To maintain steerage, junks had to exceed the current's speed or risk drifting out of control. In the New Rapids as elsewhere, junks were known to explode in collisions with rocks, with teak beams, planking and cargo flying in all directions.

Junk captains often enlisted the services of local pilots. Our *lao ban* decided not to stop. Rather, he would make the run himself through the north slit. White froth boiled over the submerged shoals and around jagged rocks which had fallen from the cliffs above.

In light of this ominous forecast, we passengers moved to other parts of the *wu ban*. The major and Wang Shi went aft to join the *lao ban* at the tiller. I ventured to the bow to stand with the first officer and his sixteen sweepmen. My move was not the wisest. Abruptly the rock-strewn channel became shallower and swifter with more ominous reefs and shifting sandbars.

Suddenly, as the boat plunged into an enormous eddy, we at the bow were showered with spray. We were into the *Xin Dan* Rapids, where we had run into hours of painstaking troubles on our upward trip. I followed the first officer's recommendation to return to the passenger hold.

Back in our tight space, we heard the skipper giving instructions for our encounter with deadly Head Rapids. Oarsmen were ordered, "Pull harder on port side!" then, seconds later, "Starboard! Pull like hell!"

We got through the Head Rapids safely only to be soon confronted with second and third of the *Xin Dan's* challenges. Though rough and nerve-wracking, the combination of the swift current, the skillful steering of the *lao ban* and the steady labors of the oarsmen and sweepmen successfully pulled us through the fearsome ordeal.

In only a few minutes, before we could recover from the *Xin Dan's* turbulence and our nerves, we were into the minor *P'ing Su* cataracts, a prelude to the more perilous *Niugan*, or Ox Liver and Horse's Lung Gorge. With almost the same speed as we had hurled down upon these feared *Xin Dan*, we surged into the next perilous rocks.

On the north bank there were four or five stone slabs shaped like a liver. Above it was a rock shaped like a lung. In 1900 when foreign imperialist war ships invaded the Xiling Gorge, they heedlessly bombarded these landmarks and destroyed half of them. Only two miles long, this section compensated for its shortness with fragmented cliffs and underlying ridges and troughs (anticlines and synclines) across which the river ran. The movement of silt and the river's rush against the gravel banks created deadly whirlpools.

Without letup we were pitched into another pair of rapids that jerked and ook the junk. We were thrust into the troublesome pair, *Gua Tong* (Suspended Beam)and then into the *Da Dan* (Big Rapids), both notorious for their dizzying swirls and eddies.

With the spray of the Da Dan still upon us, the *wu ban* headed toward the entrance of the dreaded Kongling (Pierced Mountain Straits). Toward the middle of Xiling Gorge, it was considered the worst of the Long River's cataracts. The river made an S-turn across submerged reefs along the shores, while a narrow strip of rocks obstructed the center of the channel. Captain Cornell Plant, forty-five years before, had considered it one of the most dangerous perils of the Xiling Gorge. His description was of "an immense black rock, some fifty feet high at low level, it sticks upright in midstream, surrounded by a number of smaller ones. During low water level, the south bank passage becomes impassable. The north channel, the only other way through, narrow, crooked and studded with dangerous submerged rocks."

In midstream the Kongling rocks bisected the channel, leaving only narrow passages between the shore at a sharp bend in the river. It was in this stretch, in December, 1900, that the German steamer Sui Hsiang, one of the first iron ships, had been wrecked on her maiden voyage. The captain and many of the

*Courtesy Lyman Van Slyke*

*ung-Ling Rapids From A 19th Centry Chinese Illustration*

crew and passengers had drowned within seven minutes.

Our *lao ban* told us of the heights and narrows we were about to see in *Kongling Shoal* and the perilous rocks we must avoid–First Pearl, Second Pearl, Third Pearl, Chicken Wings and the Come-to-Me Rock. The choice of the channels could not be decided in advance. The speed of the current depended on the water level, which was low in winter, exposing rock hazards, and high in summer, threatening unpredictable flooding.

A minor race called Ox Gorge was found at the *Kongling's* entrance. On the south bank a slab of rock atop the mountain looked like a person leading an ox. *Niu Shan* (Ox Mountain) spilled rock into the channel which lies just below the surface of the river. Because of these obstructions, in previous centuries it often took several days to pass through in sailing upstream. Ox Mountain remained in sight most of that stretch of the journey.

A strident shriek came from the *tai gong* at the bow. The warning he shouted was akin to: "Man the battle stations!" The crew snapped to. The skipper waved us passengers to our space in the well forward of him. "Great danger ahead," was all he had time to say.

At our side the cook gave us the explanation we needed: "Down there the river turns sharp right, then sharp left. At each elbow, giant boulders loom like dragon mouths, where the river seems to gobble up every boat it can."

"After the second elbow comes a long string of rocks in midstream as forbidding as the *Kongling's*. Beyond that come whirlpools, often bigger than the ones we've already gone through." Further descriptions were cut off by another piercing order from the bow.

Narrow already, the channel closed in even more. In a flash, every available hand–including the cook–manned an oar or a bowsweep. Our present course dead-ended straight against boulders at the foot of a cliff. We saw the crook of the channel, but dead ahead were the boulders. The torrent became more violent as it struck the rocks, bursting into spray and foam. Already, with the current and our crew's terrific exertion, we were running close to ten knots. Before these elbow rocks were reached, we would be going even faster.

Above the roar of the river, no orders could be heard, so flags were used. The nearer we came to the rocks, the more violent became our *lao ban's* frantic movements. Every ounce of strength was thrown into the oars and sweeps. Our collective fate depended upon nothing slipping, nothing breaking. Split second timing was essential. Yet even if we negotiated the first elbow, there was another to the right and a reef in midstream!

We were swept toward the jagged boulders of that first elbow. The cool headed judgment of the *tai gong*, the speed drummed out by the pace-setter, the exact pulling of the oarsmen, the right push on the sweeps and the skip er's faultless handling at the tiller–all these required perfection, if we were to ve through the next fifteen minutes.

Hearts pounding, stomachs in our mouths, we passengers were ready to hout, "Move men! Speed the rhythm, drummer! Move something! Move verything! For God's sake, *lao ban,* give the order and steer right!" But the *lo ban* didn't speak and didn't budge. Seconds became hours of dread. When : already seemed too late, the skipper finally shot his hand out to the right. The weepmen, reinforced by spare pullers, swung the giant *yulow* on the portside ith superhuman effort. The oarsmen exerted extra strength. The junk esponded to the *lao ban's* split-second swing of the tiller and rounded the cor- er. What a miracle!

Then ahead, to the right and very close, was a larger rock mass. The current roke and jumped in gigantic clouds of froth. Again boulders seemed ready to ash crew, cargo and passengers into a thousand shards. Each crew member ept the drummer's rhythm, no more, no less. The skipper was motionless, ilent as steel.

Our big *wu ban* charged straight into the center of the surge. The major, Vang Shi and I were sure the *tai gong* had overshot his mark. A man of little iith in moments of terror, I moved to port, opposite to that which looked like . was going to be the inevitable crash side. I braced myself for my last seconds n earth.

The *tai gong* threw out his left hand. The frenetic drummer rushed his gong ito an infernal beat. Every muscle worked feverishly. Every throat yelled, some hrieked, and the skipper pounded another gong. Each man performed the vork he understood. With less than fifty yards to spare, we cleared the rocks. 'he crew faded, and dead silence reigned. Then an exuberant cheer exploded, ising up to *Yu*, the great god of the river.

Around a bend, we came to the town of Nan Dao. On a promontory stood s seven-storied Needle Pagoda. Beyond, on the south bank, was the village of aomintzi, with the rocky beach and pristine shoreline where we had moored or the second night upriver. Farther along we passed the jewel-like village of *Iuang-ling* (Yellow Peak), whose beauty we had missed the week before. In atural camouflage of feathery bamboo, it was flanked by *Huang-ling Shan* Yellow Peak Mountain). Lying above the clustered houses was a delicate, red-olumned temple, its tiled gray roof supported by ornate eaves pointing sky-vard.

The surrounding bamboo provided junk builders with material for their tow ables. From this district, the *lao ban* told us, came the best trackers. If they urvived, they often rose to the dignity–and prosperity–of skippers.

Around the next big bend of the Long River we approached and passed one f the feared points going up river: the mouth of *Long Dong* (Dragon Cave).

This was a likely nemesis. Here we were vulnerable to the The Dragon's Mouth! Going downriver, we passed *Long Dong* without incident. We now realized our upriver escape from the Dragon's Mouth in this spot was tame compared with the escapes from the other Three Gorges' hazards. We know understood that in the Xiling Gorge the River Dragon is ready and waiating at many dangerous places to devour entire *wu bans* crews. The *Kong Ling*, the *Xin Dan*, the *Xie Dan* and the *Dragon Spine Rocks* all were Dragon Mouth experiences.

"You can rest easier for a bit," continued the skipper. "For travelers going downriver, the *Huang Ling Miao* (Yellow Peak Temple) is a welcome sight. It tells voyagers they have survived some of the river's chief dangers."

Cliffs again narrowed the river as we approached the next and last chasm, the Yichang, or Lamp Light Gorge. Its name hinted at the murky atmosphere created by steep cliffs which blocked much of the daylight. The western entrance opened into a lake. On the north bank we could see trackers hauling a large cargo junk that inched its way against the current. At the eastern end a mountain seemed to cut off all exits, but once again, an outlet appeared when the boat was almost upon it.

Skipper Chung gave this chasm another name, the Shadow Play Gorge. Mountain peaks rising a thousand feet or more from the banks sparkled in the afternoon sun. Above the cliffs were odd-looking peaks with cylindrical rock jutting up into the sky. The skipper suggested we imagine we were watching motion picture. On Maya Hill were four rocks which resembled the four char acters in the Chinese mythological novel Pilgrimage to the West. The Monkey *King Sun Wukong* looking ahead acts as the vanguard of the group. The Pig *Baje* climbs the mountain leading the horse. The priest *Xuan Zhung*, the master, sits up straight and the Monk *Sha* carries the Buddhist scriptures with shoulder pole. When viewed from a distance and silhouetted against the setting sun they looked like characters in a shadow play.

On its south shore, the spring foliage of azaleas, ferns, primroses and maiden enhair fern presented splurges of color. Our oarsmen and sweepmen rowed up into smoother waters toward the right side of the foreboding reef that now lay ahead. As the current quickened, the crew resumed its work at the oars and the sweeps. The *lao ban* and his *tai gong*, having brought us through the seething waters of the *Kongling Shoal's* Elbow Rocks, performed yet another navigational miracle and shaved the reef with little to spare. By now the two officers had our full confidence, though in the next few seconds, it was again tested.

An unexpected warning shriek came from the *tai gong* at the bow. We were running head-on into one of the giant whirlpools below the reefs. In the sym phony of our voyage, it felt like this was Rondo: *Allegro vivace!* We were on the outer edge of a funnel that was about 20 feet deep at its center. Logs were aught in the circling water, then after several turns, they reached the center, ᵉere sucked down and disappeared.

Caught on the outer edge, our forward movement was arrested. For a ᵐoment, the whirl was barely able to rotate our vessel. Over the side, the cone ᶜraight below gaped like the mouth of an enormous sea monster. The junk's ᵘndred-foot length more than spanned the watery pit, nevertheless, we ᵉemed doomed. Then, with a terrifying midship shudder, we felt the swirl's ᵛortex under the boat's keel. The oarsmen's perplexity turned to fear, since ᵗheir blades had no bite in the water.

Within seconds, however, the *wu ban* began to revolve, as if around the ᵖivot of the vortex. We passengers could not figure out what was happening. ᵀhe spinning was not a frenzied, out-of-control stampede, yet we found our-ᵉlves becoming more unstrung with every turn. Caught in this dizzying futil-ᵗy, we were flooded with anxieties. Would the thin wood planking of the junk ᵒold? How could we escape this devouring funnel? What force could pull us ᶜlear?

I flashbacked to years before in Boston when, in clinical training, I had lis-ᵗened with the labored conscientiousness of a novice therapist to the manic tur-ᵐoil of a client who "felt himself spinning out of control." Now, in my viscera, ᶦ felt what this man had spoken of with such agony.

"In this pit, Doc," he once told me, "I'm spinning in an explosive turmoil ᵒf mind, body and sex. There's no escape from the pressures coming at me ᶠrom 360 degrees. I can't shove off the tumultuous forces all around me. Time ᵗands still. No one appears to save me.

"My insides are pummeled. My mind whirls in confusion. I'm dragged in, ᵇanged around, pulled under. Thoughts zoom past like bullets, hitting me but ᵗot passing through, lodged inside, piercing me. My will is bludgeoned, my ᵉnergy sapped."

"My mind blows, panic strikes my heart. Round and round, ever-spinning. ᵀo peace, no meaning. One thought crashes into another, one feeling crushes ᵃnother. I'm powerless, fragile, breaking into thousands of pieces."

He had experienced a peculiar dissociation of his senses: Nothing around ᵗim lasted for more than a moment, and as one moment followed another, it ᵛas as though he alone continued to exist. He was a fixed point in a whirl of ᶜhange, a body poised in utter stillness as the world rushed through him and ᵈisappeared.

"Clong, clong, clong" went the drummer's gong. "All oars and *yulow!*" ᵇhouted the *lao ban*. Every crew member pulled with all his might: Those on ᵗhe outside of the swirl pulled against it, while those on the inside strained with ᵗhe spin. Eight sweepmen, directed by the *tai gong*, lowered a small length of

one sweep forward from the bow pulling out of the spin. As his men gained o
the pressure and felt more confident of not being thrown overboard, little b
little, more of the sweep was extended.

We inched out of the center as the drum kept up its feverish pace. Th
sweepmen's desparate efforts succeeded in pulling the bow up and out. In sev
eral minutes, we were out of the whirl and headed toward a deeper channel.

Wang Shi during our downriver journey often had been moody and tense
suggesting he was dealing with a cauldron of thoughts and emotions that h
was not expressing. The hazards we had passed through appeared to have sug
gested the ultimate binds we encounter in life. The crew's mastery of life-and
death challenges, seemed to reflect his own struggles and strategies in life.

"The whirlpool," Wang Shi said, "reflects the tumultuous condition of ou
country. The river's surge suggests the unrest and confusion of the Chines
people. We swirl about, unable to choose from possible solutions: moder
technology, Western mercantilism, a renaissance of Confucian values and socia
structures, Western democracy, Christian values. We cannot seem to pull our
selves out of the whirlpool. As Mr. Thompson observed, with a shallow reli
gious life and a confusion of beliefs and practices, we Chinese have no ropes t
grab onto to pull us from this spin."

"The United States and Western European countries are also in thei
whirlpools," the major said. "With our World War II victory scarcely te
months behind us, we are over-confident about technology and a feeling o
mastery over the world. The truth is that, despite our technological achieve
ments, our perpetual preparation for war, our self-centered culture and ou
shallow spiritual life shows that we are not really as sure as we would like t
think. In our confusion we no long can boast with easy confidence about ou
technological progress as we did only a short time ago."

As we philosophized, a gorgeous sunset framed the pillared sentinels at th
Xiling Gorge's eastern exit. The river took on a golden glow as it relinquishec
its terrors and spread out before us for miles into the Jiang An Plain. By night
fall we had swung past Yichang's seven-storied pagoda and found a moorin
near the central steps below the South Gate.

Parting from the junk brought a poignant and humbling sense of finalit
Sensing the inadequacy of any ordinary farewell, our skipper presented eacl
passenger with an over-sized calling card with his signature and red-sealec
chop. "Let this be a certificate," he said, "of your completing the journey fron
Wanxian on board my *wu ban*."

We had become part of their company—lice, sweat, garlic and all. The offi
cers, cook, trackers, oarsmen, sweepmen, drummer—the entire company—hac
woven a tapestry of skill, knowledge and friendship in only two days that woulc

st a lifetime. In a flash, sadness gripped us as we saw the crew sitting, almost athetically, under their mat roof midships. Too poor to go ashore and cele-rate their victory over the river, they were tied to unending toil.

Our return to Yichang was a reality we couldn't grasp but had to face, as we ade our way to the mission hostel. At the South Gate the three of us queezed in among four other passengers in a dilapidated taxi designed to ccommodate four. So compacted were we that the driver tied the doors osed, lest he lose one of his passengers in transit. With every bounce over pot-oles, we were made aware of the deterioration of China's war-weary vehicles.

Squeezed face to face, amid powerful garlic and other odors, we were ssaulted both by China's diet and its overpopulation. When we arrived at the ission gate, the driver had a hard time extricating his tangled passengers and eir luggage.

Safe and quiet that evening in the mission guest room, the major, Wang Shi nd I were still engrossed in the inadequacies of our leave-taking from the *wu an*, the river and the crew we had come to appreciate and respect. We emained tense, expecting some new crisis to be thrown at us by another set of pids or some other whirlpool.

The three of us were preoccupied with our internal searches for meaning in e convulsive grandeur of the past twenty days. Our minds still traveled on the ushing, copper-colored waters, past chasms and promontories, palisades and lens, temples and pagodas. Around us were the trackers, oarsmen, sweepmen, rummer, cook, *lao ban* and *tai gong*. Under us was the sturdy junk that had heltered us, taken us through dangers and passed beautiful places.

Always around us was the Great River with its persistent current, swirls and ataracts, shoals and whirlpools. Metaphors and symbols would forever alter ur understandings of the challenges and meanings of the greater journey that fe presents. We felt a rare emotion, an indefinable mixture of paradoxes: anger nd love, elation and despair, pain and joy. Though we remained troubled by any things we did not understand, new imperatives reached deep within us.

Before putting these musings to sleep, I looked out our window at the river would now always respect and feel attached to. I smiled at the moon, which ad transformed the mile-wide waters into an inviting stretch of shimmering lver, flowing past this ancient and now reviving city.

# Treasured Recollections Meet Tragedy

The next day Wang Shih and I rendezvoused with the major and his fellow pilot and took off from the Yichang airport for our return flight to Nanjing En route, high in the sky following the eastward course of the Long River, the three of us were still journeying the Three Gorges.

The river's dizzying eddies, incredible vistas, mysterious chasms and elegant pagodas would not let us go. Neither would the *wu ban's* faithful oarsmen sweepmen, first officers and skippers, nor the cavalcade of teachers, priests elders, merchants, missionaries and other personalities we had met. Those experiences glowed in living symbols in our imagination. The journey into the Three Gorges had become a treasured part of our autobiographies.

Back in the capital city, as each of us quickly were engrossed in our separate schedules, it was hard to believe that the journey was an accomplished fact. The card the savy downriver skipper had given us, however, was a confirmation of our completing the round trip journey. In stepping off the junk in Yichang we had more than returned to our starting place; the expectations which initiated the journey had been realized a hundred times over. Our odyssey, though only a few days compared with Ulysses' 12 years, still, like his, encouraged us to continue making new discoveries.

Wang Shi, the major and I decided to meet every few weeks to sort through our reminiscences and put them into a meaningful whole.

The Long River dominated our flashbacks. The Dragon's Mouth hadn't devoured us, but the great river's minutiae and immensities had absorbed us and etched deep markings in our thoughts. Though we traveled but a fraction of its full length the river's variegated aspects shaped our journey. We had been microcosms of pouring rivulets and floating driftwood, gnawed by the mysterious animalcules of the river. We were one with the remarkable alchemies that shaped the water. We became the water during those few weeks, rising and subsiding according to its rhythms. Loren Eisley's description came alive for us "If there is magic on this planet, it is contained in water."

The rushing waters, always but a few feet away from our low-slung junk, in a flash could claim us. One of the corpses floating by could well have been one of us. Within the waters was some primeval dark and passing shadow, a principle that had waited in the depths long before the advent of living creatures–what the Chinese call the River Dragon.

Our journey through this short section of the Long River was symbolic of our life journey. The eddies and whirlpools were like life's inconsistencies and opposing forces. Life offers an enchanted world of bamboo groves trimmed ith azaleas, as well as rock-strewn rapids, landslides and quicksand.

The journey through all the Dragon's Mouths had tested aspects of our-lves–skill, persistence, timing, talents, intelligence, confidence and faith. acing risks and handling anxieties demanded courage, as well as trust. In times f crisis the crew's exercise of these unique human qualities transfigured com-loners and forced surrounding, frightening demons into retreat. Vicariously, ; passengers, the challenges surrounding us put our mettle on the line. Ours ecame the story of Gilgamesh, who journeyed to the boundaries of life in his uest to conquer death, as well as America's pioneers, who pressed through the rdeals of the Great Plains, Rocky Mountains and Donner Pass to the Pacific. ike Dante, we journeyed from hell through purgatory and, finally, to paradise.

We were evolving from within as we continued this journey–becoming more vare and allowing our horizons to be expanded. We were more acutely aware f how our preconceptions affect how we cope with events. We saw anew how pping patterns affect the persons we become. We saw how much the world eeds people who have accurate assumptions. For the major and me, whose nvictions were religiously rooted, the Long River's gorges expanded our ppreciation for God's creation. In the midst of nature's magnificence we und sustenance and in its threats we found quickening. Also the Chinese pirations for themselves and their country resonated with our own and gave is journey into the Long River's gorges transcendent meaning.

As to the people, we were in 24-hour-a-day touch with Chinese. On board, ur lives had depended on the skill and toil of tens, and even hundreds, of hinese whose ancestors had plied these waters for centuries. They manifested their riverine ways, outlooks and spirits nurtured over the centuries by the ythms and whims of the Long River.

During the day we talked and ate with the crew and at night slept beside em. When they fished from the gunwales, we helped them haul in their tches. Several times, we had applied our arms to help the rowers. We had veated, stumbled and stooped with trackers over boulders, through quicksand d in their low tunnels.

In the towns, we had walked with over-loaded brine workers, shared the essures of over-burdened mission staff, discussed ultimate questions with ders on the Guizhou steps, been challenged by visionary teachers in Wanxian, njoyed the music of a *Linyang* lute player, meditated amid clouds of incense ith Buddhist novitiates and survived swashbuckling bandits.

Chinese interpersonal relations intrigued us. A phrase Wang Shi used often as *guanxi*, "relationships" or "connections." The English equivalents, how-'er, don't capture its scope. The Chinese use it frequently to refer to ties and bligations in families, neighborhoods and work-places. It identifies influence d status involved in exchanges between people. Being Chinese then and today, like being Chinese at the time of the first emperor, Qin Shi Huang L (220 B.C.), is less a commitment to Confucius, Mencius, Lao Tze, Chuan Tze, the Legalists, or the motherland than to one another–billions of sma relationships blending into one great whole. Ties to family and clan, insister commitment to the idea of "being Chinese" and viewing themselves as household, a jia, even their self-consciousness about the non-Chinese worl binds the world's most populous nation. "China is a small town of one billion people," journalists Jay and Linda Matthews correctly wrote (1984).

In the people-compacted conditions in which we lived, we saw how Chines manage to keep sane in their tightly packed places and relationships. Th patience and grace the Chinese have developed for living in constricted qua ters never ceased to amaze us, especially the positive aspects of 'saving face' considering the effects on the other person of what you think, say and do i social relations.

The many Chinese who shared their lives with us were tolerant of our fo eign ways. They put up with our cleanliness obsession and smiled at our exa peration over their careless hygiene. We, on our part, tried to adjust to som of their seemingly inconsistent ways: what the major described as "outer opt mism and inner pessimism" and their "reluctant compliance" (they might sa they agreed, but then do the opposite!) They nodded their heads at our indi vidualism, while we shook our heads at their submission and lack of freedom They disappointed us when they accepted oppression, then surprised us wit the ingenuity with which they outwitted it.

Individually, the Chinese could be engaging, but in the aggregate the could be exasperating. As one Beijing foreign correspondent (1993) observed "The Chinese will continue to enjoy their food, tell jokes, take naps, spin tale of the Three Kingdoms, cast yarrow sticks, consult the *I Ching* and atten cricket fights no matter what the next few years bring."

As Westerners, the major and I tended to break up complex problems an solve the pieces in sequence. We talked of planning, preparing blueprint assembling material and personnel. Not so the Chinese crew faced with repai ing the rock-punctured hull of our *wu ba*n; the task immediately generated int a social enterprise with each person offering differing suggestions. One desig nated foreman or supervisor didn't take charge. Each exigency was not dea with systematically. For the major and me, the approach we observed seeme disorganized. Noticing our perplexity, Wang Shi assured us the repairs wer proceeding according to the Asian "holistic approach." Like Chinese idec graphs, construction projects are approached as whole pictures. Wang Shi reminded us that the *wu ban* did get repaired–the Asian way.

The terrors of the rapids shook us into facing our anxieties. Faced with mo tal dangers differences between the crew's "Chineseness" and our "Wester ness' didn't matter–we both trembled.

Fear from minor threats was taken as part of life by the crew. Greater fears necessitated an immediate propitiation to demonic forces. In life-threatening happenings, it was as if fate was striking and persons were vulnerable to the inevitable. Yet the crew's response to the two trackers who were whipped into the river was *meiyou banfa*–there's no alternative. This was the fear that wells up from helplessness in the face of famines, floods, epidemics and poverty.

The anxiety we experienced was personal: anticipating being wiped out about to be rammed in the *Xin Dang*, or about to crash Goose Tail Rock, or caught in the whirlpool–the major and I were challenged to deal with the root causes of our anxieties.

We had left the known, for the untested and uncertain. Fears of those brushes with death continue to surface decades later. The journey taught us much about facing our own mortality, jarring us from our usual denial of it. The journey's frightening situations brought home to us our limitations, vulnerabilities and finiteness. Those decisive moments drove each of us to say, "I am!"

Humans, in contrast to other animals, said theologian Reinhold Niebuhr, anticipate future contingencies and their perils. Anxiety is the concomitant of freedom and finiteness. Existentialists from Kierkegaard to Tillich speak of the inevitability of anxiety, its crucial role in the development of individuation, freedom and responsibility. Anxiety, according to Tillich, is one's reaction to the threat of nonbeing, the threat of meaninglessness in one's existence. The capacity to bear anxiety is a measure of the strength and flexibility of the individual.

In those days we learned much of China's five magnificent millenniums. Evidences of the civilization's rich and long history jumped out incessantly. Wang Shi, obligingly, never tired of answering our questions about Chinese history.

The past obsesses the Chinese in part because there is so much of it. The longest continuing civilization, China can document its history back to the *Xia* (Hsia) dynasty, 5,000 years ago. The past matters to the Chinese in down-to-earth ways, affecting everything from entertainment to politics. For all their concern with post-war reconstruction, Chinese at that time seemed to spend an inordinate amount of time looking backward. In China, historical dramas lead box-office sales, and the more ancient the story, the better. Chinese scientists, we were told, look to the past for inspiration. Writers argue over modern problems by repeating old stories, a technique that fails to warn ordinary Chinese of how pressing today's problems are.

An historical awareness permeates the people of China more than it does most Westerners. Talking with our westbound first officer or with Wang Shi often made the Han (210 B.C.- 205 A.D.), Tang (618-905 A.D.) and Ming

dynasties (1368-1644) seem relevant to our present situation. For the untu
tored commoners, however, history has to do with their parents and grand
parents. To take part in the boatmen's conversations and concerns opened u
references to their ancestors. Chinese accept that history is the story of huma
development. Oarsman Liu used to say, "We do not know the answers yet, bu
I believe some of the old questions are going to drop away."

We felt the gnawing hunger of the teachers and students for things t
change, for the world to be a better place, where people could appreciate on
another more fully and where we could be better persons.

Along with the repeated signs of greatness and glory of China's history w
were confronted with the price of pain, tragedy and death for its indomitab!
*laobaixing.* Everywhere we saw wasted humans, injustices crying out for right
ing. Thoughtful Chinese told of how, when the war with Japan had ended
their hopes for basic changes were high. Only nine months later disillusion
ment reigned.

Wang Shi explained how China's history had progressed like a spiral–risin
and falling, rising and falling again. One after another self-serving dynasty wa
toppled by bloody rebellions. The Chinese have survived so many empire
rebellions and invasions that anticipation of change has become a nation
myth.

It was clear to Wang Shi that the 500,000,000 Chinese in 1946 were in th
midst of political unrest, economic collapse and psychological despair. H
hoped China could accomplish a peaceful transition. Needed was a new equi
librium brought about in a way different from the bloody revolutionary upheava
that have characterized every change of government in the last 4,000 years.

Wang Shi made us aware of how proud the Chinese–commoners and aris
tocrats alike–are of their culture. Widespread is a desire to again position thei
country as the Middle Kingdom, the center of the world. It's a kind of 'we're
number-one' mentality.

The hope to improve China's lot is reflected in what today's People
Republic calls "the four modernizations" of agriculture, industry, science an
the army. In 1946 the Chinese were not burdened with Western-style individ
ualism's emphasis on material success and self-gratification. Rather, they move
along a road on which directional signs were, at best, unclear, and at wors
conflicting. But further conversation often revealed that many Chinese se
"progress" chiefly as a way to achieve simpler, more modest pleasures of hom
and family.

In addition to learning much about Chinese people and their history in ou
journey we were sobered in many ways. The journey was not without its shad
ows. Dangers, chaos and injustices often had confronted us. The continuin
turbulence that often surrounded us was a menacing chaos. Then the impac

f pervasive social ills was relentless: the victimizing and miseries of the track-rs and their families, the corrupt landlords and officials the Wanxian faculty xcoriated, the exploited youths in the salt pits of Yunyang and Guizhou, the eality of bandits' threats, and the rapaciousness and depravity of Szichuan easants reported by our Hubei cook, all revealed serious injustices.

Having survived the dangers described by the doom sayers and shared /ords of judgment against human beings' inhumanity to their kind, our out->ok was less naive. The people who surrounded us continually wanted to "be ı touch"–to connect. The journey often seemed to be the story of people eeking stronger relationships–not only with others, but also with nature and istory. These multi-faceted relationships stretched our tolerance and taught s to appreciate those markedly different from ourselves. We were pressed to nd a sense of order at the heart of danger, chaos and injustice. It entailed eeping in touch with a power higher than ourselves.

In this journey we were shown events and people that pointed us toward ternal principles. We were confronted with finalities. We saw that order is at /ork in the midst of physical, social and moral chaos. The *I Qing* hexagrams' roken lines were balanced by the full lines. The crew's casting of yarrow sticks /as symbolic of their hope for stability when oblivion threatened. There was ıore than mere counting. There were other evidences of respect for elevated tandards and estimates of a higher power. In time and in eternity the last word •elongs to the Creator.

Over the months and into the next year (1947), added responsibilities fre-uently prevented Wang Shi, the major and me from meeting. Wang Shi's ınthusiasm seemed worn. Self-consciously he talked of the added teaching load o which he had been assigned. In the spring, however, without notice, he did ot join us for one of our regular meetings. Concerned, we tried to contact im, but were unsuccessful. His associates at the university remained close-ıouthed regarding his where abouts.

Alarmed, we sought out and eventually reached his wife. Devastated, she old us of the fate that had come to him. Weeks before Wang Shir had been aken out of his classroom and detained at the local police station. He was harged with "subversive activities." No word from him or about him had ome since then.

"Detention," in those days, was ominous. It meant being held incommuni-ado, and subjected to interminable interrogation, deprivations and indignities. 'he feared eventuality was that he'd be turned over to the dreaded ¡uomindang secret police for torture.

The major and I, together with two university administrators, sought in vain ɔ contact him. We went through a maize of departments and officials seeking ɔ gain his release. We were denied the chance to visit or even communicate with him. Though we tried every appeal to the point of begging for his life the government officials said simply: He's been ordered put to death."

Months after his arrest he'd been taken from his cell, assigned to a particularly sadistic executioner who was notorious for garroting victims slowly to prolong their agony.

Authorities at the university, all already suspect, counted it unsafe to talk about Wang Shi and other instructors who had 'disappeared.'

We pieced together what he must have experienced prior to his arrest. He was increasingly discouraged in the early months of 1947. By no means a revolutionary, we knew he felt violence is less effective than reforming the present order. With the country's economic and political conditions rapidly worsening however, he saw that the needed changes were more fundamental than he and his confidants had earlier estimated. But the reactionary government blocked reform at every turn. Officials who questioned the status quo were being removed.

Wang Shi and his activist friends refused to support a system in which they lacked the right to think, express ideas and make decisions for themselves. They had no desire to continue to be the tools of others.

His wife, sobbing, reported that Wang Shi and his associates found that no matter how fervently they spoke, taught, wrote and worked for "improvement" and "positive changes," nothing was accomplished. Those at the highest levels of government feared change. The paranoid and corrupt system was set in concrete.

Wang Shi and his friends found that they were stone-walled by every authority they contacted. Thus stymied and frustrated, they decided to "go active." Wang Shi wrote and distributed stronger and stronger protest tracts and organized cells of "searchers for a better way." University professors warned him about the risks he was taking when the Nanjing government would not tolerate criticism, much less courageous and forthright dissent.

The major and I joined Wang Shi's associates at a private memorial gathering, realizing anew how much we were indebted to him. He had served as our interpreter, lecturer, advisor and fellow passenger. He helped us "see" China mountains and waters (shan shui), its people and its 5,000-plus years of civilization. He breathed life into the dry bones of Chinese history. He gave us clues to the intriguing mysteries of Chinese culture and its people. His perceptive questions about missionary work added a needed perspective.

In him we found a powerful intellectual and a deeply concerned patriot. He often challenged our superficial verbiage, made us stop to explain and evaluate. Often he pulled in appropriate references to the wisdom of Confucius, Lao Tze, Chuang Tze and Gautama Buddha. Despite the likelihood that a creed

ember was an informer for the Guomindang secret police, he did not hesi-
te to vent his righteous indignation against the government's unconcern for
e people.

His view of history and humanity kept him from the extremes of either
nrealistic optimism or debilitating pessimism. He reached for a position which
rovided his life a center of reference. Acutely aware of the flux and contra-
ictions within history, for the most part he lived in his head, not in the sen-
al world. Though intellectually inclined and disciplined, however he sus-
ined an empathetic wonder about all existence. His was a burning concern
at his country would make radical changes to usher in a new social order. The
lief of China's victimized masses was his central passion.

At the Yuan Memorial Temple in the heights above Zigui, Wang Shi had
ointed out approvingly a plaque honoring the ancient hero Li An: "He sought
live out the inexorable moral law." This tribute applied well to Wang Shi.
e had deep respect for the moral law which operates through cosmic yin and
ang forces. For him "the inexorable moral law" was to be observed by indi-
iduals and societies alike in the five cardinal virtues: benevolence or love (ren),
ghteousness *(yi)*, reverence *(chung)*, wisdom *(zhi)* and sincerity *(xin)*.

As he threw his considerable energy and creative ideas into struggling with
ternal and, external contradictions, he asked: "How can the world be made
better place?" His anguished reach for the moral life was persistent. Though
e was reluctant to acknowledge it, Wang Shi's deep concerns showed a reli-
ious consciousness.

In ensuing months, the major and I grieved over the tragic loss of our
emarkable young colleague. In our sadness we found new meanings for the
946 journey. Abruptly my association with the major ended as well, when in
e fall he was transferred back to an airbase in the United States.

As time slipped away, I concluded that what I had gained was both less and
ore than I had expected. Less because I had been absorbed in the details of
avel; more because changes were subtle, slow in taking effect. The journey
ad helped me make sense of China's post war months. I knew that the stock
f new images and experiences would multiply rather than reduce the pressures
f my life.

It's doubtful that I became any clearer on how to find a "richer and fuller
fe," or re-arrange the way I approached it. This journey, however, helped clar-
y and strengthen my sense of responsibility to take hold of opportunities and
ach out in effective social service.

The journey tested and deepened my faith. Going through the rapids
equired faith in the physical vessel and the crew. Schooled in logic and com-
rtable with order, I found the discontinuities we faced difficult: the palisades,
ternately inviting and threatening; the skies, sometimes azure and other times

dark; the trackers with their courageous strength and yet always with their entrapment in poverty. Taking part in Catholic mass and Buddhist vespers gave me an awareness of the searchings and validities of other faiths. I recognized forces at work in persons, events and nature that are not determined by what can be seen, touched, smelled or heard.

My faith in the Creator, in humanity and in myself was made more substantial. My conception of God had to be enlarged to embrace all of this. A restrictive and exclusive view of God would not contain all I had experienced and felt. Allowing God to include contradictions, quieted my doubts and helped affirm a universal God that was both immanent and transcendent. wondered if any other journey would ever match those 20 days. But I had learned anew how our imaging and behavior patterns affect the new beginnings we journey into. I had gained deepened meaning of T. S. Eliot's line "We shall not cease from exploration." Years later I was to return to the Long River. In my mind, it had remained unchanged, but, of course, we both had changed and are changing even now.

# Decades Of Radical Change

*New Luxury Liners Ply Three Gorges Beginning in 1980's*

In the second half of the twentieth century China turned from its age-old non-interference response with the Three Gorges' geography and launched accelerating programs to tame the river dragon. For millennia the gorges, with their fascination and threats, were accepted and adapted to without efforts to alter their geography. This series of natural wonders was considered sacrosanct and impervious to change. Beginning at the mid-century China, addressed the perennial challenge of the troublesome physical aspects of the Three Gorges, determined to bring the river dragon under as complete human control as possible.

Early in 1950 feasibility studies were begun for a master-plan of dams and locks for the chasms. In the same decade, steps were taken to clear the Three Gorges' navigation hazards, to open channels from Yichang west to Wanxian. Engineering innovations, so long opposed by vested interests and rationalized as threats, began to be permitted.

In the '60s the government's China International Travel Service (C.I.T.S.) developed tourism in the gorges. A fleet of diesel-powered passenger and freight ships were built. As the fleet multiplied and navigation problems were overcome, the songs of trackers hauling loaded junks inch by agonizing inch against the current were replaced by the grinding motors of tugs and sleek four-decker river liners.

One of the fleet, the *Kun Lun*, launched in 1962, was designed to entertain visiting heads of state and other foreign dignitaries. It was of similar length (300 feet) and tonnage (2,300) as the Long River fleet's other vessels that carry Chinese travelers. The difference, in this "classless" society, is one of class.

While the other boats accommodate 700 to 900 passengers in five classe (starting with second down to sixth class–there is no first class), the delux *Kun Lun* was a one- class vessel accommodating less than 100 pampered pas sengers.

In the 1970's the C.I.T.S. sought increasing overseas contacts and join ventures. Lars Eric Lindblad, adventure traveler, chartered the *Kun Lun* an organized one of the early cruises to the Three Gorges. Marked changes wer initiated: Socialist propaganda, dingy flea-infested hotels and drearier mass produced dormitory-style chop suey were replaced with a semblance c Western luxury.

In May 1982, 36 years after my maiden voyage, and again in 1984 an 1991, I returned to the Yangzi Gorges. The recent journeys were safer, quick er and more comfortable, but far less adventurous. My 1946 journey had bee much like that taken by travelers for more than 4,000 years. The 95-foo Sichuan junk in which I had first traveled had been no motor ship, but rathe had inched upstream with a square rig sail, oarsmen, sweepmen and a sweatin column of trackers. My subsequent excursions were aboard sleek, 275-foot long, diesel-powered, quadruple-decked steel ships.

On the May 1982 voyage, the study group I was leading booked passag downriver from Chongqing to the eastern entrance of the gorges at Yichang In two days we would cover 400 miles, the same distance that had taken m 13 days up and five down in 1946. Early on the morning of our departure, late-model tour bus took us from our spacious guest-hostel through the his toric city of Chongqing to the river's edge, 350 feet above the ship's mooring When we reached the last gangplank, two girlish, trimly dressed officers greet ed and escorted us to our eight-person cabins. Even before we had settled ou bags, stewardesses entered with cups of tea.

At 7:00 a.m., the scheduled departure time, the ship gave four powerfu whistle blasts. The dockmen first cast off the upriver lines. The current caugh the bow and pulled it out toward midstream and the ship completed its U-tur downstream. In minutes we passed where the mile-and-a-half-wide Jialin poured into the Long River and swept downstream toward the smaller rive ports to the east.

The ship's pulsing twin-screws kept our downstream surge ahead of th river's, allowing us only glimpses of passing scenes: junks struggling against th current, Taoist temples tucked inside orchards and bamboo groves, and a occasional hillside pagoda. We found the spacious dining salon on the to deck, far aft. Five circular tables for eight were spread with rice gruel spice with pickles, hardboiled eggs, Chinese crullers and steamed rolls. Passenger requesting bacon, eggs, coffee, toast and assorted jams were also accommc dated. Cheerful, young ladies served attractive dishes and gave us solicitou attention.

Afterward, groups of eager students and steamship guides surrounded us, practicing their English with descriptions of one after another historic spot along the shore. "The plain on that side is the site of the bloody battle when the *Zhu* forces defeated the Lu kingdom's army in the 3rd century." 'That pagoda on the hill was built in honor of General Chang's victory over the *Zhu* in the Sui dynasty." "That palisade up ahead on the right is the one referred to by Li Bai, the famous Tang dynasty poet." "That pagoda was built to dissuade heaven from sweeping the wealth of nearby settlements away in flood waters."

Soon our attention was directed to a massive, 300-foot-high rock on the north shore and the 18th-century, 11-storied Buddhist temple perched on its steep slopes. This was *Shi Bao Zhai*, literally, Stone Treasure Stronghold. According to legend, rice for the monks had flowed from a small hole in the stone floor until, one day, a greedy monk enlarged the hole to obtain more than his share, upon which the rice stopped altogether and has never flowed again. Today visitors who climb the tortuous spiral staircase are rewarded with a magnificent view of the river and surrounding countryside.

The stop at the salt-processing town of Guizhou was brief, with time enough only to take on additional shipments and a few passengers. The purser informed me that within the last three years, mechanized pumps had been installed in the salt refineries, replacing the slave labor that had appalled me in 1946.

In the early afternoon on the north bank, the ancient walled city of Fengdu, once a major tax-collection center for river traffic, came into view. Its buildings, set on stilts, looked as if they were climbing the rugged hillside. After our M.S. *Zhou Jun* moored, we were met at the foot of the gangplank by our local guide. Short, wiry, animated and mustachioed, he greeted us enthusiastically, unperturbed by the torrential thunder storm. He introduced himself as Liu En-ming and with his assistant rushed to help us as we struggled in the deluge to raise umbrellas, button raincoats and slip on overshoes.

"Welcome to Ghost City, capital of the netherworld of the Tang and Song dynasties," he began, impervious to the drenching rain that made every step on the slippery deck and cross boards life-threatening. The stone steps leading to the bus parked far above were a torrent of mud.

Despite the nonstop downpour, the intrepid Mr. Liu kept up his spiel: "This famed Ghost City was once the capital of the Ba Kingdom in the pre-Qin years and later a famous Taoist scenic spot during the Eastern Han dynasty. Countless captivating folk legends surround this mystic city." On he went, while we slipped and slid, trying to find the next step. We could care less about the Ba Kingdom of 3,000 years ago; what captivated us were the raging waters.

Benevolent ghosts must have helped us, for we managed to survive the climb without a single plunge. Soaked and encrusted with mud, we boarded a bus waiting on the upper road.

Without missing a beat, our guide continued, "Fengdu has the distinction of Taoists esteeming it as the significant 46th among China's 72 'luck lands.'" Whether these 'luck lands' referred to a pre-history lottery or to the vaunted 'Eastern Islands' where the Elixir of Life is stored remained a mystery. Instead it seemed more likely that Fengdu was one of the 72 centers where one's following of the Taoist Divine Way could be enhanced. We got the message that we were especially privileged to be in a key city that manifests the Tao as the physical and moral order of the world. Here we had the inside track to the Way of reason, truth and perfect virtue.

The driver appeared benign, but once behind the wheel, he became a speed demon who careened the bus through narrow cobblestone alleys, euphemistically dubbed 'boulevards.' We sped past Western-styled buildings interspersed with century-old shops. When spaces between buildings widened, we saw rice paddies and thatched cottages which transported me back in time. Near misses with pedestrians, cyclists and overhanging shop displays were heart-stopping.

Mr. Liu, trying bravely to ease our discomfort, switched his narrative to Fengdu's famous *Yue Lan*, Ghost Festival, celebrated during the middle of the seventh lunar month. Hungry ghosts who emerge from hell and wander the Earth are appeased with food, wine, entertainment and paper money. All streets, shops, warehouses, temples and huts come alive, he assured us. Merchants and officials parade symbolic papier-mâché treasures, sent out of respect for the city by neighboring towns and prefectures.

"Folk customs and culture operate in radiant splendor," he offered, reminding me for a brief moment of the publicity-minded skipper on the voyage down the Yangzi in 1946.

The lurching bus sped up the hill before jolting to a stop in front of the Confucian temple in the city's central plaza. As we stepped off the bus, still soaked with rain and now further drenched with perspiration, Mr. Liu presented each of us with a fan and announced, "Considerate ghosts have turned off the rain. The burning of joss sticks and candles in the temple over there has not been in vain."

Waving our fans to relieve the oppressive humidity, we mounted the thousand steps leading to Ghost Lair Hill. Mr. Liu promised, "Whether or not we glimpse a ghost, we definitely will catch a spectacular view of Ming Shan and Shuangui Shan, Fengdu's illustrious twin mountains."

As we plodded up the slippery steps toward Ghost Pinnacle Pavilion, our persevering guide supplied us with stories of ghosts that populate the area. "Mention of the Ghost City abounds in classic novels, such as *Pilgrims to the West and Romance of Fantasy Gods*. These ghosts are not altogether evil, mere-

mischievous. They delight in disrupting order, making valuable papers fly way and shaking items on shelves. Some may be hellion ancestors acting out the pranks they wanted to play while still alive. Invisible and elusive, these things are very disconcerting. When you think you've avoided them, they slip back to confound you again."

We were disappointed at the summit to find that none of the Pinnacle temple ghosts were out to greet us. The view, however, was superb.

In returning to the temple at the plaza, we chose an alternate way that took us over a suspension foot bridge, which, in its eerie swaying, suggested that the Fengdu ghosts might be trying to do us in with their tricks after all.

In the late afternoon the sprawling city of Wanxian appeared on the north bank. At an elbow in the river, the ship completed a half circle from the south shore. We passed a wide tributary and caught sight of the city's renowned arched Tang dynasty bridge silhouetted by the sunset. We docked at pontoons at the foot of broad stone steps leading to the south gate.

After the gangplank was pulled to the lower deck, solicitous student guides led us across floats to the steps rising out of the river. At the crest two local guides took us to a waiting bus.

Apologizing, one guide explained that the planned visit to the showcase silk factory, usually operating its swing shift at this hour, had to be canceled. The thunderstorm three hours earlier had damaged power lines, necessitating a plant shutdown. Instead we would take a cliff-line drive to see how the city was expanding into the hills east and west beyond the remnant of the old wall.

Mr. Yang, the older of the two guides, began his rehearsed descriptions of Wanxian. Its oranges, tangerines, peaches and sweet potatoes were famous nationwide. Textiles, plaited bamboo, leather-tanning, silk-spinning and weaving were important local industries. As Sichuan's fourth-most-important industrial center and port, it boasted a population exceeding 375,000.

A new three-lane thoroughfare hugged the route of the dismantled city wall. We were driven to the crowded arcade outside the north gate. Exploration of the yet-open shops was brief. From the gate's remaining tower we gained a view of tiers of rolling hills replete with corn and sunflower fields stretching to the purple mountains on the horizon. The lighted estates on the terraced hillsides, our guide assured us, no longer were occupied by exploiters of the people, rapacious landlords and unprincipled interest sharks. Instead, these villas now housed schools, institutes and other agencies serving the people.

With only inches to spare, the tour bus honked its way through the north gate and back to the old city. The thousand-year-old cobblestone way through the heart of the city was no more. A broad new avenue had been slashed along the route to facilitate auto traffic. The picturesque memorial *pai-lous* had bee[n] dismantled. Reaching the central plaza we gained a view of the elegant bridg[e] towers we had seen from our mooring. We stopped nearby at a large trad[i]tional-style store to eye silk samples.

Back at the south gate we lingered in the park overlooking the river's ben[d] The vantage point provided a spectacular array of lights outlining bulgin[g] warehouses, docks with night-shift stevedores and junks of all sizes flankin[g] one another along the shoreline as far as we could see. The brevity of the vis[it] did not allow me to visit the mission or the sacred hilltop cemetery where ov[er] three decades before Harlow, the major, Wang Shi and I had spent a pensi[ve] morning.

Students holding flashlights helped us negotiate the slippery steps to th[e] ship. Reaching the gangplank we were hailed by a gentleman lounging in h[is] underwear and perched on a stool. Continuing to cool himself with his larg[e] black fan, he invited us to sit with him and share his tea.

Introducing himself as Liu Meng, a native of a downriver town and th[e] ship's chief engineer, he accelerated his fanning. As if we had known each oth[er] for years, he engaged us with questions: What did we think of Wanxian? Wh[at] was our 'study group' studying? Though it was near midnight, just three hou[rs] before his ship was scheduled to sail, his curiosity wouldn't let us go. He pa[r]layed our responses into larger questions, particularly about the United State[s] Is shipping on the Mississippi thriving? The size of river boats? The life of th[e] people along its shores? Then, how is it that democracy works? How do yo[u] get people to vote? How do you get rid of corrupt officials?

Timed to allow it to enter the gorges during daylight, our ship remained [at] its Wanxian mooring until 3:00 a.m. Navigating the swift river during darkne[ss] required the assistance of an extra river pilot. Searchlights at the bow pierce[d] the darkness off the starboard and port sides, showing the shoreline and chan[n]nel between the lights blinking on beacon boats.

Before dawn, in the distance on the north shore, we spotted the lights [of] Yunyang. The searchlights flashed over the south bank, where, during th[e] Three Kingdoms period (220-280 A.D.), historic battles had been fought b[y] armies of the rival kingdoms of *Shu*, *Wu* and *Wei*. At the eastern section of th[e] old battlefield, the ship's searchlights illuminated the Song dynasty memori[al] to the *Shu* Kingdom's General Zhang Fei, who had been assassinated by reb[el] officers.

The river turned golden, reflecting the rising sun, while a purple glo[w] spread over the distant peaks. The Sichuan plains gave way to hills that fa[st] became mountains. The eager students, roused before daybreak, resumed the[ir] self-appointed role of telling us about the history and lore of shoreline spots

First there was the city of Yunyang with its brine-processing works sendin[g]

ouds of white pollutants into the sky. Not far away we sailed by Guizhou.
nly a short distance eastward was Baidicheng, or White King City. The rising
in emblazoned the temple on the peak that commemorated heroes of the
hree Kingdoms period, while accentuating the 800 stone steps leading up to
. Below was the hallowed hill where the Tang poet Du Fu had lived.

The accelerating current harbingered our approach to the *Qutang*, the most
esterly of the gorges. The awesome Gui Gate came into view. From the
eight of the ship's bridge we gained a spectacular view of the awesome
romontory. A sharp right turn was required to enter the gorge itself, since
ere the river is only 350 feet wide.

In this dramatic and much fabled section, the Long River was forced
nrough a narrow passage like the throat of an hourglass. When shores squeeze
ne river, the current becomes swifter, while its subsurface depths are more
nan 400 feet. This lent credence to the legend that the gorges were created by
ne mythical emperor Yu the Great, who hacked apart a mountain range with
giant axe in order to drain a lake which had submerged most of what is now
ichuan province. Geologists, on the other hand, contend that the gorges were
ormed some 70 million years ago by massive water erosion, which occurred
fter a major movement in the earth's crust squeezed two adjoining mountain
anges.

Only eight miles long, the Qutang's luminous, sandstone walls were in
ome places almost a mile high. Each dangerous bend, cloud-enshrouded peak
nd weirdly shaped boulder carried its own name and legend.

Before we realized it, we were into the waters of the once-feared *Da Yehtan*
Rapids. As it plowed through one after another enormous eddy, our steel hull
huddered with propellers alternately racing and then biting the convulsed
raters.

Often the stone walls shut the sun from view, casting long shadows on the
urbulent waters. Terraced fields of corn, mulberry and orange trees could be
een when a break came in the vaulted walls. Clusters of flowers punctuated
revices.

Along the north bank, the now-empty tunnels were stark reminders of the
enturies of trackers who had hauled junks upstream. I was transported back to
ny first, much more harrowing journey and the spot where our two trackers
vere whipped off their narrow tow paths into the river.

On the south bank the Meng Liang Staircase, deep etching in the sheer
liffs, could be seen. It was an upward zigzag of square holes cut into the
romontory for timbers to be inserted as rungs to climb upon. The most com-
non legend has it that the holes were carved by the bodyguard of a murdered
ong dynasty official who was attempting to recover his master's corpse.

After passing two temples set back amid orange groves, our ship approache and soon moored at Wushan. Named after a mountain once believed inhabit ed by witches, it actually presents a bewitching individuality unique among th cities of the Three Gorges. It is tucked into a cove on the west side of th Daning tributary, which marks the boundary between Sichuan and Hube provinces.

The plan was for us to board one of the sleek, 28-seat, motorized sampan for an hour's excursion through the Three Lesser Gorges of the Daning. As w stepped off the shaky gangplank to board the sampan, the heavens unloade torrents. Determined to carry out the day's itinerary, our Wushan guides led u toward a reserved launch. Boatmen in yellow ponchos helped us, person b drenched person, to pick our way across shaky planks and bobbing pontoons

At the bow of the boat readied for us, we picked our way through a tangl of ropes, hooks and bamboo poles. Once seated, water dripping from abov and splashing from the sides, we watched the two poling bowmen and the tw rope-pulling sternmen try to maneuver our sampan free of the ten-deep row o boats that hemmed us in. At the same time, our soaked guide tried to maintai our enthusiasm. In time, the frustrated boatmen declared their efforts in vain They helped off-load us and escorted us up the long flight of stone steps to waiting bus.

The bus sped through the city's narrow streets and uphill along perilou switchbacks. The dashing ride up the steep bank took us skidding aroun curves that so frightened us we forgot our drenched condition. Careenin around a bend and onto a stone bridge spanning the Danning chasm, ou guide said, proudly pointing upstream, "There they are!" In the gray of th downpour, we saw the outlines of the intriguing mini-gorges: first *Longmen* then *Bawu* around a bend and then in the distance the *Dizui*.

On the precarious drive back to the great stone stairs above our mooring though still drenched, we listened faithfully to our animated guide's storie about the jeweled miniature gorges. Eventually we were returned to the ship well briefed in region's lore. Aboard the M.S. *Zhou Jun*, we changed into dr clothes and regained a degree of composure.

Within an hour the ship cast off and headed for Wu Gorge, the second an most serene of the three main gorges. On Goddess Peak, the highest mountai along the Long River, stood a 40-foot stone pillar which resembled a maiden believed to be the youngest of 12 fairies who bring good luck and guide ship through the river's dangers. Other points of interest included the Kong Min Tablet with an inscription written by Zhugeliang, a noted *Shu* prime minister

Farther downriver on the south bank, we passed Badong, an industrial cit whose erupting chimneys and steaming brine vats created a blot on the other wise impressive landscape.

Mid-morning we docked at the small city of Zigui. We were relieved that the rain abated before we were to begin our tour. We wound through narrow cobblestone alleys to reach the elaborate Qu Yuan Memorial Hall and Temple. Inscriptions on black granite slabs in the gardens gave tribute to this renowned warrior and counselor. Off to the side, in work sheds, skillful stone cutters with mallets and chisels were fashioning perfect ideographs on new stele (stone slab).

Back aboard the ship we were asked to prepare for the tour's gala finale: the captain's dinner. Later, at the farewell banquet, toasts to Sino-American, Sino-Japanese and Sino-European friendship abounded, followed by gulps of fiery 140-proof *maotai*, a sweet red wine and Tsingtao beer (made with mineral water from Lushan).

Following the banquet, the waitresses who had served us well for two days became entertainers. They sang and danced, finishing their production with a "style show" in which they appeared in up-to-the-minute, self-made dresses and suits, designed from their collections of Vogue and Haute Couteur. Svelte in their modeling poses, here in China's hinterland, they flaunted Parisian sophistication.

The next day, early in the afternoon, we sailed into the Xiling, last and the longest of the gorges (almost 40 miles).

Until the late 1950's, the Xiling was the most feared of the three gorges. The western approach into which we came had for millennia terrorized junkmen with the treacherous *Yehdan* rapids, caused by landslides during the 9th century that piled obstructions in the channel. The three successive rapids which comprise Xin tan and cover a mile and a half of the river, namely, Head Rapid, First Rapid and Second Rapid, were especially difficult for large upbound cargo junks. Head Rapid was the worst of the three. Until the channel was improved in the 1950's, the current could build up to 14 knots. I recalled how in 1946 junks had to exceed the velocity of the current in order to keep from drifting out of control. If they missed the proper openings and failed to attain sufficient speed, they were doomed.

At the midpoint of the gorge lay the worst of the Long River's rapids, the feared *Kung-ling Shoal*. In addition to the *Kung-ling* itself, junks had to avoid First Pearl, Second Pearl, Third Pearl, Monk's Rock, Chicken Wings and the seductively named but deadly Come-to-Me Rock.

Twenty years before (1955) those serious navigational hazards had been dynamited and dredged clear. This section now open, I found it hard to believe that the channel could be so tame. Sailing through the Xiling four decades later lacked the drama of the past. The dreaded *Yehdan*, with rocks blasted and channel dredged, had been renamed New Rapids to reflect its new placidity. Then came the Yellow Ox Gorge, no longer threatening. The enormous Deer

Horn Rocks (Kung-ling shih) nemesis, so feared by boatmen for two millen nia, were no more. The entire obstruction had been blasted away in 1951. Th deadly Come-to-Me Rock had also been cleared. Dragon's Mouth Cave an Rapids, no longer dangerous, are now known as "the new and friendly Drago Mouth."

Although it is scenically overshadowed by the Qutang and the Wuxi gorges, the Xiling is impressive for its serrated banks interspersed with orang groves. We focused telescopes and cameras on its ubiquitous farmhouses an temples in bamboo groves. The Xiling's eastern part was, and still is, famou for its four smaller gorges, the Gorge of the Sword and Book on the Art c War, the Horse Lung and Ox Liver Gorge, the Kung Ling Gorge and th Gorge of Shadow Play. The Huang Ling Temple, first built during the Thre Kingdoms period and reconstructed during the Tang dynasty, rose up a moun tainside east of Shadow Play gorge.

Eager students surrounding us elaborated accounts of these parts immor talized by their poets and dramatists. Our guide summed up their message Happy is the person who takes these treasured experiences of the Three Gorge journey seriously, because it's of the stuff of history that is relevant today.

We Westerners agreed: the story of journeying this portion of one c China's life-giving rivers dramatizes how history has a way of flowing alon; rivers.

In response, several of us were carried away as we expanded our reply: I Biblical days of the Middle East were the Nile and Euphrates. In Ezekial a rive flows from the temple and sweetens the Dead Sea. At the end of Revelation we are told of the "life-giving river" which flows through the city, shining lik crystal, flowing through the throne of God. The streets of the shoreline citie are transformed by its loveliness and power. Much of Revelation has to do wit death and destruction–as with the Long River's Three Gorges. At the comple tion of our '46 odyssey we were aware that new directions could be taken. Th present was full of opportunity and justified high expectations. Christocentri as Revelation is, it tells how, like a river, the Son of God becomes a power i us, surging up as an inner energy of transforming potency.

In China the Yangzi, Yellow, Min, Pearl and Han rivers each have their lor legends and history. In other continents were the Ganges, the Amazon, th Congo and the Zambezi. Later, the Volga, Danube, Rhine, Thames Mississippi, Colorado and Yukon were channels of history.

The students listened politely to our globalizing the significance of rivers i world history, but in the end returned to make certain we appreciated the spe cial features of this section of China's Long River.

Old anxieties flashed as we approached where for millennia the Xiling's east ern rapids had raged and taken their fearful toll. In minutes, however, we saile

rough the once-perilous stretches. Not distracted with dangers, we had time
） appreciate the changing shoreline. In minutes we sailed through the sentinel
alisades, known until the '40s as The Gates of Hell.

The mountains to the west gave way to a plain that stretched to the eastern
orizon. Our ship slowed to follow another that was moving into the locks of
1e mile-and-a-quarter-wide Gezhouba Dam west of Yichang.

The reality of cement and steel gave way to a frightening flashback when I
ad been in the 95-foot junk on this same stretch of river. I was immersed in
nages of the wooden craft caught in the giant whirlpool, swirling out of con-
·ol as if it were a toy. Once again it was vivid to me how helpless we mere
umans can be against nature's power. In 1946, no lock or dam had held the
ver in check.

My present role of gawking tourist paled in comparison to my earlier part
s an adventurer. Then I was a participant in a life struggle with the great river.
Jow I was a mere sightseer. It seemed a travesty now to travel in such safety
nd security.

A journey like mine in 1946 will never happen again. I felt a sense of sad-
ess and loss. The struggle had been costly in blood and sweat for the boat-
1en and in anxiety for us passengers. But in 1946, on board the *wu ban,* we
·ere far more intimate with the gorges.

Entering the lock astern of the other ship, we saw the 110-foot-tall gates on
1e upper (western) side close behind us. Then the gargantuan gates inched
pen on the downstream end. The 60-foot-deep body of water on which we
oated rushed past the forward gates. As the waters subsided, our ship moved
1to the lower level of the Long River.

The M.S. *Zhou Jun's* animated captain gave a positve estimate of the
iezhouba dam and locks. He cited its success as an engineering feat and its
gnficant contribution to the region in enhanced electric power and naviga-
onal improvement. He pointed out that its completion provides arguments
>r both advocates and critics of the much larger Three Gorges dam farther
·est. Advocates, pragmatists and nationalists say, "Look we did it and we can
gain accomplish even greater feats." Critics, including archeologists, ecolo-
ists and humanitarians, counter with, "The mega-dam is three times as big,
rill cost billions more than China can afford and will exact the human cost of
,000,000 displaced residents and the cultural loss of 1,300 known archeo-
)gical sites."

The captain said the problems of planning and completing such an enor-
1ous project are hard to imagine. He added that the country's propaganda
pparatus has hailed the proposed mega-dam's power generation, flood con-
·ol and shipping facilitation. But despite its advantages, the real costs–of con-
truction, relocating millions of people and instituting the needed measures to

protect the river's life–have not been told to the people. He was sure that the approaching millennium, along with its benefits, the country was in f  many problems with the projected mega-dam.

His observations were cut short when the first officer called him to com mand the docking of the ship. He, indeed, was precient in putting his finger c the key points about the project that would arouse controversy.

As the setting sun focused on Yichang's 900-year-old, needle-like pagoda, returned to the place where in '46 the major, Wang Shi and I began ou odyssey into destiny. Completed was an up-to-the-minute experience of th radical man-made changes in the Three Gorges area that had taken place dui ing the decades following 1950.

# The Three Gorges In The New Century

As jorneyers into the Long River's Three Gorges we survived the killer apids, absorbed the beauty and majesty of nature's riverscapes, lived for three weeks elbow to elbow with westward and eastward crews of 95 and 75 sinuous p-river boatmen and ashore visited with trackers, towns people, veteran missionaries, enthusiastic Chinese teachers and pastors, and all the while enjoyed aving at our side Wang Shi, an articulate renaissance Chinese instructor. Returing to the gorges 40 and again 50 years after the initial 1946 journey, we were able to see amazing changes in this section of the Long River as new ways f taming the River Dragon were in progress. As to the nature of ourselvles and our involvement in the day-to-day events of these journeys, the gorges symbolized the importance and fact of change and flux. In bringing the accounts f these contrasting 1946 and 1996 Three Gorges' journeys to a meaningful lose, what lessons were gained about Chinese and ourselves as Westerners?

## THE *QIN GU* (FOREVER) COLLAGE OF THE CHINESE

The 1946 journey gave the major and me the most intense, immediate, lose and powerful impressions of the Chinese uniqueness. In the 17th centuy of the K'ang-xi emperor a Jesuit's description said that "his bearing, his figre, the features of his countenance, an air of majesty tempered with mildness nd kindness, inspire at first sight love and respect for his person and announce om the very first the master of one of the greatest empires of the universe." n 1960 Joseph Needham, Cambridge professor, returned from his China jourey and began his monumental seven-volume account of China and the Chinese. In the next decade Ramond Dawson, Oxford don, who had already ublished six difinitive books on China, wrote another that he entitled *The Chinese Experience.*

No match for these and countless other beautiful and exhaustive estimates, he major and I gained, nevertheless, a short but authentic and intense Chinese xperience. Every minute of our journey, however, brought demonstrations of ow the intriguing countrymen ate, slept, dressed, joked, related to one anoth-r, made decisions and revealed the world view by which they lived and died. t close range we saw how they dealt both with society's opportunities and vils and nature's treasures and hazards. We resonated with how they sought ɔ realize their personal well being and how they responded to the responsi-ilites and ambiguities of their own inner selves. These travels reflected the Chinese life journey.

We found the Chinese know well their rivers. To speak of rivers opens up the variety of circumstances that engage the Chinese. Whether it's the Amu the Yellow, the Wei, the Min, the Han, the Pearl or the Li, the Chinese kno well that they are both sustained and harried by them. Their waterways hav carried the hearts and souls of the people from place to place for over five mi lennia. What the African American poet, Langston-Hughes, wrote about h people also applies to the Chinese: "I have known rivers, ancient dusky rivei and my soul has grown deep like the rivers." Wang Shi told how artists an poets had enshrined the river in Chinese culture.

The crews' comments and reactions to the Yangzi's power and capriciou ness unfolded vivid images about the dragon metaphor they applied to th Long River. The Long River's real dragon, however, is no mere order of ange ic beings or demons flapping about in the sky. It reflects the river peoples' sens of the tremendous potential in the concept of *powers*. The dragon metaphc applies to the river, but also offers a way of interpreting the realities of China institutions, structures, and systems. The river's *powers* are both visible *an* invisible, earthy *and* heavenly, institutional *and* spiritual. There's an oute physical manifestation (rushing currents, navigational possibilities, buiding portfolios, personnel, trucks, fax machines) and inner spirituality, or corporat culture, or collective personality. The Powers aspect of the river dragon ar simultaneity of an outer, visible structure and an inner, spiritual reality. It w; a spiritual aspect that is not easy for people steeped in materialistic though and pursuits to grasp.

Though each of these important aspects deserve elaboration, at the 20t century's end every consideration of the Three Gorges focuses on questior about the building and consequences of the Three Gorges' mega-dam.

## SURGING DEBATE OVER CONSEQUENCES OF MEGA DAM

Before the 1950s the gorges, as they always had been from the beginnin of history, were one of the country's teasured natural wonders. This section c the river had always aroused aesthetic appreciation, and, since it seemed to hav a reference to the people's destiny, it evoked awe. Though respectful of th Long River's passage through the gorges, travelers were continually vulnerab before its multiple hazards. Like the dragon metaphor applied to it, the gre; river was viewed as both benevolent and dangerous. For generation upon gei eration this remarkable, but perilous, series of imposing chasms have both trou bled and challenged Chinese. Instead of five millennia, compress the time hor zon from 1946 to five decades and what do we find? The journeys during th second half of the twentieth centry reveal the response of monumental soci and technological efforts to bring the river dragon under human control. Th gigantic engineering project in process is producing upheavels of such magn tude that they can only be compared with the stupendous geological convu sions that formed the gorges millions of years ago.

The results of the present enormous engineering, financial and political efforts to tame the River Dragon are problematic. This colossal project is more than physical change, altering the geography. This is a wholesale coordination of human resources–scientific, economic and organizational. It includes displacing and relocating millions of inhabitants. Winners are big merchants and financiers, large and small vendors and all too many corrupt parasites. Losers are the displaced millions, ecologists, archaeologists and historians whose pay-dirt sites will be flooded and many conscientious citizens' whose convictions go unheeded. Future generations will be burdened to pay off the project's sky-high debt and to repair the ecological damages that will occur. These considerations necessitate charting the *pros* and *cons* of this vast project to alter the Three Gorges.

The enormous present project is focused on the easternmost gorge, the Xiling. Deeply etched memories remain of how this prized section of the Long River was: With all of its hazards, it was exalted for its stunning riverscapes, majestic walls and quiet coves. Pagodas graced its peaks, memorial tablets dotted its banks and shrines remained tucked in the corners of its inlets. Its golden waters thundered through tumultous rapids and then settled in the enchanting hush of tree-lined tributaries. The fisermen's and villagers' thatched houses and farmers' vertically plowed fields, fascinated travelers, suggesting pristine simplicity and harmonious communities. For thousands of years the lofty limestone cliffs resounded with chants of toiling trackers symbolizing the peoples' response to the horrendous obstacles that they sought to overcome. Poets and painters were inspired by its awesome beauty. Westerners could easily resonate with the spell of the Xiling chasms and imagine them as natural amphitheaters for the profundities of Beethoven or Brahms' symphonies and also the romace of Straus' waltzes. When one sailed through the awesome East Gate palisades, spotted the Huangling Temple nestled in the orange groves, and passed the yawning Three Travelers' Cave's entrance–known as "The Dragon's Mouth"–the metaphor of a powerful but maverick river dragon seemed plausible.

Today, at another *fin-de-siecle*, instead of lofty promontories impervious to change, it is the river's flux and rush that best symbolize the predominate character of the renowned Three Gorges. The tyranny of geography is being batted by the all-out applications of technological change. Now, at the turn of the century, a mega-dam in this famed Xiling Gorge is three years into its building and 11 years from its scheduled completion in 2009. After eons of evolving in nature's slow way, the gorges will be altered forever–in just fourteen or fifteen years.

Thus, in the late 1990s, instead of say the melodious flow of a Grieg's liquid composition, the music is rather that of Stravinski's most strident symphonies. The cacophony now is one of blasting, roaring, of earth-movers, behemoth cranes, rock-crushing towers, 20-ton dump trucks and thousands of jack hammers. Tens of thousands of workers crowd the Xiling's shores a *Sandouping*. Cliffs are being gouged to carve out enormous locks to accom modate 10,000 ocean-going cargo ships. As critic Dai Qing, national renowned journalist, has said, "If the gorges could speak, they would plead fc mercy."

The plans are as awesome as the river itself. A work force of 40,000 ar building the 610-foot-high dam that will span 6,864 feet. A lake nearly 40 miles long and almost 600 feet deep will be formed, allowing ocean-goin freighters to reach 1,500 miles inland to Chongqing, a city of 15 millior Generators producing 18,200 megawatts of electricity–some 15 times the out put of a typical 1,200-megawatt nuclear reactor–are being made. All for an est mated US $17 billion. The dam will be the world's biggest hydroelectric pro ducer and potential lifesaver for tens of thousands by controlling floods tha have plagued the Long River over the centuries. The dam will improve th transfer of freight between China's east and west, by making it possible fc heavy barges and 10,000 ocean-going ships to reach the heart of Sichuan. Th increased economic mobility will facilitate the flow of information and expan commerce, increasng the lure of greater profits. Despite the powerful *pros* an *cons* that swirl about the mega-dam's consequences and the prospect of huma ingenuity doing further ecological damage to the area, the Three Gorges wi long endure and continue to be beneficial to numbers of Chinese. Such is th official scenario.

## SERIOUS ECONOMIC QUESTONS MULTIPLY

Economic uncertainties about the project present an array of problem Questions arise over the claim that this stupendous alteration of the area geography will create in the region a society and culture conductive to ecor mic growth. It is not clear how the project will enable the people living in less-advanced economy to realize a more-advanced economy. Critics sketc dark economic consequence of the project. They point to indications of th project being a US $40-billion boondoggle. Corruption on a grand scale pe meates all aspects of the project, siphoning off already inadequate sums sc aside for attacking China's long-standing social problems. Indications are tha the dam's accelerating costs have never been honestly reported. It is feared tha once foreign banks face the real costs of the dam they will be reluctant t extend loans needed for the project's completion. Already concerns mour with the World Bank, sociologists, anthropologists, geographers and educator

A more optimistic estimate points to the significance that this vast proje was conceived and organized by Chinese. Chinese engineers, financiers, mar agers and officials are demonstrating their know-how and their competenc The fact that it planned and organized such an immense effort shows the worl how China has demographic mass, economic dynamism, critical geograph placement and growing military might. The mega-dam's progress and scope underline how China is the world's fastest growing economy. Most economists predict that China will overtake the United States as the world's largest economy sometime in the next 25 to 30 years.

## Inhabitants Face Hardships

Demographic or sociological problems accompany the mega-dam project. As many as two million residents' homes will be flooded. Many disgruntled farmers are being forced into marginal higher land. Others will no longer be able to cultivate reeds for paper making, cut grass for fertilizer and gather medicinal herbs for sale. Untold thousands of villagers on the tributaries and lakes who live on plants that rely on the river's seasonal surge and ebb will be affected. The homes and work places of more hundreds of thousands villagers and town people will be wiped out. Ther River Dragon speaks of the enormity of the experience of being dislocated: It speaks to the flux and powers of movements for individuals and communities.

One wonders also whether China's rich cultural inheritance will be rendered irrelevant by the revolution in communications that will bring VCRs and satellite dishes to the remote villages and, with them, the homogenizing influence of the mass media. If so, perhaps all that are left to determine the capacity for growth are the government's economic policies toward money, trade, property rights and education. Signs of bourgeois decadence abound: Diversion of public construction funds into private pockets, fancy resort villas for visiting dignitaries on choice hilltops, Party secretaries' sons cruising the new roads in Rolls Royces, thriving casinos and brothels.

## A Gamut of Political Questions Emerge

The mega-dam project also presents a gamut of knotty unresolved political quesitons. According to Dai Qing, a strident critic, the dam serves as a metaphor of China's changing society, a microcosm of what is happening in the whole of China. "It is a very special case in China," she said. "The politicians seeking power who support the Three Gorges project have all the characteristics and mind set of China's old society that maintain control with a one-party authoritarian political and economic system. The current regime has little regard for the individual and allows no democratic discussion. These are all characteristics of the old system."

Those who oppose the dam, on the other hand, Dai Qing points out, include intellectuals, scientists and environmentalists. They are against this project not only for technical and financial reasons, but for the dangers it presents to the environment, public safety and preservation of China's ancient roots. These people have the characteristics or features of the new society. They are independent thinkers. Concerns over the mega-dam mount with sociologists, anthropologists, geographers, archeologists and educators. They are concerned with human rights and can express their own opinions. Now they are asking for an open democratic debate on this crucial enterprise that concerns the fate of the whole nation. Beyond the economic, social and political objections, the damaging ecological, consequences of the gargantuan project loom large. She sees in the project's ambiguities not only gross misuse and waste of resources but evil. She and other resisters acknowledge that the gorges' dangers and obstacles must be addressed, but only after much open debate among citizens and in forums of China's strongest mind. She sees that serious ethical issues are being disregarded. The recognition is that one of the most pressing questions facing the world today is: How can we oppose evil without creating new evils and being made evil ourselves?

Dai Qing and other Chinese resisters to the mega-dam believe that they are backed by caring people worldwide. The undemocratic political bureaucrats, they believe, have pushed this project through on ideological grounds and without a consensus. Though the world's most populous nation and rising great power, China is kept by its government in the mind-set of the Cold War. Its political leaders maintain a communist ideology that, while weak among the masses, justifies their hold on power.

In China's history, unlike the River Dragon that continues (forever), "the Command of Heaven is not forever." This simple idea with far-reaching consequences was articulated in a court song commemorating the founding of the Zhou dynasty in the middle of the 11th century B.C. The idea was invented to help legitimize the new dynasty which usurped the power of its predecessor. The rationalization invented was that the revered founders of the Zhou dynasty had rightfully banished the previous Shang dynasty because their last ruler had foreited the Mandate of Heaven by his tyrannical behavior.

This concept of the Mandate of Heaven also broke apart the previous cozy arrangement in which a king's position was derived from his connection to his royal ancestors, who were in turn his connection to the high ancestral divinities, including Heaven. This simple idea made possible the notion that leaders had moral responsibilities to perform in the interests of the welfare of the led. In his sophisticated work, *The World of Thought in Ancient China*, Benjamin I Schwartz, a Harvard University historian, explores how Chinese thinkers dealt with the twofold problem of why humans, and rulers in particular, go astray rather than maintain the order that was confirmed for the Zhou (Chou) kings by Heaven. He shows how the vanguard of society can recognize its responsibility and develop the means to restore that normative order. The word Confucius used that comes closest to "moral responsibility" is *ren* (Wade-Giles=*jen*). Professor Schwartz defines *ren* as "refering to the inner moral life of the individual person that includes a capacity of self-awareness and reflection." The rulers who implement the good society must enhance the welfare of the common people and the common people of China have a mandate to struggle to ealize this vision. In this regard, it appears that the United States had best forge its mainland China policy by the same standard we once applied to Taiwan, whose external policy mattered more to us than its internal order, which was far from democratic but improving.

## DIRE ECOLOGICAL CONSEQUENCES

In estimating the ecological consequences of the mega-dam, many complex and critical questions have been given short strift or ignored. The fast rising mega dam will alter if not destroy one of China's greatest natural landmarks–the stretch of racing water, sharp cliffs and soaring green peaks treasured by Chinese in the way Americans love the Grand Canyon. Magnificent scenery and archeological sites will be lost beneath the waters. The cliffs and heights of the 150-mile-long Three Gorges will remain, but they will no longer soar high above the water, since the dam will create a 400-mile lake.

Opponents of the project fear the effects of the massive lake that will be formed. They say it will create a gigantic inland cesspool, fouled by 265 billion gallons of raw sewage each year and the effluents from the flooding of 1,000-year-old landfills. Water supplies to millions will be threatened, presenting the specter of disease and the extinction of aquatic species. Heavy siltation could jam sluiceways, leaving the dam vulnerable to collapse in a severe flood.

According to the Institue of Hydrobiology in Wuhan, the dam will severely reduce the numbers of more than half the river's 160 species of fish and curtail vital spring floods that coax fish from Lakes Dongting and Poyang into the river to spawn. It will hold the water temperature below the 64 degrees F. which many fish require to lay eggs. The drastic ecological overhaul demanded already has proven close to impossible. And what will become of the 140,000 fisherman?

The dam will disrupt the Yangzi's estuary by reducing the flow during the dry season and causing sea water to move upriver. From the dam to the estuary, river life will probably suffer the loss of silt and nutrients as these back up in the dam's reservoir. The relatively corrosive water will scour away shoals that make up the habitat of the Yangzi River dolphin, pushing the treatened species closer to extinction–less tan 200 are alive today. Other endangered wildlife include the Yangzi River sturgeon, Siberian crane and Yangzi River alligator.

## INTERNAL SIGNIFICANCE OF THE MEGA-DAM

Debate about the consequences of this immense project are more important than routine travel information for tourists. At issue are more than the disruption of land, community and economic-biological units a large number of Chinese have lived by. These revolutionary changes sweeping through the Three Gorges are similar to those sweeping across the planet. The man-made changes are of increasing significance not only for China but for the entire world. Technological development has leaped into hyperdrive and changed our life's fundamental character. As residents of earth at the end of the 20th century, all who have counted on the permanence of "continuity," are having to accept flux and rapid change, and fast learn how to cope with them.

A big question arises: Is this progress? Along with its promised positives, the mega-dam project, though justified as a part of modernizing the country, will have a host of negative consequences. The burden of its costs and gigantic efforts will long shadow China's economy and polity. Engineering expertise, building materials and human labor expended on this physical project have depleted resources that could have been applied to education, health and welfare institutions. For China and other countries to underestimate or fail to face these fundamental changes is perilous. The furor associated with these developments represents more than  a political-economic and ecological debate.

The successful building of the mega-dam demonstrates how fast the country's industrial and technological capacity and involvement in international trade is advancing. The building of the mega-dam gives evidence of China's economic modernization which will transform it into the world's greatest export power, dwarfing even Japan's influence in the world economy. No effort to regulate international trade and global transfer of sensitive technology or weaponry can succeed if China is not a part of it.

There are political and historical reasons, according to the specialist Charles William Maynes, to be concerned about China's rise that have nothing to do with ideology. He reasons that every major country, including the United States, upon reaching a stage when it was able to project its military power internationally has done so, usually with unfortunate consequences for its neighbors. At the same time, to complete and realize the benefits of this project China needs a period of external calm in order to attend to domestic deficiencies. These conditions reinforce the motivation to work for international stability. Only states of its size and power can mount or prevent the kind of regional or global struggle that could jepardize world peace.

Implications for the family of nations when China achieves the completion of this stupendous project are not clear. It can be predicted, however, that the successful finishing of the mega-dam will further demonstrate China's gathering technical, organizational and power capabilities. Then, for example, if China's Dickensian horror in its orphanages and abuse of civil rights continue the international community should not hesitate to at least call these horrors and abuses to the attention of the Chinese government. At the same time those from other countries should work with the National People's Congress and relevant Chinese ministries to help them correct such ill-treatment. Other nations should work with Chinese universities and the Chinese judiciary to strenghten legal education for judges and to improve judicial administation.

## LESSONS ABOUT OURSELVES AS WESTERNERS

A few impressions about Chinese gained by the major and me from our 1946 journey in the gorges were given at the beginning of this Epilogue. There followed a listings of the questions surrounding the gorges' mega dam that is being built. The lisings draw on the store of experiences from fifteen years residence in the country with the addition of information gathered about China and Chinese later in subsdequent tours.

This brings us to a needed summary of what we Westerners learned about ourselves. Today, for both Chinese and Westerners, life's Protean style is characterized by constant shifts in identification and belief. Like the river's currents and eddies, our lives are churned as a result from such broad factors as the velocity of historical change, the revolution in mass media, and the effects of 20th century genocides. The self can no longer be considered a fixed concept: It is continually "in process," and the stress is upon movement, innovaiton and trasformation.

It would be interesting to examine the contrasts and commonalities of how Westerners and Chinese seek their personal well being, how they respond to the ambiguities of their inner lives, how they make decisions and give evidences of their contrasting world views. But space and time do not permit that. Suffice to report that, personally, the experiences of journeying in the region's unique vistas and vicissitudes in 1946, and again several times during decades following, gave me deeper moral and spiritual insights–a claim that practical and secular persons will want proof or at least an explanation.

## THE INDIVIDUAL'S SELF RESPONSIBILITY

The realization comes afresh that life's journeying requires us to investigate and transform ourselves with decisiveness and discipline. A 1998 American bumper sticker reads: "Prevent truth decay; be true to yourself." Twenty-five centuries ago Confucius said. "What the superior man seeks is in himself *(Analects 15:20)*." Twenty centuries ago Jesus raised the question, "What will a man gain by winning the whole world, at the cost of his true self? (Mt. 16:26)"

Each person's journey, according to his/her particular individuality, as Confucius taught, "Is to seek wisdom, benevolence, responsibility *(ren)* and fortitude. *(Doctrine of the Mean, 20:8)*." Westerners see this as application of what may be called "personal quality control." People are to monitor themselves with questions such as: 'Am I trustworthy?' 'Am I disciplined to have sufficient inner strength to be unafraid and faithful to my guiding purposes?' 'Can I allow myself to be present to another because I can trust my responses?'

Character sufficient to survive the winds and battering of life's chasms and rapids is shaped not so much from without as from within. Yangzi boatmen hold that the river dragon lies in wait for drifters. However that may be, those with religious faith generally agree that there is judgment and retribution for drifters the irresponsible ones. Navigating the Long River's gorges allowed no place for naïveteé, pretension or overconfidence. Going upstream was to labor against the current. Going downstream was to move fast enough ahead of the downward surge to maintain steering control. Along life's journey persons cannot linger indecisively. On the great River of Life, to drift is to die.

The "inner journey" is yet a foreign territory for many. But indecisiveness on these matters of personal discipline invites destruction. The discipline required however, is more than a matter of casual whim; it is a matter of intention and the cultivation of faith's resourcs. The challenge is to continue on the journey of discovery and involvement. Such journeying is illuminated and encouraged by faith's light and power. As the person of faith brings his/her insecurity, unforgivingness and immature thoughts and behavior patterns to the Creator, freedom from pain and weaknesses and empowerment to live a new way come.

On our 1946 journey, the major, Thomspon and I talked with each other about this. The Chinese crew's tendancy to slip into a time of *xiu xi* (described as rest and restoration) often seemed more than loafing and escape from tension. They were letting "their souls catch up with their body." For the major and me this sort experience came from placing our lives beside quiet waters where the spirit of God could brood upon it and empower it. It meant including in our journeying intentional reaching toward God.

## THE SELF'S OUTWARD JOURNEY

Social concern needs to go along with personal discipline. People moving toward an enriched inward journey are drawn also to the outward journey–involvement with the world's human and natural needs. Jesus said "Love your neighbor as yourself." Because of His closeness with his Heavenly Father, Jesus knew that responding to the people's screams are linked to appreciating the evidences of how the Creator responds to our screams. Life lived close to one's center enables persons to give more freely one to another.

Faithful journeying, inward and outward, fortifies us to cope with the central human struggle which is in the realm of the moral and spiritual. The tension is not so much between what is "within history" and what is "beyond history," between the "this worldly image" and the "otherworldly truth"; the tension is between the will of God, which is both within history and beyond, and the will of man, which is solid enough within history to continue doing a great deal of damage! "No social ethic can be constructed on New Testament grounds, for instance", Walter Wink points out in his *Engaging the Powers (1992)*, "without recognition of the role of 'Principalities and Powers' in sustaining and subverting human life."

Exclusiveness vanishes before this inclusive and broad summons. Crucial is the rediscovery by numerous grass-roots movements of the importance of community and a sense of place. Work to spread justice and righteousness becomes an imperative for the one dedicated to servanthood for persons and communities. The Rev. Pan, in Wanxian, went to the heart of our directive when he quoted. "And what does the Lord require of you but to do justly, love mercy and walk humbly with your God. (Micah 6:8)."

A responsible stewardship of the earth and "all that is in it" is a crucial part of being accountable in "journeying outward."

"Nature cries for reverence," writes Dai Qing, the Chinese journalist. "Along with better understanding and skill at manipulating it, the created universe demands respect, appreciation and care. Dire consequences follow from the anthropocentric view of human culture as being in opposition to nature, which is thought to have merely instrumental value, i.e., to be of value only to the extent that it is useful to humans. All living systems, including the planet, need to be protected as a whole, as being creative and self-organizing, a view that is being developed in the new science of complexity.

## SPIRITUAL INSIGHT AND TRANSCENDENCE

To confront the problems of our time, which include elements of both reality and transcendence, we do well to discard outdated paradigms. We need to take stock of the emergence of the postmodern ecological visions of conditions crucial for the survival of humanity in the 21st century. Instead of seeing the universe as a machine composed of elementary building blocks, scientists have discovered that the material world is a network of inseparable patterns of relationships and that the planet as a whole is a living, self-regulating system. The view of the human body as a machine and of the mind as a separate entity is being replaced by one that sees not only the brain but also the immune system, the body tisssues and even each cell as living systems. Evolution is no longer seen as merely a competitive struggle for existence, but rather as a cooperative dance in which creativity, cooperation and the constant emergence of novelty are the driving forces.

We come, then, to reinforce the assertion that insights about the spirit were gained on these journeys into the Long River's gorges. In these experiences the major, Thompson and I in making such an affirmation stood on a basic assumption. We felt that the suggestion of transcendence that can be derived is not the utterly transcendent mystery of philosophers and mystics. God–the Transcendent One–is active but more than an event, for He is the ultimate Power. He is a being but more than some neutral entity. God's activity and being are more than those of a divine that allegedly lives in a far-off eternity uncontaminated by the ordinariness of time and space. It matters to this Transcendent One that we experience events sequentially. Openness, contingency and freeedom in temporal affairs are of crucial concern for God's eternity.

This then is to recognize another universe of discourse–transcendence. It is a supersensible realm that can not be known by the senses. People holding this view preserve a privileged "spiritual" realm immune to confirmation or refutation–at the cost of an integral view of reality and the simultaneity of heavenly and earthly aspects of existence. In New Testament times, people did not read the spirituality of an institution straight off from its outer manifestations. Instead, they projected its *felt* or *intuited* spiritual qualities onto the screen of the universe, and perceived them as cosmic forces reigning from the sky. What the people of the Bible experienced and called "Principalities and Powers" was in fact real. They were discerning the actual spirituality at the center of the political, economic and cultural institutions of their day. The spiritual aspect of the powers is not simply a "personification of institutional qualities." On the contrary, the spiritual aspect of an institution exists as a real aspect of the institution even when it is not perceived as such.

When ears, eyes and hearts are tuned to appreciate the full significance of the Long River you begin to search for the Almighty who formed the gorges, the rivers' source in the Tibetan highlands and the navigable 1500 mile stretch from the gorges to the China Sea. Is that so odd? You and I are reminded that we can say nothing and do nothing so as to be recognized by anybody who doesn't know us. Neither can God.

Awareness and faithfulness to God–the transcendent and imminent One–whether of concept, imagery or faith, can grows gradually and from below or within. To decree it is futile in writing and, no doubt, in life. Some friends, in all sincerity, report that deep down in their souls they hear no messages from 'above.' They ask, "Is God dead? Are we being fooled that there is a living personal God working to redeem what He has made?" And they ask, "Where is the evidence?" Still others, the action-oriented say, "Granted that in theory the world is the arena of a 'higher powers' concern. Lets get on with the work of living! This meditation, this silence business or time to develop a quiet center where you can consider the 'transcendent' is not for me. There's not that much time!"

Shakespeare once undertook to document divine Providence by finding "tongues in trees, books in the running brooks, sermons in stones, and good in everything." But what do the gorges say when the river's whirlpools spin and threaten to drag you into oblioion? If your trackers are jerked into the seething "brook" and drowned, what's the title of the book? And as for stones, if they're like the one that drove a hole in our *wu ban* or like the menacing Dragon Spine Rock, where is there a sermon in them? How dare we talk about the "good in everything"? Any one chasm of the Three Gorges can throw enough mortal dangers at the journeyer to turn such piety into a maniac's laughter!

Dispite these contrary indicators, the Long River's flow was a constant reminder of the manifestations of the Almighty's life-giving power. The current–pulsing power and provider of buoyancy for junks and ships–was a metaphor of the Creator's nature.

On the 1946 three-weeks journey in China's Three Gorges, as on the river of life, the major, Wang Shi and I sought to remain receptive to intimations of matters of the spirit and transcendence. As we resonated with the boatmen's toil, through the light and shadows of the chasms and rapids, we sensed an unfailing presence. As we struggled through the gorges we heard reassuring melodies speaking out of the chaos and suggesting a cosmic order and harmony. As we listened, the music we heard mattered! The Old Testament verse from 1 Samuel: "Hitherto hath the Lord helped us, (7:12)." made sense. It was like an echo. You could hear it carom off the chasm walls, out of the millennia. In life we live on the moving edge of time which we call the present–gone before you can finish a sentence about it. On that edge we can confidently read God into the past and just as confidently read him into the future, never mind what the world seems ready to hurl in our faces.

The will to hear the promptings of God and to respond grows in people as they live in structures which point to the inward and the outward. People do not come to wholeness without both movements. But because we're not whole, the reminder increases the "dialogue of conflict." The movement toward the resolution of this human struggle is enhanced with being an involved part of a vital convenant group on a corporate mission.

The integral worldview that is emerging in our day takes seriously the ancients' outlook, but combines them in a different way. Few of us in the West can any longer think that God, the angels and departed spirits are somewhere in the sky, as most ancients including the majority of Chinese, literally did. The image of the spiritual as "withiness" is not, howeer, a flat, limited, dimensionless point. It is conterminous with the universe-an inner realm every bit as rich and extensive as the outer realm.

The cries of exultation that flash across the otherwise somber landscape of the Book of Revelation express joy at being freed from the paralysis induced by the pseudo-trinity of the Dragon and its two Beasts. Freedom means release to expose their seductions to others. The passion that drove the early Christians to evangelictic zeal was fired by relief at being liberated and by the determination to set others free.

This exuberance arises from the conviction affirmed in this book's Preface. It is the assurance that the world process means something to the Creator God. He is not a separated self-sufficient entity who, driven by whim, creates what he wants and saves whom he wants. Rather, the eternal act of creation and continued concern for it and humanity is driven by a love which finds fulfillment only through the other one who has freedom to reject or to accept love. God, so to speak, drives toward personal fulfillment and the appreciation of everything's essence. For the eternal dimension of what happens in the universe is the Divine Life itself. It is the content of the devine struggle and blessedness seen in the *Qin gu*, "Forever", aspects of China's Three Gorges.

THE END

# Bibliography

Baker, Janet. Seeking Immortality: Chinese Tomb Sculpture. (Santa Ana, CA.: Bowers Museum of Cultural Art, 1997).

Ballard, W.L. "Aspects of the Linguistic History of Southern China," Asian Perspectives, XXIV (2), 1981 (163-83).

Bird, Isabella. The Yangtze Valley and Beyond. (London: John Murray, 1899, reissued, Virago Press, 1985).

Brodbeck, L. Emma. China Farewell. Alhambra, CA.: Self-Published, 1970).

Cooper, Arthur. Li Po and Tu Fu. (Harmonsworth UK: Penguin, 1973).

Crow, Carl. Handbook for China. Shanghai: Dodd, Mead and Co. 1924).

Chung-Li Chang. The Chinese Gentry. Seattle: University of Washington Press, 1974).

Dai Qing. The River Dragon Has Come, New York: M.E. Sharpe Publishers, 1998.

_____. Yangzi! Yangzi! Debate over the Three Gorges Project, (Earthscan Public Ltd., 1996).

De Riencourt, Amaury. The Soul of China. (New York: Coward-McCann, 1958).

Eberhard, Wolfram. China Minorities, Yesterday and Today. (Berkeley: Wadsworth Publishing, 1982).

Fairbank, John K. And Edwin Reischauer. East Asia and the Great Tradition. (Boston: Houghton Miffin Co., 1960).

Fei Hsiao Tong. Towards a People's Anthropology. (New York: New World Press, 1981).

Fitzgerald, C.P. China: A Short Cultural History. (New York: D. Appleton-Century & Co., 1938

Griffth, Samuel B. (Trans.) Sun Tzu: The Art of War. (London: Oxford 1963).

Hersey, John. A Single Pebble. (New York) Knopf, 1963).

Hinton, William, Fanshen. (New York: Randam House, 1966.)

Historical Low Water Survey Team from the Changjiang River Basin Planning Office and the Chongqing Municipal Museum. "A Study of Historic Low Water Levels in the Yichang and Chongqing Sector of the Upper Reaches of the Changjiang," Wenwu, 1978. Translated in Abstracts Vol. 9, (86-98).

Hosie, A. Three Years in Western China, (New York: Dodd, Mead and Co., 1890). Hucker, Charles O. China's Imperial Past. (Stanford, CA.: Stanford University Press, 1975).

Knapp, Ronald. Chinese Landscapes: The Village as Space. (Honolulu: University of Hawaii Press, 1992).

Latourette, Kenneth Scott. The Chinese: Their History and Culture. (New York: Macmillan, 1943).

Lip, Evelyn. Chinese Geomancy, (Singapore: Times Books International, 1979).

Little, Archibald. Through the Yangtze Gorges. (London: Sampson Low, Marston & Co., 1898).

Lo Kuanchung. Romance of the Three Kingdoms. (New York: Pantheon Books, 1976).

Luo Erhu. "Preliminary Study of the Cliff Tombs in Sichuan," Kaogu Xuebao, 1988, (133-137). In Chinese.

Ma, L. and A. Noble (eds). The Environment: Chinese and American Views. (New York: Methuen and Co. Ltd., 1981).

MacGowan, J. Sidelights on Chinese Life. (London: Kegan Paul, Trench, Trubner & Co. Ltd., 1907).

McKenna, Richard. The Sand Pebbles. (Greenwich, Conn.: Fawcet, 1962).

Pannell, C. And C Salter (eds). China Geographer Number 12: Environment. (London: Westview Press, 1985).

Service, John (ed.). Golden Inches: The China Memoir of Grace Service. (Berkeley, CA: U.Calif. Press, 1991).

Shi Weixiang. "Two Illustrations of the Fu Tian Jing from Dunhuang's Mogao Caves," Wenwu, 1980 (9) (44-48). Abstracts, Vol. 11 (1632-35).

Schwartz, Benjamin I. The World of Thought in Ancient China. (Cambridge, Mass.: Harvard University Press, 1985).

Topping, Audry R. "Ecological Roulette: Damming the Yangtze," Foreign Affiars, Vol. 74, No. 5, September/October 1995, (132-148).

____. "Dai Qing, Voice of the Yangtz River Gorges," (Earth Times, Jan. 14, 1997).

____. "What now for Three-River Gorges?" (Earth Times, Jan. 17, 1997)

Van Slyke, Lyman P. Yangtze; Nature, History and the River, (Menlo Park, CA.: Addison-Westley Publishing Co., 1988).

Waley, Arthur. Translations from Chinese, (New York: Knopf, 1941).

Watson, Burton. Su Tung P'o, Selections from a Sung Poet.

Werner, E.T.C.A. A Dictionary of Chinese Mythology. (New York: The Julian Press, 1961).

Williams, C. A. S. Outline of Chinese Symbolism and Art Motives.

Wood, Bernard. "Origin and Evolution of the genus Homo, Nature, Vol. 355 1992 (783-790).

Worcester, G.R.G. The Junks & Sampans of the Yangtze, (Annapolis: Naval Institute, 1971).

Yang Qunxi, "The Cultural Sequence c Prehistoric Cultures in the Xiling Gorg Area," Chinese Cultural Relics Newspaper, Nov. 11, 1992. In Chinese

Yichang Museum. "Summary of Archaeological Fieldwork during Preparations for the Three Gorges Dan Construction." JHKG 1986 (1).

Zich, Arthur. "China's Three Gorges Before the Flood," National Geographic Magazine, Vol. 92, No.3, September 1997 (1-33). (Shanghai: Kelly and Walsh Ltd., 1941).